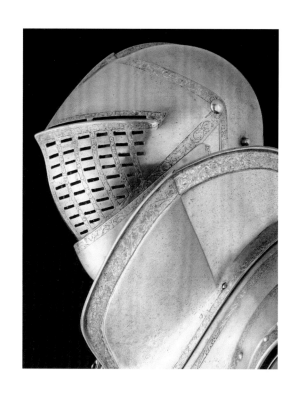

HENRY·VIII
ARMS·AND·THE·MAN

HENRY · VIII
ARMS · AND · THE · MAN
1509–2009

This book was published to mark the exhibition Henry VIII: Dressed to Kill

at The White Tower, Tower of London 3 April 2009 – 17 January 2010

EDITORS:

GRAEME RIMER, THOM RICHARDSON, J P D COOPER

ROYAL ARMOURIES   Historic Royal PALACES

The Royal Armouries and Historic Royal Palaces would like to thank
the following for their help in sponsoring and realising our ideas:

Mixed Sources
Product group from well-managed
forests and other controlled sources
www.fsc.org Cert no. SA-COC-1487
© 1996 Forest Stewardship Council

Royal Armouries Museum, Armouries Drive, Leeds LS10 1LT

© 2009 The Trustees of the Armouries

First published 2009

ISBN 978 0948092 626

Printed in Great Britain by Taylor Bloxham

CONTENTS

I know that I speak for my fellow Trustees when I say that, in marking the 500th anniversary of Henry VIII's accession to the English throne, the Royal Armouries has created a very special contribution; in fact one of those special offerings that stands out and reminds us why museums and heritage sites are so important to our cultural life.

As Chairman of the Board of Trustees of the Armouries, I take tremendous pride in introducing this superb publication to you and commend the wonderful exhibition, *Henry VIII: Dressed to Kill*, that it accompanies.

So why is this so special? Not only is its subject one of England's most famous and flamboyant monarchs, not only a sporting hero of great prowess, not only the man whose passions influenced and shaped this country but Henry was also the founding father of the national collection of arms and armour. Some of the arms and armour featured in this book and on display at the Exhibition, have formed part of the Armouries collection since Henry VIII ordered them to be made almost five centuries earlier. Even more exciting is that some of 'the ones that got away' are also featured, thanks to generous loans from the Royal Collection and several other museums and galleries across the world.

As if this continuity of objects was not in itself enough, the added dimension of our strong partnership with Historic Royal Palaces enables us to stage *Henry VIII: Dressed to Kill* within the White Tower at HM Palace and Fortress of the Tower of London, the very building which Henry VIII would instantly recognise if he were to return on his 500th anniversary. This remarkable conjunction of historic site and artefacts has provided the starting point for more research and different interpretation, involving some of the leading writers on the Tudor period, stunning new photography and analysis, using state of the art scanning technology.

I believe that the end result is a significant addition to our knowledge about Henry VIII and especially the legacy of arms and armour that he left. Perhaps even more important is that we will, I hope, introduce Henry VIII to many who know little about him and help to inspire the next generation of researchers to discover even more about this fascinating man.

My personal gratitude goes to everyone who has helped bring the opening of this grand exhibition and the publication of this fine book to fruition.

Ann M Green

Ann M Green
Chairman
Board of Trustees of the Royal Armouries

TOWER OF LONDON

LEEDS

FORT NELSON

Henry the Man. Henry the King. Henry the Warrior. Every facet of this most famous of English monarchs captures the imagination and provokes debate. The world 'knows' Henry VIII largely through a series of striking portraits that serve to create a larger-than-life image. So how do we get closer to the real man?

Time has destroyed much of the intimate evidence of Henry's life – his exquisite clothes and many personal documents are dust. Nothing exists in such a complete and spectacular way as Henry's personal armours. Every contour, whether of the slim young athlete or the massively overweight older man, was measured and shaped by highly skilled armourers to fit their royal client exactly. Henry the man fought, sweated and posed for the nation inside these fabulous metal carapaces. Five centuries later, through the joint efforts of the Royal Armouries and Historic Royal Palaces, we can marvel at the artistry of these armours and almost feel the physical presence of the King through the dazzling exhibition that is *Henry VIII; Dressed to Kill*.

We are very excited by the collaboration between our two organisations that has resulted in the staging of this unique exhibition against the superb backdrop of the White Tower. On behalf of Historic Royal Palaces I congratulate the Royal Armouries on this insightful – and highly readable – collection of essays that accompanies the exhibition and adds hugely to our knowledge of Henry the Man, the King and the Warrior.

New audiences will thrill to the display of armour under the spotlight, and the themes of fashion, style and the exploration of monarch as celebrity will resonate with many of the younger visitors, inviting them to explore further. It is vitally important that we continue to work together to preserve this unique collection for the nation. I am confident that, together, we will rise to the challenge.

Charles Mackay
Chairman
Board of Trustees of Historic Royal Palaces

FOREWORD

RICHARD HOLMES

MEMBER OF THE BOARD OF TRUSTEES OF THE ROYAL ARMOURIES

Had my life taken only a slightly different path I might have spent my career in the Royal Armouries rather than as a university teacher. In the 1960s I worked there briefly and with great pleasure, though with little distinction: I recall being introduced to a stiff brush and a cannon barrel, and asked to show progress at the day's end. I decided that a year's postgraduate study in the USA was an offer I could not refuse, and so the die was cast. But much of my passion for history is triggered, now as then, by places or artefacts. I do not believe that one can understand a battle without visiting the field upon which it was fought, or really grasp the significance of a weapon without feeling its weight and understanding its mechanism. I have collected weapons all my adult life, not, to be sure, with the fortune-funded determination of the great collectors, but with enough modest enthusiasm to have the occasional piece of interesting metal-work in my study. Becoming a Trustee of the Armouries was like a happy marriage at the end of a long courtship. I look forward to the Henry VIII exhibition with genuine excitement because it brings together a wonderful collection of artefacts in one of the land's most iconic settings, the White Tower in Her Majesty's Palace and Fortress of the Tower of London. Why, the very name is enough to make me doubt the decision I took all those years ago.

Even forty years ago a youth with his scrubbing brush was struck by the fact that a mighty bronze gun told him something about the technology of the age in which it was cast, a little about the ruler whose emblem it so proudly bore, and hinted at what its ball, trundling above the sea, might have done when it hit the bulwarks of a hostile warship. I might not have put it in such terms, but even then I would have recognised that arms and armour are a multi-faceted phenomenon. In most cases they have a primary purpose related to war or hunting, though in many instances, often paralleling the fur and feathers of the natural world, they were actually designed chiefly to impress, to exalt or to advertise. There is more than a little symbolism shared between the exaggerated form of the codpiece (an appendage intended, at least in theory, to protect the genitals) of some of Henry VIII's armours and the mating display of the peacock. Sometimes the distinction between utility and show is stark: a black-from-the-hammer munition-quality set of pikeman's armour from the Civil War of the 1640s has little in common with the lacquered plates and vivid silk cording of a samurai armour made at a time when Japan was emphatically at peace. Sometimes it is more subtle: armour designed to protect its wearer in the field or in a tournament may nevertheless, as this exhibition shows so well, embody the very best artistry of its day, with an attention to external detail which would have contrasted starkly with the sweaty reality of the body it safeguarded.

Technology, which lies at the heart of the development of arms and armour, did not follow a smooth or easy path. There were plenty of blind alleys (like Henry VIII's breech-loading gunshields, ingenious in theory but surely impractical in real combat), several long straights where relatively little changed, and steep slopes and sharp corners where innovation followed innovation with bewildering speed, sometimes con-stituting part of what historians are fond of calling a 'military revolution.' Similarly, regional and national preferences helped influence style and design, and just as technology was often imported (the steady westwards drift of the stirrup from its origin in the east is a classic case in point) so too distinctive styles of arms and armour became fashionable outside their land of origin. The exhibition contains an Innsbruck-made helmet presented to Henry by the Emperor Maximilian I, which was originally part of a characteristically fluted suit in the style now known by the Emperor's name, and then represented the apogee of continental fashion. Although the nation-state had not yet solidified across Europe – this would take another century beyond the Henry's death – the process was already well under way. It was already becoming clear that a state could not claim genuine independence if it relied on importing arms, particularly the top-quality armour which was the peak of technical perfection at the time. In this context Henry's armour workshop at Greenwich, established in 1515, was deeply significant: so too was the fact that it was closed in 1649, when King Charles I was executed and England briefly and unhappily became a republic.

It is abundantly clear, then, that arms and armour do not exist in a vacuum, but are intimately connected to the society from which they spring, although that relationship is often anything but simple. The Royal Armouries' Henry VIII exhibition was always intended to do more than state the obvious by focusing on the royal armours, striking and magnificent though they are. It was instead designed to tell us more about the king himself, a vigorous sporting hero in his youth, long before he became fat and heavy-jowelled, made more cruel and dangerous by the constant pain of ulcerated legs. His armours testify to his skill in that ultimate manly game, the tournament, and other exhibits reflect his interest in 'real' (royal) tennis, football, hawking and archery.

Most arms and armour was not made for the king and his nobles but for humbler warriors altogether. Though, properly speaking, the British regular army was not to come into being until the Restoration of Charles II in 1660, Henry's military establishment was not to be scorned. The Yeomen of the Guard and the Gentlemen Pensioners provided him with personal protection at just the time that his courts ensured that 'overmighty subjects' with their own armed retinues (which had contributed to instability during that untidy succession of lethal baronial brawls usually termed the Wars of the Roses) would no longer be tolerated. Although we tend to remember his navy because of the ill-starred *Mary Rose* (the arms and armour found aboard her are well-represented in this exhibition), royal warships, mounting heavy guns to fire broadside, represented the best of new technology and embodied Henry's desire to rule the narrow seas. His coast-defence forts, their great drum-towers designed to mount artillery, were also at the cutting edge.

Although most soldiers in Henry's armies still plied the '*bill and bow*' that their fathers would have recognised (bows from the *Mary Rose* are one of our best sources of evidence for the great war-bow which had once provided kings of England with such a notable military advantage), it is not hard to sniff the wind of change. The 1485 battlefield of Bosworth, where victory brought his father, Henry Tudor, to the throne as Henry VII, has still not been located with certainty: archaeologists yearn from just a few of those bullets that help them site 17th-century battles with growing certainty. In contrast, the traditional site of the 1515 battle of Flodden, where Henry's lieutenant the Earl of Surrey crushed the Scots, has been confirmed by the discovery of metal and stone cannon-balls. The bad-egg stink of black powder, the crash of cannon and the thud of small arms were already emerging in grimy contrast to the splendour of knightly armour, although it would have taken remarkable prescience to predict that, little more than a century later, firearms would dominate the battlefield. Yet even in Henry's reign gunnery had ceased to be a black art and was becoming a science, as the specialist's tools in the exhibition, like a gunner's rule and shot gauge, demonstrate.

Just as the exhibition itself seeks to put the arms and armour of Henry's age into its wider context, so this catalogue goes beyond the narrowly curatorial to tell its reader more about a period which, even if scholars now shrink from that notion of a '*Tudor revolution in government*' that was current when I was a Cambridge undergraduate more than half a lifetime ago, was of enormous national significance. It witnessed the creation of a personality cult, with all its attendant iconography, that a modern spin-doctor might envy; a court life that saw a peripatetic medieval monarchy increasingly settling in palaces that reflected the ruler's grandeur; the break with Rome (its implications no less constitutional than religious) and the steady hardening of royal authority over all aspects of national life, as well as the development of England's military and naval power with its largely successful use against the French and Scots. There are articles on the food, dress, and medicine of the age, and the very special relationship between the Armouries and the Tower, where they were housed for so long, demands a piece on the Tower as palace and fortress.

History resists easy codification, and although we often choose to see the reigns of Henry and his father ushering us from the medieval to the early modern world we may doubt if contemporaries were as aware of radical change. Yet the reign of Henry VIII is certainly one of those hinges upon which time's gate swings hard. There could be no doubting the implications of the 1533 Act in Restraint of Appeals, whose preamble proudly affirmed:

This realm of England is an empire...governed by one supreme head and king...unto whom a body politic compact of all sorts and degrees of people...be bounden and owe next to God a natural and humble obedience.

We cannot tell what things might have been like without Henry and his passions, martial, marital and monarchical, but this exhibition and the catalogue it supports gives us an insight into a nation he did so much to shape.

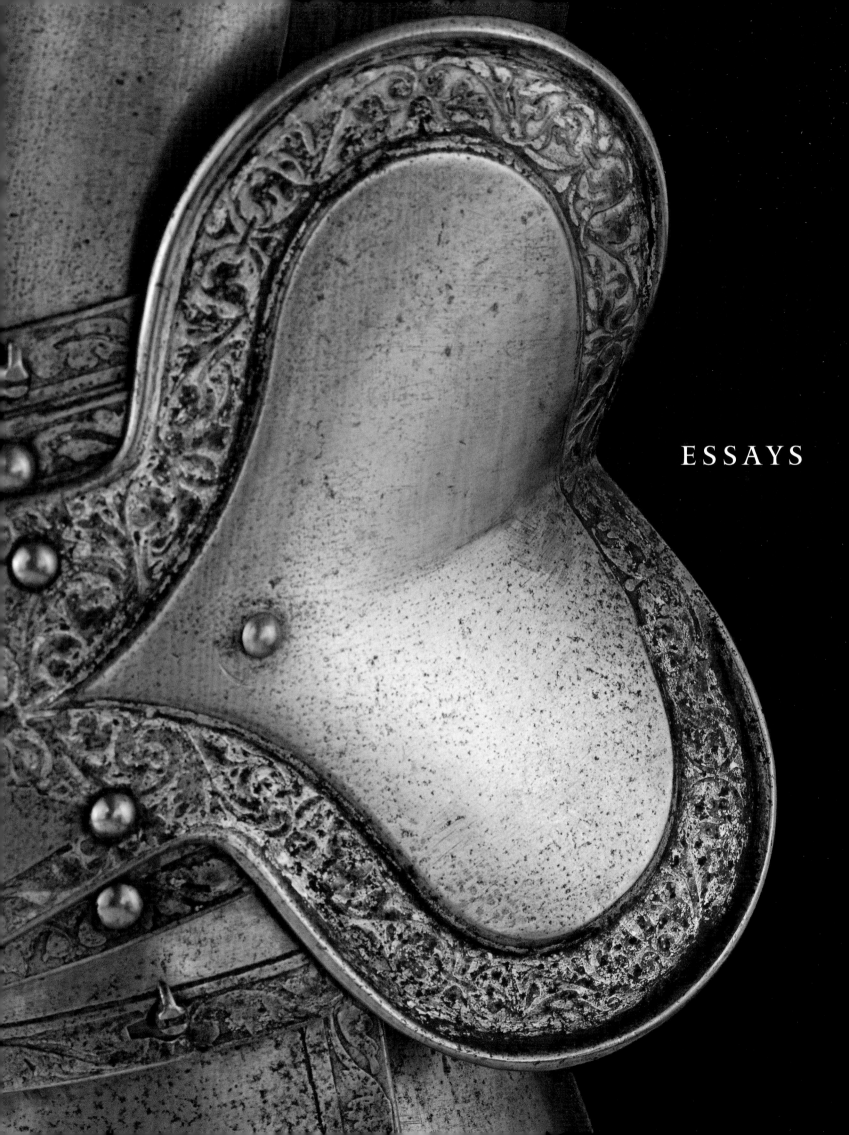

ESSAYS

Er zoch darnach in niderlaud
Zů hilff dem könig von Engelandt
Bald sampten sie ein here groß
Die Frantzosen solichs verdroß
Ir maniger der nider lag
Terzauon ward geschleyst Tornay sich gab

{ I }

HENRY VIII:
POWER AND PERSONALITY

J P D COOPER

*Love him or loathe him, Henry VIII is indisputably the most recognisable king
of England. John Cooper's introductory essay explains why the reign of Henry
VIII has often been seen as a point of balance between the medieval and
modern worlds. The scale of his achievements provoked powerful emotions
among his own subjects, from worship to dread. In his warfare and diplomacy,
his break from Rome and his patronage of magnificent Renaissance culture,
Henry proclaimed his sovereignty over a kingdom that was fast becoming one
of Europe's great powers. But his reform of the Church opened up great
fissures in society, and his government of Ireland and the north of England was
challenged by massive rebellions. Five centuries after his accession to the
throne, the debate about Henry VIII remains as intense as ever.*

Fig. 1 Maximilian I
and Henry VIII at the
battle of the Spurs,
from *Der Weisskunig*,
1514, an engraving
by Hans Burgkmair
(1473–1531).

W hy is Henry VIII the most celebrated king in English history?
The answer used to be simple: he liberated his subjects from
the tyranny of Rome, and he founded the Royal Navy. For the
Victorians and Edwardians, these ranked among the great
achievements of the British nation. Henry VIII had the courage to assert his
independence in defiance of the Pope and other foreign powers, and the vision
to provide a Bible in the language of the common people. Under his rule
England became a sovereign state, governed by monarchy but in consultation
with council and parliament, thus avoiding the spiral into absolutism that would
blight the European continent. By recognising that England's strength lay in its
navy rather than a standing army, Henry set the course for the future defence of
the realm and, within a generation or two, its imperial outreach. If his father
Henry VII looks like a medieval king, struggling against over-mighty subjects
and pretenders to the throne, then Henry VIII appears as a true prince of the
Renaissance, presiding over a nation that was strong, splendid and free.

Tho: Moor L'Chancelour

Fig. 2 Sir Thomas More, about 1527 by Hans Holbein the Younger
(1497/8-1543). The Royal Collection © Her Majesty Queen Elizabeth II

Traditional certainties about the essential rightness of the Church of England and the British Empire have long since passed away. We have lost that Victorian confidence that the virtues of the British constitution can be traced to an alliance between monarchy, parliament and gentry established during the Reformation era. And yet King Henry VIII remains defiantly centre-stage, a celebrity rivalled only by his daughter Elizabeth. Henry V was a more successful warrior, James VI and I a better theologian, William III a surer model for a constitutional ruler, but it is Henry VIII's portrait that sells the souvenirs in the gift shops of England's historic houses. The likeness captured by Hans Holbein, calculated to inspire awe in its viewers, has become a logo for the whole Tudor brand. In schools, Henry VIII and his dynasty survive within a history curriculum that is dominated by the dictators of the 20th century. He and his six wives inspire frequent biographies, popular histories, novels and television series. The intricacies of Henrician politics, religion and government are the subject of intense academic research in universities on both sides of the Atlantic. The perceived connections between

past and present may have faded since Queen Victoria's day, but Henry VIII remains relevant to contemporary culture in a way that no other English king can match.

Henry was a ruler who provoked powerful emotions in his own time, ranging from devotion to dread. His accession in 1509 was welcomed by political class and commons alike amidst an atmosphere of relief that the oppressive regime of Henry VII had ended in a peaceful transfer of power. The new King's chivalric outlook and open manner of keeping court promised a fresh alliance with the nobility, and humanist scholars praised Henry's intellect and learning with real enthusiasm. As Thomas More (fig. 2) wrote in a Latin epigram for the coronation, '*This day is the limit of our slavery, the beginning of our freedom, the end of sadness, the source of joy*'.[1] Henry's early military offensives in France and Scotland, and his patronage of the latest styles in art and architecture, bespoke his aspirations for parity with the far wealthier King of France and the Holy Roman Emperor. His father had placed England on the international map by forging a profitable alliance with Spain; now Henry VIII was claiming to broker the balance of power in Europe. Briefly, with the ceremonial signing of a treaty of universal peace in 1518, London was at the diplomatic centre of the western world.

Without a legitimate male heir, however, the stability of the English commonwealth was more apparent than real. The urgent need to settle the succession led Henry, previously a loyal son of the Catholic church, into schism with Rome and an accompanying campaign of religious reform. The royal supremacy over a national church remains Henry VIII's most lasting political legacy, to this day a contested keystone of the English (if less obviously the British) constitution. The nature and extent of the King's commitment to religious reform has been endlessly debated. Those who want to believe in Henry VIII as a Protestant monarch point to his licensing of sermons and scripture in English, his antipathy towards superstition and relics, and his intention to replace monasteries with schools. On the opposing side may be cited Henry's burning of evangelical preachers, his defence of clerical celibacy, and his personal devotion to the miracle of the Mass. The chronicler Edward Hall and the Protestant martyrologist John Foxe struggled to make sense of these contradictions, just as later historians have done. Henry VIII certainly thought of himself as a reformer, but his vision of church and state was of his own construction. As his biographer J J Scarisbrick has put it, Henry '*was his own theologian*', his religion '*a highly personal admixture of new and old*'.[2]

If the doctrinal and liturgical significance of Henry's Reformation is open to interpretation, then the same cannot be said of its political impact, which was profound. By fostering printed polemic and public debate, by mobilising factions for and against, the controversies over religion added an unprecedented ideological dimension to English life. As the age-old scramble for patronage and position became complicated by questions of faith, so the royal court evolved into a dangerous and febrile place, of shifting alliances and betrayed friendships. Those who miscalculated and lost their footing, like Anne Boleyn and Thomas Cromwell, paid with their lives. The poet and ambassador Sir Thomas Wyatt, who probably watched Anne's execution from his own cell in the Tower, was moved to write a wrenching lament: *'These bloody days have broken my heart'*.[3] A few radical voices began to compare Henry VIII to the tyrants of the classical world. Thousands of ordinary people in the provinces were also drawn in, whether criminalised by the new treason laws, or incensed to march in the Pilgrimage of Grace, or estranged from their neighbours on grounds of their belief. In their support, their protests, or simply their decisions to be obedient, the English population was politicised on a wholly new scale.

The great events of the reign, and their lasting consequences, go some way towards explaining Henry VIII's tenacious hold on historians and the broader national memory. Had there been no crisis of the succession and no break from Rome, English Protestantism would very likely have remained oppositional and underground, a disparate association of evangelical students, merchants, and converts from Lollardy. Without the legislative reformation of the 1530s, statute law and parliament would not have achieved the pre-eminence that MPs in later years would recall as a precedent. The dissolution of the monasteries, and the Crown's realisation of its assets to fortify the south coast and fund another war in France, prompted a revolution in land ownership of which the gentry were the principal beneficiaries. Several of the great families of English history owe their fortunes, and their country houses, to successful manoeuvring for the spoils of Henry VIII's assault on the cloistered life. Add in the administrative reforms of Thomas Cromwell (which generated many of the records which historians now use to analyse the regime), and the transformation of Ireland from a lordship of the English crown to a dual monarchy, and the humble beginnings of a system of poor relief, and it is not difficult to make a case for Henry VIII's reign as a point of balance between the medieval and modern worlds.

For a full explanation, however, we must also be alert to the ways in which the King presented himself to his people and to posterity. Henry VIII was acutely aware of the relationship between imagery and authority, as his father Henry VII and grandfather Edward IV had been, but the span and splendour of his own achievements clearly outclassed those of his royal predecessors. In palaces and portraits, ceremonial and the printed word, the language of statutes and sermons, Henry and his government exploited the royal image to the full. Geoffrey Elton wrote of a *'full-scale propaganda campaign'* during the 1530s, although he also reflected on how little we know about its actual impact.[4] Similar reservations have been raised about the sumptuous visual culture of Henry VIII's court: who saw it, and how many of those people really understood what they were seeing?[5] And yet it must be significant that Henry chose to invest his limited resources so heavily in the cultivation of magnificence. Henry VIII was the first English king whom his subjects could actually recognise by sight, thanks to the portraits on his coinage and the title page of the 1539 Great Bible. No previous English regime had made such concerted efforts to communicate with the subjects that it ruled. Foreign visitors, too, were impressed. As the papal nuncio to England reported to Isabella d'Este, Marchesa of Mantua in 1517:

'...the wealth and civilization of the world are here; and those who call the English barbarians appear to me to render themselves such... blessed and happy may this country call itself in having as its lord so worthy and eminent a sovereign, whose sway is more bland and gentle than the greatest liberty under any other'.[6]

It is within this context that many of the objects in the exhibition, *Henry VIII: Dressed to Kill* should be viewed: as an armoury of courtly splendour and display, the means for Henry VIII to assert his symbolic status at the summit of the English aristocracy and to compete with his brother princes in Europe.

How ought we to assess the kingship of Henry VIII? Sixteenth-century people judged their rulers according to criteria assembled variously from Scripture, from English history, and – among the educated elite – from their reading about the virtuous and tyrannical regimes of ancient Greece and Rome. Henry VIII himself thought in similar terms. As a young king he fashioned himself as another Henry V, campaigning in France and commissioning a translation of Titus Livius's biography of the victor of Agincourt.[7] In the years of Reformation he looked to the Old Testament and the sacred kingship of David and Solomon for guidance and affirmation.

His illuminated psalter of 1542 portrays Henry VIII as King David with striking candour, slaying the giant Goliath and kneeling before an angel in penitence, and a Holbein miniature of about 1535 casts him as Solomon receiving the homage of the Queen of Sheba (fig. 3). The walls of his palaces were hung with tapestries telling the same stories, resonant of the royal supremacy over the church.[8] The Roman Emperor Constantine was another potential model, offered up to Henry by his advisors to endorse the supreme headship.[9] Behind the elaborate imagery and theorising, however, lay some basic assumptions. A good king saw justice done in his dominions, defended his people and took them to war when the cause was right, and matched piety with princely magnificence. Henry VIII never doubted that he had been placed on the throne to fulfil these duties in the eyes of God. What some of his subjects welcomed as a time of liberation, however, others lamented as a descent into tyranny.

WARRIOR

War was the great constant in Henry VIII's life. He could inhabit other roles when circumstances dictated: early in his reign, the courtly lover of Katherine of Aragon; in middle years the scholar and theologian, poring over the dossiers which explored his powers as supreme head of the Church; and at last the Solomonic judge, executing Protestants for heresy side-by-side with Catholics for treason. But it was in the field in northern France, or surveying the royal dockyards and coastal artillery batteries, where Henry was most obviously in his element. Three times he led his nation to war with France, allied with his father-in-law Ferdinand of Spain and the Emperor Maximilian (fig. 1) in 1512–14, with Maximilian's grandson and successor Charles V in 1522–5, and with Charles once again in 1543–4. Henry sailed to Calais in 1513 to lead the French campaign in person, riding around camp to encourage his rain-drenched troops and entering the captured towns of Thérouanne and Tournai to hear *Te Deum* sung by his own choir. He took inordinate pride in the battle of the Spurs, a cavalry skirmish in which several French standards and high-ranking nobles were captured, although Hall reveals that Henry himself remained a mile behind the action on the advice of his council of war.[10] His next trips to France were more diplomatic. In 1520 Henry strove to outdo Francis I in magnificence at the Field of Cloth of Gold (fig. 3 and 4), the two kings fighting on the same side in the tournaments, although Henry cannot have been pleased to concede a wrestling match to his great rival. They met

Fig. 3 Solomon and the Queen of Sheba, An engraving of about 1534 by Hans Holbein the Younger (1497/8-1543). The Royal Collection © Her Majesty Queen Elizabeth II

again in 1532, at a critical moment in the great matter of Henry's marriage and the succession. Anne Boleyn travelled to Calais as effectively a queen in waiting. Her apartments backed onto the King's, Henry was emboldened by Francis's apparent declaration of support, and Anne was pregnant with Elizabeth before the year was out.

By the time that he returned to France at the head of an army in summer 1544, Henry was a changed man: obese, feverish, and frequently in dreadful pain from the ulcers on his legs. But although he was carried around his private apartments on a chair, and hoisted to the upstairs of his palaces by machinery, Henry still managed to get into the saddle to review his troops. He relished the siege of Boulogne, where he had the chance to see English artillery in action, and supervised the garrisoning of the town when it fell to him in September. When Charles and Francis concluded a bilateral peace four days later, Henry fought on alone. During the invasion scare of 1545 he toured his new coastal fortifications, dined aboard the warship *Great Harry*, and witnessed the sinking of the *Mary Rose* in the Solent. For Henry, the winning of Boulogne seems to have been more important than the keeping of it; or perhaps he yielded to advisors who could see the financial cost of maintaining the King's ambitions in France. Conquests were negotiated away with surprising speed. By a treaty of June 1546, Boulogne would remain an English territory for eight years, at the end of which France would buy it back for £600,000. But the siege alone had cost this much; and more than £400,000 was then spent on garrisoning the town. During the 1540s Henry haemorrhaged over £2 million on his land wars in France and Scotland and on the navy.[11] This was eight or ten times the ordinary annual revenues of the Crown.

Faced with such a huge deficit, the government was forced to call on parliamentary taxation and loans, to dispose of monastic land, and – most damagingly of all – to manufacture money by debasing the coinage. The strain on resources was very great. Tournai was sold back in 1518. Boulogne was returned to France four years early and at a knock-down price by the government of Edward VI. Meanwhile the French enjoyed symbolic victories of their own, as when Brighton was burned in 1514 and raiding-parties ravaged the Isle of Wight in 1545. The army that Henry mustered for his last French war was impressive in size, probably the largest deployed abroad until the reign of William III, but Venetian observers contrasted the courage of the English soldiers with their outdated kit. Bad weather, or the want of food and drink, lured infantry away from the field of combat in spite of orders to stand firm.[12] In the judgement of one historian, Henry VIII's armies *'had fallen badly behind their opponents in the race for modernity'*, and were fortunate not to meet the French, with their superior provision of handguns and higher proportion of mercenaries, in an open fight.[13] Henry postured as one of the big three in Europe, but the sober truth was that his military resources laboured far behind those of the French King and the Emperor.

Since 1337 English kings had claimed to be rulers of France and Henry VIII took some pride in the title, minting coins in Tournai inscribed '*Henricus Dei Gratia Franciae et Angliae Rex*' and accepting oaths of allegiance from his French subjects as the Duke of Suffolk crossed the Somme in 1523.

And yet the Pale of Calais, the last outpost of the empire re-established by Henry V, was governed as an English town and would gain the right to return MPs to Westminster in 1536. There was another flurry of interest in the French title when Francis I was captured at Pavia in 1525, news which Henry greeted with exultation, but lack of funds and unrest at home meant that he was unable to pursue his advantage. Overall his attitude towards France seems to have been more opportunistic than dynastic. By the early 1540s, the Reformation and England's consequent diplomatic isolation had created ample strategic justification for going on the offensive to pre-empt a French assault from the new naval base at Le Havre.

War with France generally also meant war with Scotland. Although a 'British' policy was beginning to emerge by the early 1540s, based on a mixture of force and diplomacy, Henry's interest was not consistent. Scotland could, perhaps should, have been the more important theatre, but for Henry it always played a secondary role to France. When James IV's herald formally defied Henry VIII in the camp outside Thérouanne in August 1513, Henry stayed on in France. When James met his death at the devastating Scots' defeat at Flodden Field a month later, the victory belonged to the Earl of Surrey and to Katherine of Aragon, acting as regent in Henry's absence. Loyal to chivalric tradition, Henry sent his queen tribute and high-born prisoners from his conquests; Katherine, however, could reply with the bloody coat of a King of Scots. In the 1540s the initiative against Scotland was once again left to a senior military commander, the Earl of Hertford, who proved ultimately unable to capitalise on the English victory at Solway Moss and the death of James V. In 1544 Hertford burned Edinburgh, while Henry watched the bombardment of Boulogne. The '*Rough Wooing*' of Scotland carried on into Edward VI's reign, but hopes for an Anglo-Scots union turned to ash when the infant Mary Queen of Scots was betrothed to the Dauphin.

Throughout his life Henry took an almost childlike delight in technology and gadgets: clocks, navigational instruments, automata, and above all guns. He was especially proud of the great bombards, made by Hans Poppenruyter of Mechlin and named after the twelve apostles, which accompanied him to Tournai in 1513. Henry VII had taken steps to found a domestic armaments industry, and Henry VIII established a foundry making cast bronze cannon in 1511, but the scale of his military activities compelled him to import weapons from the Low Countries and Italy. In 1545 he ordered 200 cast-iron guns of the type pioneered by William Levett, a Sussex gun-founder and clergyman, although they could not all be

supplied in the two years left to the King. Most of them were intended for Henry's beloved navy. The construction of a standing royal navy had begun under his father, but Henry VIII turned the five vessels that he inherited into a force of 50 by 1544. The ships that he built were floating gun-platforms, with disastrous consequences for the *Mary Rose* (fig. 4), refitted to house more ordnance than she had been designed to carry. Henry VIII took a personal interest in naval architecture, and appears to have designed the small rowed galleys built for the final French war. The real innovation,

however, lay less in the ships than in the administrative structures created for their maintenance and deployment. The Council for Marine Causes that emerged in the mid 1540s has been called '*the most effective and sophisticated system of naval management in Western Europe*' and the origin of the later Admiralty.[14]

Reviewing Henry VIII as warrior, we are left with the impression that he had something to prove. Unlike his father, he had not won his throne on the battlefield; and unlike his elder brother Arthur, he had not been sent as a boy to the

Fig. 4 Detail of *The Embarkation at Dover*, painted about 1520–40, artist unknown. The painting shows a number of Henry VIII's ships in 1520 as he prepared to set sail for the Field of Cloth of Gold, where he would meet King Francis I of France. Among then may be the *Mary Rose*. The Royal Collection © Her Majesty Queen Elizabeth II

God and the Tudors still held firm. Not everyone shared Henry's enthusiasm for war: the humanism fashionable at court and in the universities was supposedly pacifist (though also admiring of classical military virtue), and Cromwell referred to the acquisitions in France as '*ungracious dogholes*' in the Parliament of 1523. But the cult of chivalry, and the keen spirit of competition between the princes of Renaissance Europe, stirred Henry's blood as the business of government never could. In Wolsey he found an able manager of military logistics, and a minister who enthusiastically laid plans for the invasion and partition of France. By the early 1540s, with Thomas More and Thomas Cromwell both dead by execution, there was no-one of sufficient stature to advise a policy of caution.

MAGNIFICENCE

The waging of war and the making of peace offered Henry VIII the chance of glory on the European stage. At a time when notions of the state were only beginning to develop, 16th-century warfare was still presented as an engagement between kings, a personal contest of allegiance and honour. The cannon that Henry commissioned for his navy were decorated with the royal arms, as were the castles that he built along the Channel coast. Treaties of peace were illuminated with princely heraldry. According to the medieval doctrine of the king's two bodies, Henry VIII *was* England, and this was nowhere more evident than in his foreign policy. But war was expensive and fast becoming more so, unsustainable in the long-term and potentially destabilising at home, as proved by the protests in London and East Anglia sparked by the 1525 'amicable grant'. Henry's forces were engaged in active campaigning for perhaps eight of his 38 years on the throne, excluding the raids endemic to the Scots border and Gaelic Ireland. At other times the projection of royal authority depended on artistic culture and ceremonial, the universal language of power of Renaissance Europe. If Henry lacked the manpower and the income that the French king had at his disposal, he could at least create the illusion of majesty. David Starkey has summarised the strategy: '*by behaving and spending like a great power Henry was accepted as one*'.[16]

Welsh marches to learn how to govern. In the early 1520s Henry spoke of his trust in God that Francis I would '*make a way for him as King Richard did for his father*'.[15] The remark reveals something of Henry's psychology. The defeat of Richard III at Bosworth was the foundation myth of the dynasty, proof that Henry VII and his line were ordained to rule. The fact that Henry VIII invoked this memory in the context of the French war implies that he was seeking to emulate, and exceed, the achievements of his own father as well as those of Henry V; to prove that the covenant between

Fig. 5 *The Field of Cloth of Gold, 1520,* painted about 1545, artist unknown. The Royal Collection © Her Majesty Queen Elizabeth II

Grand claims have been made for the artistic, architectural and literary patronage exercised by Henry VIII, and with good cause. Historians often borrow a 20th-century vocabulary of 'propaganda' to characterise the portraits, palaces and books commissioned by the King, although this requires caution: the audience of most royal imagery was limited, and there was certainly no Tudor propaganda machine to compare with those developed by modern governments. The early 16th century had words of its own to describe the display of power expected of the sovereign. Sir Thomas Elyot wrote of the 'majesty' of monarchy, and indeed Henry VIII demanded to be addressed as 'Your Majesty' rather than the humbler 'Your Grace'; the practice continues to this day. 'Magnificence' was another term of art, discussed by the later 15th-century legal theorist Sir John Fortescue and recalled in Henry VIII's reign in the title of a play by John Skelton, who had once been Henry's tutor. Magnificence meant more than simple opulence or luxury; it was the proper use of royal wealth, a means to maintain the stability of the estate royal. Edward IV had renamed the parts of the royal household inhabited by the king as the 'house of magnificence', and Henry VII followed his example by pouring money into prestige building projects, buying up plate and Flemish tapestries, and judging tournaments at court. Although he is usually remembered as dour and miserly, placing the nobility on probation and retreating to the security of his privy chamber, more recent studies of Henry VII have found him to be a ruler fully aware of the equation between art and power.

This was the world of splendour in which Henry VIII grew up. One of his earliest memories would have been the feats of arms held to mark his creation as Duke of York in 1494. At the age of ten he led the wedding party of Prince Arthur and Katherine of Aragon through the pageant-strewn streets of London. For his own coronation procession in June 1509 he wore a doublet of white cloth of gold, embroidered with precious stones, and his velvet robe was trimmed with ermine. All things were conducted according to precedent. The final part of his journey was made on foot, under a canopy borne by the barons of the Cinque Ports and preceded by nobles, bishops, and the Abbot and monks of Westminster. Henry had prepared for his enthronement with cleansing and prayer, and the solemnities that followed – being anointed by the Archbishop of Canterbury, donning the crown of Edward the Confessor, surrendering it again to the saint's shrine in the Abbey – was a sacramental affirmation of monarchy as a divinely appointed order. Ceremonial of this sort was more

than spectacle or liturgy; it was a ritual of participation on the grandest scale, intended 'to *bind together the ruler and his most important subjects*'.[17] Within the Abbey the clergy predominated, while at the ensuing feast the nobility waited on the royal party, their order of precedence having been settled by a court summoned for the purpose. Later in the reign the symbolic bond between king and political nation was visualised in the christenings of the royal children, the costly gifts exchanged at court each New Year's Day, and – more controversially, given some key absences – the coronation of Anne Boleyn.

Henry had spent the last summer before his accession practising in the tiltyard at Richmond, on one occasion observed by his father. He matured into a courageous jouster, and his success is evident in the score cheques kept by the heralds (cat. no. 11). His favourite opponent was Charles Brandon, Duke of Suffolk, who in 1515 married Henry's younger sister Mary (fig. 6); one observer enthused that they were like Hector and Achilles. As the lance charge on heavy warhorse was progressively replaced by artillery on the battlefield, so the tournament became more symbolic and historicised, its costumed participants dismounting to dance with the ladies of the court. But jousting was still a risky business. Riding with an open visor in 1524 left Henry with a helmet full of splinters, and a bad fall in 1536 could have killed him; as it was, two hours of unconsciousness may have persuaded him to leave the sport to younger men. Jousts had an important political dimension, representing the hierarchy of influence within the royal entourage (Brandon's rise was clear for all to see) and stamping an image of English power on the minds, and the correspondence, of the foreign envoys in whose honour the events were often held. Watching from the new stands at Greenwich in 1517, the ambassadors of France, the papacy and the Empire were treated to a magnificent display in which Brandon answered the King's challenge and hundreds of spears were broken. Steven Gunn has described the meeting between Henry and Francis I at the Field of Cloth of Gold (fig. 5) three years later as a case of '*tiltyard diplomacy*', when 150 French and English courtiers jousted and fought on foot over the course of several days: a substitute for the real warfare to which they would soon enough return.[18]

In terms of the visual arts, the reign of Henry VIII occupies a sort of debatable land between the late Gothic and the Renaissance. His father had dabbled in the new styles emanating from Italy and Burgundy, although the overriding impression created by the Henry VII chapel at Westminster is

Fig. 6 Henry's younger sister Mary and Charles Brandon, Duke of Suffolk, by Jean De Mabuse, 1515. © The Earl of Yarborough

square, flat and uncompromising. The same features can be found on the great seal, in the plea rolls, and in the title pages of the Coverdale and Great Bibles that depict the King in majesty presiding over a united English commonwealth. Comparing the Whitehall cartoon with Henry VIII's armour reveals how Holbein played with perspective, broadening the shoulders and lengthening the legs of the King. Holbein's vision is echoed in the iconography of the young Edward VI, whose kingship was presented as a continuation of his father's.

Portraiture was central to the artistic Renaissance, and Henry VIII's court offered an environment in which it could flourish. Not only the King but politicians, gentlemen, clergy, women; all were captured by Holbein, with an apparent speed and deftness that reminds the viewer of a modern courtroom sketch-artist. Architecture offers another perspective on royal splendour. Henry VIII has been characterised as 'certainly the most prolific, talented and innovative builder to sit on the English throne', a monarch who kept plans and drawing instruments close by him in his study, just as he took an active role in the design of ships, guns and castles.[20] The building works that Henry carried out at Hampton Court and Whitehall during the 1530s mirrored those of Francis I at Fontainebleau. And yet Hampton Court remained a vernacular rather than a classically proportioned structure, rendered more fashionable by the application of terracotta roundels made by Giovanni da Maiano; a sort of bolt-on Renaissance. Inside the King's houses, a profusion of heraldry on ceilings, furniture and domestic objects would have overwhelmed any references to the antique. At Whitehall, meanwhile, the citizens evicted when their houses were cleared to make way for the sprawling new palace paid a high price for the King's magnificence: proof, for some, of Henry's inclination to tyranny.

The history of art and architecture can offer us a window on Henry VIII as both a Renaissance and a Reformation king, reinforcing our perception of his reign as a turning-point between the medieval and the modern. Just as interesting, however, are images that imply continuity with the past. One of Holbein's first commissions when he arrived in England was a 'plat' or panoramic map of the siege of Thérouanne, hung in the banqueting house at Greenwich for the benefit of the French peace delegation of 1527. This is now lost, although we know that Holbein received the large sum of £4 10s. in payment. Given the diplomatic context, both the subject and the King's behaviour were provocative: Henry deliberately drew his guests' attention to the canvas hanging on the back of the triumphal arch through which they had

of a final triumph of the English medieval. Henry VIII, by contrast, has been credited with 'the transformation of the English court' on a Renaissance model.[19] The claim depends substantially on the presence of Hans Holbein, 'King's painter' by 1536 and the finest portraitist to work in England until van Dyck was employed by Charles I. Holbein was a versatile artist, and his work for Henry VIII varied dramatically in scale. The famous panel in the Thyssen collection measures a mere 279 x 203 mm (11 x 8 in), its small-ness some-how emphasising the massiveness of Henry's frame, while Holbein's preliminary drawing for his group portrait mural at Whitehall stands 2.5 m (8 ft) high. Rather like the Hilliard image of Elizabeth I, however, the face was constant:

just passed.[21] The same theme gained renewed relevance towards the end of the reign. A map-like painting of the battle of the Spurs, and a panel depicting the same encounter together with the meeting of Henry VIII and the Emperor Maximilian and the sieges of Thérouanne and Tournai, both held by the Royal Collection (fig.7), have been dated on internal evidence to about 1545, some three decades after the events that they portray.[22] By then Henry VIII was again at war, fortifying himself with the memory of his first French campaign. Late in life, it was as a warrior rather than a reformer of the Church or a paragon of Renaissance virtue that Henry VIII chose to be painted.

So much for courtly magnificence; what of the king's humbler subjects? Away from London and outside a coronation, opportunities to catch sight of the monarch were few. Henry generally went on progress during the summer months, when sickness raged in the capital and the latrines of the royal palaces had to be cleaned, albeit only once to the north of England and never as far as Wales or Devon. We know less about Henry VIII's travels than we do about Elizabeth's,

VANE

Fig. 7 Detail of the meeting between Henry VIII and Maximilian I in 1513, painted about 1545. In the background the towns of Thérouanne (left) and Tournai (right) are depicted under siege.
The Royal Collection © Her Majesty Queen Elizabeth II

Although it could serve as a diversion from the tedium of government, hunting was also part of the business of kingship, giving Henry the opportunity to show off his considerable horsemanship and make contact with a wider proportion of the political nation than was able to attend the jousts as court. Sometimes royal progresses were disrupted by pestilence, as in 1517 and 1528, when Henry isolated himself from his subjects as best he could. On a tour of the West Country in 1535, Henry and Anne avoided plague-ridden Bristol and stayed instead with Nicholas Poyntz at Acton Court, a moated manor house redecorated with a Renaissance-painted frieze, Spanish earthenware and Venetian glass. Given the aristocratic focus of progresses by this date, the argument that it dissuaded the conservative west from rising with the Pilgrimage of Grace in 1536 probably over-estimates its political impact.[24]

More promising in terms of the King's public propaganda is the ceremony of touching for the '*King's evil*'. Like the kings of the high middle ages, Henry VIII placed hands upon selected worthy subjects to heal them from the skin disease of scrofula, a practice perhaps revived by his father after a period of disuse. He also consecrated the Good Friday cramp rings that were thought to protect against epilepsy, and distributed them via his envoys to foreign courts as proof of his sacred kingship.[25] Neither seems to have been affected by the Reformation. Progresses and royal healings were traditional ways of bringing royal magnificence to the provinces and the people, but Henry and his advisors also innovated. The English Bible carried Holbein's image of Henry VIII into every parish in England, although the impact of this '*consciously planned act of mass propaganda*' was reduced when restrictions were imposed on those wishing to read the Word of God for themselves.[26] A similar point may be made about the coinage, also sometimes praised as a type of royal propaganda. The coins of the 1540s bore a very recognisable new profile portrait of the King, but contemporaries were probably more concerned that their precious metal content had been reduced. Henry VIII's final issue of gold sovereigns showed him seated on a Renaissance throne, with orb and sceptre and the union Tudor rose at his feet. A sovereign, however, was beyond the means of all but a few of his subjects.

and recovering the responses of the crowd beyond stock reports of rejoicing is next to impossible. His earliest progresses look rather like his father's, receiving the homage of significant towns in return for redress of grievances. In 1510 he visited Salisbury and Southampton, while the following summer he and Katherine were hosted by North-ampton, Leicester, Coventry and Warwick during a splendid progress through the Midlands. As the reign drew on, however, Henry preferred to stay in country houses where he could hunt in the company of his nobility and courtiers.[23]

Early in his reign there was a chance that Henry VIII might acquire the title which he craved to compete on an equal footing with the rulers of Renaissance Europe, the 'Catholic kings' of Spain, the *most Christian kings* of France and the Holy Roman Emperor. In 1512 Pope Julius II briefly bestowed on him the crown of France and its style *'roi très chrestien'*, even dangling the lure of a coronation in Paris. This episode, half-obscured by the later drama of the Reformation, is important for illustrating Henry's abiding concern with his own sovereignty. In the event Henry had to be satisfied with a lesser honorific, 'Defender of the Faith', granted by Leo X in recognition of the *Assertio septem sacramentorum*, a refutation of Martin Luther in which the King had a hand. The Pope seems to have intended the dignity to be personal to Henry, but this is not how he chose to receive it, and a statute of 1543 decreed that it was hereditary to the English crown. The title was the end-product of years of petitioning by Wolsey, during which Henry had impulsively offered his army, his navy, and his own command of a papal crusade against Islam.

Henry's aversion to writing and preference for giving orders by word of mouth has left relatively little autograph evidence of his perception of his powers as king. Much must be extrapolated from the public rhetoric of the regime. In October 1530, for instance, Henry's increasingly aggressive attitude towards the papacy was reflected in the Latin instructions sent to his agents in Rome: *'in our kingdom we are supreme, and so rule, that we recognise no superior'*.[27] By 1533 the language of diplomacy had solidified into statute law. To quote the famous English preamble to the Act of Appeals,

'this Realme of Englond is an Impire, and so hath ben accepted in the worlde, governed by oon Supreme heede and King having the Dignitie and Roiall Estate of the Imperiall Crowne of the same'.[28]

Henry did made some marginal annotations to the *Collectanea satis copiosa*, a manuscript collection presented to him in 1530 in defence of his spiritual supremacy.[29] But there is no equivalent of, say, the bulk of writing in which James VI and I set out his vision of monarchy. This gaping hole in our knowledge of Henry VIII has left historians free to speculate about the extent to which Henry VIII was working out a model of his sovereignty for himself, or whether (as seems more likely) its elements were presented to him for his revision and approval. The question of origins is critical, because without the break from Rome and the royal

supremacy there would in all likelihood have been no overhaul of the liturgy and doctrine of the English Church, at least not in Henry's reign.

It would be too reductive to explain the Henrician Reformation exclusively in terms of the king. Many other factors came into play: the gathering presence of Lutheran ideas in the universities, Inns of Court, and a scattering of towns; the influence of leading evangelicals such as Thomas Cranmer and Hugh Latimer; the growing impact of print. But none of these would have been decisive had Henry VIII not been won over to the cause of reform. For a monarch so sensitive to dynastic continuity and his own honour, the prospect of an unresolved succession was appalling. Far from being the libertine of Catholic propaganda, Henry came genuinely to believe that his union with his brother's widow was adulterous and condemned to be barren. The marriage to Anne Boleyn, and the supreme headship of the Church that authorised it, promised both the chance of a male heir (thus fulfilling a king's greatest obligation to his people) and the opportunity to assert his sovereignty. It was at about this time that Henry VIII decided to update the coronation oath of England. A reference to the liberties of *'holie church'* was struck through and replaced with *'the holy chirche of ingland'*; new clauses limited the oath to matters *'nott prejudiciall to hys crowne or Imperiall Jurisdiction'*; the coda *'with hys consent'* was appended to a reference to the laws and customs made by the people.[30] Whether Henry acted on behalf of his successors or believed that he could somehow retrospectively amend the terms of his own oath, we cannot say. If the former then he was frustrated, since the oath reverted to its traditional formula for the coronation of Edward VI in 1547. Whatever its intent, this rare document in Henry's own hand is a vivid testimony to his burgeoning confidence as a ruler, and proof that Thomas More was right to fear that he had the makings of a tyrant.

Henry's faith is difficult to define. Neither the break from Rome nor the dissolution of the monasteries is necessarily the clear evidence of the King's Protestantism that it has sometimes been taken to be. The royal supremacy over the Church can be interpreted within a longer-term trend towards imperial notions of kingship, pre-dating the Reformation and shared with the monarchies of continental Europe. Stephen Gardiner, Bishop of Winchester and an orthodox Catholic, found himself able to write in its defence, basing his argument on reason as well as *'the most certain voice of God'*.[31] No doubt Gardiner wanted to protect his position at court, but his humanism seems to have made him sympathetic to the idea of a godly and reforming monarchy. As for the monasteries and friaries, a process of dissolution had begun under Wolsey and could also be represented as humanist in inspiration. If the vigour had largely gone out of the cloistered religious life, then its resources could be diverted to funding education, new dioceses, or even the building of roads and bridges. This may well have been Cromwell's plan before the threat of invasion required that ex-monastic revenues be diverted into castles, ordnance and the navy. In his own devotions Henry VIII gave mixed signals. He never had much time for pilgrimage or purgatory, but he shared this attitude with reformist Catholic thinkers. He excoriated the translator William Tyndale as a heretic, yet read his *Obedience of a Christian Man* with relish, and authorised an English Bible that was largely Tyndale's work. He outlawed the saints' plays that had catechised the illiterate without ever losing the hostility towards Luther that had won him his papal title of 'Defender of the Faith'.

Henry VIII's religious policy was not only idiosyncratic but inconsistent. Between 1536 and 1538 an intensive campaign brought reform to the parishes, where devotional lights were snuffed out and sermons preached on the usurped authority of the Bishop of Rome. Shrines were looted and fraudulent relics exposed; the 'holy blood of Hailes' was found to be the blood of a duck rather than Christ. Royal injunctions, the Act of Ten Articles and the '*Bishops' Book*' sanctioned a kind of watered-down Lutheranism, with little sympathy for cults of the saints or prayers for the dead. Then, to the horror of the evangelicals, the Henrician Reformation went into reverse. In 1539 the Act of Six Articles (a '*whip with six strings*' to Protestants) reaffirmed traditional Catholic teaching on confession and communion in one kind, followed in 1540 by the fall of Cromwell, implicated by association with the heretical party at court and in Calais. In 1543 the '*King's Book*' rejected justification by faith and affirmed the real presence in the sacrament of the altar. Henry's death was marked by requiems and his funeral was thoroughly traditional in its iconography, his coffin attended by banners of the Trinity, the Virgin and St George. And yet Henry had retained to the end his self-fashioning as a reformer. In 1541 he commanded the destruction of shrines which he had discovered on progress in the north of England, and the '*King's Book*' voiced his satisfaction that his dominions were being cleansed of hypocrisy and superstition.

Why the return to conservatism at the end of the 1530s? There are two broad schools of thought among those seeking to explain the spinning weathercock of Henrician religion.

One of these, based on the study of the politics and personalities surrounding the King, argues that Henry was influenced in sometimes contrary directions by the courtiers and clerics orbiting him. The second prefers to see Henry playing a skilful game of his own, steering the ship of state on a middle course as his daughter Elizabeth would do after him by allowing factions to compete for his favour. Both approaches tend to make religious policy the crucial determinant of Henry's kingship; neither has a monopoly on the evidence. The suddenness of Thomas Cromwell's fall from grace – further elevated as Earl of Essex in April 1540, executed in July – and Henry's glowering complaints that he had been tricked into disposing of the best minister he ever had, imply that Cromwell's enemies were able to turn the King's suspicion of heresy and notoriously quick temper to their own advantage. On the other hand, the idea that Henry VIII was a weak or indecisive monarch flies so far in the face of common sense and received opinion as to be unrecognisable outside the academic sphere.

The evidence to resolve these competing interpretations once and for all does not exist. Probably it never did; personal monarchy leaves an inconsistent paper trail. The best that we can do is to set the shifting politics of religion against Henry's own understanding of his kingship, insofar as we can reconstruct it. The didactic literature of the period offers some clues. From Thomas More's *Utopia* to Thomas Elyot's *The Boke named the Governour*, humanist writings constantly stressed the importance of good counsel to virtuous monarchy. Henry VIII knew that an uncounselled king could fall into tyranny and he acted accordingly, choosing both traditionalists and reformers for his advisors and balancing the influence of the privy council with that of the privy chamber. The varying tone of religious policy might represent the flow of information and advice received, and the flexibility demanded by political circumstance, rather than any weakness or indecision on the part of the king. Meanwhile the central pillars of the Church remained unshaken throughout the final fifteen years of the reign: the supreme headship, the Latin Mass, and a celibate clergy.

One of these three elements, of course, was a radical departure from the past, although not as Henry's propagandists presented it and not as the King himself believed. For Henry the royal supremacy was a recovery rather than an invention, upheld by the '*dyvers sundrie olde autentike histories and cronicles*' cited in the Act of Appeals. Denying the novelty of the supreme headship required some tendentious reasoning and a highly selective reading of the authorities: Richard Rex speaks for many, both approving and opposed, when he describes the transfer of ecclesiastical loyalty from Pope to King as '*a constitutional revolution of the first order*'.[32] Some scholars have gone further. More than a century ago the Anglican theologian J N Figgis interpreted the royal supremacy as an '*emphatic assertion of unfettered sovereignty vested in the king*', and there have been several subsequent discussions of the 'Tudor despotism'. What Figgis also noted, however, was the stress on obedience that predominated in apologies for the Henrician Reformation, outweighing any abstract theorising about monarchy.[33] Henry VIII undoubtedly took a high view of his own sovereignty, causing it to be proclaimed through print and the pulpit and aggressively policed by the law of treason. In the sense that he asserted the royal supremacy and healed his subjects with the royal touch, he promoted the divine right of kings. But he spoke a different political language from James VI and I, who would lecture the House of Commons that '*kings... by God himself are called gods*'. The reign of Henry VIII did not start England on a high road to the civil war of the 1640s.

The imperative of obedience was not restricted to the Church. In the hands of Thomas Cromwell it became a means to gather together ancient territorial liberties and sanctuaries and subsume them into one empire. In England this was either a revolution in government or a piece of legalistic house-keeping, depending on interpretation. In Wales its impact was unquestionably profound: representation in Parliament, the extension of English common law, and the forging of a permanent relationship between the provincial elite and the English Crown. Henry VIII faced barely a whisper of dissent from Wales, in spite of a Reformation that must have cut deeply into popular religious culture. Across the water in Ireland, however, a major rebellion in the mid 1530s forced the English government to reassess its traditional policy of ruling through the local nobility. The history of Ireland in Henry VIII's reign is of such complexity and interest that it really deserves an essay of its own. 'Ireland' itself is little more than convenient shorthand, as there were really two or even three communities – the Pale around Dublin, the broader area of English influence, and the Gaelic territories – divided from each other by language, law, custom, and increasingly religion. Questions of sovereignty, already acute in Ireland, were made more so by a Reformation that could never quite decide how to proceed: whether in the Irish language, thus attempting to evangelise among the ordinary people, or to impose the gospel in English as a means to civilise Gaelic culture. For his part, Henry VIII was reluctant to divert resources from the war in

France, and rejected the call from the Irish council for a decisive conquest of the island in favour of refortifying the Pale as an English enclave on the Calais model.

When change in Ireland's constitution did come, it was engineered by Henry's viceroy and council in Ireland rather than the king himself. The idea of recreating Ireland as a kingdom rather than a lordship of the English crown was floated by the English-born Bishop of Meath in 1538 in the context of the royal supremacy over the church.[34] Two years later it took shape in a letter from Lord Deputy St Leger advising Henry to assume the title of King of Ireland, on grounds that:

'*...they that be of the Irissherie wolde more gladder obey Your Highnes by name of King of this your lande, then by the name of Lorde thereof; having hadde heretofore a folisshe opinyon amonges them, that the Bisshoppe of Rome shulde be King of the same*'.[35]

The reference to the Pope was a skilful lure. Henry's understandable concern that he lacked the revenues to assert his honour and dignity in Ireland was overcome, and the Irish Parliament duly proclaimed him King in 1541, the Bill read out in both English and Irish. Celebrations were staged in Dublin, with bonfires, a salute of guns, feasting in the houses and wine in the streets. Lords and gentry rode to St Patrick's Cathedral to hear Mass sung by the Archbishop, and the Act was proclaimed to a crowd of 2,000 people to the sound of the *Te Deum*. St Leger was beside himself: that Henry VIII should be presented with another imperial crown was '*no lesse to my comforte, then to be agein rissen from dethe to life*'. Sending Henry a pair of silk gloves, he apologised for so simple a gift from one '*that wold as gladly presente yow with the empier of the hoole worlde, if it were in him to gyve*'.[36] St Leger's fawning words are a reminder of the stifling atmosphere of flattery that surrounded Henry VIII in his later years.

CONCLUSION: MONARCHY AND TYRANNY

In 1902 A F Pollard, one of the most influential historians of his generation and the first modern biographer of Henry VIII, described him as '*the most remarkable man who ever sat on the English throne*'.[37] Henry may have been egotistical, despotic, tempted along the path towards tyranny; but he was also a statesman of vision and judgement, instinctually attuned to his people, and a mighty advocate of the national interest in England's hour of need. Without him, claimed Pollard, the storm of the Reformation would have broken with an even greater destructive force: '*Every drop of blood shed under Henry VIII might have been a river under a feebler king*'.[38] His admiration for Henry is all the more intriguing in light of Pollard's affirmed Liberalism and respect for England's unique constitutional development. The realm flourished because of, and not in spite of, Henry's strength as a ruler. To quote Patrick Collinson's essay on Pollard in the *Oxford Dictionary of National Biography*, it was during Henry's VIII's reign that England was set on its '*predestined course towards greatness and a kind of political perfection*'.

The intervening years have been less kind to Henry. While acknowledging that he was revered by his people as the '*quintessence of Englishry*' and a focus of national pride, Scarisbrick was damning in his final verdict: '*rarely, if ever, have the unawareness and irresponsibility of a king proved more costly of material benefit to his people*'.[39] His life of Henry heralded a procession of academic books and articles reinterpreting the Reformation as a time of uproar and misery, with churches left despoiled and their congregations bereft and bewildered. New histories of court politics have questioned the reality behind the icon of royal power, stressing the manipulability and even vulnerability of the king. Others have revived the discussions of tyranny that began in Henry's own time, not only in Catholic circles but among his own advisors, servants and friends: the humanists More and Elyot, the poets Wyatt and the Earl of Surrey. Pollard wrote of the '*dictatorship*' of Henry VIII, albeit before that word acquired its 20th-century meaning, and with the proviso that he was also strictly speaking a constitutional monarch.[40] A century later, one commentator has described the '*strikingly totalitarian*' tone of the King's policies and ambitions, with no such qualifications.[41] Film and television have tended in the same direction, for obvious reasons. Fred Zinnemann's 1966 adaptation of Robert Bolt's *A Man for All Seasons* contrasted Paul Scofield as Thomas More, a beacon of calm and conscience, with the raging vindictiveness of Robert Shaw's Henry VIII. More recently, the BBC's *Tudors* has introduced US and British television audiences to a smaller, sexier, but just as power-crazed King Henry.

Five hundred years since Henry VIII's accession, is his reign something to celebrate? As so often with the towering personalities of the past, there is a split between the professional academics whose opinions are highly critical, and a popular memory which echoes Pollard in admiring Henry in spite of his many failings. Generations of children, for example, learned from H E Marshall's *Our Island Story* of 1905 that King Henry was a bad and selfish man and died a cruel tyrant, but that he also placed a Bible in every English church.[42] The exhibition, *Henry VIII: Dressed to Kill*, at the Tower of London in 2009 offers a chance to reassess Henry VIII according to criteria that are sensitive to historical context, and to rebalance our analysis of his kingship. The historiography of the reign has focused disproportionately on the 1530s, the era of the Reformation and revolution in government, when rich seams of minable documentation were laid down. The first half of the reign and the 1540s have been less fully explored. But these were the times when Henry went to war, living his own definition of what a King of England should be. Focusing on the material and ritual culture of the Tudor court – the sorts of evidence that until relatively recently made historians wary – enables us to see a fuller, and sometimes finer, side to Henry VIII. Investing in magnificence could pay handsome dividends: France may have been dissuaded from an enterprise against England as much by Henry's aura of majesty as by his royal navy.

Summing up the evidence of Henry VIII's reign, a judge would have to take account of a unique combination of destruction and rebuilding. Henry taxed and spent his subjects' money, upset their understanding of salvation, brutalised the north of England and neglected his other kingdom of Ireland. A medieval devotional landscape of monasteries, shrines and sacred drama was laid waste. He executed hundreds on grounds of disloyalty (though not so many as has sometimes been claimed), and fostered a climate of fear around him that intimidated many more into keeping silent. A fissure opened up between papists and heretics, Catholics and Protestants, with incalculable consequences for the future of the British Isles. If this is the case for the prosecution, then that for the defence lies in palaces and castles, warships and many of the objects in the exhibition, but also in the English Bible, a precociously active Parliament, and (depending on your point of view) the sovereignty of a nation-state. Henry VIII faced the greatest popular rebellion between the 1381 peasants' revolt and the civil war, but the Pilgrimage of Grace did not seek to depose him, as did uprisings against Henry VII, Mary and Elizabeth. If inconstant in religion, then he adhered to the cause of reform as he interpreted it, and kept up a cycle of private devotions that are astonishing by the standards of today. The last word should be given to the English people, ringing their church bells and singing Requiem Mass at the news of Henry VIII's death: in mourning and in fear for the future they were united as never before.

Notes and references page 334.

{II}

FAITH AND POLITICS

LUCY WOODING

Henry VIII was brought up to believe that he was the instrument of God, and his faith was deeply held. Lucy Wooding's essay explores the contradictions of a king who broke away from the Roman Catholic Church, but continued to attend Mass every day; who hated Luther, but commanded the destruction of sacred images and the translation of the Bible into English. Henry's belief that he was a new King David led England into a Reformation that transformed the appearance of every parish church, and politicised the nation as never before.

On 30 June 1513, in the fifth year of his reign, Henry VIII landed at Calais, on his way to make war against the French. The sea was black with ships, and the sound of the guns firing the welcoming salute could be heard back across the Channel in Dover. It was two days after Henry's 22nd birthday, and the young, handsome, athletic king, over six feet tall, made an imposing martial figure. Over a German-made armour he wore a tunic made of white cloth of gold which bore the red cross of St George, and he wore another badge of St George in his hat. His first action was to ride to the church of St Nicholas and to ask God's blessing on his venture. Among the many who had accompanied him to France were over 100 members of the Chapel Royal, priests and musicians, that the King might hear Mass on a daily basis, even as he campaigned in the field. When the campaign achieved its first concrete victory, capturing the town of Thérouanne, the Chapel Royal sang *Te Deum*, the ancient Christian hymn of rejoicing and thanksgiving, in the town church in celebration of the victory.[1]

This mingling of military and religious activities was reflected at a deeper level in the King's war aims. Determined to renew his ancestral claims to French territory as soon as he came to the throne, it had taken several years of patient diplomacy to forge the necessary alliance, but now England formed part of a so-called 'Holy League' with the Holy Roman Empire, Spain and the Papacy. Henry's intentions were hallowed by divine approval, or so he claimed, partly because he was attacking the French in retribution for their aggression in Italy. Pope Julius II had promised that if Henry won he could take the title of 'Most Christian King', which formerly had belonged to the Kings of France. The formation of this Holy League had been sealed by a solemn oath taken at St Paul's Cathedral back in April, and the twelve great cannon that travelled with the King as the centrepiece of his armaments were named the 'Twelve Apostles'. Henry's cause was also just, he maintained, because he was claiming back lands that were his by right of inheritance. As a marching song of the time insisted, the English were fighting the French 'in the quarrel of the church and in the right'.[2]

It is easy to dismiss this kind of religious rhetoric as empty. To the modern mind, it might seem analogous to the pious protestations made by politicians today to justify their own foreign policy aims, which are in fact based on more crude calculations about economic realities such as the price of oil. For Henry VIII too, warfare offered the possibility of considerable wealth through territorial gains, and his soldiers also hoped to profit from their loot, or from the ransoms paid for any captured French nobles. Yet what Henry hoped for more than anything else was glory. He went to war in search of the kind of magnificent reputation won by Henry V a century earlier. The battle of Agincourt in 1415 is still today a name to conjure with, a victory with the same nostalgic force and patriotic overtones as Blenheim, Trafalgar, Waterloo or the battle of Britain. Henry VIII made a conscious attempt to achieve something of comparable stature. Before his departure for France, he had commissioned someone to write the life of Henry V, and he modelled his behaviour closely on that of his illustrious predecessor.[3] As Shakespeare later recorded, on the night before the great battle, Henry V walked quietly around the camp, listening to and encouraging his soldiers. A century later, Henry VIII was to do the same. Military success, however, could not be had for the asking, and the best Henry managed in 1513 was the capture of the town of Thérouanne and the city of Tournai. Even so, Henry's propaganda managed to elevate the battle of the Spurs to the status of an important victory, as its depiction in paintings and prints shows.

Henry VIII's thirst for glory, and his insistence that his every political move be given the gloss of religious sanction, tell us something of profound importance about Tudor politics. Nowadays a political leader might choose to project an image of strength, military success, or moral standing in order to boost his ratings in the polls, or improve his chances in a forthcoming election. Tudor politicians, and above all,

Tudor monarchs, were engaged in a more subtle and anxious process. Their desire for the sanction of religion was a bid to secure their authority in a fiercely religious age, and they were concerned to justify their actions not only because of their subjects' religious convictions, but also because of their own. Even military success was seen not purely as a demonstration of their strength, but as an indication of divine approval. To rule England in the 16th century it was vitally important that God was seen to be on your side. Success in battle, or in any other field, including the procreation of healthy male children, was taken as a direct indication of God's support and sanction. Without divine sanction, not only might your popularity suffer, but so too would your self-belief, and the aura of kingship would be tarnished for ruler and subject alike.

The complex relationship between Tudor politics and religion was far more than the manipulation of a superstitious population by a series of intelligent and educated rulers. It was the central fact of a political system which rested far more heavily on ideological convictions and moral obligations than any system we know today. The king could not use elaborate administrative structures or coercive powers to enforce his authority; he relied on his ancestry, on precedent, on ritual, but above all on his own personal ability to compel respect and obedience. Without standing army, police force, civil service, or the powers of the modern judicial system, he had to make his subjects obey him because they wanted to do so. This was still a long way from democracy, not least because the allegiance and obedience of his wealthier subjects was far more important than that of the peasantry, who had other social and economic constraints to keep them in their place. Yet even the views of the peasantry could be important in times of rebellion. Tudor monarchs were obliged to fashion an image for themselves with all the determination of the modern celebrity, with a great deal more at stake than just their personal success. On their ability to dazzle, impress and convince hinged the security of the realm. It was in many ways rule by sheer force of personality.

And in an age when religion gave meaning to almost every aspect of daily life, when faith permeated every intellectual proposition, when devotional traditions coloured every aspect of popular culture, a successful personality was inevitably one with a strong element of piety. This was clearly a belief universally held; the heroes and heroines of the 16th century were those distinguished by their devotion to their God. Henry V had won the battle of Agincourt against the odds; to contemporaries (as Shakespeare again makes clear) he had done so because he was a man of integrity, a man of stern principles, and in the 15th and 16th centuries, integrity and principle could only dwell within a Christian world view. It was no accident that Henry V as a king had also been energetic in his pursuit of heretics, had reformed the existing monasteries and founded new ones. The coronation service, with its elaborate ritual of acclamation, oath, anointing, robing, crowning and blessing, transformed kings into figures with religious as well as secular authority. Henry VIII was believed to have healing hands, and like every monarch until Queen Anne in the early 18th century, he regularly performed the ritual of laying-on of hands to heal disease. One of the most important days of the year at the royal court was Epiphany, when in honour of the Three Kings visiting the Christ child, Henry wore his purple robes of state and his crown. At points like this, the identification between divine majesty and royal kingship was complete. For all the Tudors, including Henry himself, the greatness of their king was necessarily reflected in his closeness to God.

Henry VIII was brought up to be a hero. The role models he was given in his youth would have been those displayed to every child of noble or royal status being raised during the Renaissance. Some of these role models were classical, like Alexander the Great or Julius Caesar, but more were biblical heroes such as King David, King Solomon or King Josiah, or rulers from the Christian past such as the Emperor Constantine or the Emperor Charlemagne. Henry's most immediate education would have been that which he received from the example of his father's reign. Henry VII had a weak dynastic claim to the throne; the two pillars of his reign were his victory at Bosworth in 1485 and his marriage to Elizabeth of York, which effectively ended the civil wars of the 15th century by uniting the Lancastrian and the Yorkist lines. He ruled, therefore, as victor and peacemaker, but he was careful to reinforce his moral standing by ostentatious and consistent piety, and lavish religious patronage. The chapel which Henry VII built at the east end of Westminster Abbey to house his tomb proclaims his majesty, asserts his right to lie entombed among his fellow kings, and at the same time declares his subservience to God. Henry VIII, who paid for the completion of his father's tomb, would have understood the visual message only too clearly (fig. 2).

Throughout his life, Henry would consider his religious obligations to be one of the most central aspects of his life and his kingship. This was not a cynical decision to manipulate his image through the appearance of piety; it was something more fundamental than that. Henry was a very religious man, odd though that sounds to modern ears, and his religious

Fig. 2 Bronze effigies of Henry VII (1457–1509) and his wife, Elizabeth of York, by Pietro Torrigiano (1472–1528), Westminster Abbey, London.
© The Bridgeman Art Library

convictions, although at times idiosyncratic, show every sign of having been sincere. Throughout his life, the King attended Mass every day, and in great state on Sundays and feast days; he gave alms regularly to the poor; when his first child was born, on New Year's Day 1511, he went on a pilgrimage to Walsingham to give thanks; every major occasion of his reign was marked by a religious ceremony. When good news came, his choir sang *Te Deum*; in times of trial, threatened by plague or a French invasion, processions and litanies were ordered throughout the kingdom. It is also important to appreciate that Henry had a deeply religious approach to the sacrament of marriage, ironic as this may seem. When he came to the conclusion that his first marriage to Katherine of Aragon had been a sham, an illegal and immoral union, he based his view on the Bible, and the prohibition in *Leviticus* against marrying a brother's wife.[4] Katherine, many years before, had been briefly married to Henry's older brother Arthur, who had died after only a few months. Henry's discovery of the relevant passages in *Leviticus* was akin to a religious revelation, and however convenient this conclusion might have been, it was one he clearly felt deeply. Even more telling was the fact that he and Anne Boleyn refrained from sexual relations throughout the long years of waiting for the divorce, until by the end of 1532 it became clear that she would be his queen.[5] On one level, Henry had tired of one woman and found another to replace her. But in his own understanding, he had discovered that his first marriage had offended against God's law, and he wanted his second marriage to be pleasing to God.

Yet Henry's relationship with his maker was far from servile. Henry knew himself to be God's anointed, and thought of himself as one of the kings of the Old Testament, a royal figure like King Solomon or King David. Particularly in the latter part of his reign he liked to have himself depicted accordingly, and his own private psalter showed the King, in the distinctive headdress he favoured, as King David, playing his harp (fig. 3). This identification meant he expected God's favour, and demanded divine approbation as of right. When it was not forthcoming, when his enterprises failed, or his baby sons died, it meant that something was amiss, and Henry was adept at blaming everyone but himself. It also meant that he was not afraid to deal in an authoritative manner with the Church. In Henry's eyes, this was part of his prerogative as king.

Historical appreciation of this aspect of Henry's character has been muddied by conflicting interpretations of the Reformation, for it was in Henry's reign that England's long and complicated journey towards Protestantism began. Once upon a time, when this was viewed with unashamed triumphalism as a move from bigotry and superstition to the true faith, Henry was seen as a man responding to the needs of his subjects when he severed England from the Papacy, and set up an independent and reformed Church. Later on, when historical opinions changed, the destruction of English Catholicism began to be seen as a terrible act of high-handed violence perpetrated against the treasured beliefs and traditions of the population at large. Henry was seen as the worst kind of reformer, one bent on his own aggrandizement and enrichment as he took power from the Pope and wealth from the monasteries. His own religious convictions were assumed to be negligible, his ambitions entirely mercenary and personal.

In recent years, this view has been reconsidered yet again. No easy answer is possible. Henry broke with the Pope, destroyed the monasteries, smashed the images which had encouraged the populace (or so he said) in idolatry, and introduced the English Bible. This all looked like the beginnings of Protestantism. On the other hand, he steadfastly

Fig. 3 Henry VIII depicted in his psalter as King David. © The British Library Board

rejected the doctrines of the Lutherans, upheld the Latin Mass, the seven sacraments, the celibacy of priests and many other traditional aspects of the faith. This looked like 'Catholicism without the Pope', or so it has been argued. Many commentators have taken refuge in the view propounded by one of the first people to write the history of Henry's reign, namely John Foxe, whose *Book of Martyrs* became one of the most important books in English culture. Foxe, not wanting to stress Henry's Catholic side, but rejoicing in his more Protestant moments, claimed that Henry was well-intentioned but easily influenced, that his wives and councillors had too much sway over him, accounting for the apparent vacillations in policy. Yet many of us who have studied Henry have found this picture deeply unconvincing; this was not a man easily swayed by those about him.

The contradictions in Henry's approach to religion begin to make more sense if we place them more firmly in the context of both his religious ambitions and his political concerns. The breaking point was to come in the crisis of 1529–32, when Henry was seeking to have his first marriage to Katherine of Aragon annulled. Her child-bearing days were over and his only legitimate child was a daughter, Princess Mary. Meanwhile, an added imperative came from the fact that Henry had already fallen in love with the woman he intended to make his new queen, Anne Boleyn. Even then it took Henry's discovery of the biblical passage which confirmed his own feelings to really add force to his request for a divorce. He felt that he was doing God's will. He was surprised, and outraged, to discover that not everyone saw it this way. Under pressure from the Holy Roman Emperor, Charles V, who was Katherine of Aragon's nephew, the Pope was unable to give his agreement to what was by no means an unusual request. The subsequent stand-off between Italian Pope and English King was to end in a rupture, the declaration of Henry himself as 'Supreme Head of the Church of England', and the rejection of centuries of English allegiance to the Roman pontiff. To many observers at the time and since, this seemed like a display of exceptional arrogance and ambition in the service of the King's own personal whims.

We need to take a step back from the indignation of the ages, and appreciate that, whatever Henry's private lusts, this was for him a religious matter. His first marriage was clearly against God's will, because despite Henry's piety, his sons kept dying. This put a religious complexion on what was also a major political issue. In 1529 Henry had been on the throne for twenty years, and throughout that time had been desperate to secure the succession with at least one healthy male heir. It is important to remember that Henry's father had taken the throne in 1485 on the back of an era of civil war and unprecedented dynastic upheaval, which had seen five kings deposed, and three of them murdered. A fourth had died at the battle of Bosworth which brought Henry VII to the throne, and for many years there was no assurance that Henry VII might not himself be deposed and murdered. Henry VIII had been brought up under the shadow of his father's insecurities, and the memory of what were later termed the 'Wars of the Roses'. He knew only too well that all the achievements of his magnificent reign would count for nothing if he had no legitimate male heir, and that the realm would likely be plunged once more into civil war at his death. The merciless vengeance he exacted on any of his subjects who seemed to threaten his dynasty was a testimony to his insecurity. He might have been besotted with Anne Boleyn, but in the end she too would die a terrible death in the interests of dynastic security when she too failed to give him a son. Henry's ambitions were for the peace of his realm, not just for his own emotional needs.

Just as importantly, Henry's own particular crisis emerged during an extraordinary era in church history, when many long-standing attitudes were being questioned and there were increasing demands for church reform. Again it is important to understand the nexus between politics and religion at this time. The desire to reform the Church meant on the one hand the revival of scripture, the purging of superstition and the education of the clergy; on the other hand, it meant an end to papal corruption, the secular political ambitions of the papal states, and the backing of reform by princes educated according to newfound Renaissance principles. Long before Henry had given up on Katherine of Aragon's fertility, he had begun to endorse new ideas, both promoting the new 'humanist' learning which encouraged a return to the beliefs and morals of the early Christians, and curbing the powers of the clergy within England when they seemed to challenge his own authority.

Henry had already cast himself as a church reformer in the early years of his reign; it was part of his self-fashioning as the epitome of a Renaissance prince. If he was warrior, sportsman, poet and musician, he was also scholar and theologian. He encouraged the study of Hebrew and Greek in the universities, the original languages of the Bible, and he encouraged Erasmus (fig. 4), who in 1516 brought out the first new translation of the New Testament to appear for centuries. The new Renaissance interest in ancient languages

Fig. 4 Portrait of Desiderius Erasmus (1466–1536); by Hans Holbein the Younger (1497/8–1543). © The Bridgeman Art Library

meant that people were returning to the Bible and finding new inspiration and excitement there. They began to argue the case for a more educated clergy, for schools which taught piety alongside the classics, for an end to the immoral living of some clergy and for more university colleges to educate the next generation. This movement had swept across Europe. In due course it would give birth to Lutheranism, and the other forms of Protestantism, but it began as a movement for reform within Catholicism. Henry himself wrote a book against Luther in 1521, in itself a startling act for a king. In it he argued passionately for papal power, and traditional Catholic doctrine. But the significance of it was that a king had for the first time entered an arena which previously had been the preserve of popes and their scholars. In the ferment of new ideas about church reform, secular princes were to have a huge role to play, as were the laity at large, helped by the transmission of ideas through the new medium of print. No church would ever look the same again.

To begin with, this new era looked like the dawn of a golden age. So Erasmus thought when he compared the efforts and enthusiasm of Henry VIII, Pope Leo X and others. He wrote 'I feel the summons to a sure and certain hope that besides high moral standards and Christian piety, the reformed and genuine study of literature and the liberal disciplines may be partly reborn and partly find new lustre'.[6] But the political implications of this new interest in church reform soon burst upon the European scene. Luther's radical version of the new ideas began to tear the German lands apart. And when Henry came up against the pope's unwillingness to free him from Katherine, he began to think in more ambitious terms. It is highly significant that for Henry, the central aspect of his case came from the Bible, from the prohibition in the *Book of Leviticus* against marrying a brother's wife. The rights and wrongs of this case were argued all around Europe, in royal courts, diplomatic exchanges and an array of universities. But at root the point was that Henry was challenging the papacy with a higher authority; the Word of God itself.

It was on the basis of scripture, and some rather dubious claims about early Church history, that in the early 1530s Henry shaped the doctrine of the Royal Supremacy. He claimed that kings of England had always been heads of their Church (a point he had made in public long before the divorce case loomed) and that the Pope's claims to supremacy over Christendom were entirely unjust, in no way rooted in the Bible but the expression of papal greed and corruption. He denounced the Pope, took charge of the Church himself, banished Katherine, and married Anne Boleyn. The final, ironic twist to this drama came in September 1533, when the new queen gave birth, not to the expected prince, but to a daughter, Elizabeth. Nonetheless, Henry was to continue with his bludgeoning of the English Church and his frightening domestic upheavals alike. Anne lost her head, and his third queen, Jane Seymour, finally produced the long-awaited prince, nearly 30 years after Henry had come to the throne.

It is important to understand that in all these twists and turns of policy Henry held on to the idea of himself as a godly prince, a pious reformer, a scholar and a theologian bent on purifying the Church and returning it to its original state of morality and true doctrine. The consequences of this idea may have varied but the idea itself remained central to his convictions. He wrote to Erasmus in 1527, 'we have felt for several years, and now feel, that very thing; our breast, incited without doubt by the Holy Spirit, is kindled and inflamed with passion that we should restore the faith and religion of Christ to its pristine dignity... so that... the word of God should run freely and purely'.[7] Once his supremacy was established in fact he went on to exercise it in a wide array of religious policies, bent on fulfilling his own rhetoric and acting the part of Old Testament king to the hilt. It was not Protestant and it was not Catholic either, although Henry liked to call himself a Catholic. It was a kingly Reformation, a bid for Renaissance glory, an attempt at a biblical revival, all in one devastating gesture of royal piety and magnificence.

Two lasting images make the point that Henry was so anxious to transmit, which kept the propaganda machinery of his government busy from the 1530s until the day he died. One is the mural by Holbein (fig. 5) which was enshrined at the heart of Tudor government, on the wall of the Privy Chamber, now destroyed, but still available to us in a 17th-century copy. The shadowy presence of Henry VII and his queen, Elizabeth of York, is the backdrop to the now iconic portrayal of Henry VIII's majestic figure, Jane Seymour his modest counterpart. At the centre, a Renaissance-style pilaster bears a Latin verse glorifying Henry's achievement, and in particular the way it outshone even his father's reign. The verse concludes:

And in truth, to this steadfastness Papal arrogance yielded
When the sceptre of power was wielded by Henry the
Eighth,
Under whose reign the true faith was restored to the nation
And the doctrines of God began to be reverenced with awe.[8]

To Henry himself, his religious policies were clearly his greatest triumph.

Fig. 5 *Copy after Holbein's Whitehall Mural* (1667) by Remigius van Leemput (1607–75). The Royal Collection © Her Majesty Queen Elizabeth II

The Whitehall mural was an image for the privileged few at the heart of government, and for the King himself. A second, equally telling image was disseminated by one of Henry VIII's most important achievements, and perhaps his most lasting legacy, namely the official English Bible, which was to be placed in every parish church of the realm. In this image Henry spoke more directly to a greater number of his subjects than in any other place, or through any other medium. On the title page of the Great Bible Henry was depicted enthroned in majesty, as a kind of secular Christ in glory (fig. 1). He was shown declaiming from scripture as he handed out copies of the English Bible to clergy and laity on either side. Lower down the page the dissemination of the Word of God was shown, and at the base of the picture, the grateful populace were shouting their acclamation, not to God, as might be expected, but to Henry himself. '*Vivat Rex!*' and '*God Save The Kynge!*' we see issuing from the mouths of his newly enlightened subjects. The identification between King of Heaven and King of England was complete.

The rest of Henry's reign was to be deeply coloured by the extraordinary religious and political initiative of the Royal Supremacy. It became the central test of both political loyalty and religious orthodoxy. Those who denied him on political grounds or on religious grounds were persecuted with equal viciousness. Catholics like Thomas More, John Fisher, or the London Carthusians, died brutal deaths. Protestants who enthusiastically welcomed his break with Rome, yet transgressed against the central Catholic doctrine of the Mass, also died horribly. For many, Henry's legacy was chiefly one of destruction and despair. In particular, he targeted the monasteries, claiming that they were corrupt (as indeed some were), knowing that they were wealthy, not caring that they were in many parts of the country a vital and treasured part of society. The north of England most notably suffered Henry's wrath, when the northern counties rose in revolt against his dissolution of the monasteries in the rebellion called the Pilgrimage of Grace. Henry's fury at this was all the more deadly, in that this rebellion was at first a serious threat to him. Once he had managed to gain an advantage over the rebels, he persecuted those loyal to the monasteries and the Catholic past they represented with savage vengeance. Abbots were hanged from the spires of their abbey churches, and their bewildered supporters – who could not believe that the King could really have intended such devastation – died swinging from a gibbet. All over England the empty shells of our former monasteries stand to this day as a sobering testimony to the force of Henry's evangelical and authoritarian vision of himself as a godly king (fig. 7).

Fig. 7 Rievaulx Abbey, North Yorkshire. © English Heritage Photo Library

The strength of Henry's vengeance was a direct consequence of the new political order he had created, which combined the royal right to political obedience with the religious obedience previously the preserve of the Church. Once Henry had declared himself Supreme Head of the Church, anyone who disobeyed him had added an offence against God to their offence against the King. More worryingly, it was no longer possible to obey the King whilst maintaining an independent or private understanding of one's own faith. Thomas More opposed the Supremacy, but tried to seek refuge in silence, professing his loyalty to the King. This was unacceptable to Henry, who demanded acceptance of his religious settlement also, and Thomas More went to the block. Many were to fall victim to this new and terrifying nexus between divine and human law. Thomas Cromwell, who served the King so well but was unable to conceal his Protestant leanings, went to the block on the same principle, that Henry required complete submission to his religious formulations as an integral part of political conformity. Factions at court, who in earlier times had organised themselves around a particular domestic or foreign policy agenda, now began to take on different religious allegiances. Henry's intermingling of the sacred with

rion, that Chzift hath left here with vs;so that I beleue, we néed no vnwzitten verities to rule his

Lord, so be it,

By me Anne Askew.

The order and manner of the burning of *Anne Askew*, *Iohn Lacels, Iohn Adams, Nicolas Belenian*, with certaine of the *Counsell sitting in Smithfield*.

Fig. 8 The Martyrdom of Anne Askew, John Lacels, John Adams and Nicolas Belenian at Smithfield. A woodcut from 'Actes and Monuments' by John Foxe (1516–87), published in 1563. Private Collection © The Bridgeman Art Library

the secular had made the Crown at once much more power-ful, and much more resented, and had given new levels of complexity and anxiety to the business of Tudor politics (fig. 8).

Henry was always savage in his persecution of any who opposed him. His wives, his chief ministers, his relatives, his nobility – all bore the brunt of his wrathful indignation when he deemed that they had betrayed him. The more constructive aspects of Henry's religious policies also need to be recognized, however. The proceeds of the dissolution did not all go into his wars. He also founded new cathedrals (appropriating the abbey churches) and university colleges; he transformed the parish churches of his realm, taking away many of the trappings of the Catholic past and installing his English Bible; he stirred up great achievements

in the fields of learning, art, architecture and music. In his brutal, domineering, yet intelligent fashion, he was reconfiguring both kingship and Christianity side by side. His arrogance on both counts is astounding, but then he had been brought up to believe himself the instrument of God. He was also the first king to be called 'Your Majesty', and in every gesture he lived up to this image. He built palaces, founded a court armour workshop, bought jewels and tapestries; hunted, danced, played, fought and married on a scale never before equalled by an English monarch. That Henry's reign was so extraordinary, that it left such an arresting legacy to his successors, that it had such an impact on English society, was in large part a consequence of the profound and inescapable relationship between politics and religion.

Notes and references page 334.

{III}

WARFARE IN HENRY'S REIGN

STEVEN GUNN

Although he could play the peacemaker when diplomacy demanded,
Henry VIII was never happier than when leading his nobility to war.
Steven Gunn explains how the glorious memory of Henry V and the Hundred
Years War spurred Henry VIII to renew the military campaign in France.
Tournai and Boulogne were captured for a while, and two great defeats were
inflicted on Scotland. Coastal artillery forts were built to protect the kingdom
against invasion. The cost of conflict, however, came not just in lives lost
but in the squandered resources, ruined coinage and raging inflation that
would afflict England for years to come.

Fig. 1 Flodden Field,
James IV lies dead and
the Scots begin to flee.
From *Der Weisskunig*,
1514, an engraving by
Hans Burgkmair
(1473–1531).

For Henry VIII and those around him, war was something great kings did. His father-in-law, Ferdinand of Aragon, had taken Granada from the Moors and beaten the French to overrun Naples. Louis XII of France, to whom Henry married his sister, had conquered Genoa and Milan. Maximilian of Habsburg, the Holy Roman Emperor who joined Henry on his first campaign, had won his spurs rescuing his young wife's inheritance in the Netherlands from the advancing French. Then he had written about it in an autobiographical chivalrous romance. Henry's own father had taken the Crown on the battlefield of Bosworth, kept it at Stoke and Blackheath and fought the French, the Scots and the Irish; and he passed for cautious, parsimonious and peace-loving.

Henry's young contemporaries were struck from the same metal. Francis I of France came to the throne in 1515 and at once crossed the Alps to defeat the Swiss pikemen, the greatest mercenary army of the age, at the epic battle of Marignano. Charles of Habsburg, succeeding Ferdinand in his Spanish kingdoms in 1516 and Maximilian as Emperor in 1519, was slower off the mark. But territorial disputes with the French along the Pyrenees, in Italy, in

Burgundy and in the Low Countries brought war after war from 1521 until he retired, exhausted, to a Spanish monastery in 1556. Whenever he freed himself from that struggle, he turned to block the spread of Ottoman power across Hungary and the Mediterranean, relieving Vienna in 1529 and 1532 and attacking Tunis in 1535 and Algiers in 1541. And when the French and the Ottomans allowed, he mobilised against the defiant German Protestant princes, crushing them in 1547 at the battle of Mühlberg.

There were voices raised against this tide of war. Most famous was that of Desiderius Erasmus of Rotterdam, leading light of the spiritually earnest Northern European wave of the Renaissance rediscovery of ancient learning. In his *Praise of Folly* of 1511 and his essay *Dulce bellum inexpertis* – '*War is sweet to those who know nothing about it*' – of 1515, he argued trenchantly that war was bestial, unchristian, and unworthy of the enlightened rulers who now graced the thrones of Europe. He was an authority on the subject from several angles, an expert on the Bible and the classics who had grown up in a Netherlands ravaged by mercenaries, helped to educate Charles and met Henry as a boy on his trips to England.[1] When it suited them, princes could take this argument on board, trumpeting the blessings of peace and their own wisdom in achieving them. Henry did so impressively in presiding over the conclusion of a treaty of universal peace in London in 1518. But all too often the siren call of war drowned out the voices of Erasmus and those who thought like him.

History drove kings to war. The great kings of the English past had been warriors, from Richard the Lionheart and Edward I, victorious over Saracens, Welsh and Scots, to Edward III and Henry V, triumphant over the French at Crécy, Poitiers and Agincourt. It was kings like these whose deeds surrounded Henry at court, from the armoured sculptures his father had installed at Richmond Palace through tapestries and paintings to books: Both the *Agincourt Carol* and a translation of Froissart's *Chronicles of the Hundred Years War* were printed in Henry's reign. One of Henry's closest friends, his admiral Sir Edward Howard, surely knew the King's mind when he wrote to him in 1513 '*I pray God … send you as much victory of your enemies as ever had any of your noble ancestry*'.[2] Henry V in particular was a model for Henry to follow, and on his first campaign in 1513 the young King seems to have deliberately acted out scenes from his namesake's campaigns. Beyond these comparatively recent English predecessors stood the great models of chivalrous kingship glorified in the romances, Arthur, Charlemagne and

more. And as the romances' version of the past came under challenge from the new canons of scholarship – and Henry faced the embarrassment of an official court historian, the Italian Polydore Vergil, who denied King Arthur's existence – so classical models of conquest, Alexander, Scipio, Caesar and Constantine, were held up to ambitious kings.[3]

The past provided not just examples, but also incitements to war. Henry inherited Edward III's prizes of Berwick and Calais, which the Scots and French felt duty bound to retake if they could. His own ancestral claims were larger, to Normandy, lost under John and again under Henry VI, to Gascony, the last of the old Angevin provinces to fall in 1453, and to the French throne, claimed by every English king since Edward III. Over Scotland, ruled by its own kings back into a mythical past, he claimed overlordship as Edward I had done. Over Ireland, largely controlled by Gaelic chieftains whose lineages reached back before the Norman invasions, he claimed the lordship granted by the pope to the Angevin kings and then, from 1541, the kingship of the whole island.

It is hard to say how far Henry's subjects expected him actively to pursue these claims, though it was difficult for anyone to deny him the right to appeal to the judgement of God in battle to vindicate them. In a society concerned with the maintenance of honour it was also hard to argue against the King's need to assert his honour against other kings who challenged him. On a more practical level, the English could expect Henry to defend the realm, as he had sworn to do in his coronation oath. That legitimated his grand fortification campaigns, his naval expansion and the huge musters held when invasion threatened. It stretched to cover aggressive, sometimes disproportionately large, responses to raids by the Scots and the Gaelic Irish. And perhaps it justified potent interventions in the wars of the great European powers. In the Wars of the Roses the succession to the English throne had become at times the plaything of the French, the Scots and the Burgundian rulers of the Netherlands. Henry VII had had to fight, to bargain, to choke off trade to prevent his neighbours from patronising rival claimants to his crown. Under Henry VIII the French still harboured a Yorkist pretender until 1525 and after 1533 rulers loyal to the papacy might use Henry's break with Rome to justify his deposition. In such circumstances military commitments bought allies and military demonstrations deterred those who might think Henry and England an easy prey.

Internal pressures too drove Henry towards war. Many noblemen felt rather uneasy in Henry's England. At court they were edged from power by monopolistic ministers, rakehell favourites and low-born lawyers. In the country their influence was undermined by centralising law courts, royal dependence on the gentry in local government and restraints on their recruitment of retinues of political and military followers.[4] War made noblemen feel at home. They could follow in the footsteps of the ancestors who had won their titles on the fields of France. They could recruit men with the King's blessing, dress them in their livery colours and family badges and bond with them on campaign. If all went well, they could win the King's confidence, gratitude and reward: from Henry's first great campaigning season of 1513 came the Howard dukedom of Norfolk, the Brandon dukedom of Suffolk, the Somerset earldom of Worcester and the Stanley barony of Monteagle. No wonder the peerage served Henry almost to a man. In 1513 there were 34 peers neither too young nor too old to fight, and all but one turned out against the French or the Scots or at sea.[5]

Some contemporaries probably thought of war as a social safety valve, giving runaway apprentices and other disruptive types the chance to work out their aggression on foreigners rather than swelling the criminal classes in England; certainly this had been put forward as a respectable argument in favour of war in parliament in the 1470s.[6] Alliance with the Netherlands against France also guaranteed England's major export trade in cloth from London to Antwerp, and with it the employment of tens of thousands of potentially restive clothworkers. As Henry's reign went on and religious division deepened, so the beneficial effects of war in pulling the country together against a common enemy also became more attractive to him. In 1544 he neatly tied together his military adventurism and his idiosyncratic blend of old and new religious traditions by ordering all his subjects to pray in processions for the success of his campaigns using a new vernacular text of the litany.[7] By the end of his reign, however, more dispassionate social, economic, religious and strategic analysis than Henry's was coming to suggest to English policy-makers that his brand of extravagant war-making was something England could not afford.[8]

Henry's wars were the product of these attitudes and expectations, but they were also the product of the European power politics of his day. France was England's traditional enemy, but England's resources were too small for her to challenge France alone. Unlike the French kings, Henry had no standing army and no regular direct tax revenues. Even when he could persuade parliament to top up the customs on trade and the revenues of the crown lands with grants of direct taxation for war, the population he had to tax was perhaps one-sixth that of France.[9] What Henry needed were allies against the French. Fortunately for him other powers concerned to limit French power in Italy and the Low Countries readily played that role, but they did so at times and on terms that suited them. On the other hand, while England was more than a match for Scotland, which had little history of taxation and did not even pay its armies, relying on their serving for 40 days unpaid, the Scots could generally call on their ancient allies the French to assist against English aggression. And while English armies could make headway against the less well-armed Gaelic Irish given sufficient time and numbers, it was only when resources were not needed for more glamorous conflicts that they were devoted to Ireland, and they seldom stayed devoted for long.

War was in the air from the start of Henry's reign, but 1511 saw a distinct quickening of the martial pulse. The statute of Winchester of 1285 was re-issued, prescribing what arms and armour men of each social rank should possess. Henry's naval patrols intercepted and killed Andrew Barton, a leading Scottish captain whom the English accused of piracy. Henry's understanding with his father-in-law Ferdinand led to the dispatch of English archers to assist in an abortive crusade to North Africa. His understanding with the guardians of Charles of Habsburg, currently betrothed to his sister Mary, brought a similar force to the unsuccessful siege of Venlo, part of the interminable wars between the Habsburg rulers of the Netherlands and the francophile Dukes of Guelders. Undaunted, Henry pursued the diplomacy necessary to under-pin a full-scale war against France and in November concluded a Holy League with Ferdinand, Venice and the Pope.

The war in 1512 was mostly fought at sea, with raids on the Breton coast and sweeps of the Channel to capture French ships. An indecisive battle off Brest was marked by one particularly horrific incident, in which two ships grappled together had exploded and burned with the loss of many lives. The year's only land campaign was a fiasco in which the Marquis of Dorset's army, shipped to Spain to begin the reconquest of English France with the far south-west, was instead used by Ferdinand to cover his flank as he overran the kingdom of Navarre. Dorset's men drank too much, mutinied and came home. It was an inauspicious start for a reign of memorable conquest. The next season started equally ill. In spring 1513 Henry's admiral, Sir Edward Howard, frustrated at the inability of his sailing ships to get to grips with the French galleys guarding the Breton shore, was killed in the attempt to storm them from his own smaller rowbarges.[10] Henry now put all his effort into his own campaign in France.

Fig. 2 *The battle of the Spurs, 16 August 1513*, painted about 1513, artist unknown. The Royal Collection © Her Majesty Queen Elizabeth II

Henry's army, funded by grants of taxation and the remaining fiscal surpluses of his father's reign, was huge, perhaps 30,000 strong, twice the size of any English army in the Hundred Years War. He meant to achieve solid results with it and therefore settled down to two sieges in succession, first of Thérouanne, then of Tournai. Each fell in turn, affording Henry the pleasure of riding into Tournai on Sunday 25 September in full armour, on a barded horse, under a silken canopy, to receive the submission of his new subjects. Equally satisfying was a victory in open battle over a French relieving force. Admittedly it was a small affair, but it yielded aristocratic prisoners and it could be given a suitable name – the battle of the Spurs, from the speed with which the French tried to get away – and it could be repeatedly represented in the art of Henry's court, as in several panoramic paintings (fig. 2). Henry got what he wanted from his first war, then,

Meanwhile a far bloodier contest had taken place on the bleak uplands of Northumberland. James IV of Scots, eager to win glory, to avenge Barton and to meet his obligations to his French allies, marched south in August with perhaps 40,000 men, rapidly taking the castles of Norham, Etal, Chillingham and Ford. Thomas Howard, Earl of Surrey, a veteran of Bosworth who had campaigned against James around Norham in 1497, led an army of some 26,000 Northerners and East Anglians to meet him at Flodden on a drizzly 9 September. After a bold manoeuvre by Surrey to cut off any Scottish withdrawal, hard fighting, Scottish pikes against English bills, began at 4pm and lasted until after dark, so that no-one knew for certain until first light next day that the Scottish King, ten earls, thirteen barons and perhaps 10,000 Scots lay dead on the field (fig. 1).[12]

For the next nine years diplomacy took over from war in Henry's plans as the pattern of European politics repeatedly rearranged itself. Dissatisfied with his allies, he made peace with Louis XII in 1514, then manoeuvred against his successor Francis I, only to strike a deal with him for the return of Tournai under cover of a general European peace by the Treaty of London in 1518. Their friendship was splendidly celebrated as they met at the Field of Cloth of Gold in 1520. With the Scots, meanwhile, Henry maintained frail truces, and in Ireland he experimented with a larger army than normal, 1,000 men strong, in 1520–1, but to no lasting effect. The Anglo-French amity crumbled in 1521–2 as Charles of Habsburg, struggling to co-ordinate his vast but disparate dominions, offered Henry attractive terms for an alliance against France.

This time, though there were again naval raids on the Breton coast, fighting was concentrated on the borders of Picardy and Artois, where Henry's forces and those Charles raised in the Netherlands could most easily co-operate. In 1522 they managed only a desultory sweep through the French countryside and a failed siege of Hesdin. In 1523 they promised much more, taking towns deep in France, crossing the Somme and heading for Paris, only to falter and retreat when it became clear that the rebel French Duke of Bourbon would not be arriving to help them. Again it was Henry's allies who drew most benefit, as Habsburg troops overran Friesland while the French were kept occupied.[13] From Scotland, meanwhile, the pro-French regent, the Duke of Albany, led an abortive invasion of England in 1522 and a failed siege of Wark Castle in 1523, while in between these two ventures the English burnt Jedburgh. Renewed truces recognised the futility of this fighting and as plans for a grand

the admiration of his friends and the respect of his enemies, but in a pattern that would repeat itself, the real benefits went elsewhere. Maximilian, who accompanied Henry on campaign though without adding any significant financial or military contribution, saw two troublesome French strongholds eliminated from the borders of the Habsburg Low Countries. Thérouanne was more or less razed and Henry was left to fortify and garrison Tournai as a costly white elephant.[11]

enterprise against France, led by Henry in person, foundered on Habsburg awkwardness and widespread refusals to pay taxation in England, Henry gave up on the European war too, making peace with France in August 1525.[14]

Henry's next two wars were his strangest, and neither amounted to much. In 1527–8, wanting to put pressure on Charles, who was understandably obstructing Henry's efforts to annul his marriage to Charles's aunt, Katherine of Aragon, Henry drew ever closer to the French. At length, and rather reluctantly, he declared war on Charles, but plans for an attack from Calais into the Netherlands foundered and an embargo on the cloth trade hurt England more than Antwerp, forcing Henry into a truce.[15] Turning increasingly to domestic solutions to his marital problems and the quarrel with the papacy they provoked, Henry then reined in his international adventures. It was more his inattention than his ambition that sparked his next war. In 1532–4 the usual cross-border reiving escalated into a desultory series of clashes on the Scottish border. Neither side showed much will to calm it down until the French brokered a settlement.[16]

In the mid 1530s, as he consolidated the break with Rome, Henry had to mobilise not against external enemies but against internal dissent. The first challenge came in Ireland. In summer 1534 the Fitzgerald Earls of Kildare, the leading magnates of English Ireland, angry both at Henry's religious changes and at their own displacement from the governorship they had held repeatedly since the 1470s, led their extensive network of followers into revolt and drew in various Gaelic lords to support them. It took fourteen months for the 2,500 men sent over to regain control, and Tudor Ireland never returned to the light-touch government that had characterised the Kildare years.[17] The next revolt posed smaller administrative and strategic challenges, but a more immediate political threat. In autumn 1536 first Lincolnshire and then all the northern counties rose up against the dissolution of the monasteries, against Henry's taxes and his unpopular ministers in the Pilgrimage of Grace. Loyal noblemen near at hand – the Earls of Shrewsbury and Derby in particular – levied men to stem the spread of rebellion, while great musters in the south provided an army for the Duke of Norfolk, son of the victor of Flodden, to lead to Doncaster to confront the rebels. The forces were too evenly matched to risk battle and a truce, pardon and disbandment were followed by the King's exploitation of further unrest to isolate and punish his opponents.[18]

Henry's attack on the Church gave him new sources of income; from monastic lands and goods and heavy taxation on clerical incomes. He needed it to defend himself, not just

against these domestic opponents, but also against the alarming prospect of an alliance of powers still loyal to Rome against his schismatic kingdom. In 1539 that threat became very real. Charles and Francis, weary of another round of war, made peace and began to plot against Henry. He responded with a massive display of defensive strength. Men were mustered across the country and the London militia were pointedly paraded before the ambassadors attending his court. Ships were massed at Portsmouth and a vast campaign of fortification was set in motion, ringing the coast from Cornwall to Northumberland with characteristic round-faced artillery forts, some not just paid for with monastic money but even built from monastic stone. Henry's isolation even led him briefly to sacrifice his marital happiness on the altar of an alliance with the German princes as he married Anne of Cleves. But normality soon returned, as Henry repudiated Anne in favour of the more enticing Catherine Howard and moved steadily back towards an alliance with Charles against Francis, their amity having proved predictably frail.

Henry's last years saw a return to war on the grand scale. He aimed to revive the French conquests of his youth, some might say to compensate for the painful fact that Catherine Howard had not found him as exciting a husband as he had hoped and had had to be executed for adultery with several younger courtiers. Before he could venture to France, however, there were matters to be settled with the Scots. James V had proved impervious to Henry's avuncular advice and remained stubbornly attached to both the papal obedience and the French alliance, even standing Henry up when he thought they had arranged a personal meeting in 1541. Once again they drifted into war. Henry licensed raids across the border, one of which resulted in an embarrassing defeat at Haddon Rigg in August 1542. A large but aimless English invasion of the eastern Lowlands was followed by a major Scottish incursion at the other end of the border. Haddon Rigg was avenged as the Scottish army disintegrated, ambushed at Solway Moss, but the battle's true significance lay in the haul of high-ranking Scottish prisoners. When James died three weeks later – some said from shame – they, suitably entertained at the English court, provided the nucleus for an anglophile party prepared to marry his infant daughter Mary to Henry's son Edward. This marriage, agreed by the Treaty of Greenwich of July 1543, promised to achieve what Edward I and Edward III had failed to do, to bring Scotland under permanent English control. No wonder most of the Scots soon repudiated it. No wonder Henry fought to make them carry it out, sending his armies with naval support to burn Edinburgh in 1544 and repeatedly lay waste to Jedburgh, Kelso and much of the Borders. But this 'Rough Wooing' did not bring the marriage any closer, and it was left to Henry's successors to work out how best to draw 'Great Britain', a term first coined at this time, into being.[19]

Meanwhile Henry geared up for war with France. In February 1543 he agreed an offensive alliance with Charles and in June he declared war, sending his ships out into the Channel and 5,000 men to help defend the Netherlands. His great effort came the next summer, as he landed at Calais with some 40,000 men to march on Paris from the north as Charles, advancing through Champagne, attacked it from the East. That was the agreed plan, but Henry, tired at last of doing all the hard work and seeing his allies reap the rewards, simply settled down to capture Boulogne, diverting the French by detaching part of his army to besiege Montreuil. Charles, frustrated, made a separate peace with Francis, but Henry got his conquest, entering Boulogne in triumph on 18 September. It was the great prize of his autumn years and he was determined to keep it. He fortified it, garrisoned it, sent his boldest captains to defend it – including the reckless poet Henry Howard, Earl of Surrey and the man who had burnt Edinburgh, Edward Seymour, Earl of Hertford – and turned a deaf ear to his councillors' advice to give it back to secure peace.

For nearly two years the French fought to recover Boulogne. In the process they put a fleet into the Solent, prompting the action in which the *Mary Rose* sank, landed men on the Isle of Wight, and lost their king's favourite son, dead of plague in the siege camp. Peace talks brokered by Charles and a parallel set brokered by the German Protestants both failed. But finally, on 7 June 1546, a treaty was agreed by which Henry would keep Boulogne for eight years, after which the French would have to buy it back, if they could. Henry had won, but at an astonishing price. Where Henry's wars had cost around a million pounds in 1512–14 and half a million in 1522–5, his last four years of war had cost around two million, costs to which the attempt to secure the Scottish marriage and hold onto Boulogne would add another million within four years of his death. Only about a third of this came from taxation, though parliamentary grants came thick and fast and were topped up with forced loans, benevolences and other levies raised without consent, apparently hitting mercantile wealth especially hard and damaging the urban economy. A further third came from the sale of Crown lands, mostly those confiscated from the monasteries, an expedient

that undermined the long-term financial security that the dissolution might have given the Crown. Worst of all, a third came from debasement of the coinage, as the mint adulterated silver coins with base metal in order to give the King more money to spend. Before 1542, English silver currency was 92.5 per cent silver, but by April 1546 it was down to 33.3 per cent. Sterling fell on the foreign exchanges, stimulating cloth exports as English goods became cheaper abroad, but domestic inflation rose out of control and after 1550 retrenchment – including the return of Boulogne to the French – was unavoidable to restore Crown solvency, purify the coinage and repair the national economy.[20]

Taxation, inflation and the sale of monastic land were probably the effects of Henry's wars most obvious to his subjects. Only the inhabitants of the immediate borders against Scotland and Gaelic Ireland, of the Channel Isles and the Calais Pale, and of the few coastal districts raided by the French saw war at first hand, as all too many continental Europeans did in Henry's day. Yet we should not underestimate the everyday impact of war. Henry ordered musters regularly, and all men between sixteen and 60 were expected to attend. He insisted that all his male subjects should practise with the longbow on Sundays and holidays, and records of fatal accidents when arrows went astray show that many obeyed. Towards the end of the reign parishes were expected to maintain arms and armour to equip soldiers raised locally and some had to sell church plate to buy them. Coastal towns had to improve their fortifications and buy guns for their walls; a few, like Hull, found themselves more or less taken over by Henry's strategic garrisons. Ship owners, captains and sailors faced danger from the French and Scots at sea but might be tempted by the huge profits of privateering against the King's enemies. The iron industry was boosted by the demands of gun-founding. Propaganda pamphlets mocked the proud French and craven Scots, reported on Henry's victories and drove home the message that every Englishman should serve the King in defence of the realm. Public celebrations, with bonfires in the streets, church bells ringing and barrels of beer, greeted the triumphs of Flodden, Tournai, Edinburgh and above all Boulogne.[21] In strategic terms, Henry's wars may have been without result: four years after his death, the English crown held no more land in France or Scotland and not much more real authority in Ireland than it had done at his accession. But that did not mean that Henry's wars were without importance for his people or for the history of his reign.

Notes and references page 334.

Hier is het beleeh hã eerwaen
ghecouterfeÿt nã Edieuen

Suyden

Oest

Graue de
espijnoijs

Noerden

{IV}

HENRY'S ARMY
AND NAVY

DAVID LOADES

Henry VIII may have lacked the income to maintain a standing army,
but he could still muster huge numbers of men to fight in France.
In this essay, David Loades traces the modernisation of England's land forces
as the longbow gradually gave way to pikes, handguns and cannon.
Developments at sea were more dramatic. Henry fancied himself as a
naval architect and by the end of the reign had assembled a fleet of 50 ships,
armed with the latest artillery and supported by a network of
royal dockyards. The system of naval administration established by
Henry VIII set the course of England's future supremacy at sea.

Henry VIII saw himself as a warlike king, and put his mettle to the test on three separate occasions. He fought the French (and briefly the Scots) from 1512 to 1514, the French alone from 1522 to 1525, and the French again from 1543 to 1546. These last campaigns were both preceded and accompanied by invasions of Scotland which hardly counted as wars, and he also had to deploy military force against the Pilgrimage of Grace, a domestic rebellion, in 1536. Of Henry's 38-year reign, foreign wars therefore occupied only about eight, so it is necessary to keep such activity in proportion.

The military system which he inherited in 1509 was deeply rooted in the past, and reflected the fact that England had not fought a serious continental war for over 50 years. In the later middle ages, armies were raised mainly by commissions of array or by indenture. Commissions were normally issued to those noblemen who were tenants-in-chief, and thus considered themselves to be

Fig. 1 Battle of the Spurs, 1513, woodcut, 1553, by Cornelis Anthoniszoon.

© Rijksmuseum, Amsterdam

his natural companions in arms. They then raised their own retinues of followers for the king's service, and initially paid them, recovering their expenses at the end of the campaign. The indenture was a contract whereby a professional soldier undertook to raise so many men (with whom he may have had no prior contact) for a given period and at a given rate of pay. The contractor would then be given so much money 'in prest', to pay his men for a month or three months, at the end of which time he would expect a further advance. The men so raised were, in effect, mercenaries, but they were English (or Welsh), and could be expected to show a natural obedience to their employer – which did not preclude the occasional mutiny when the money ran out, as happened in France in the 1440s and 50s. The other military force consisted of the county levies, the descendants of the Anglo-Saxon *fryd*, which in theory embraced every able-bodied male between the ages of sixteen and 60, but they were not supposed to be used outside their counties of origin. The levies were required to provide their own weapons, but were essentially an untrained home defence force, and were useless for overseas campaigning.[1]

Henry VII had been only too aware of the military potential of the private retinues, and had taken steps to curtail them by a system of licences, being very anxious that the deployment of violence should be a royal monopoly. For the same reason he had developed an artillery train far more powerful than any individual nobleman could have afforded. Armies were very expensive, and by 1500 only the king had the resources to deploy a force of any size. So, although many English noblemen by that time were frustrated by the lack of opportunity to display their traditional warlike prowess, they knew better than to attempt to revert to the practice of private warfare which had so bedevilled English politics in the reign of Henry VI. By 1509 the secret of military organisation was delegation by commission.[2] Henry VIII may have wished to be his own commander-in-chief, but he knew perfectly well that he could not discharge in person all the multiple tasks which were required for the making of war. A treasurer of the war was needed to handle the money, with deputies wherever necessary, and that required a commission. Victuals also had to be provided, and although a system of purveyors was in place to provide for the royal household, they could not possibly cope with such a massive increase in their responsibilities. So further commissions were required. In 1512, therefore, commissions of array were issued to expectant nobles, the management of money and provisions was similarly delegated, a Lieutenant was required to safeguard the north, and the Lord Admiral was given his instructions. All these were issued under the great or privy seal. Nor could the actual arming of his host be done from domestic resources. Bows and arrows might be available locally, but English armourers could not be expected to cope with the sudden demand for swords, bills and body armour, most of which had to be purchased in the Low Countries. There was a gun foundry at Hounsditch, but its output was small and guns of all sizes from harquebuses to cannon had similarly to be bought from places such as Mechlin.[3] Not surprisingly, the war was already over twelve months old before Henry was able to lead an army royal of between 30 and 40,000 men to the siege of Tournai.

Just as there was no such thing as an 'English army' unless one was specially raised, so in 1509 there was no such thing as a Royal Navy either. Before guns came into use at sea there was no significant difference between the hull design of a merchantman and a warship. By simply mounting prefabricated fighting platforms, or 'castles' on the bow and stern of a commercial ship, she could be converted for fighting purposes, and the castles were easily removed when the ships returned to civilian use. The only English king between the Norman Conquest and the Tudors who showed any real awareness of the importance of sea power was Henry V, and the fleet of 30 or so ships which he assembled to fight the war of 1415–20 was decommissioned and sold off as soon as the fighting was over.[4] It was simply beyond the resources of the Crown to maintain so large a fleet in peacetime. By 1450 the navy had been reduced to nothing, and the office deputed to look after the king's ships was discontinued. For the remainder of the 15th century, the sea was 'kept' and piracy curtailed by extending the system of commission and indenture to privately owned fleets. This was cheap, but not particularly effective, and led to the development of private warships, which could be (and were) occasionally turned against the Crown. It was Henry VII who had begun, in a small way, to build a permanent navy. Within months of his accession he ordered the construction of two large new warships. These were carracks on the Portuguese model, and were subsequently named the *Regent* and the *Sovereign*. They were designed to carry guns, albeit serpentines, and the *Regent* was equipped with over 200 of them. Two ships do not make a navy, and Henry had no intention of waging war unless he had to, but he was nevertheless making an unequivocal statement. He was a 'sea king', and intended to be respected as such. The *Regent* and the *Sovereign* were not the largest ships ever to be constructed in England; that honour belongs to Henry V's *Grace a Dieu* of 1,400 tons, but at 750 and 600 tons they were still large by the standards of the time – too large to cross the Hamble bar – and that required a new dock to be constructed at nearby Portsmouth. This was done in 1495–6, and with the addition of a forge and a storehouse created the first embryonic naval base.[5] Apart from that, Henry contented himself with replacing the six or seven modest-sized vessels which he had inherited from his predecessor, so the navy which he bequeathed to his son was not very much larger than it had been in the 14th century – but it did include two state-of-the-art warships.

As far as we know, neither of these ships fired a shot in anger as long as Henry VII lived. However the fleet was deployed in the summer of 1497 in support of the Earl of Surrey's somewhat perfunctory campaign against James IV – a retaliation for the latter's support for pretender to the throne Perkin Warbeck. About a dozen vessels were deployed in transporting an English army north, led by the *Regent* and under the command of Lord Willoughby. Apart from the *Regent* only two or three of these were the king's own ships, and what they did is unrecorded. They seem to have got as far as the Firth of Forth, although that was well beyond where the army was operating, and their presence there may have owed more to the weather than to any intention.[6] Both the *Sweepstake* and the *Mary Fortune*, which were royal ships, expended quite a lot of arrows, and significant quantities of gunpowder and shot, but there is no record of their ever being in action, and 'wastage' or some other accounting fraud has been suggested. Most of the weapons issued to the fleet were returned unused, and the whole campaign lasted only a couple of weeks. Such a war hardly rates as a serious military commitment, but it was just about all the experience that English fighting men had had in the twenty years or so before Henry VIII's war with France began in 1512.

However enthusiastic he may have been by that time, neither Henry nor his subjects were experienced fighting men. However, unlike his father, the young Henry was deeply interested in the technology of warfare, and particularly in ships and guns. Immediately after his accession, he commissioned two new men-of-war, and in the design of one of these he took a personal interest. The *Mary Rose* was the first ship in England, and probably in Europe, to be built with gunports. There were only two or three of these on each side, but they marked the first capacity for broadside firing big guns to be mounted on a deck below the level of the gunwales.[7] We do not know exactly where, or by whom, the *Mary Rose* was built, but the special affection which he always showed for the ship indicates that the King had a hand

in her design. A few years later the *Great Harry* was also built with gunports, and in 1515 the *Great Galley*, a galleasse following the Venetian model, similarly expressed the King's interest. Much later in his reign, after 1540, Henry also seems to have been responsible for the introduction of rowbarges. These were small galleys of about twenty tons and mounting two or three medium-sized guns. Just what purpose they were intended to serve is not clear, because they were too small to take on the full-sized French galleys, and not powerfully enough armed to trouble a sailing warship. They may have been intended for scouting, or pursuing small pirate vessels, but the fact that they were sold off immediately after Henry's death suggests that the Admiralty did not share his enthusiasm. The King was ambivalent towards oared vessels. Apart from the rowbarges, as we have seen he master-minded the *Great Galley*, and commissioned the *Galley Subtle* in 1544. He also caused four medium-sized galleasses to be built in 1546. Nevertheless, when the *Great Galley* was rebuilt in 1538 she was converted into a sailing ship and renamed the *Great Bark*. At the end of his reign the *Subtle* was the only pure galley in English service.[8]

Apart from experimenting with galleasses, which was not particularly original, ship design changed in only one way during Henry's lifetime. In the 1530s sailing warships, like the *Grand Mistress*, began to be built without the towering castles which had characterised the carracks. Their profile was closer to that of the galleasse, only without the oars, and resembled that of the later galleon.[9] Existing carracks, like the *Mary Rose* and the *Great Harry*, continued to be rebuilt in their original form, only with many more gunports, and reinforced frames. Others, such as the *Jesus of Lubeck*, were purchased, but the new ships which were being built had lower lines. How they were constructed below the waterline we do not know, and it is likely that they lacked the smooth profile of the galleons, but the absence of castles indicates a tactical switch away from grappling and boarding towards stand-off gunnery. This is confirmed by the greatly increased number of broadside heavy guns which are shown in the *Anthony Anthony Roll* (fig. 2), an inventory of the navy completed in 1546.

Guns changed more dramatically than ships during this period. In 1514 the *Great Harry* had carried only twelve 'grete peces of yron'. The great majority of her guns were wrought-iron (that is built up in strips), and were accompanied by 'chambers'. These wrought guns had a relatively low muzzle velocity. About half such weapons were 'brass', that is of cast bronze, and many are listed as being of Flemish or Spanish make. At that time only the major

Fig. 2 The Mary Rose, from the Anthony Anthony Roll, 1546. © The Pepys Library, Magdalene College, Cambridge

warships carried great guns at all, the standard weapon being the anti-personnel serpentine. The big guns were of a variety of calibres, and many of them fired stone shot, which broke upon impact.[10] In 1545 the same ship was carrying over 30 big guns (cannon, demi-cannon, culverin, demi-culverin, port pieces and slings). These were of both iron and bronze, and if the archaeological evidence of the *Mary Rose* is any guide, some wrought and some cast, as before. They were, however, of English make and their combined firepower would have been much greater. English gunfounding had been transformed by the opening of the Wealden foundries in 1543. The King had promptly ordered 200 of their largest product, but it is unlikely that many of these had been delivered by 1545.[11] Such guns also fired cast-iron shot, which had much more

penetrative capability against the hull of a wooden ship. The bores were standardised, and the shot consequently interchangeable. Muzzle velocity had also been increased by the introduction of corned gunpowder (hydrated and sieved to produce standard granules) as opposed to the earlier serpentine powder, which had been prone to separate out in storage. By the end of the reign, Henry's warships were primarily floating gun platforms, and that was beginning to have a marked affect upon fighting tactics at sea.[12]

In 1530, when Thomas Audley had issued fighting instructions to the fleet, it was still anticipated that the standard form of engagement would be 'one on one', and that gunfire was essentially intended to intimidate an enemy before boarding took place. The real effect of artillery was only at very close quarters, and the instructions were largely concerned with the protocol of combat – the admiral to grapple with the opposing admiral, and so on. Fifteen years later, when John Dudley issued similar instructions, the whole emphasis had changed. The fleet was now organised, like an army, in 'battles', and it was envisaged that the ships would sail, and fight, in formation. They were to keep their distance one from another, and sail between the enemy ships in order to deploy their guns on both sides. Grappling and boarding might still be necessary, but the main purpose of gunfire was now to cripple the enemy before coming to close quarters, or even to sink him, which was by this time a distinct possibility.[13] Years later, at the time of the Armada, veteran Spanish captains were recalling that 40 years earlier the English had developed a style of fighting whereby their guns were aimed low, to hole their enemies below the waterline, rather than high, to damage his masts and rigging. They warned Philip to expect no less in 1588, but their memories went back to the end of the reign of Henry VIII.[14] However, of the line ahead tactic which so impressed the Spaniards at the later date, there is at this stage no sign.

Apart from an abortive attempt to help Ferdinand of Aragon against the Moors, Henry's first deployment of land forces came in the late summer of 1511, when he sent 1,500 men to assist Margaret of Savoy against the Duke of Guelders. These were partly archers and partly gunners. They were raised by indenture and acquitted themselves well in a limited campaign. By contrast, the Marquis of Dorset's Guienne expedition of the following summer was a fiasco. Neither the victuals nor the reinforcements promised by King Ferdinand were delivered, and the army eventually mutinied, returning home in commandeered ships.[15] This lesson was not wasted upon Henry, who, when he led an army royal of about 30,000 men to Picardy in 1513, placed the supervision of the logistics in the capable hands of Thomas Wolsey. This large army was raised mostly by commission of array, but a small nucleus was provided by the Royal Household itself, spearheaded by the King's new bodyguard, the 50 or so Gentlemen Spears. Altogether the Household contingent numbered about 500, most of who served on horseback as Gentlemen-at-Arms. Sir Thomas Wyndham oversaw the commissions of array, and acted as one of the treasurers, while Sir John Daunce was the other treasurer, who oversaw the victualling operations. Both were kept on short rein by Wolsey, and performed with conspicuous success.[16] The English still favoured the longbow and the bill as their chosen weapons, but this rather out-of-date weaponry was compensated by excellent artillery (thanks to the King's commitment), and very good cavalry They did not, in any case, have to fight a pitched battle, because the so-called 'battle of the Spurs' (fig. 1 and fig. 3) was merely the ambushing of a relief column for the besieged town of Thérouanne. Thérouanne and Tournai were taken, thanks to good siege guns, while Louis XII's main army was tied up elsewhere. It was a successful campaign, but more a test of logistics than of field fighting.

Much more significant in that respect was the battle of Flodden, fought against the invading Scots on the 9 September, while Henry was sitting before Tournai. James IV had seen the English preoccupation in France as too good an opportunity to miss, and had crossed the border at the head of about 30,000 men, many of them armed with modern pikes and with good artillery support. The Earl of Surrey (just about the only senior English soldier not in France) hastened north, gathering the levies of the midland and northern counties as he went. These were raised by the sheriffs, and consisted of the more able and better armed of the available men. Everyone understood the danger posed by a Scottish invasion, and there seems to have been no resistance to the call. Thanks to the energy of the ordnance officers, he was able to call on an adequate number of good guns, and these were sent north by sea. Eventually he had about 15,000 men, adequately equipped, but by no means superior to their opponents. When the armies clashed by the Tweed, the outcome was decided partly by the skill of Surrey in choosing his ground, and partly by the superior fighting qualities of the English when it came to a melee.[17] At very close quarters the pikes were useless, and the English archers came into their own. James IV and 5,000 of his subjects perished on a field which they should have won by all the logic of warfare.

In 1511, in preparation for the war which he intended, Henry VIII had mustered his subjects – not because he intended to use the levies overseas, but in order to assess his potential resources. This was one of the reasons why the levies were available to the Earl of Surrey in 1513. Having done that his recruiters in 1512 and 1513 knew where to look, and who to use as local agents. Apart from a few hundred gunners, Henry does not appear to have used foreign mercenaries in any of these campaigns. Nor does there seem to have been any great problem at this time in re-absorbing demobilised soldiers and seamen back into civilian life. The mariners, in any case, probably stayed with the ships for which they had been 'taken up', the indenture system being used for naval recruitment no less than for the army. What was different

Fig. 3 Battle of the Spurs. From *Der Weisskunig*, 1514, an engraving by Hans Burgkmair (1473–1531).

when the war came to an end in 1514 was that Henry retained the war fleet which he had built up over the past three years, instead of disposing of it, which had been the ancient custom, and which had been followed by Henry V. Instead new docks and warehouses were built at Woolwich, Deptford, Erith and Portsmouth, and two new officials were added to the existing Clerk of the Ships; the Clerk Controller and the Keeper of the Storehouse.[18] There was as yet no Admiralty, and the only unity of management lay with Cardinal Wolsey, but there was a standing navy, and a rudimentary infrastructure.

In 1522, when he was again contemplating war against France, the King commissioned a full military survey of the entire country. Returns from nearly 30 counties disclosed 128,250 able-bodied men, divided into different categories according to wealth and the kind of weapons with which they could be expected to provide themselves.[19] The return of weapons was extremely diverse (where it was completed at all) and mostly very traditional, although the occasional handgun or harquebus revealed that things were beginning to change. It was from this reservoir of manpower that the commissioners and contractors who recruited the expeditionary forces of 1522 and 1523 drew their soldiers. The weaponry was for the most part irrelevant, because only gentlemen were encouraged (or allowed) to provide their own equipment for campaigns. The rest were provided when the men had been mustered, and were supposed to be returned on demobilisation. Neither of the resulting campaigns was successful, but that was not because either the men or the weapons were substandard. The reasons were political in both cases. Ten thousand men were sent over in 1522, an effort which required the mobilisation of a dozen royal warships, and the 'taking up' of numerous transports, including some Spaniards who happened to be in the right place at the right time.[20] Wyndham was again the treasurer, but this time the logistics, particularly the provision of the carts needed to transport the guns was defective in spite of Wolsey's vigilance, and that contributed to the failure of the campaign. In 1523 a larger army, led by the Duke of Suffolk, fared even worse. The Duke's strategy failed to co-ordinate with that of the Emperor and a promising advance on Paris came to nothing.[21] The logistics were not to blame this time, but the whole strategy of the campaign was a mess, and by the end of it Henry was running out of money. In both 1523 and 1524 the navy was also deployed in strength, but nothing was achieved beyond a bit of coastal raiding. Perhaps this was because no enemy fleet appeared, or perhaps Henry's strategic imagination had deserted him.

For the next fifteen years England was theoretically at peace, although the tensions created by the King's repudiation of papal jurisdiction necessitated a certain level of military preparedness. The garrisons at Berwick and Calais were constantly reinforced, and a Channel guard of small warships patrolled the Narrow Seas and up the east coast. The budget for maintaining the Royal Navy grew from around £1,000 to about £5,000, and that did not include the re-building programme, which was mostly carried out in private yards and paid for by extraordinary warrants. The only military operation which took place during these years was that required to confront the Pilgrimage of Grace in October and November 1536. The rebels were alleged to number 30,000, and were drawn from those same northern levies which in ordinary times would have been called upon to resist the Scots. However, their weapons were basic and their leadership divided. The Duke of Norfolk, who went against them, had fewer men, and since they were drawn from the southern levies he could not entirely trust them. However, he did have an efficient artillery train and a stiffening of foreign mercenaries, who had no desire to be exposed to local hostility. There was eventually no fighting. The King appeared to compromise, and the rebels, most of who did not want to try conclusions with the Lord's Anointed, in due course dispersed.[22] There were political lessons to be learned from the Pilgrimage, but militarily it was a mere *chevauchée*.

1539 was rather different. The Emperor and the King of France had patched up their differences at the treaty of Toledo, and Henry had good cause to fear a papally inspired crusade against him. Musters were again held throughout the southern part of England, and the fleet was mobilised. However, the most significant consequence was the decision to build a string of artillery forts along the south coast. These, of which Walmer and Deal are surviving examples, were built in the French fashion, with low bastions and immensely thick walls. They were intended as gun emplacements, rather like the pillboxes of the Second World War, and intended to withstand battering by the same means. At the time of their construction they were state-of-the-art fortifications, and the King built over a dozen of them at immense cost.[23] The crisis passed, and they were never put to the test, but they remain as a monument to the military ambitions of the man who created them. By the end of 1539 Charles and Francis were at each other's throats again, but Henry's military ambition had been rekindled and in 1542 he entered into another imperial alliance, with a view, once again, to seizing control of a part of northern France.

Remembering what had happened in 1513, he decided this time to take the Scots out first. Using a minor border infringement as a pretext, he launched a brief but destructive raid into the Scottish lowlands in October 1542. James V walked into the trap. The following month in retaliation he launched 20,000 men into the 'Debateable Land' north of Carlisle. This force had been hastily assembled, and was neither well- equipped nor well-trained. On the 25 November it was caught at Solway Moss by a smaller, but much more professional English force under the command of the Earl of Hertford. Part of Hertford's force consisted of German mercenaries, and the battle was virtually a rout in the course of which a large number of Scottish nobles were captured. James V died soon after, and was succeeded by his week-old daughter, Mary, which prompted Henry to seek a settlement by marrying the infant Queen of Scots to his own son, the five-year-old Edward.[24] After seeming to agree to this, the Scottish regent, the Earl of Arran, then changed sides and the Scots repudiated the settlement at the end of 1543. Henry was extremely angry, and decided upon a serious punitive strike in the spring of 1544. This took the form of a seaborne assault on Edinburgh, commanded by the Earl of Hertford with the support of the Lord Admiral, Viscount Lisle. About 15,000 men, who had originally been mustered for the delayed attack on France, were switched instead to Newcastle, where a fleet of 68 ships was also assembled at the end of April. Bad weather delayed the fleet, and the victualling commissioners were cheated by the purveyors, but the whole force was embarked in about two days, and landed near Leith on the 3 May. Scottish resistance was brushed aside, the town was plundered, and Edinburgh taken by assault – only the castle holding out. English cavalry raided as far as Stirling, and both Edinburgh and Leith were burned.[25] The ships were then loaded with plunder and captured guns, and returned to Newcastle, while the army made its way back to Berwick overland, burning and destroying as it went. The 58 privately owned ships which had been taken up for the expedition were then paid off, and the ten royal ships sent south to join the forces mustering for the attack on France. About 2,000 of the soldiers were retained to strengthen the northern garrisons, and the rest were also sent south to join the main muster. In spite of problems with the victuals, this large-scale raid had been a model of efficiency by 16th-century standards. Unfortunately it failed in its political objective and the 'Rough Wooing' was set to continue.[26]

Henry's attack on France in 1544 was an act of unmitigated aggression. In 1513 there had at least been the excuse of the Holy League, and in 1522 there had been aggression on both sides, but in 1544 the main reason was the King's declining health and his need to prove again his warlike credentials. He paid little attention to the needs of his ostensible ally the Emperor, and that alliance fell apart even as the campaign proceeded. In July 1544, with the King in personal command, perhaps as many as 50,000 men were launched against Boulogne. The preparations had been meticulous. Musters had been held all over the country, and on this occasion there was 'a new phenomenon; armies composed of levies officered by gentlemen, whose patronage ties created military clienteles'.[27] This was a variation on the system of indentures, because the individual bands were quite small, and the King appears to have paid their wages directly from the start. It has also been described (with some exaggeration) as 'the last hurrah for the royal affinity in war'. The King did, what was technically unlawful, and recruited directly from the musters, using the local gentry as the officers in order to minimise resistance to the imposition. About 35,000 men were raised by this means, of which 3,500 were cavalry, and to them were added some 10 or 12,000 mercenaries – mostly Germans. The English counties also contributed nearly 2,000 draft horses, 282 carriages and 564 carts.[28] The whole operation, which was budgeted at £250,000 in fact cost £650,000 and well-nigh bankrupted both the Exchequer and the Court of Augmentations.

Although Picardy was a rich province, the victuals were provided out of England, and a fleet of some 150 ships was mobilised to transport the army and to act as victuallers. Boulogne was duly besieged, without any regard to the Emperor's campaign further south, and captured on 17 September, thanks partly to the efficiency of the English artillery, and partly to the failure of the French to mount a relief operation. There was plenty of skirmishing around the fortress and in the suburbs of the town, but nothing like a major battle. The Dauphin led an army into Picardy which forced the Duke of Norfolk to abandon the siege of Montreuil, but came too late to relieve Boulogne, and there was no pitched battle during the campaign. The English navy, however, revealed its new capability by bombarding the fortifications from the sea, and the surprise of this, as much as the damage, contributed to the surrender of the garrison.[29] The Emperor, however, made a separate peace on the same day that Boulogne surrendered, and left Henry to defend his conquest as best he could against the power which Francis I was bound to bring to its recapture.

Although they had not been particularly prompt to do so,

by 1545, the English had adopted most of the military developments which had been taking place in Europe over the previous half century. Archers, although they were still used, had slowly given way to harquesbusiers and pikemen. Such weapons were beyond the ken of the ordinary militiaman, and required special training for their effective use, but an increasing number of English officers and sergeants had experienced service in the imperial armies, and were capable of giving such training. Unlike the English, the Emperor's armies were permanent, and recruited their soldiers wherever they could get them. Warfare was endemic in Europe, although the English only participated from time to time. However, by the end of Henry's reign an English army would consist of demi-lances (heavily armed horsemen), light horsemen, pikemen, harquebusiers, billmen and archers. Only the Scottish borderers were largely unaffected by these changes, and they were skirmishers rather than battle soldiers. Only in one respect had the English moved rapidly, and established a precarious ascendancy, and that was in gunnery. English siege trains were as good as any, and in naval gunnery she led the world.

This was put to the test in 1545 when French admiral Claude d'Annebaut led some 120 ships into the Solent in an attempt to knock out Portsmouth. His real objective was Boulogne, but realising that the garrison was being supplied by sea, he decided to try and seize command of the Channel by depriving the English fleet of its base.[30] Lord Lisle, with a similar number of ships, was waiting for him in the harbour and a great naval battle seemed certain. It did not happen, partly because of the weather, partly because of English gunnery, and partly because plague broke out among the French ships. D'Annebaut backed off, and having dodged a battle with Lisle, who came after him, landed most of his soldiers in Picardy and demobilised his fleet. Boulogne remained in English hands, and the only significant loss to

Henry was the sinking of the *Mary Rose*, through '*negligence and misadventure*', rather than enemy action.[31]

By the time that this confrontation took place, Henry had increased the size of his navy, by purchase and building, to over 50 ships of all sizes. This represented a massive investment, and was costing almost £20,000 a year to run and maintain, irrespective of the expense of using it. In order to manage this fleet, and the five or six dockyards, anchorages and store bases which it needed Henry created in 1546 a new department of state, the Council for Marine Causes, otherwise known as the Admiralty. In place of the three uncoordinated officers who had previously carried that responsibility under the king's chief minister, there was now a committee of six fully salaried officers, with a staff of clerks and servants. All the money was now channelled through the Treasurer of the Navy, and although it was to be another ten years before it was given a defined budget, the Admiralty had a properly institutional existence and responsibility from the beginning.[32] It was probably modelled on the Ordnance Office, and it constituted the most efficient system of naval management in Europe at that date.

Henry ended his reign as he had begun it, in precarious peace. Over 38 years he had built up-to-date fortifications, and developed his army more or less in line with his continental rivals. However, he had transformed the navy, turning it from an occasional event into a professional service with a substantial infrastructure and a permanent base. During his last war he had also officially licensed privateers, and had thus authorised a revival of the private warship.[33] This amounted to the creation of an auxiliary navy of armed traders who were to come into their own during the long and troubled reign of his daughter Elizabeth. Having spent most of his life insisting upon his royal monopoly of force, he ended his reign by compromising it.

Notes and references page 334.

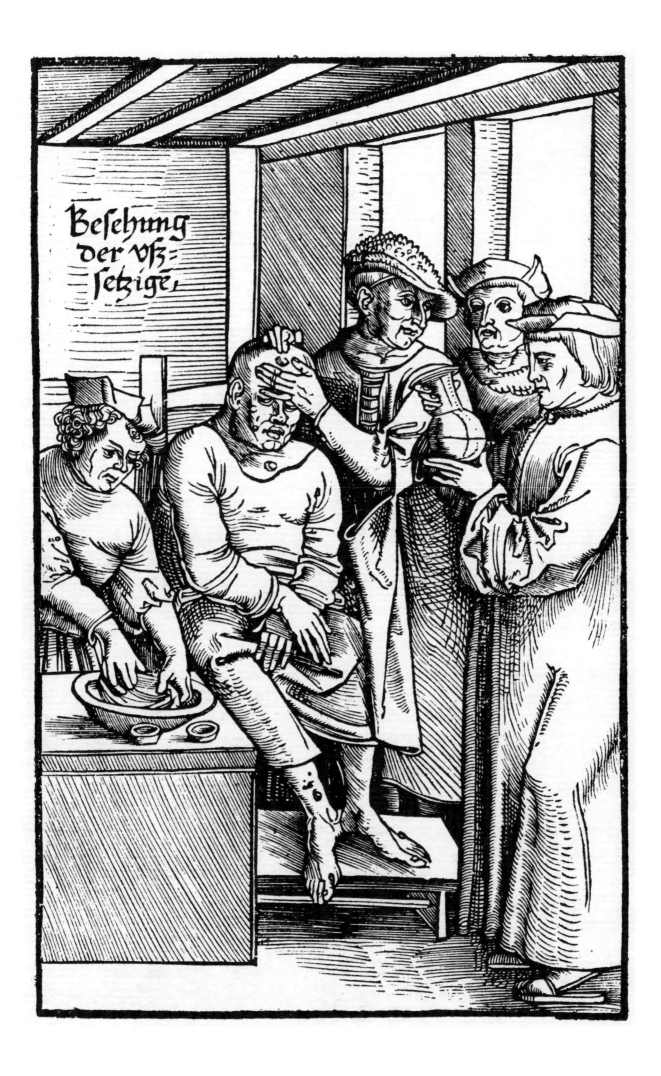

Besehung
der vß-
setzigē.

{V}

THE TREATMENT OF INJURY AND DISEASE

ERIC GRUBER VON ARNI

Just as warfare and weapons were changing fast in the early 16th century, so medicine and surgery were also developing rapidly. Eric Gruber von Arni outlines some of the improvements in medical care, particularly with regard to that for soldiers on campaign. He outlines the part played by printed books and illustrations which accelerated the spread of new discoveries and techniques amongst physicians and surgeons. The author draws on contemporary accounts to explain how new treatments were trialled, such as Ambrose Paré's discovery that gunshot wounds could be better treated by poultices than by boiling oil. He also outlines progress in the treatment of diseases such as smallpox, typhus and tuberculosis, which affected far more troops than wounds in an era where lack of hygiene was a constant threat.

Fig. 1 Physicians examining a patient. The physician on the right is observing the patient's urine. From *Feldbuch der Wundartzney* (Fieldbook of wound dressing) by Hans von Gersdorff, 1517. (Also figs 2–10).

Even before Henry VIII's accession vast changes were taking place in the practice of medicine and surgery. Most importantly for the purposes of this essay the period brought final recognition of the concept that, when soldiers went to war, medical support should accompany them. Meanwhile, the whole pattern of warfare was changing. With the wider use of gunpowder, firearms and pikes were steadily replacing the bill and the longbow.[1] By the beginning of the 16th century, changes were also taking place in the medical world as physicians and surgeons began to organise themselves into self-governing professions. This had been achieved mainly as a result of the expanding influence exerted by the spread of printing presses that had been steadily increasing in numbers through the previous century, especially in London. Illustrations in medical works began to develop from their origins as mere decorative or schematic images becoming more naturalistic and descriptive aids to understanding. Detailed woodcut illustrations could transmit ideas and concepts much more quickly and more clearly than the written word whilst the increased production and availability of medical textbooks brought widespread changes in medical learning, not simply to academic readers but also to lay audiences who could now access books for the first time.

Medical teaching was also in the process of assimilating several significant shifts in direction and emphasis. The theories of Hippocrates (460–370 BC) and Galen (about 129–216 AD) both revolved around a principle which held sway for over a thousand years whereby disease was held to be the result of an imbalance of the four natural bodily humours. These linked changes in human personalities, moods, well-being or illness with the four natural elements of air, earth, fire and water. A sanguine personality, serene and unruffled, was linked with air, whilst melancholia, stubbornness or insolence was relative to earth. A choleric personality was bold and exuberant and favoured fire whilst the phlegmatic was idle or foolish and associated with water.

The first and most significant change to this approach was the emergence of the so-called 'chemical physicians' who offered treatments specific to particular diseases. One of the leaders of this movement was the Swiss physician Theophrastus von Hohenheim, otherwise known as Paracelsus (1493–1541), the founder of clinical pharmacology and therapeutics. Paracelcus discarded the teachings of Galen and the principles of the four humours and taught physicians to substitute therapeutics for alchemy, whilst attacking witchcraft and astrology. He taught that for every disease or ailment there was a specific remedy and dismissed any separation of medicine from surgery. He experimented widely in the analysis of various substances, introduced mineral baths and published works on the specific diseases suffered by miners.

As the century progressed, the standard of education amongst both physicians and surgeons rapidly improved. The Flemish physician, Andreas Vesalius (1514–64) was the first to teach that a study of anatomy was essential to the accurate diagnosis of disease and its treatment by specific remedies. Whilst the teachings of Vesalius were widely resisted, his effect on Renaissance medicine was significant and his teachings were most clearly demonstrated by one of his disciples, the greatest contemporary military surgeon, the Frenchman Ambroise Paré (1510–90) whose contribution to surgery is discussed later in this essay.

Throughout their history, physicians, surgeons and apothecaries have struggled between themselves in attempts to enlarge their individual influence to the detriment of their rival professions, despite the fact that each was working towards the same goal – the improvement of the health and well-being of patients. There were two categories of surgeon practising during Henry VIII's reign; master surgeons and barber surgeons. Master surgeons, who had received academic training and many of whom had seen army service, formed themselves into a guild in 1368–9. Fifty years later, in 1421, they combined with physicians but this unhappy liaison was dissolved in 1518 when the physicians were granted a Royal Charter by Henry to form the College of Physicians. One of the College's main privileges was the prevention of any non-member practising physic within seven miles of London without a special licence.[2] This monopoly was the cause of continuing friction between the physicians and surgeons throughout the century and beyond, the former attempting at every turn to prevent surgeons from administering internal medicines and restricting them to the application of external salves and lotions.

Barber surgeons, who were less qualified than master surgeons and whose work included bleeding their patients, cupping, applying leeches, administering enemas and extracting teeth, as well as treating the bruises and breaks associated with falling from horses during either tournaments or battle, had been granted a separate charter by Edward IV in 1462, becoming a city company some 56 years before the physicians.

Henry VIII maintained a strong and abiding personal interest in the study of medicine. In 1528, during an outbreak of plague in London, he spent a considerable amount of time with one of his personal physicians, Dr Butts, and dabbled in concocting remedies that were later included in a published work *A book of plaister, spasmdrops, ointments etc. devysed by the King's Magestie, Dr Burts* [Butts], *Dr Chambers, Dr Cromer and Dr Augustine*. In one of his love letters to Anne Boleyn, the King wrote of his great affection for Butts who had been sent to the future queen when she was sick claiming that '*he will love* [him], *if he can, more than ever*' if he succeeded in curing her of her illness.[3]

During Henry VIII's reign, the master surgeons were incorporated into a fellowship which led, ultimately, to the granting of a charter by the King in 1540 which brought about an amalgamation with the barber surgeons and the foundation of a liveried Company known as 'The Masters or Governors of the Mystery and Commonalty of Barbers and Surgeons in London'.[4] The following year, an Act of Parliament exempted surgeons from '*bearing arms or being put upon watches or inquests*'. They were also granted the important annual privilege of being authorised to receive and use the bodies of four persons *condemned, adjudged, and put to death by the due order of the King's law of this realm* for anatomical dissection.[5]

The most notable army surgeon of the latter part of Henry VIII's reign was Thomas Gale, author of a seminal work on gunshot wounds as well as a translation of ancient surgical texts. Gale served in the expeditions which Henry undertook in alliance with the Emperor Charles IX and continued in service through the reigns of the King's successors. He was present as principal medical officer at the siege of Montreuil in 1544 where he refused to imperil the lives of eleven soldiers by attempting to remove bullets, the position of which he was uncertain.[6] Three years later, at St Quentin, a force of 1,000 Horse, 4,000 Foot and a train of Artillery was supposed to be accompanied by 57 surgeons although Gale was subsequently forced to complain that he had experienced considerable difficulty in achieving this number due to a national shortage of adequately qualified practitioners. He wrote to Queen Elizabeth:

'I have myself helped to furnish out of London in one year seventy-two surgeons, who were good men, which served by sea and land, and were well able to serve – and all Englishmen. Now there are not thirty-four of the whole company of Englishmen, and yet the most part of them be in noblemen's service, so that if we should have need, I do not know where to find sufficient men.'.[7]

Gale also reflected upon the difficulties he had experienced as a result of the presence of innumerable quacks who pursued the army in search of gullible customers and preyed upon the superstitions and credulity of the soldiers. He later recorded that *'when at the wars of Muttrel, in the days of that most famous prince Henry VIII, there was a great rabblement that took upon them[selves] to be surgeons'*. He went on to describe this rabble as including *'sow and horse gelders, tinkers and cobblers … and dog-leeches'* notorious for their proprietary cures. The high death rate amongst the victims of these ghouls forced the Duke of Norfolk to order Gale and his colleagues to investigate the situation. Their subsequent findings highlighted the fact that large numbers of unqualified impostors present with the army were actually drawing the pay and allowances of regimental surgeons. That they were able to do so was possible as a result of the contemporary system in which commanders were free to recruit their own staff, including physicians and regimental surgeons. Little or no control was exercised over the qualifications, experience or abilities of those appointed. As far as noblemen were concerned, when they went to fight, whether by land or sea, they continued the medieval tradition of taking their own surgeons with them. Thus, in 1513, Lord Bergevenny who accompanied the King to France, took John Yan, a barber surgeon of Chelmsford with him in his retinue. Even private gentlemen would sometimes secure the services of their own barber surgeon for their personal use. Amongst the 57 surgeons at St Quentin, the staff of the Duke of Somerset, the Lieutenant and Captain-General included two surgeons whilst his senior subordinates, the Lieutenant General, the 'High Marischell' (or Quartermaster General), the General of Horse, the Captain-General of Footmen and the 'Master of Ordynance' were also each authorised to retain surgeons amongst their various staffs, the latter being the first recorded instance of a surgeon being specifically attached to the artillery train.[8] The perceived difference in social status between the horsemen of the cavalry and the foot soldiers of the infantry was reflected in variations of the authorised pay for surgeons inasmuch as those attached to the Horse received two shillings a day compared to the one shilling for those serving with the Foot. Obviously, this was an encouragement to the better qualified or experienced to favour the cavalry where their work would receive greater social status and remuneration.[9]

From the middle of the 16th century onwards, although the company remained the primary basic element of any army, regiments began to appear as temporary accretions of a variable number of companies united for a specific task or campaign, however temporarily, under the command of a colonel. In the footsteps of this arrangement came the appearance, for the first time, of the regimental surgeon – a member of the colonel's staff, whose task was to co-ordinate the work of the individual component company surgeons. As the naval service of the period acted more as a transport platform for the army rather than as a separate fighting force, the same basic principles applied at sea. However, when attempts to recruit sufficient masters and mariners for his ships proved inadequate, the King was forced to approve the use of the age-old practice of impressing sufficient men for the task, including surgeons.[10]

The everyday hazards met with by those employed in hard physical work – such as moving and loading heavy guns, working with gunpowder, handling sharp weapons, close proximity to active heavy horses and, on board ships, managing sails, halliards, blocks and tackle – were inevitably accompanied by a multitude of major and minor injuries. Whilst minor wounds were commonly treated personally by the individual or by his companions, more serious injuries involving the control of bleeding, removal of embedded material and suturing were treated and cared for by the surgeon. Traumatic wounds were seldom allowed to heal naturally. They were invariably sutured to encourage suppuration as, for centuries, it was believed that the appearance of 'laudable pus' was an essential element in the promotion of successful healing. Subsequent elaborate dressings of the wound with salves and ointments were also intended to promote the same result.

However rough and ready, contemporary methods employed in the treatment of fractures differed little in most respects from those surviving into modern times. The concepts involved in correcting deformity with traction and im-mobilisation with splintage were well appreciated (fig. 2).

Frequently, on-going maintenance of support for the affected limb was provided with firm bandages impregnated with egg white, flour, pine resin, comfrey root, ointments and salves which set hard to form either a rigid splint in much the same way as plaster-of-Paris and resin casts are used today. For the armoured knight or wealthy victim, not only could he hire

the services of a private physician or surgeon, it was even possible for an armourer to construct anatomically correct splintage, under medical supervision, using pieces of armour fitted with fine screw adjustments to suit the clinical requirement (figs 3 and 4). These metal adjustable splints for arms or legs look very similar in appearance to external fixators and would have been used in a manner similar to modern orthopaedic practice. The technique of using external fixation of fractures using pins inserted into bone was first employed in 1840 by Malgaigne.

Dislocations of joints, particularly the shoulder, were also reduced with the help of a variety of various extension apparatus based upon a winch (fig. 5).

Serious pelvic and spinal injuries were highly problematic for the surgeon to care for inasmuch as the only treatment possible would have been sedation and rest. If the patient survived, such injuries, together with unreduced fractures of the femur where shortening of the limb occurred, could all lead to permanent, lifelong disability. In complicated cases where traumatised bone ends were exposed and the wound was contaminated with soil, clothing and other material,

Fig. 2 Applying traction to a fractured lower leg.

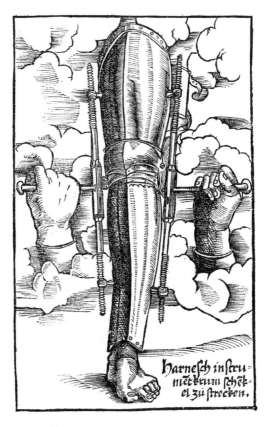

Figs. 3 & 4 Adjustable external fixation devices constructed using arm and leg armour.

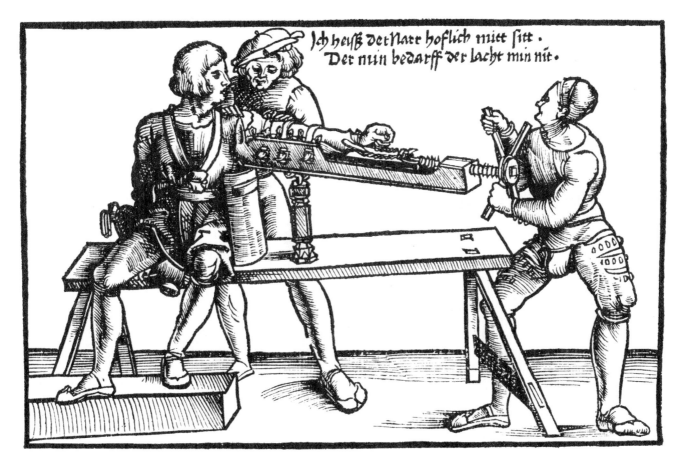

Fig. 5 Reducing a dislocation of the shoulder.

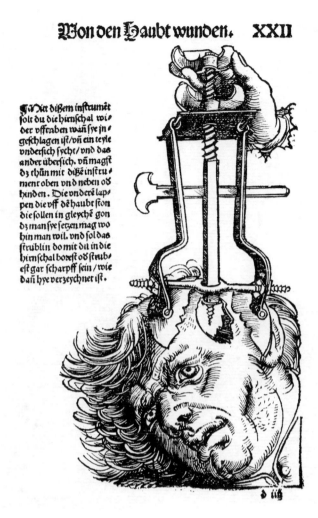

Von den Haubt wunden. XXII

In bet disem instrumēt solt du die hirnschal wider vffrůben wañ sye jn = geschlagen ist/vñ ein teyle vnderfich sycht/vnd das ander übersich. vñ magst dz thůn mit disē instru = ment oben vñ d neben od hinden. Die vnderē lap = pen die vff dē haubt ston die sollen in gleychē gon dz man sye setzen mag wo hin man wil. vnd sol das strüblin do mit dū in die hirnschal borest od strub = est gar scharpff sein / wie dañ hye verzeychnet ist.

Fig. 6 Skull fragment elevator in use.

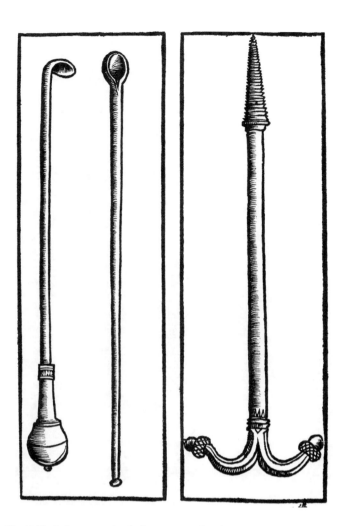

Fig. 7 Tools for extracting bullets or arrowheads.

infection of the bone would rapidly occur and amputation of the limb became an invariable sequel.

Although head injuries, where fractures of the bones were not displaced, could lead to concussion, when internal bleeding was not excessive the injured soldier or sailor might well survive without surgical intervention. Trephining was, however, extensively practised to reduce intra-cranial pressure for more serious head injuries when internal bleeding was exerting pressure onto the brain, as well as for epilepsy and even migraine. If the fracture included displacement of a bone fragment causing pressure on the brain, instruments designed to elevate and secure the fragment were available (fig. 6).

The weapons of Henry's reign differed little in their effects from those of the Wars of the Roses and earlier times. They were designed to produce crude, extensive injuries upon the victim. The slashing and stabbing effects of edged weapons, the *armes blanches*, such as swords, rapiers and daggers, as well as lances, halberds, war hammers and other polearms,

produced incised wounds, possibly severing muscles and tendons or causing penetrating puncture injuries to abdominal organs such as the stomach, liver, spleen, intestines or kidneys. Dependent upon the force of the blow, they could also inflict underlying bone fractures or penetrating injuries of the head, chest or abdomen with further concomitant damage to internal organs. An increasing incidence of gunshot injuries as a result of the widening use of gunpowder was of particular note in this period. Although cannon had been in existence since the reign of Edward III, and were first recorded in the open field at Crécy in 1346, the introduction of gunpowder did not materially affect the operations of war until the 16th century. Burns, either superficial or severe, could be inflicted by the careless handling of gunpowder as '*these devilish engines of warre*' became increasingly common. The use of the bow had begun to decline but, as the presence of a large stock of longbows found during recovery of the warship, *Mary Rose*. demonstrates, they had not yet completely fallen

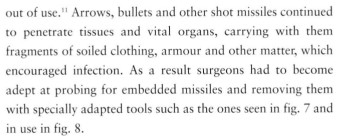

Fig. 8 Bullet extraction

Fig. 9 Applying cautery to a wound

out of use.[11] Arrows, bullets and other shot missiles continued to penetrate tissues and vital organs, carrying with them fragments of soiled clothing, armour and other matter, which encouraged infection. As a result surgeons had to become adept at probing for embedded missiles and removing them with specially adapted tools such as the ones seen in fig. 7 and in use in fig. 8.

The new natures of wounds caused by firearms – either shot by the enemy or due to the soldier's piece exploding accidentally during firing, possibly as a result of faulty casting – was appalling to both surgeons and wounded alike. Contemporary opinion held that gunshot wounds were 'venomous', and boiling oil was the recognised treatment supported by prayers, incantations, exorcism and charms.[12] John de Vigo, a 16th-century writer, recommended surgeons to cauterise such wounds either with irons made from iron, bronze or, best of all, gold, heated until they were red hot or with boiling oil of elder mixed with a little treacle (fig. 9).

An unknown surgeon, writing in 1536, recommended a recipe in which two new-born puppies were boiled in two pounds of oil of lilies until the flesh had fallen from their bones. Earthworms purged and cleansed by steeping in wine were then added to the mixture which was subsequently strained and '*two drachms of turpentine and an ounce of spirit of wine*' added to the resulting liquor. This, to modern eyes, vile preparation, known as 'oil of whelps', enjoyed a considerable reputation amongst surgeons in the treatment of gunshot wounds whilst other contemporary surgeons kept the wound open by inserting cylindrical or conical plugs, known as 'tents', and applied aromatic oils.[13] This latter treatment was probably not as ill advised as may be thought at first reading. Delayed closure of a gunshot wound until all foreign matter, non-viable tissue or sepsis has been removed is normal surgical practice today.

Writing in 1517, the master surgeon Hans von Gersdorff wrote an extensive essay on the surgery of war from which

Fig. 10 Amputation of a leg.

almost all of the illustrations used in this essay are taken. His text provides us with vivid descriptions of his surgical techniques including the form of his pre-operative preparation for elective or planned amputation of a leg (fig. 10). Prior to operating the patient was offered the Holy Sacrament and the surgeon invoked divine assistance. All of the required tools and equipment were collected together and arranged in the order that they would be used. His description then continued:

Prior to making your incision, draw the skin firmly back and bind the skin tightly with a tourniquet. Then tie another cord close to your first tourniquet, leaving a space of about a finger's breadth between the two. Make your incision between the two so as to make a flap that will form a good stump. Pull the flap back on itself then take a saw and cut through the bone. Having divided the bone, remove the tourniquets and pull the flap and muscle firmly forward to cover the bone end and form a stump. Take a bandage, which has been thoroughly moistened until wet, and use it as a pressure dressing to arrest bleeding and retain the skin and flesh over the wound. Afterwards apply a styptic and a good thick compress. Finally, cover the stump using the bladder of an ox, bull or pig that has been trimmed so as to completely encase both the pad and the stump, and bind it on with a cord.[14]

Von Gersdorff continued his description with instructions for the post-operative care of the patient. On the third day the stump was well soaked in warm soapy water prior to removing the bandages in water. The exposed stump was washed clean and a fresh dressing applied over an application of egg white to seal the wound. Tow (teased out hemp fibres) was then bandaged over the stump to form a thick, protective pad. Subsequently, the wound was bathed daily and a mixture of herbs and honey, which has known antiseptic properties, was then applied for as long as deemed necessary.

The eminent Frenchman Ambroise Paré was another enlightened surgeon of the period who worked tirelessly to ease the lot of wounded soldiers (fig. 11). He began life as a rustic barber's apprentice. Arriving in Paris in 1529, he gained an in-depth clinical experience working in the Hôtel Dieu, a prominent hospital for the poor of Paris. Afterwards he chose to become an army surgeon and, in 1536, during the various wars of religion currently raging, he joined the force sent by the French King Francis I into Piedmont where they besieged the city of Turin. Despite his total inexperience in the treatment of gunshot wounds, the young and relatively inexperienced Paré worked as a front-line surgeon. He had read the works of de Vigo regarding '*wounds made by fiery engines* [that] *do participate of venenosity*' and, even though

Fig. 11 Ambroise Paré aged 45 years.

he knew that such treatment caused severe pain to the patient, he endorsed the practice of applying cautery either with irons or boiling oil.

However, one night his supply of oil ran out and, using what came to hand, he applied a poultice of egg yolk and oil of roses mixed with turpentine which seemed to ease his patients' suffering. The following morning, fearing the worst, he inspected his patients' wounds and was surprised to find that, contrary to his normal experience with boiling oil, the wounds appeared healthy and free from the red, angry swelling that was normally present. He subsequently resolved never to use cautery and boiling oil again and, in later life, introduced several other innovative techniques including the application of ligatures to blood vessels severed during amputations, massage as a routine element of his post-operative care for his patients' recovery and the invention of many other surgical techniques and instruments that were soon adopted by other army surgeons.[15]

Throughout the history of warfare sickness and infection have caused far more deaths than injuries sustained in battle but, in general terms, the standards of military medicine in Henry's reign, as distinct from military surgery, remained far behind those of civilian medicine, which itself was in a less than exalted state. Had greater attention been paid to field hygiene much suffering through the deprivations of communicable diseases might have been avoided.[16]

Fevers, food-related illnesses, lung infections, venereal disease as well as worms and parasites and a host of skin diseases all linked together under the generic title of '*leprosy*' were all frequent, unwelcome visitors amongst the armies of the day. Although contemporary terminology is sometimes obscure, malaria, typhus and plague figured largely amongst the infections that produced severe fevers in their victims and there is no doubt that they, along with smallpox and tuberculosis, were amongst the primary killer diseases of the period. Nevertheless, dysentery, commonly called the '*bloody flux*', probably caused more deaths than any other infection in Renaissance armies. Their irregular, nomadic existence, unreliable food sources, lack of preservatives, poor transportation and corruption in administrative circles all combined to predispose soldiers to the disease but, as most water supplies, especially in towns, were contaminated, infection was almost inevitable.

Cold, wet winters brought bronchitis, pneumonia and tuberculosis in their wake and cross-infection increased as troops huddled together in whatever shelter and warmth was available. Influenza was prevalent and several epidemics occurred throughout the Tudor period, one particularly serious outbreak in 1510 being as devastating as that of 1918/19. In addition, several unspecified and mysterious epidemic diseases arose and vanished as quickly as they came. In particular, the nature of the so-called '*sweating sickness*' which ravaged the country during five severe epidemics, killing mostly members of the higher echelons of society and then disappearing, has never satisfactorily been established, although it may well have been caused by a mutation of the influenza virus. The disease first appeared when Henry VII landed at Milford Haven and subsequently ravaged his army after the battle of Bosworth to the extent that his coronation had to be postponed. Two Lord Mayors of London died of it within a week, and people walking about in the streets would fall down dead without warning symptoms; but the epidemic was all over within a few weeks. It was only following the disastrous progress of the sweating sickness coupled with the endemic outbreak of syphilis which swept across Europe during the early years of the 16th

century that doctors began to classify specific signs and symptoms into separate disease entities.[17]

Syphilis was frequently confused with both plague and leprosy. One theory has it that the disease was brought to Europe following the discovery of the New World but modern research appears to indicate that it was present, particularly in the Near East, much earlier. Mercury had been used for skin conditions for many years and the skin rash present during the secondary stage of the disease's progress soon drew physicians' attention to the use of the metal as a potential cure for syphilis. Mercurial preparations were applied to the patient's skin. This treatment brought with it all of the signs of mercurial poisoning including loosening of the teeth in their sockets, ulceration of the mouth and profuse salivation.[18] By 1529, the sexual nature of its transmission was recognised and a quack's handbill from the period coined the expression '*A night with Venus and a month with Mercury*'.

Surprisingly, remarkably few records survive to throw light upon the almost annual ravages of bubonic plague, a disease carried by fleas, which was particularly prevalent during the summer months and which continued to appear regularly throughout the Tudor period. Letters and a few extant plague-bills indicate that these outbreaks were frequently severe and tended to follow in the wake of periods of famine. Powerless in the face of such a powerful foe, physicians, taught that all epidemic disease was due to '*fowle, contagious ayre*', struggled to provide any effective care. In his work *The Castel of Health*, Sir Thomas Elyot pronounced that '*the causes whereby the ayr is corrupted be specially four: the influence of sundry stars, stagnant waters, carrion and overcrowding*'.[19] Henry was so in agreement with these opinions that, for the first time in English history, he introduced quarantine laws.

Smallpox had always flourished in the Middle East but writers during the Tudor period considered it to be a new disease in England and coined its name to distinguish it from the Great Pox, syphilis. As the years progressed, the effects of this disease seem to have become both more potent and endemic. By the end of the century, it was accepted belief that almost everyone would suffer from it at some time in their lives. In response, the Court initiated a special code of quarantine regulations, primarily to prevent direct access to the Sovereign. Shortly after Henry's death the quarantine laws were formulated in the Code of the Lord Protector Somerset in 1547.

Typhus or gaol fever became common in England during the Wars of the Roses. Boorde, who was committed to the

Fleet Prison in 1549 wrote in his *Breviary* 'This infirmitie doth come of the corruption of the ayre, and the breath and fylth the which doth come from men, as many men do be together in a lytle room having but lytle open ayre'.[20] The close confinement found in prisons provided an ideal environment for encouraging the spread of this louse-borne disease – conditions frequently identical to that of the hovels which soldiers made for themselves (or expropriated from the civilian population) during cold weather and in which they huddled together for warmth.

Malaria was also endemic in parts of the Low Countries and in England, especially the Fens where it continue to appear as late as Victorian times. Boorde's *Breviary* also mentions the several manifestations of this infection, including the malignant form which affects the brain and progresses to mania and death.

Scurvy was common throughout the Tudor period, particularly amongst seamen. Their diet contained no vitamin C and the disease became the commonest cause of death in the Fleet. During his voyage round the Cape of Good Hope to the East Indies in 1497, Vasco da Gama lost almost two-thirds of his crew of 160 men to this disease alone.

In summary, the wars of the Renaissance raised a vague awareness within society of the medical needs of common soldiers who fell sick or were wounded in battle but, as the majority of soldiers were recruited from the lowest social classes, an inherent disdain for such people persisted amongst the upper classes from whom military commanders were drawn. Monarchs, nobles and officers might occasionally distribute largesse but more often sick and wounded soldiers and sailors were expected to look after themselves, seek the help of friends, relatives or local civilians or pay for their treatment and frequently forfeit their wages. The state's attitude of indifference was reinforced by the universal belief that disease and pestilence were the results of divine intervention sent as a punishment for wrongdoing. Astrology was also a powerful element in decision-making and the governance of peoples' lives. Aloofness, inherent prejudice and maladministration prevented any real progress being made with regard to the reform of casualty care and welfare. The Poor Laws introduced at the very end of Queen Elizabeth's reign attempted to alleviate the plight of the discharged soldier but it was not until 1642 and the onset of a civil war that Parliament finally recognised the State's duty towards the sick or wounded soldier and established a pension facility for those who had suffered in its service, as well as for the widows and orphans of those who died.[21]

Notes and references page 334.

Fig 1. The Tower of London, 1547. Artist: Ivan Lapper.

1. White Tower
2. Wardrobe
3. Queen's Lodgings
4. Lanthorn Tower
5. Wakefield Tower

6. Mint Street
7. Legge's Mount
8. St Peter ad Vincula
9. Artillery Store
10. Brass Mount

{VI}

THE TOWER OF LONDON IN THE REIGN OF HENRY VIII

GEOFFREY PARNELL

Henry VIII spent little time at the Tower of London, preferring to live at his other palaces. However, Dr Parnell charts several important roles of the Tower at this period. From its function as a state prison, especially for people of high rank, to its continuing purpose as a stronghold and garrison, the Tower was useful in many ways. However, its main role was to house government departments that needed a secure environment, such as the Jewel House, Royal Mint, Record Office and offices of Ordnance and Armoury. The author examines Henry's involvement in the preparations for the celebrations at the Tower before Anne Boleyn's coronation. The King never stayed there afterwards – but the inventory on his death in 1547 shows the Tower's importance as a royal storehouse.

At the beginning of Henry VIII's reign the Tower of London was still an occasional royal residence, but in the words of the later Tudor chronicler Raphael Holinshed, rather more '*an armourie and house of munition, and thereunto a place for the safekeeping of offenders, than a palace roiall for a king or queen to soiourne in*'.[1] The function that has captured the public's imagination above all is the Tower as a state prison – a dark and mysterious place where famous personalities languished en route to a bloody death on the scaffold. Like any castle in England the Tower's role as a prison was incidental, largely brought about by the close proximity of the royal courts at Westminster. It was ideally positioned, therefore, to become a secure and convenient location to hold prisoners of rank. This was particularly so during the religious and political upheavals of the 16th and 17th centuries, but even then it represented a rather minor strand of the daily life of the fortress when compared to the work of the household and early government departments operating within the site.

Most of these organisations had evolved from the medieval Wardrobe, the body tasked with maintaining and issuing all manner of royal possessions from clothing, jewels, ornaments, coined money, books and accounts, to arms and armour. The Tower provided a secure environment in which goods could be stored and managed by the Wardrobe and the various specialist sub-sections, into which it fragmented throughout the Middle Ages. By 1509 these included the offices of Ordnance and Armoury, the Royal Mint, the Record Office, the Great Wardrobe, the Jewel House and even the Royal Menagerie and their staff. Add to the list of residents the Constable, his deputies and their households, the body of the Yeoman Warders and their families, state prisoners and their relatives and/or servants, not to mention the occupants of a number of inns, and it is not difficult to imagine what a crowded and potentially chaotic institution the fortress presented.

The myriad of domestic houses that once accommodated the Tudor inhabitants of the Tower have now largely disappeared

with the notable exception of the Queen's House, the official residence of the Governor (fig. 2). Located in the south-west corner of the Inner Ward against the medieval curtain walls, this large L-shaped timber-framed building can be seen on the 1597 survey labelled 'The Lieutenant Lodgings'. It was erected in 1540 for Sir Edmond Walsingham, the then Lieutenant of the Tower, after many requests and complaints about the condition of the earlier lodging that occupied the site. Close inspection of the extant building reveals vestiges of an earlier medieval stone building, it is thought these form part of the house built for the Constable between 1361 and 1366. The east-west range of the present house seems to have contained the grandest rooms, including a fine first-floor hall in the penultimate western bay and a great first-floor kitchen in the most easterly, both are now divided horizontally, but were originally open to the roof. The former must have been rather old fashioned by the standards of the day, but in any event the Queen's House now represents one of the few remaining domestic houses still to be found in London dating from before the Great Fire of 1666.

Fig. 2 The Queen's House and its surroundings in 1720. 1.29

THE FORTIFICATIONS AND THE GARRISON

It was, of course, the need for security that resulted in so many early Tudor institutions congregating within the walls of the Tower, and the maintenance of these walls was the routine and important responsibility of the Surveyor of the King's Works. That said, it is perhaps surprising to observe that with the exception of works to strengthen the western entrance towards the end of the 15th century, including the provision of an artillery bulwark and the building of the surviving wedged-shaped gun tower against the Byward Barbican, little effort was made to upgrade the defences since the great works of Edward I in the late 13th century. In particular no effort was made to equip the outer *enceinte* with artillery bastions to carry and resist heavy guns, or reduce the vulnerable heights of the medieval towers. It has been suggested that the two large 'bastions' on the north-east and north-west corners of the outer curtain wall date from the reign of Henry VIII, but recent archaeology investigations have demonstrated that they originated as open-backed

structures contemporaneous with the rest of Edward I's *enceinte*. Brass Mount, on the north-east corner is probably the '*bulwerke in the mynte*' mentioned in March 1559 with the recommendation that it should have '*a brycke or stone wall made on the inside therof and to be filled full with earthe*' and the Haiward and Gascoyne survey (fig. 3) shows that this had been done by 1597.[2] By comparison, Legge's Mount was not enclosed until the 17th century, evidently sometime before 1682–3 when a brick vault was removed and the building raised to its present height.

Instead of artillery bastions the Tudor defenders relied on cannon mounted on the leads of existing building and on a few timber platforms planted between them. In 1534, for example, the French ambassador noted that Henry VIII had had guns mounted on the roof of the White Tower to command the City, and guns in this position can be seen on the 1597 survey. It was probably the weight of these guns that resulted in substantial repairs being carried out to the roof of the building in 1535–6, including the replacement of one of

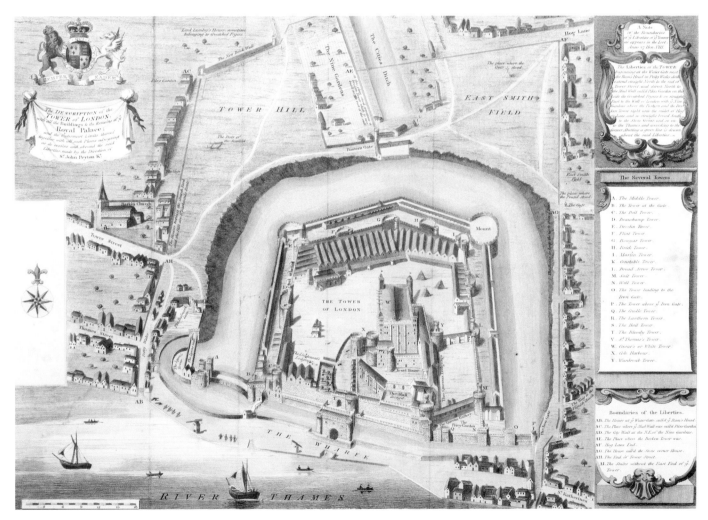

Fig. 3 Survey of the Tower and its Liberties by Haiward and Gascoyne in 1597. I.573

the massive tie-beams and the reinforcement of all the others. Interestingly, there is an account of the White Tower battery in action during the Thomas Wyatt rebellion of Mary I's reign. This suggests the arrangement was less than effective for as Protestant rebels approached the fortress in February 1554 an anonymous eyewitness noted that *'ther was shot off out of the White Tower a vi or vii shot, but myssed them, sometimes shoting over and sometimes shoting short'*.[3]

The men operating the guns were almost certainly the Tower gunners, a permanent attachment employed by the Office of Ordnance who lodged and trained at the fortress and whose descendants eventually went on to form the core of the Royal Regiment of Artillery in 1716. At the time of Henry VIII's accession there were already an unspecified number of gunners on the establishment; the number was subsequently fixed at seventeen when detailed instructions were issued to the Constable in 1555, by 1597 the number had risen to 140. The other important element in the day-to-day guarding of the fortress, before the setting up of the first permanent military garrison in the time of the Commonwealth, was the body of Yeoman Warders. In 1509 regulations for the Constable and his deputies required four Yeoman Warders and as many gunners, artificers, etc, as was deemed necessary to guard the entrance to the Tower from *'the first opening of the said gate to till the last shutting'*.[4] In 1555 it was decreed that nine Yeoman Warders and gunners were to perform the task during the day and six at night. These numbers may appear small for such a large building containing stores and equipment of national importance, but in an emergency the force could be augmented by men from Tower Hamlets who *'owe their service to the Towre … for the defence of the same'*.[5]

THE ROYAL LODGINGS AND THE CORONATION OF ANNE BOLEYN

While plans for a major overhaul of the great circuit of walls and towers of the Tower were drawn up by 1532, the works commissioned in the early summer of that year, in fact, centred around the royal lodgings and at a time when it was reported that arrangements were to begin for the King's marriage to Anne Boleyn and her coronation. Since the early 14th century it had been the custom for the royal party to lodge at the Tower on the eve of coronations.

The core of the royal lodgings at the Tower had been located in the Inmost Ward immediately to the south of the White Tower since the 12th century. In 1506, however, Henry VII enlarged these limits with the addition of a court to the east, comprising a new gallery intersecting gardens in the fashionable continental style. The subsequent works undertaken for Henry VIII represented not so much a further expansion, but rather an effort to modernise and make serviceable the existing ceremonial rooms. In this respect, however, it is worth noting that the contemporary accounts include references to wainscoting, mantelpieces, etc, being *'wrought with Antyk'*, thus indicating the first recorded use of classical decoration at the Tower.[6]

The 1532–3 refurbishment of the Tower's royal apartments – the King's concentrated in and about the Lanthorn Tower and the Queen's side comprising a range running between the Wardrobe and Lanthorn towers – seems to have been conducted at a frenetic rate. Thomas Cromwell, in his own words, was obliged to *'to sende in to all the places of this Realm for provysyon of the same by the kinge's commyssyon'*.[7] In October 1532, John Whalley, the paymaster at the Tower, was able to assure Cromwell that he had a work-force of some 400 men engaged on the project and that building operations were going well. On 5 December the King himself viewed progress with the French ambassador, and returned four days later with Anne Boleyn to show her what was being done.

The King's Gallery, erected in 1506 between the Lanthorn and Salt towers, was repaired together with the Council Chamber located mid-way along its length. Either side of the range new gardens were laid out, the larger one to the north was known as the Great or King's Garden, that to the south the Queen's or Privy Garden. Elsewhere in the King's apartments expensive repairs and alterations were carried out, two of the principal rooms being the Great Watching Room, adjoining the Great Hall, and the Great Dining, or Presence, Room beyond. Similar all-embracing repairs and alterations were executed in the queen's lodgings, though in the case of her Privy and Dining chambers, plans to refurbish the interiors were abandoned and the structures entirely rebuilt.

The medieval Great Hall, to the west of the King's apartments, was evidently in a very poor state and a complete reconstruction was recommended. The proposal seems however, to have been abandoned, and in the final weeks leading up to the arrival of the royal couple at the end of May 1532 the works accounts reveal hasty efforts to repair the existing walls and roof of the building. Within the building the walls were roughcast and all the timberwork treated with yellow ochre. At the western end the builders created an unspecified chamber for the Queen, while in the middle of the hall a dais was constructed *'where the hight table do stande'* and in the centre a *'chair of state'* was made for the King.[8]

Elsewhere the kitchens had to be overhauled and got ready for the royal supper while a row of seven timber-framed chambers with offices beneath was built against the outside of the curtain wall between the Wakefield Tower and Cold-harbour Gate (fig. 4). The 13th-century private lodgings of Edward I in St Thomas's Tower were rebuilt and partitioned as apartments for the Lord Great Chamberlain and the Lord Chamberlain. The work of the master carpenter, James Nedeham, the extant timber-framed structure, albeit much altered and repaired, is the principal survivor from this building campaign still to be seen at the Tower.

Whereas the main focus of the pre-coronation celebrations was the royal lodgings, attention was also paid to the White Tower, the great donjon that formed the architectural centrepiece of the fortress and a backdrop to the refurbished

Fig. 4 Row of seven timber-framed buildings erected against the curtain wall north of the Wakefield Tower in 1533. A drawing by T H Shepherd made shortly before the buildings were taken down in 1846. © Guildhall Library

palace complex. Works included repairs and alterations to the exterior of building and the fitting out of a chamber within for the creation of eighteen Knights of the Bath. The former saw the pilasters repaired and new battlements provided. The four corner turrets were given new lead-covered cupolas surmounted by great weather vanes that were decorated by the celebrated Italian painter, Ellys Carmayan. The ogee-shaped devices still survive, though the Henrician vanes were removed during the Commonwealth and the existing ones added in 1668.

The tradition of creating new Knights of the Bath on the eve of important royal events such as coronations and marriages had long been an accompaniment to the royal sojourn at the Tower and, at least during the Tudor period, the White Tower seems to have hosted the event. The accounts indicated that this took place on the top floor of the building in the larger west room that was provided with eighteen tubs and equipped with rails 'to be hangid for the knights of the Bathe'. Having completed the ritual bathing and instruction the party proceeded to a nocturnal vigil in the chapel. There is no evidence that this was the Chapel of St John in the White Tower, which by now may have performed a non-religious role anyway. The more likely setting was the Chapel of St Peter ad Vincula, in the north-east corner of the Inner Ward, which had been completely rebuilt in 1519–20 following a fire in 1512, and offered a more spacious and imposing venue for such a solemn ceremony.

Following the celebrations that preceded Anne Boleyn's coronation there is no evidence that Henry VIII ever stayed at the Tower again, Anne only returning for the trauma of her trial and execution. The irony is that the next public use of the old medieval great hall was the Queen's trial and involved 'a great scaffold' being erected close to where her own chamber had been formed only three years earlier.[9] Tower myth states that Anne stayed in the Lieutenant's Lodgings (the Queen's House) at this time, but the lodgings were not built until 1540 and contemporary accounts make it quite clear that she was permitted to stay in her former apartments. Nor is there any truth in the assertion that she was executed on the so-called scaffold site located in front on the Chapel of St Peter, for this was an invention of 1862 to please Queen Victoria, and wrongly laid out on the site of the ancient graveyard of the Tower that was in use until the early 19th century. In fact Anne's 'private' execution, evidently witnessed by hundreds of spectators, took place in front of the Tudor Ordnance House to the east on ground then known as the Green, or Green Hill, which is known to visitors now as the Parade Ground.

THE OFFICES OF THE ARMOURY AND THE ORDNANCE

During the early 15th century two separate organisations emerged from the Privy Wardrobe that specialised in the supply, storage and administration of weapons and equipment needed by the armed forces on land and at sea. The Office of the Ordnance concentrated on explosives, cannon, handguns and the more traditional bow and arrow, the Office of the Armoury concerned itself with armour and edged weapons. Most of their stores were held at the Tower and senior officials were provided with lodgings on site; the Master of the Ordnance, for examples, had accommodation in the Brick Tower along the north inner curtain wall. In 1513 monies were advanced for improvements that evidently saw the upper storey largely rebuilt and an extension added to the east, all this was done in brick, hence the name of the building.

During the reign of Henry VIII the Ordnance in particular enjoyed a sustained period of expansion, and under the mastership of Sir Christopher Morris (1536–43) important appointments were created, namely the Lieutenant, Clerk of Deliveries, Surveyor and Storekeeper. Subsequently, during the 1540s, financial reforms were also set in motion that saw payments beginning to be made through the Ordnance treasurers from monies voted to the Office in advance of requirement.

Military storehouses, workshops and official lodgings could be found in most parts of the Tower, sometimes in surprising and unlikely places. The great competition for available space was not unique to the Henrician era; for example in 1382 the queen's *camera* had to be cleared of chests of armour to accommodate a visit by Anne of Bohemia, while five years later piles of stone cannon balls were hastily removed from the Great Hall in advance of Richard II's arrival at the Tower to celebrate Christmas. That said, by the start of Henry VIII's reign most military stores were concentrated on the western half of the Wharf and on the hill immediately north of the White Tower. The *'house of ordnance'* on the hill was clearly the largest and most important and it was in this building that stands were contrived for Henry VII and his entourage to watch a great tournament in May 1501. In 1514 the ordnance storehouse was demolished and replaced with a building to house the King's artillery, bows and arrows. However, the new building proved to be a rather ephemeral affair for by the autumn of 1533 it was judged *'lykly to falle downe'*. Following some remedial efforts the decision was taken to replace the building and in 1545–7, Sir Francis Flemyng, Lieutenant of the Ordnance,

was issued with nearly £3,000, *'to erect and newe buylde one house wherein all the kinges maiestie Store and provicion of Artillerie Ordnance and other Municions maye be kepte and garded and bestowed'*.[10] The accounts show that the new storehouse comprised a wooden frame erected on brick footings, with brick chimneys. The roof was covered in lead, and the masons were paid for stone paving, windows, door frames and fireplaces. Joiners set up racks for hanging weapons, some of which were installed in special rooms *'wherein all the kinges maieties rich Weapons of his own person should be kepte'*, thus indicating that the accommodation was to be shared with the Armoury Office.[11] The new building can be seen on the 1597 survey. In plan, at least, it was the largest building ever to be erected at the Tower, and probably incorporated offices for clerks, etc, and possibly even lodgings, for in 1552 the Lieutenant of the Tower was ordered *'to remove Doctor Tunstall, late Bishop of Duresme [Durham] from his lodging in thordnance Howse to summe other mete place, for the sayd Ordnance Howse must be occupied otherwise by the Officers of the same'*.[12]

THE WARDROBE AND THE JEWEL HOUSE

By the beginning of the 16th century the rump of the old medieval Wardrobe had divided into two separate organisations. The Great Wardrobe, which had its headquarters near Baynard's Castle on the western edge of the City, was responsible for the supply, transport, storage and maintenance of the royal furniture, while the Wardrobe of the Robes dealt with robes and all household liveries. Both came under the auspices of the Lord Chamberlain's department and both had offices and storehouses at the Tower of London, though much of this was shared.

The accommodation allocated to the wardrobes was located in and adjoining the eastern annexe to the White Tower. This was a large two-storied stone building probably dating from the 14th century, but incorporating the 12th-century Wardrobe Tower in its south-east corner, the remains of which still stand (fig. 5). In 1532 a new range, measuring 31 m x 7.3 m (101 ft x 24 ft) was added on an east-west axis between the Wardrobe and Broad Arrow towers. This probably replaced an earlier building and accessed the interior of the Broad Arrow Tower where excavations in the basement of the tower in 1980 revealed a deposit of early 16th-century glass and pottery, some of it of high quality with traces of the royal insignia.

The inventory taken at the time of Henry VIII's death in 1547 illustrates just how valuable were the contents of these

Fig. 5 *The Great Court of the Tower* by T Malton, 1799, showing the 14th-century annex of the east side of the White Tower. I.96

buildings with numerous beds, carpets, canopies and tapestries being listed (fig. 6).[13] The collection became one of the great sights to be seen at the Tower and by the end of the 16th century foreign visitors began to provide breathtaking accounts.

Surviving medieval accounts indicate that the jewels and plate of the English monarchy were stored in the White Tower during the reign of Edward III and quite possibly earlier. By the beginning of the 16th century these important possessions were the responsibility of the Keeper of the Jewel House and his staff and in 1508 a new depository was constructed against the south side of the White Tower. In 1535, and at a time when Thomas Cromwell held the post of Keeper, this structure was re-roofed while another very nearby, older, building described as adjoining the King's Buttery, was entirely rebuilt. The new building was composed of brick with Caen and Reigate dressings and roofed in lead. The windows were protected with iron grilles and the lead downpipes were decorated with badges and arms. Within this building the

joiners made presses, cupboards and almeries in which to keep plate and jewels, while settles with lockable lids were provided '*to put in records or enny other wrytyngs or juells*'. The renewal of these facilities improved operations at the Tower with the former containing the removable plate, and the new building functioning as a standing jewel house where precious items, less frequently called upon, could be stored. Like the wardrobes, the collections in the jewel houses were shown to paying visitors to the Tower by the end of the 16th century, although the practice may have started some years earlier.

THE RECORD OFFICE

In the early 1530s the Wakefield Tower and its adjoining chamber block in the south-west corner of the Inmost Ward were described as '*the tower and lodgyng of the kyngis Reco'ds*'.[14] These buildings were erected in the 1220s, and

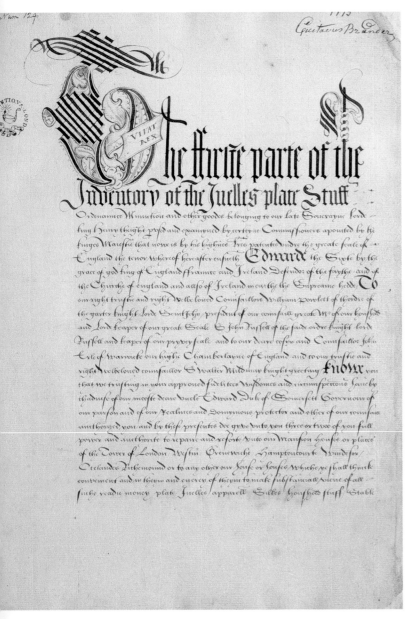

Fig 6. *The Inventory of King Henry VIII*, commissioned after Henry's death in 1547 by his son Edward VI. © The Society of Antiquaries of London

their upper floors originally formed part of Henry III's private lodgings. It is not clear when they became the nucleus of the Record Office at the Tower, but it might have been as early as 1360 when the records were removed from the White Tower for the imprisonment of King John of France. The eastern half of the chamber block was granted as a residence to the King's Bowmaker in February 1474 and remained in the hands of the Ordnance until the 19th century, despite repeated attempts by the Record Office to recover possession. The office received no attention during the building programme of Henry VIII's time, but by this time functioned as more than a repository as accounts show that the public could consult the records having first made an appointment and paid a fee.

THE MINT

Exactly when the Mint began operations at the Tower is not known. Recorded regulations suggest that it might have been as early as 1248, but by 1300, when the Warden of the Mint was instructed to build a furnace house 122 m (400 ft) long at the Tower, it would seem that operations were partly, or wholly, within the Outer Ward, where they remained until 1810. By the early 16th century a variety of Mint workshops and offices stood here, to which more were added in 1514, when the Prior of Bartholomew's was paid for '*new making and transposing storehouses and coining houses in the Mint*'.

The coinage reforms of 1526 increased the Mint's work significantly and as a result its buildings at the Tower received considerable attention. Unfortunately it is not possible to determine where the individual buildings stood, but archaeology has demonstrated that about this time assaying was being carried out in the extreme north-west corner of the Outer Ward against the rear of Legge's Mount.[15] Here, during the modernisation of a warder's lodgings in 1976, the remains of a small Tudor building were recorded (fig. 7). The building had been constructed against the inner face of Legge's Mount, in a lean-to manner, when the Tower stood as an open-backed bastion. The remains comprised the lower part of a vaulted cellar, containing a well, with a ground floor quadrant room to the north. Within the latter were the remains of a furnace, incorporating two key-shaped hearths and an ash pit; the furnace was linked to the cellar by means of a culvert, possibly intended as an air duct; all were constructed in brick. A range of metalworking finds were recovered, including crucibles used for melting copper, or one of its alloys, and small cupels made from bone ash and used to test the purity of silver. A further group of finds, consisting of globular pottery flasks, with long thin necks, were probably used to distil nitric acid employed to dissolve out silver from gold-silver alloys. All these finds, together with the nature of the excavated furnace, indicate that the building was connected with assaying – the process of testing the proportions of metals in alloys. Indeed, a survey of the Mint taken in 1701 labels a building adjacent to the east side of the excavated site as '*formerly part of the Assay Masters*'. In order to determine more precisely when these operations had been carried out a process known as archaeomagnetic dating was carried out. This involved calculating the direction of the earth's magnetic field when the furnace was last fired. When the data was compared with results from other dated sites, it was possible to calculate that the furnace had probably been heated for the last time between 1530 and 1560.

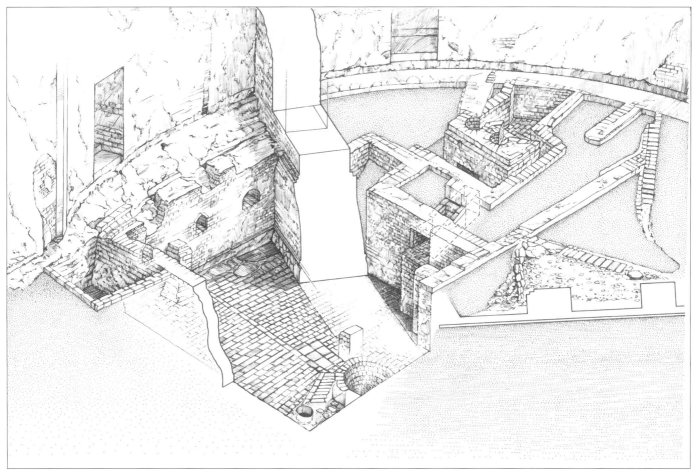

Fig. 7 Cut-away illustration of the remains of the Tudor Mint Building excavated in Legge's Mount, 1976. © English Heritage

CONCLUSION

In October 1597, 50 years after the death of Henry VIII, Sir John Peyton, newly appointed Lieutenant of the Tower of London, prepared a declaration on the state of the fortress for Queen Elizabeth that begins with a list of its principal functions:

First yor Maties Royall Stores of Amunytions for warre, wth the dangerous Charge of yor Highnes Magasyns of Powder

Secondly, yor Ma:^{ties} rich Treasures, of Jewells, Plate, and furnytures

Thirdly, yor Highnes Recordes

ffourthly, the office of the Mynte

ffifthly, the Prysoners for causes of state [16]

This list echoes the descriptions of the Tower provided by the contemporary historians Raphael Holinshed (see above)

and John Stow and affirms the role of the Tower as the Crown's central arsenal and the headquarters of its offices of state. In summary, therefore, the unique role of the Tower of London in England's history is inextricably linked to the development of the Wardrobe and its sub-departments in the Middle Ages – a process well under way before the era of the Tudors and one that was only enhanced by the efforts of by Henry VIII and his ministers. The extraordinary role that a medieval castle in the centre of London continued to play in the political life of the realm during 17th and 18th centuries, and even beyond, has more to do with the mechanics of bureaucracy than a colourful (if misleading) view of historical events.

Notes and references page 334.

{VII}

FOOD AND DINING
AT HENRY'S COURT

PETER BREARS

Food and drink played a very important part at Henry VIII's court, but films have given us a false impression that bears little or no resemblance to reality. Peter Brears cuts through these images of gluttony and boorishness to reveal the highly organised – and costly – arrangements to feed the King and his court. He details the layout of the kitchens, the range of foodstuffs used and the variety of dishes prepared. The author shows the tremendous differences in menu between the household staff and the King himself, and reveals the way Henry was protected against any attempt to poison him. The elaborate ritual of serving food to the King is also described and the question is raised of the likely effect of his diet on Henry's weight and health.

Fig. 1 The Royal Clock Salt, French, about 1535. The only surviving piece of Henry VIII's tableware given to Henry by Francis I, and a truly magnificent example of goldsmithing of the period. © Courtesy of the Goldsmith's Company

There is now a well-established concept of what the meals and manners of Henry and his court were like, having been informed by several generations of historical films. Following Charles Laughton's depiction of Henry in Alexander Korda's 1933 film *The Private Life of Henry VIII*, we see him as a lascivious gargantuan, grabbing handfuls of gross food, and cramming almost all of it into his flabby, podgy face. Such images may win Oscars, but they have nothing whatsoever to do with reality. One of Henry VII's great achievements was to instruct his sons in all the skills required for powerful, effective kingship. These included military exercises and jousting, physical recreations from tennis to hunting, and intellectual interests and abilities in languages, literature and music. Even more important was their knowledge of manners, for it was manners that established a person's place in the social hierarchy. Unless trained by skilled masters, it was impossible to pass oneself off as a gentleman, noble or prince, since the established etiquette was so complex that imposters were readily exposed and disgraced. It was therefore inconceivable that Henry should ever display bad manners, especially when dining in state or in public. As we know from other sources, he was a most fastidious monarch.

The organisation of the food supply for the Henrician court of around 1,000 to 1,500 people was one of the country's major industrial-scale operations.[1] Its managers claimed a long tradition of efficient excellence descended from their service to the legendary kings Lud and Cassibellan.[2] Their working practices had been honed under sequential medieval kings, but still lacked the degree of tight control which Henry and his Chancellor, Cardinal Wolsey, now required. Their first major revision, the Eltham Ordinances, were introduced in 1526, Thomas, Lord Cromwell making further substantial improvements in the Greenwich Ordinance of 1539–40.[3] Now the whole of domestic life of the court was supervised by a Lord Grand Master in the person of Henry's brother-in-law Charles Brandon, Duke of Suffolk. His duties were shared with two other great officers, Sir Thomas Cheyney, as Treasurer, and Sir John Gage as Comptroller. The bulk of their day-to-day responsibility was undertaken by Sir Edmund Peckham as Cofferer, four lesser Masters of the Household, and Clerks of the Comptrollment, Spicery, Kitchen and the Greencloth.[4] All these officers met around their green-baize-covered accounting table in the Counting House early every morning to plan and control every aspect of the house-hold's domestic management.

Some foodstuffs, such as fruit, vegetables and game, might come from the royal estates, but these were always insufficient to meet the demands of feeding such a great court. As a result, the vast majority of all the raw foods and drinks had to be bought in. Some impression of the scale of this operation is given by the annual costs of provisions purchased for each division of the household in 1540.[5]

		(at 2008 prices)
For the King	£1,520 12s. 4d.	£456,184.50
For his Officers	£6,369 18s. 2d.	£1,911,973.00
For the Queen	£1,520 12s. 4d.	£456,184.50
For her Officers	£2,680 1s. 1.25d.	£804,016.86
For Household staff	£6,250 19s. 6.75d.	£1,875,292.50
Fuel, utensils etc	£4,445 2s. 6d.	£1,333,503.70
Total cost	£22,787 5s. 0d.	£6,836,175.36

In order to control such massive expenditure, the Officers of the Greencloth determined the price which should be paid for each individual item when purchased by the accatery of beef and fish, and their purveyors of poultry, wheat, ale, wine and other provisions. They also drew up contracts with both London city companies such as the Poulterers, and individuals, to supply foods at pre-determined prices. Samples of each

commodity were carefully checked for quality and value before being conveyed into the larders, any employee found guilty of fraud or inefficiency being given a week in the Marshalsea, the Knight-Marshal's prison in Southwark, or losing a week's wages.[6]

As the Officers of the Greencloth kept the keys of every larder and kitchen, one of their first tasks every morning was to open up the larders. Here they supervised the cutting up and measurement of the ingredients for that day's meals, then locked up the larders once more, and opened up the kitchens so that cooking might begin. On returning to the Counting House, they then received reports on what had been consumed, how many meals had been served the previous day, their clerks then recording the quantities and values, to ensure that all was within the predicted budgets. Next they issued keys to the pantries, butteries and dining areas, so that tables could be set for dinner, to be served at 10am. At this time they took their places in offices adjacent to the serving hatches, so that they could count all the dishes of food leaving the kitchens. In this way they could check if any had gone missing, and arrange investigations and punishments accordingly. The same procedure was then repeated when supper was served at 4pm.

The kitchens built at Henry's new palaces were all designed to achieve the maximum administrative and practical efficiency. The largest and most complete of these is at Hampton Court Palace (fig. 2). Built in 1529–31, it occupies a massive largely two-storey block measuring some 128 m x 27 m (420 ft by 90 ft), running along the cool north side of the Base Court.[7] Entered by its own porter-controlled gate, the first quarter of the block was largely devoted to administration, the Officers of the Greencloth directly above being able to see everything and everyone entering or leaving. Here all purchased supplies were brought in along with the 'oven-ready' fresh meats and poultry, the breads and the fuel, all pre-prepared in external premises. Next came the stores etc, for dry foods, the larders for fresh foods, then the kitchens, and finally the dresser or serving-hatches from which the food was distributed. In all, there were some 60 separate rooms, each with its designated purpose, and arranged in logical order. It was essentially a huge food-processing plant, larger and more efficiently planned than any factory built until the early stages of the Industrial Revolution.

Within the royal court, food was required for seven separate dinning areas: (1) the King's Privy and Secret Chambers, (2) the Queen's Privy and Withdrawing Chambers, (3) the Privy Council's Chamber, (4 & 5) the Great Watching Chambers for the King's and Queen's officers, (6) the Great Hall for the household staff and lesser visitors, and (7) the Counting House,

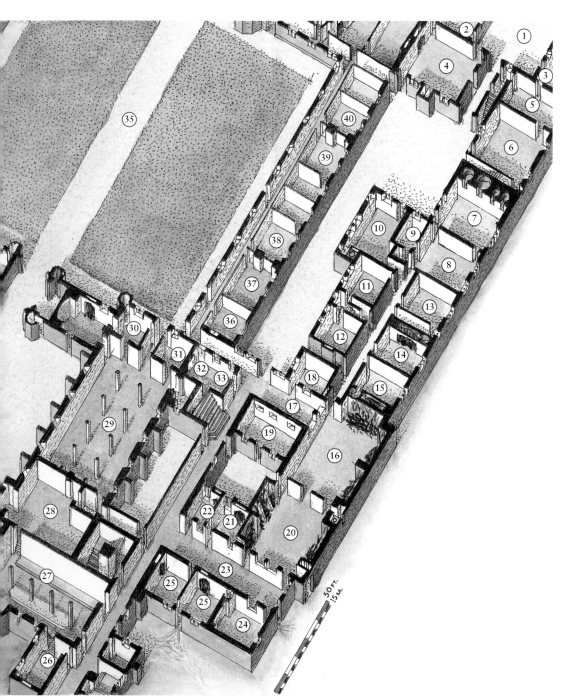

Fig. 2 Henry VIII's kitchens at Hampton Court. As completed about 1531, these kitchens demonstrate a highly advanced approach to factory-like food production, all being arranged for the maximum practical and administrative efficiency. From the Back Gate down to the cellars beneath the Great Hall, they incorporate:

1. Greencloth Yard
2. Chandlery
3. King's Coal House
4. Clerk Comptroller's Room
5. Bottle House
6. Dry Fish House
7. Pastry Bakehouse
8. Pastry Workhouse
9. Pastry Boulting House (?)
10. Boiling House
11–12. Wet Larders
13. Dry Larder
14–15. Hall Place Kitchen Workhouses
16. Hall Place Kitchen
17. Hall Place Surveying Place
18. Hall Place Dresser Office
19. Pewter Scullery
20. Lords' Side Kitchen
21. Lords' Side Dresser Office
22. Silver Scullery
23. The Great Space
24. Lords' Side Workhouse (?)
25. Clerk of Kitchen's Lodgings
26. Drinking House
27. Great Wine Cellar
28. Privy Cellar
29. Beer Cellar
30. Great Buttery
31. Privy Buttery
32. Pantry
33. Almonry
34. Fountain Court
35. Base Court
36–40. Lodgings

kitchens, where, due to their workload, staff took their meals in their places of work.[8] Dining elsewhere was strictly forbidden, for it encouraged waste and theft.[9]

To serve all these areas there were four separate kitchen departments (1) the King's Privy Kitchen (2) the Queen's Privy Kitchen (3) the Lords' Side Kitchen for their officers, the Privy Council and senior officers of the Counting House, and (4) the Hall Place Kitchen. Each had its own staff, equipment and pre-determined menus to supply food of the appropriate quantity and quality to each dining area. These are best

considered separately, starting with the mass catering required to serve the hundreds of people who dined in the Great Hall.

To be eligible to take meals here, or anywhere else at court, it was first necessary to have the approval of the Officers of the Greencloth, this being known as the Bouche of Court.[10] Anyone not authorised in this way by reason of their employment within the court, or the express permission of the Officers, would be rejected. Those who dined in the Great Hall were household staff, lesser courtiers, or their servants. Their diets were quite basic. For dinner, each lower servant received half a loaf of wholemeal bread, 227 g (8 oz) (uncooked weight) of both boiled beef and veal, with oatmeal and vegetables as pottage, and one and 0.75 lt (1 ¼ pt) of ale. The upper servants, meanwhile, had three-quarters of a wholemeal loaf, 255 g (9 oz) boiled beef as pottage, 227 g (8 oz) each of roast veal and pig, goose or rabbit, with 1 lt (2 pt) of ale. Equivalent quantities of ling or cod were served on Fridays and Saturdays, as these were fish days, when no meats might be eaten.[11] The Hall Place Kitchen was provided with a large boiling-house where the 1 kg (2 lb) joints of meat or fish, each large enough to serve a 'mess' of four people, could be boiled together.[12] Further large copper boilers stood on iron frames in the deep fireplaces of the kitchen itself, so that collectively perhaps 200 joints might be boiled at one time.[13] When the meat was tender, it was hooked out, and left to rest while oatmeal and pre-boiled and chopped vegetables were stirred into the remaining stock to form pottage.[14] This was then ladled into pewter dishes, each to serve a mess of four people, and sent into the hall, closely followed by the boiled meat or fish.

Within the Great Hall, long, narrow trestle tables had been set up, their tops covered with lockram (coarse linen) table-cloths, and their sides lined with benches.[15] Having entered and washed their hands at tables bearing communal ewers of water, basins and towels, each person now took his place. Before him would be a trencher, probably a flat piece of wood, to serve as his personal cutting-board, an ash-wood bowl to serve as his cup, and a communal group of loaves, saucer of mustard, salt cellar and probably a leather ale-pot, for each mess of four people. After saying grace, he would sit down, use his own eating-knife to cut his portion of bread into fingers, and use his own spoon to drink from the communal mess of pottage. When the meat arrived, he would use the thumb and first two fingers of his left hand to grasp the piece he wanted, using the knife in his right hand to cut it off. Holding it down on his trencher, still with his left hand, he would then cut it in pieces, put down his knife, and use the thumb and first two fingers of his right hand to dip the meat into small portions of either salt or mustard on his trencher, and carry it up to his mouth. In this way he could never contaminate the joint with his saliva, nor place his 'cack-hand', used when at the latrine, near his lips.[16]

In theory, dining in this way should have been a pleasant, orderly experience, but in practice it was fraught with numerous vexations. The tableware might not be of the cleanest, for example; the wooden cups being;

Old, black and rusty, lately taken from some sink;
And in such vessel drink thou often time,
Which in the bottom is full of filth and slime,

And in that vessel thou drinkest oft I wis,
In which some states [important men] or dames late did piss.[17]

The table service might also be purposely inefficient, especially when the waiters expected to have the leftovers for their dinners.

Slowe be the servers in serving in alway,
But swift they be after taking meat away,
A special custom is used them among,
No good dish to suffer on the board too long.
The hungry servers at the table stand
At every morsel hath eye to thy hand...
Because that thy leavings is only their part,
If thou feed well, sore grieved is their heart.

If a dish was particularly pleasant, it might be hacked by ten hands, those from one's own mess, and others joining in from those at both ends of the table.

And if it be flesh, ten knives shalt thou see
Mangling the flesh and in the platter flee;
To put there thy hands is peril without fail,
Without a gauntlet or else a glove of mail.
Amongst all these knives thou one of both must have,
Or else it is hard thy fingers whole to save,
Oft in such dishes in court is seen,
Some leave their fingers, each knife is so keen,
On finger gnaweth some hasty glutton,
Supposing it is a piece of beef or mutton...

Finally there was the nature of the food itself. Though nutritious and plentiful, particularly by contemporary every-day standards, it was dull, predictable, monotonous and basic. This was a matter of domestic policy, for not only did it make best use of the available finances, but it also emphasised the fact that those dining in the Great Hall were unworthy of anything better. To ensure that they fully appreciated the benefits of hierarchy, all the delicious food intended for the Lords' tables was deliberately paraded under their noses at every mealtime:

...though white and brown [bread] be at one price
With brown shalt thou feed, lest white make thee nice...
The Lords will always that people note and see
Between them and servants some diversity.
Though it to them turn no profit at all,
If they have pleasure, the servant shall have small...
And costly dishes a score may [the servants] tell;
Their greedy gorges are wrapt with the smell;
The daintiest dishes which pass through the hall
It were a great labour for me to name them all...
And then is their pain and anger fell as gall

When all passeth by, and they have none at all.

The diet for the Lords was certainly superior in variety, quality and quantity, including for dinners:[18]

Sunday, Tuesday & Thursday	Monday & Wednesday	Friday & Saturday
	1st Course	
Pottage	Pottage	Pottage
Beef	Beef	Ling
Mutton	Mutton	Salmon
Veal	Kent Capons	Plaice or Gurnard
Swan or Goose	Beef Olives	Haddock or Whiting
Kent Capons	Veal	Conger Eel
Rabbits	Rabbits	Pike
Delicacies & fritters		
	2nd Course	
Pottage	Lamb	Burt
Heron or Bittern	Rabbits	Bream or Tench
Lamb or Chicken	Cocks, Plover	Sole, Salmon or Trout
Cocks, Plovers	Tart etc	Tarts
Tart	Fruit	Fruit
Fritters	Eggs	Butter
Fruit	Butter	Eggs
Butter		
Eggs		

In addition to wholemeal bread, there were fine white manchet loaves, as well as ale, there was hopped beer and wines.

The lords' food was cooked in the Lords' Side Kitchen. This too had a separate boiling house, but on a smaller scale, for it only prepared the pottage. The boiling of the more delicate dishes, and the labour and fuel consuming spit-roasting of the best meats took place in the specially equipped wide-arched fireplaces. One had a pair of walls built out from its back wall, some 2.13 m (7 ft) apart. These provided shelter for two turnbroaches (spit-turners) at each side, and supported great iron racks on which they turned eight long spits loaded with joints, all at the same time.[19]

It had been customary for kitchen staff to work here either completely naked, or in dirty clothes smothered in grease. Due to Henry's reforms, the head cooks were now to keep their staff clean, well-dressed, and, since they now had to sweep the palace courtyards, well-ventilated and visible to all.[20] Just as in the Hall Place Kitchen, there was a separate serving hatch from which the food was checked out on its way to the Lord's dining areas. At one end of its inner side a hatch led through to the Officers' dresser office, and on to a silver scullery beyond. Since all the lords' individual and communal tableware was of solid silver, and extremely valuable, this arrangement ensured that the clerks could draw the required dishes from the scullery, pass them into the kitchen, see them filled, and then check them before they were carried up through the Great Hall, into the Privy Council, Great Watching, and King's and Queen's Presence Chambers.

Here, with fine furniture, damask table linen, and silver trencher-plates and tableware, the lords dined in considerable splendour served by ushers, sewers, yeomen, grooms and pages of the chamber.[21] The lords still used their spoons, knives and fingers in the same way as those crowded into the Great Hall, but with none of its boisterous fervour. Here there was plenty of fine food, and plenty of time to enjoy it without risk of it being carried off by the waiters. However good it was, whether boiled, roasted, baked or fried, it still fell far short of that served to Henry and his queens.

Due to his great size in later life, there has been much speculation on Henry's diet, some claiming that it had serious deficiencies which caused him to increase in bulk and fall fatally ill. All the contemporary evidence tends to contradict this, showing that he had access to the greatest range of foods, none of which appear to have caused similar effects on other members of his court. However, even if we know what was presented at his table, on the advice of his physician, there is nothing to inform us of which actual foods he preferred, and the quantities in which he consumed them. Henry's daily dinner menu comprised the following dishes, but it must be remembered that this is what was set on the table, almost like a buffet, and not which dishes he actually selected, which were undoubtedly far fewer in number.[22]

DINNERS Sunday – Thursday	DINNERS Friday & Saturday
	1st Course
Pottage	Herring
Chines of Beef	Pottage
Rammuners	Ling
Venison, stewed	Salt Eel or Lamprey
Leg of Red Deer	Pike
Mutton	Preserved Salmon
Carp or Veal, stuffed	Whiting
Swan, Goose or Stork	Haddock, Mullet or Bass
Capons of Grease	Plaice or Gurnard
Rabbits of Grease	Sea Bream or Sole
Delicacies, baked Carp	Conger Eel
Custards, garnished or fritters	Porpoise or Seal

Carp or Trout
Crabs or Lobsters
Custard
Rascalls or Flage (?)
Closed Tarts
Fritters
Fruit

2nd Course

Jelly Ipocras, cream of Almonds	Second Pottage
Pheasant, Heron, Bittern etc	Sturgeon
Partridge, Quail or Mew	Turbot
Cock, Plover or Gull	Bream or other fish
Kid, Lamb or Pigeon	Tench
Larks or Rabbit	Perch or other fish
Snype, Pullet or Chicken	Eel with Lamprey, roast
Venison Pasty	Chine of Salmon, grilled
Tarts	Crayfish
Fritters	Shrimps
Fruit with spiced sugar	Tarts
Butter & Eggs	Fritters
	Fruit
	Baked Pippins & Oranges
	Butter & Eggs

All these were accompanied by wholemeal and the finest white breads, ale, beer and wine. In addition, Henry enjoyed numerous other dishes, such as the meaty sausages from '*the wif that makes the king podinges at hamptoncourte*', and numerous presents from well-wishers.[23] These included wildfowl, sturgeon, lampreys and pears, or the pies of oranges or of quinces as sent by Lady Sydney.[24]

To prepare these dishes, there were separate King's and Queen's Privy Kitchens, Henry's at Hampton Court being on the ground floor, directly beneath his bedchamber. Not only did this enable his meals to be conveniently carried up a spiral stair to his privy- or presence-chambers, but it also kept his bedchamber aired and warm.[25] Henry's Yeoman Cook for the King's Mouth was Pero Doulx, the man who was responsible for instigating the court's taste for French cuisine. He was paid £13 16s. 8d. a year in wages, with a £10 a year clothing allowance – around £4,180 and £3,000 in 2008 values, but with all his living expenses met by the court.[26]

Henry usually dined in his privy chamber, at any time he found convenient, his meals being served by six gentlemen, assisted by two gentlemen ushers, four grooms and a page.[27] Here the tableware would be of gold, and the ceremonial precise. The gentlemen would kneel as they assayed his food

by eating samples of every dish, carved it into mouth-sized pieces and laid it on his trencher, or held up his cup before him if he chose to drink. This must have been a nerve-wracking task, for Henry had instructed them '*to have a vigilant and reverent respect and eye to his Grace, soe that by his looke or countenance, they may know what lacketh, or is his pleasure to be had or done*'.[28]

For an immensely potent display of kingly majesty, few ceremonies could compare with that of Henry VIII dining in public, either in his presence chamber, or at some great diplomatic feast. For these he sat beneath a magnificent canopy of state, a rectangular deeply valanced frame which projected from the wall high above his chair, and from which hung a back-cloth or celure, all being of the richest cloth of gold and silk, embroidered with his coat of arms. His table was covered in the finest white linen damask, woven with designs such as the Children of Israel being fed with manna.[29] Every week Anne Harris, the King's Laundress, washed, ironed and perfumed his tablecloths, napkins and towels, to keep them in perfect condition.[30]

Before Henry entered, on a day of great estate, his table would have had one of his fabulous gold saltcellars set at its centre.[31] The '*Morres daunce*' salt, for example, had a 'table' raised on a base and shank, on which stood five Morris dancers and a lady holding a covered salt.[32] With 4.16 kg (147 oz) of solid gold, 40 diamonds, nine great sapphires, 91 rubies and 150 pearls, its flashes of brilliant colour would have been truly spectacular. Before it, to his right, lay cutlery. This included a steel-bladed knife, perhaps hafted in gold, silver-gilt, rock crystal or chalcedony (a translucent quartz), and a spoon for Henry's own use.[33] Some spoons were New Year gifts, that given by the Marquess of Exeter being of solid gold, and tipped with the royal arms.[34] Here too were the carver's knives, sets such as one having '*two great Carving knives and three small, the haftes golde having Lyons upon ther heddes endes*'.[35] Over their blades was then placed a horizontal stack of trimmed white loaves wrapped in their linen port-pane. The whole of this arrangement was finally covered in a cover-pane, perhaps one of fine damask, or of lawn, embroidered with the King's beasts, fringed and edged in Venetian gold and silver.[36]

On entering the chamber, Henry would have been approached by some of his gentlemen bearing a ewer of perfumed water to pour over his hands, a basin to catch the falling drops, and a towel on which to dry his hands. In 1536/7 Queen Jane Seymour had commissioned a magnificent new set, weighing 3 kg (109 oz) of solid gold, chased and enamelled with the

King's arms, the Garter, and red and white Tudor roses .[37]

Having taken his chair, the Carver, Lord Henry Neville, knelt before the table, removed the cover-pane, and re-arranged the tableware, setting Henry's cutlery, bread, napkin and trencher before him.[38] His trenchers were usually shallow rectangular plates of silver or silver gilt, but his best was of 765 g (27 oz) of solid gold, with a hollow for salt in one corner, and all supported by six 'antique men'.[39] Now the Sewer, Sir Percivall Hart, led a procession of gentlemen ushers and daily waiters up to the right-hand side of the carver, each using the ends of his long narrow linen towel tied at the top of his left arm, to hold the gold or silver-gilt dishes of food.[40] Each in turn knelt by the kneeling Carver and Sewer, as the former cut a portion of each food, and fed it to them by way of assay, to check it was not poisoned, before placing the dishes on the table.

The Carver now began his real work. Taking his lead from Henry's glances, he served mouth-sized portions of each chosen food onto the King's trencher, from where he had only to carry it up to his lips. Each morsel had also to be given its appropriate finishing.[41] This might involve the use of a charcoal brazier called a chafing dish to re-heat the food, or saucers of sauces in which to dip it.[42] The Carver might also use silver-gilt ginger, pepper, sugar or spice boxes to sprinkle on their finely ground contents.[43] There was even a 'Strayner of gold with a roose at thendes' if Henry wished to have orange juice on his roast capon'.[44]

Whenever the King wished to drink, his Cupbearer, the Earl of Surrey, would approach the table, kneel before it, and hold up one of the great gold covered cups already filled with wine. Like the salts, some of these cups were of magnificent quality and workmanship. One of his finest, *The Dream of Paris*, had the figures of Paris and his horse, with Jupiter, Venus, Pallas and Juno on its cover, the whole having 78 rubies, eleven diamonds, four sapphires and 139 pearls, all set in 3.5 kg (120 oz) of solid gold. Such cups were most probably purely display pieces, being far too cumbersome for practical use, but others of around 570 g (20 oz) would certainly have been in practical use.[45] As he knelt, the Cupbearer would remove the lid with his left hand, hold it beneath the cup, pour in a few drops from the cup, drink these by way of assay, then hold the cup up for Henry to grasp and drink, meanwhile holding the upturned lid beneath it, to catch any drops. Having had the cup handed back to him; he would then replace its lid, and return it to the cupboard.

After the second course had been served, the tableware and crumbs etc. were carefully removed, the almoner placing token loaves into one of Henry's great alms dishes, to show that all broken meats from the royal household's tables would be distributed to the poor. For state occasions, there was a choice of two silver-gilt alms dishes, the great alms dish at 16.2 kg (35.9 lb oz), and one '*made like a shippe*' at 8.9 kg (19.6 lb).[46]

Now the table was prepared for the final hand washing by placing a towel at one end, this being up to 17.4 m (57 ft) of 68 cm (27 in) white damask or diaper linen folded end-to-end, and then across 30 cm (1 ft) pleats, to form a deep stack.[47] Having been drawn out along the table and stretched straight, a '*yard of wood tipped with silver*' was used to form an 'estate' or pleat at each side of the King.[48] The ewer and basin were then used as before, the ends of the estates being held up beneath his cuffs, to keep his clothing perfectly dry. After he had dried his hands on a shorter towel, the table was completely cleared away, so that the King could stand up to take his digestives of spicy sweetmeats. Seven hundred grams (1.5 lb) of these were served on spice plates of silver or silver-gilt.[49] If they were dry, sugar-coated spices, Henry could take them up with his fingers, but if of wet and sticky quince-paste 'marmalades', or green ginger preserved in syrup, a sucket-spoon or fork had to be used. Described as '*Spones with a suckett forke upon one stele (shaft) gilte 3 ounces*', or as '*ginger forkes*', these were only to be found in the most prestigious of households.[50]

With this final ceremony, the meal was over, and Henry could go about his business, but if he had important guests to impress, he might take them on to a 'banquet'. In the 16th century these were the most private and exclusive of entertainments, featuring the most elaborate works of the royal confectioners. For the French embassy of 1527, for example, there were '*beastes, byrdes, fowles of dyvers kyndes, and personages most lyvely made...some fighting wt. Swordes, some wt. Gonnes and Crosebowes, some dauncyng wt. Ladyes...Castles wt. Images in the same*' and even a model of the medieval St Paul's Cathedral.[51] Some of these may have been '*divers consaites for a banquet made of earth*' listed in Henry's inventory, but others, such as the figure of St George on horseback which introduced his Garter Day dinners, were probably of wax or sugar.[52]

Given the above evidence, it is clear that Henry VIII had one of the most magnificent courts in all of Europe. In modern times, when filmmakers still use Henry as a vehicle for their repressed fantasies, it is best to remember that he was a monarch of enormous sophistication. Today's actors may still bite their food like animals, but only the most uncouth of peasants ever did that when Henry was king.

Notes and references page 335.

{VIII}

DRESS AND FASHION AT HENRY'S COURT

MARIA HAYWARD

In the reign of Henry VIII clothing was an increasingly important part of court life. Maria Hayward explains how important it was for the King to dress the part, through making contacts with merchants and spending lavishly on new, luxury textiles. To maintain his place at the forefront of society and style, Henry was supported by the King's Tailor and the office of the Great Wardrobe. The author makes the point that Henry was eminently suited to leading fashion while he was young and fit, but that this was harder when he became older and fatter. The fascinating relationship between Henry's clothing and armour is explored: both were essential in creating an image of magnificence. Today much of his armour survives, but sadly his costume does not.

In 1528 Baldesar Castiglione published *The Book of the Courtier*, in which he described the ideal courtier. He covered many topics including the courtier's appearance and the comments he made would have applied just as well to a prince or king of good taste, such as Henry VIII.[1] Not surprisingly, Castiglione's courtier was quintessentially male. In a similar vein, during the reign of a monarch like Henry VIII, who actively participated in all aspects of court life and when young had prided himself on his physical prowess, male dress overshadowed female attire. Consequently, this paper will consider three specific aspects of Henry VIII's clothing: the significance of male dress at the Henrician court, the financial, social and political value of the King's clothes and the various links between the King's clothing and his armour.

Fig. 1 Henry VIII, unknown artist, about 1520. © National Portrait Gallery, London

Magnificent masculine apparel:
The importance of male dress and fashion
at the Henrician court

While people living in the 16th century might not have had the same sense of fashion as those from the 18th or 19th centuries, men's clothing evolved more quickly in the early 16th century than it had in preceding centuries. This was demonstrated by the increasing variety of garments for men and the growing range of decorative techniques used to embellish them. Equally, English male clothing had its own distinctive style but it was open to influence from styles from a number of European countries including Germany, France, Italy and Spain, each one of which was seen as having a distinctive character. In order to ensure his place at the forefront of clothing trends, Henry VIII made sure that he had first sight of new textiles and jewels being imported into England by granting trade concessions to Italian merchants and French jewellers. In a similar vein, the King allowed the leading Italian merchants dealing in luxury silk textiles to bring their wares directly to him on occasion rather than insisting that they always dealt with the Great Wardrobe.[2]

In the early 16th century, for a man of means such as Henry VIII, his wardrobe would have consisted of five staple garments: a doublet and hose which were worn over a shirt and with a gown and bonnet.[3] The King's clothes were made for him annually by the King's Tailor. Five men held this office during his reign, beginning with Stephen Jasper who had been his father's tailor.[4] In 1511 Jasper was succeeded by William Hilton and the subsequent office holders were John de Paris, John Malt and John Bridges.[5] While these men did not work exclusively for the King, he was their best and most important customer. In addition, they worked in conjunction with a range of other craftsmen, including the King's Hosier, Skinner, Embroiderer and Cordwainer to create the King's clothing and accessories. Together they created the regal image recorded in Henry VIII's portraits (fig. 1).

The King's Tailor worked for the Great Wardrobe which issued him with warrants outlining in detail the clothes that the King wanted, stipulating the type of garment, the cost, the colour and variety of fabric along with the linings, interlinings

Fig. 2 Detail showing Henry VIII arriving at Guisnes riding in procession with Wolsey, from The Field of the Cloth of Gold, an engraving after the original painting. I.224

and decoration. As such, the surviving Great Wardrobe accounts provide a detailed overview of the clothes that Henry VIII ordered between 1509 and 1547 and they record a variety of styles. For the King's everyday wear, the accounts show how colour choices and decorative styles evolved over the decades.[6]

The accounts also chart the development of specific types of sporting dress: in particular coats for hunting, tennis, falconry and the associated accessories. These clothing developments echo the sporting skills that Castiglione noted as essential for his courtier.[7] In addition, there were the King's formal robes of silk velvet or cloth of gold for the coronation, parliament, the garter, the other European orders of chivalry, the orders of St Michael of France and the Toison d'Or or Golden Fleece of Burgundy and Spain.

Political theorists such as Sir John Fortescue were well aware of the value of clothes to a monarch. In his book *The Governance of England* he placed particular emphasis on '*Riche clothes, riche furres, other than be wonned to fall vndre the yerely charges off his wardrober, rich stones...and do other such nobell and grete costes, as bifitith his roiall magestie*'.[8] As such, Fortescue made explicit the link between clothes and the concept of royal magnificence.[9] Henry VIII's clothing choices acted as an expression of his own personality and his competition with his rivals abroad, namely Charles V of Spain and Francis I of France. This rivalry was played out at events such as the Field of Cloth of Gold in 1520 (fig. 2) and the meeting at Boulogne in October 1532. For the latter event, Hall recorded that '*The Frenche kynge caused twoo gounes to be made of white veluet pricked with gold of damaske, and the capes and ventes wer of frettes of whipped gold of damaske very riche, which twoo gounes he sent to the kyng of Englande, praying hym to chose the one and to weare it for his sake*'.[10]

The social hierarchy emphasised in the King's sumptuary legislation was designed to set the King apart from other English men by his right to wear purple silk, cloth of tissue and sables. Henry made selective use of the colours, fabrics and furs that were exclusive to him so making the occasions when he chose to wear them more significant – usually events of state and the key days of the liturgical year when the King was required to wear purple and scarlet (fig. 3). The small group of Henry's clothes listed in the 1542 inventory of the palace of Whitehall fits very well with the sumptuary law including '*oone Gowne of crymsen vellet with a Caape furred with Sables with fourtie and oone peir of Aglettes of golde*'.[11] Equally, the King could tolerate a degree of flouting of the sumptuary law and on occasion he sanctioned individuals

Fig. 3 Henry VIII at prayer from the Black Book of the Garter (MS DOC 162a). © Dean and Canons of Windsor

such as Sir Henry Guildford to wear cloth above their rank as a sign of royal favour. However, Henry's chief competitors within England, the Duke of Buckingham and Henry Howard, the Earl of Surrey, both used dress on occasion to indicate their rivalry with the King.

Henry VIII was the focus of his court and his style of dress would influence those around him, especially when he was a young man. Male dress at this time emphasised physical strength by stressing the breadth of the shoulders and virility through the size of the codpiece.[12] However, the emphasis on youth started to pose a problem for the King and his tailors as he aged and his body changed shape resulting in his favouring different, looser styles such as the cassock and his use of a staff to help him walk (fig. 4). Male dress also dominated the orders placed by the King with the Great Wardrobe for livery for members of his household which was almost exclusively male.

In general, the only female livery that Henry VIII ordered was for the women who attended the royal nursery. In addition, red and black livery was issued to the King's Laundress for her attendance at his coronation and funeral.

A CONSUMING PASSION: HENRY VIII's INTEREST AND INVESTMENT IN CLOTHES

Henry VIII's interest in clothes was both personal and professional.[13] The Tudors shared a family fondness for clothes, shoes and jewellery and this was demonstrated very strongly by Henry VIII, his sisters Margaret and Mary and his daughters Mary I and Elizabeth I.[14] While Henry VII was less prone to overt displays of wealth, he used his clothes to great effect for events of state and Elizabeth of York's privy purse accounts hint at her being a woman who took a careful interest in her own clothes and those of her children.[15] An interest in clothes was something Henry VIII also shared with his nephew James V of Scotland and his rival Francis I of France – as such clothes were essential to give a monarch a magnificent appearance and dressing with style was part of being a renaissance king.

The value of Henry VIII's clothes can be expressed in a variety of ways: financially, socially, politically and sartorially. Starting with their financial significance, it is possible to divide Henry VIII's wardrobe into three strands. First, he owned a small number of items which he kept throughout his reign – namely his formal robes for parliament and the three orders of chivalry – and these can be thought of as a long-term investment. There are no references in the surviving Great Wardrobe accounts to these robes being repaired, replaced or remodelled indicating that they existed in the same style throughout Henry's lifetime. The robes for the coronation, parliament, the garter and the Toison d'Or were valued in James Worsley's inventory of the wardrobe of the robes which was taken in 1521 at £533 6s. 8d.[16] These robes had a high financial value reflecting the quality of the velvet, furs and surface decoration but other garments cost more. In addition, these robes were a reminder of the King's sacerdotal role because he wore them for crown wearing days. Equally his parliament robes emphasised his relationship with parliament which was especially important during the 1530s and 1540s when the reformation parliaments were sitting. As such their value was financial, symbolic and political.

Opposite: Fig. 4 King Henry VIII in about 1542, unknown artist, early 17th century. © National Portrait Gallery, London

The largest section of the King's wardrobe can be regarded as a short-term investment which Henry exploited in several ways. Primarily these garments consisted of clothes for everyday wear, ceremonial clothing including the clothes worn on the days when he was required to wear purple and scarlet and sporting dress. However, because there was a virtue in the King being seen to have many clothes and not to wear the same thing twice for important occasions, Henry did not keep his clothes for long. Instead, he frequently gave away his clothes as perquisites to members of his household and his court. Consequently, their additional value lay in the possibility for variety, fashionability and for having new clothes for special occasions.

Finally, there were the clothes that Henry provided for the jousts and revels for himself and others. These were essentially ephemeral items that were designed to impress the spectators with the cost of their materials and the originality of their design, to thrill those who wore them and who might be given them as a memento of the occasion and as evidence of royal favour. For the joust held on 7 July 1517 at Greenwich, Richard Gibson made a coat, base and trapper for the King, half of which was cloth of silver overlaid with a '*cut work loose of white velvet*' embroidered and fringed and the other half was of black satin with cutwork of black velvet and embroidered with blue tinsel. Bases and bards of the same colours and materials were supplied to the fourteen knights and gentlemen challengers. At the end of his account Gibson noted that they were allowed to keep their costumes, along with the waiters, yeomen, minstrels and armourers.[17] In a similar manner, after the mask held to celebrate the Anglo-French peace treaty in 1527 '*the kyng gaue to the viscount of Torayn, the masking apparel that the kyng hym self ware & also the apparel that the viscount hym self masked in, which were very riche*'.[18] Equally, the ephemeral nature of these events also meant that the King and his courtiers selected to wear blue, a colour which very rarely featured in their everyday wardrobes because of its lowly implications. For the running at the ring on 29 January and 5 February and jousts on 20 May 1516, Henry and his immediate companions wore blue and purple and blue and black.[19]

The Great Wardrobe accounts provide another way of looking at the cost of Henry VIII's clothes. These accounts were produced at Michaelmas (the end of the Wardrobe's financial year) and of the 37 that were produced during Henry VIII's reign, fourteen have survived. They include the warrants for the King's own clothing orders which ranged in value from £425 17s. 2½d. in 1521–22 to £2,240 4s. ½d. in

1538–9.[20] With the exception of the figure for the year 1521–2 which is the lowest, the expenditure on Henry's clothes generally shows a steady increase throughout the his reign. The total for the fourteen accounts was £15,544 18s. ?d. and the average was £1,110 5s. Taking the average as a base figure, the total expenditure on the King's dress for the whole reign could easily have been in the region of £41,080 10s. In a similar vein, in 1537 Francisco Giustiniani, the Venetian ambassador to France, estimated that Francis I spent 30,000 livres a year on clothing and furnishings.[21]

Unfortunately, none of the entries, including those for the Wardrobe of the Robes were valued in the 1547 inventory of Henry's possessions which was taken after his death.[22] In contrast, some of the entries in the wardrobe book of James Worsley, Yeoman of the Robes, which covered the period from 1521 to 1525, were valued. The items listed in 1521 were appraised at £10,391 2s. 4 ½d. excluding the 'goldsmiths work pearls and unvalued stuff'.[23] Of this figure, the gowns and other outer garments were valued at £6,140, while the coats, jackets and doublets were assessed at a further £2,249. The Great Wardrobe accounts and the wardrobe book both make it clear that Henry VIII regarded his clothes as an essential part of his royal image and he spent liberally.

While the discussion above has touched on the social, political and sartorial value of the King's clothing, it is worth returning briefly to these themes. Clothing, including shirts, hats and other garments formed part of the culture of gift exchange as indicated by the items given to the King at New Year's gifts. This practice reflected that the King valued clothing and such gifts could have a high financial worth. Other items, such as the granting of Garter membership and giving of Garter livery could be political in its nature, as it reflected those individuals who had the King's favour. Equally, clothing could show changing patterns of what was thought to be fashionable, as with the gradual shift from the glaudekin, to the gown and then to the cassock. Coming full circle to cost, the King's clothing was also a vehicle for displaying jewellery and jewels that were stitched to the surface as in the case of 'a Coate or Shamewe of purple clothe of golde with workes furred with Sables garded with purple vellat and enbraudred with golde And Eight ballases set in golde standing vpon the Sleves with Ten Clusters of peerle'.[24]

Having invested so much time and money in his clothes, it was essential that they were kept clean, in a good state of repair and as Henry VIII was a peripatetic king, to ensure that they were in the right place at the right time. The King's clothes required regular care and maintenance and this was reflected in the work of the King's Tailor to make, repair and remake his clothes and the Wardrobe of the Robes whose officers cleaned, stored, packed, aired and perfumed the king's clothes. Therefore the value of the King's clothes was reflected in the number of people employed to keep them in pristine condition.

Dressed to kill: The relationship between clothes and armour

According to Castiglione, the courtier's 'first duty' was 'to know how to handle expertly every kind of weapon, either on foot or mounted, to understand their finer points, and to be especially well informed about all those weapons commonly used among gentlemen'.[25] While Castiglione placed his emphasis on skill with weapons, it was implicit that the courtier would have been suitably equipped with armour and a range of textile garments that were worn under or over the armour. Items such as the arming doublet and arming hose were padded and worn under armour, in order to provide some protection and to act as a foundation garment to which elements of the armour could be secured with points, while the basecote and base, a short textile skirt, were worn over armour. They were made from expensive materials, indeed the same materials as were used for his everyday fashionable wardrobe: 'A base cote of blacke vellet embrodered with Cloth of golde' (8386). In addition, they were often made by his tailor.[26] While some items were stored within the wardrobe of the robes with the King's everyday wardrobe, others were kept with his armour such as a brigandine with sleeves covered with crimson cloth of gold (8264) and a brigandine covered with blue satin (8265) which were in the care of Erasmus Kirkenar at the Greenwich armoury.

There are no full-scale images of Henry VIII in armour which makes the miniature of him jousting before Catherine of Aragon in 1511 especially valuable (see page 112–13). The image compares well with Hall's description of the four challengers in 'their hose, capes, & cotes, were full of poyses & H & K of fine gold in bullion, so yt the grounde coulde scarce appere & yet was in euery voyde place spangles of gold'.[27] Also of note is the portrait of Sir Nicholas Carew, by Holbein or a follower of Holbein, about 1528, who was Master of the Horse, a member of the privy chamber and a close friend of the King. Unlike many of his contemporaries who chose to be painted in fashionable dress, he opted to be depicted wearing a Greenwich armour and a base, along with a fashionable black bonnet and gold coif.[28] There were two main times when the King would be seen in armour: for jousts at court or abroad and when on campaign. For occasions such at Henry VIII's two meetings with Francis I at the Field of Cloth of Gold in 1520 and at Boulogne in 1532, the King's armour was prepared with as much care as the King's clothes. For example, 'one harnesse for the kinges Majestie all grauen and parcel guilte bothe for the felde and Tilte complete' that 'was commaunded to be translated at the kinges goinge ouer to Bulloigne whiche lieth in peces parte translated and parte vntranslated by A contrarie comaundement by the kinges Majestie'.[29] However, as this entry in the 1547 inventory indicates, some of the armour was retained, while the fashionable, everyday clothes were not.

The bases and bards supplied for the jousts were often made en suite and by 1547 they were listed together at the first block entry in the charge of Sir Thomas Cawarden, master of the revels.[30] They were often heraldic in design, or incorporated symbolic motifs. When Henry VIII jousted as 'Noble Cueur Loyall' before Katherine of Aragon in 1511, his horse's bard was decorated with Hs, Ks and hearts.[31] The tiltyard, like the tennis court, was one of the few places where the King could appear as a *primus inter pares* jousting with men such as Charles Brandon, Duke of Suffolk, who was of a similar build and a similar level of skill. This was emphasised by their being dressed alike. For a running at the ring on 29 January 1516, Gibson provided clothes of blue and purple velvet 'with broad guards of blue satin and trystram knots of blue velvet laces' for the King and Suffolk, while the other nine members of Henry's team had basecoats and bards of blue damask with the same decoration.[32]

The sense of teams for the jousts was created by the clothes made for the combatants and the trappings provided for their horses and this was a recurrent theme. At the jousts held in 1527 to celebrate peace with France, Sir Nicholas Carew, Sir Robert Jerningham, Sir Anthony Browne and Nicholas Harvey, 'were apparelled in bases and bardes all of one suite' while the Marquis of Exeter was accompanied by thirteen men with bases and bards of 'one suit' 'the right sides of cloth of golde cut in cloudes engrailed with Damaske golde, the otherside cloth of syluer set with mountaynes full of Oliue braunches, made of gold all mouyng'.[33]

In terms of materials and colours for elite clothing Castiglione noted that while a courtier's clothes for everyday should be sober in colour, so making black 'the most agreeable colour…and if not black, then at least something fairly dark', he did concede that 'there is no doubt that light and gay colours are more suitable for wearing on top of armour, and it is also more fitting for holiday clothes to have

trimmings and to be ornate and gay'.[34] Analysis of Henry VIII's extant Great Wardrobe accounts has demonstrated that black was the most popular colour choice throughout his reign for his everyday and ceremonial clothes, in keeping with Castiglione's ideal.[35] In a similar vein, the revels accounts of Richard Gibson and the entry for the revels in the 1547 inventory show that bright, strongly contrasting colours were regularly chosen for arming doublets, bases and bards.

The relationship between armour and clothing can be viewed in several levels. First, armour could be ordered by sending a doublet and hose to the armourer as these would provide a rough indication of the client's body size. However, once Henry had his own armourers working in England he could guarantee that his armour was a good fit by having his armourers come to him to take initial measurements and to undertake the final fitting. Second, armour, like clothing, was required to fit well. So the King's surviving armour provides a very good indication of his body size which is especially important as none of Henry VIII's clothes have survived. As armour has survived from about 1514 to 1540s, it provides a good indication of how his body expanded over time (see Henry's foot combat armour II.6 cat. no. 1 and fig. 5). This was an important issue for Henry VIII's tailors and armourers who had to alter his clothes and armour to compensate. In contrast, the Great Wardrobe did not reflect the King's increased size in the amount of cloth that it allowed to make his clothes. For instance, tailors were given three yards of cloth for a doublet throughout Henry's life. Third, clothes and armour were designed to emphasise certain elements of the body but they placed emphasis on different parts. Clothes were designed to emphasise a man's shoulders and this was achieved by wearing many layers and with the shoulder seam on the gown placed outside the natural shoulder line. In contrast, armour emphasised the legs – an area of the male body which would become increasingly visible in the second half of the 16th century as the doublet's skirts got shorter and the knee-length gown was replaced by the shorter cloak. However, one element was emphasised on clothing and some armour alike: the codpiece. The message was clear. Henry's lack of a male heir was not the result of any physical failing on his part.

There are other ways in which close links can be drawn between dress and armour. The 'silvered and engraved' armour for man and horse belonging to Henry VIII has preserved information about elements of dress and related accessories which have not survived: namely the base and the trapper (see the 'silvered and engraved' armour for man and horse II.5 cat. no. 21).

The steel provides evidence about the shape, size, construction and decoration of items that were usually made of textile and this information can be used in conjunction with references in the written accounts.[36] The decorated band with linked H and K on the silvered and engraved base could have been created using appliqué on a textile version, while the engraved design on the trapper depicting scenes from the life of St George and St Barbara which could have been created using other embroidery techniques.[37]

In a similar vein, some armour of this period echoed decorative techniques such as slashing which was found on clothing in the German or *almain* style. However, much of the armour made for Henry by his own armourers was relatively plain and did not include such features. Even so, it did incorporate the use of silk trimmings such as fringe or the applied textile on '*oone Rounde Targette of Lether coverid with crymsen vellat alover enbraudred with Venice golde*'.[38] The armourers also worked in conjunction with a range of other craftsmen. Hans Holbein the Younger produced designs for silk passementerie and it is likely that the decorative gilded and etched borders on Henry VIII's Greenwich armour of 1540 used designs supplied by Holbein.[39]

Finally, jewellery formed an essential part of the King's everyday appearance and so it is not surprising that jewels were given as tournament prizes as a symbol of male prowess. On 20 June 1527 a number of pieces were delivered to Henry VIII including '*a black carkeyn, with a black.....having in his breast a rose of diamonds, a pointed diamond which was the price in Flanders at the justs and a fair hanging pearl thereat*'.[40] It is possible that this was one of a number of items that the King was going to have reworked to form new pieces of jewellery but other relics of the Henry's martial youth lingered until his death. The 1547 inventory included '*a Shelde conteyning prises wonne by the king in England Fraunce and Flaunders having a roose of Dyamountes in the myddes two other diamountes an Emerarde a Rubie and three peerles pendaunt*'.[41]

CONCLUSION

Clothes played an essential part in the magnificent image that Henry VIII created for himself. Clothing of this type was very expensive with the bulk of the investment resting in the materials rather than the labour. For example, on the King's warrant dated 14 July 1527, the King's Tailor, John Malt, was paid 13s. 4d. for making a shammer of black cloth of gold embroidered with purple velvet, furred with sable and the sleeves lined with buckram.[42] On a day-to-day basis, their quality and quantity helped to set him apart from everyone else at court, while in the tiltyard his choice of clothes could ally him with close friends such as the Duke of Suffolk and the leading members of his court and household. While portraiture and written documents have captured the scope and scale of Henry's wardrobe, only his armour has preserved the imposing size and shape of the body that wore them.

Notes and references page 335.

Opposite: Fig. 5 Armour of Henry VIII, Greenwich, about 1540.
RCIN 72834 The Royal Collection © Her Majesty Queen Elizabeth II

{IX}

THE LEGACY OF HENRY VIII

ERIC IVES

*In this concluding essay, Eric Ives judges Henry VIII by the issues that
mattered most to him: defending his honour at home and abroad,
securing the succession, and acting out his role as a religious reformer.
The wars of the 1540s left the Crown with a bill of more than £2 million
and a faltering economy. Henry secured his male heir in the end, although his
chequered marital history cast a long shadow over the legitimacy of his
daughters, both of whom were destined to inherit the throne. It was
Henry VIII's religious policy, however, that had the greatest impact, during his
own reign and for centuries to come: the destruction of a medieval world of
devotion, and the recreation of the Church of England as a national institution
under the governance of Crown and Parliament.*

On Thursday 30 June 1513, two days after his 22nd birthday, Henry VIII crossed the Channel to take command of the English army at Calais and begin an assault on France. On Monday 14 July 1544 the 53-year-old Henry VIII crossed to Calais once again to join his troops in an assault on his old enemy. In 1513 Henry had been on the throne for only four years, in 1544 he had only two and a half years of life ahead of him, so the two invasions effectively bracket his reign. In the years between these two expeditions which involved Henry personally, English armies invaded France in 1522 and 1523 and there were major conflicts with Scotland in 1513, 1523, 1542 and 1544–7. Henry's self-image was that of a warrior. He announced this at the very start of his reign when, in January 1510 he took part, for the first time in public, in that war substitute, the tournament. For the 1513 campaign he landed at Calais in a decorated armour known as an 'almain rivet' under a cloth of gold tunic embroidered with the red cross of England; he prepared for the 1544 campaign first by having existing armour modified to fit

Fig. 1 Henry VIII, after Hans Holbein the Younger, about 1536. © National Portrait Gallery, London

and then by acquiring a new three-quarter armour from Milan. His palaces were decorated with paintings of his exploits, particularly his defeat of the French in 1513 at the battle of the Spurs, a victory he lived off for the rest of his life. Military equipment fascinated him. His guards had gold-painted shields fitted with pistols; he himself rode into Calais in 1544 grasping a large wheellock pistol; when he died, he had 64 brass and 351 iron cannon in store at the Tower of London. In 1538 there was a danger that Francis I of France (fig 2) and the Emperor Charles V (fig 3) might invade to bring England back to its papal allegiance. Henry's response was to create – indeed to a significant degree design – a cordon of shore defences, several elements of which still survive. As for the navy, by the end of his reign this had grown to over 50 ships, and a permanent board had been set up to administer the fleet.

The importance which Henry VIII attached to war and the preparation for war is, thus, beyond question, but to what end? In 1513 Henry destroyed the town of Thérouanne, 15 kilometres south east of Calais, and added the then French city of Tournai to his dominions while the Earl of Surrey smashed a Scottish invasion at Flodden. In 1542 Henry launched a punitive raid across the Border. It was abortive, but the Scottish counter was comprehensively defeated at Solway Moss. In May 1544 he sent north 'an army royal' to *'put all to fire and sword, burn Edinburgh town, so razed and defaced when you have sacked and gotten what ye can of it, as there may remain forever a perpetual memory … putting man woman and child to fire and sword, without exception, where any resistance shall be made'.*[1] The following September Henry captured the major port of Boulogne and in 1545 a French counterattack on the English Channel coast was repulsed. Henry saw all this as vindicating his credentials as a great soldier, but what did his subjects have to show for all the king's enthusiasm? Tournai was the whitest of white elephants, costly to garrison and needing expensive refortification and after five years the city was sold back to the French. Boulogne was even more of a millstone. Fortifications there cost Henry nearly £50,000 and his son £75,000.

Henry VIII's diplomatic legacy was equally malign. In the peace negotiations with France in 1546 he insisted (against advice) on holding on to Boulogne, at least for a period, so the agreement was for England to continue in possession until 1554 when France would redeem the town for the huge sum of two million crowns. That, however, perpetuated the affront to French honour and constant irritation became open war in August 1549. England was in no position to defend Henry's trophy and the dispute was compromised in March 1550 by

Fig. 2 Portrait of Francis I (1494-1547), 1538, by Titian (Tiziano Vecellio) (about 1488-1576). © The Bridgeman Art Library

the early surrender of Boulogne in return for 400,000 crowns, twenty per cent of the sum previously specified. As for Scotland, the defeat at Solway Moss had been followed by the death of the Scottish King and the accession of his week-old daughter Mary. This created a marvellous opportunity to link England and Scotland by marrying the young Queen of Scots to Henry's five-year-old son Edward. However, instead of negotiating sensitively with the nobles captured at Solway Moss, Henry chose to revive English claims to suzerainty over Scotland and when this was resisted, launched the 1544 raid. As with the retention of Boulogne, the *'Rough Wooing'* bequeathed a situation which bedevilled the reign of his young son Edward.

There was, too, an economic cost to realising Henry's self image. War was hugely expensive. The 1512–14 conflict with France called for around £100,000, a figure equivalent to the annual income of the Crown. That black hole was probably closed by surpluses left to him by his father. Countering the invasion fear of the late 1530s was hugely expensive, and with the continuous war from 1542–6, in the north and in France, the overall bill came to more than £2 million. Government expenditure on this scale inevitably produced a surge in prices which were already rising because of population pressure. Further damage was inflicted on the economy by the severity of the taxation levied towards these military expenses. Crown land had also to be sold and when Henry appropriated perhaps 12-16 per cent of the nation's capital by dissolving its abbeys, priories, nunneries and friaries, much of this too was liquidated, so missing the chance to remedy the Crown's chronic financial vulnerability. Even so taxation and land sales covered only half of the costs of war and military preparedness, and for the rest Henry turned to fraud. The value of a Tudor coin was – or should have been – fixed by how much precious metal it contained. From 1544 Henry abandoned that principle and issued coins with the same face value but a reduced bullion content. The difference between the face value and the value of the gold or silver remaining in the coin was profit to the Crown. Between 1544 and the end of debasement in 1551, the English Crown robbed the country of £1,270,000. Pumping this extra money into circulation simply exacerbated the existing inflation, the more so since the debased coinage had been debased again and again. Thus a groat (value 4 pence) which before debasement had contained 2.55 g (0.089 oz) of silver and 0.21 g (0.007 oz) of alloy, by 1547 contained 0.83 g (0.029 oz) of silver and 1.67 g (0.059 oz) of alloy. This released enough silver to mint two extra groats for the king to spend. In three years inflation increased by perhaps 30 per cent.

The diplomatic and economic problems Henry bequeathed to his children took more than a decade to resolve. One which troubled the country for a good deal longer was his interference with the established succession to the Crown. This he achieved through three acts of parliament and the provisions of his last will. The first statute (1534) ignored his eighteen-year-old daughter Mary and declared his heirs to be his children by Anne Boleyn. In 1536 came an act which declared both Mary and Elizabeth illegitimate and incapable of succeeding to the throne. This should have meant that the next heir to the crown would be either his nephew the King of Scotland or his niece Frances Grey, the Marchioness of

Fig 3. Portrait of Charles V (1500-58), 1516 by Bernart van Orley, (c.1488-1541). © The Bridgeman Art Library

Dorset, but the act went on to accept that if Henry had no legitimate offspring 'of his body', he could nominate a successor. Since kings called Parliament and not vice-versa, using statute to recognise his right to alter the succession was totally *ultra vires*. As Robert Aske, the leader of the Pilgrimage of Grace complained, '*he and all wise men of those parts grudged at [the act] and that for divers causes. One was that before that statute, since the Conqueror, never king declared his will of the crown of this realm, nor never was there known in this realm, no such law*'.[2] Nevertheless having Parliament accept that he could disqualify his legitimate collateral heirs put Henry in a position to nominate his daughters to succeed in turn without removing the stigma of illegitimacy which he was convinced was decreed by God. In 1544 the third statute went further by naming Mary and Elizabeth to succeed conditionally, if his legitimate son Edward died childless, while at the same time confirming that they were both bastards. Finally this was restated in Henry's will and testament which also specified the conditions under which the two daughters could become queen.

Henry died sure that he had honoured God in accepting that his marriages to both Katherine of Aragon and Anne Boleyn had defied divine law, but confident that he had ensured that their illegitimate daughters could succeed nevertheless. In reality his scheming created a succession problem which bedevilled the reigns of each of his children. In 1553 Edward followed his father in nominating Frances Grey's daughter Jane as his successor, and this return to the legitimate line explains the considerable support she received. Mary then ousted Jane Grey and sought to regularise the succession by having herself legitimated by Parliament, but without cancelling her sister's claims under her father's will. This meant that when Mary had no child and the problems of her reign increased, her half-sister was all the time hovering in the background as a possible alternative. In 1558 Elizabeth did succeed, but still as her father's illegitimate daughter, and this meant that two others could claim a better title: Jane Grey's sister Katherine; and Mary Queen of Scots, who had married the son of the King of France, England's old enemy. The result was a chronic succession problem which racked Elizabeth's council and parliaments, year after year, and led eventually to the execution of Mary Stuart. Not until 1603 was the law of the succession restored by the acceptance of James VI of Scotland.

The diplomatic, economic and constitutional dimensions of Henry VIII's legacy are, however, eclipsed by the consequence of his religious policy which continues to feature in English society. When he came to the throne, the overwhelming majority of his subjects made up the English branch of the Western European catholic – i.e. universal – church. They belonged to one of two provinces – Canterbury and York – which had a certain local distinctiveness but which, with provinces in France, Spain, Italy, Germany and elsewhere, made up a single Christian church that recognised the Pope in Rome as its ultimate head and accepted him as its earthly governor. When Henry died this was no longer the case. He had broken with Rome, extinguished the authority of the Pope and brought the English Church under the authority of the English crown. The Church previously *in* England was now the Church *of* England, a national institution with the monarch as its sole head and governor. This was a massive augmentation in the power and prestige of the monarch. Instead of the King being restricted to secular affairs, he was now omnicompetent. Lesser changes reinforced this. Local

franchises and rights of jurisdiction were abolished in England and Wales, Calais was granted two parliamentary seats like any English borough, and Henry took the title 'King' instead of 'Lord' of Ireland. Unlike the takeover of the Church, these changes seem to have been made for pragmatic reasons rather than principle, but taken together the result was that Henry VIII henceforward ruled a unitary state – the first king to do so. Henry VII had been '*by the Grace of God, King of England and France*'. Henry VIII had become '*by the Grace of God, King of England, France and Ireland, Defender of the Faith and of the Church of England and also of Ireland, in earth under Jesus Christ, Supreme Head*'. To this day, Elizabeth II is '*Defender of the Faith and Supreme Governor of the Church of England*'.

Often in the past Henry's supreme headship has been seen as little more than a judicial and constitutional adjustment: 'Catholicism without the Pope'. This is very far from the truth. His Church *of* England continued to claim it was part of the Catholic Church, but only 'catholic' as now redefined by Henry. Along with what were the national churches of Spain and France, it was not 'catholic' because part of a greater whole, but because 'legitimately descended from the church as founded by Jesus Christ'. Doctrine originated with Christ as enunciated by the early Christian councils of the Church, but it was declared and enforced by divine authority vested in national sovereigns. Henry took this God-given role literally and as a King-Pope set out to reform the Church. As the legend on Holbein's great painting in Whitehall Palace declared, Henry, '*drives the unworthy from the altars and brings in men of integrity. The presumption of popes has yielded to unerring virtue and with Henry VIII bearing the sceptre in his hand, religion has been restored and with him on the throne the truths of God have begun to be held in due reverence*'.[3] Henry's 'restoration of religion' was, however, a good deal more destructive than it might sound. On a material level, the dissolution of the country's 800 or so monastic institutions was an act of massive vandalism as what still remains visible on the ground and the manuscripts which scholars rescued bear witness. But Henry destroyed ideas as well as *matériel*. Effectively he subverted the raison d'être of the late medieval church. Orthodoxy had it that the souls of the faithful departed were in purgatory being cleansed of any remaining sin and that their transfer to the bliss of heaven could be expedited by the prayers and religious devotions of the living. But dissolving the abbeys whose principal function was to pray for souls and their transfer to the bliss of heaven, implied the opposite. The value of praying to saints to assist the living and the dead was similarly devalued as shrines were destroyed and pilgrimages ended and by 1545 *The King's Primer* (which Henry claimed as his own) could announce that: '*There is nothing in the dirige [the Office of the Dead] taken out of scripture that maketh any mention of the souls departed than doth the tale of Robin Hood*'. It is difficult in the 21st century to appreciate the momentous psychological shift which this 'truth of God' demanded. Indeed, Henry himself only partially absorbed it. But in a single generation it put an end to an understanding of Christianity which for centuries had focused on the health of souls departed. Alongside this destruction, Henry took a crucial step towards a new expression of Christianity which would eventually replace the old. He licensed an official vernacular translation of the Bible which was to be available in every parish. He did not live long enough to realise how momentous was a decision which put an end once and for all to the Church's monopoly of religious belief but it would lead eventually to the religious radicalism which cost the head of Henry's great, great, great nephew, Charles I.

Henry VIII thus promoted reform, but he was not one of the reformers to whom later generations gave the name Protestant. Far from it. His concern was to hold 'a middle way', not in the sense of a compromise between the radical ideas of Martin Luther and the traditionalism of Rome, but as the virtuous mean between error on both sides. He was both reformed and orthodox, according to where from time to time he believed the twin path of reform and orthodoxy lay. Hence his radical rejection of the Pope was matched by the adamant rejection of the Protestant doctrine of salvation by faith alone. Even more vehement was his insistence on the late-medieval understanding of the ceremony of the Mass which held that when bread and wine were consecrated by a priest, they became the natural body and blood of Christ, although without changing their physical appearance. It was a work of divine power which was effective in saving the soul and in protecting against the dangers of this life. This to Henry was the miraculous core of Christianity and he would have nothing to do with any questioning of the miracle either by reformers abroad or temerarious subjects at home.

Reformed religion as established by Henry VIII was thus very much a personal construction, sustained by the will of one man. After 1 February 1534 the punishment for persisting in the centuries-old respect for the Pope was hanging, drawing and quartering. After 12 July 1539 the punishment for querying the miracle of the Mass even on a single occasion was to be burned alive. Such a tension of incompatibles could

not last. Edward VI resolved it by opting for Protestantism, Mary I by returning to Rome and Elizabeth by living long enough to see something like Anglicanism beginning to emerge. Even so repercussions continued through the ensuing centuries and it is arguable that they have yet to run their course. Bishops sit in the as-yet partially reformed House of Lords and the Church of England is the established church. The reason for this continuity is that although Henry saw the royal supremacy as something he possessed by divine right, he used Parliament to give teeth to that right. This ensured that the future arena for religious debate in England would be parliament. In countries such as France where the state continued in an established partnership with the papacy, religious dissent necessarily involved disloyalty and even rebellion. In England it led to a vote in Parliament. An important consequence followed. With statute being used to enforce religious change, the status of Parliament and the competence of its enactments changed fundamentally. Nothing was now beyond its reach. Seven parliamentary sessions in the first twenty years of Henry's reign contrast with fifteen sessions in the last eighteen years. The twelve years following his death would average a session a year. Not that Henry had any conception that Parliament would grow in status to the point where it could challenge his successors. His conviction was '*that we at no time stand so highly in our estate royal as in the time of Parliament*'.[4]

Politicising religious issues had a further and even more important consequence which is often overlooked. Pre-reformation politics can be described as 'organic', i.e. determined by networks of association – family, locality, economic interest, rivalry, status. The fundamental relationship was with the monarch and the successful monarch was one who could manage these networks to secure loyalty and acceptance of his authority. The Reformation changed this fundamentally by introducing ideology. It was no longer sufficient to be loyal, it was necessary to have the correct belief. What is more, religious commitment ceased to be a private matter and became a public test of conformity. In 1534 all of Henry's subjects were called upon to swear to uphold the rightness of his rejection of Katherine of Aragon and the legitimacy of his marriage to Anne Boleyn – which Thomas More refused to do. From 1536 all persons of importance were required to swear an oath accepting the royal supremacy. Henceforward ideological conformity and non-conformity became substantial and permanent features of English life. Under Elizabeth church attendance would become compulsory and it became an offence to attend services – catholic or puritan – where the official prayer book was not used. When Oliver Cromwell told Lawrence Crawford in 1643 that '*the state in choosing men to serve them takes no notice of their opinions; if they be willing faithfully to serve them, that satisfies*' he was harking back impossibly to a golden age before Henry VIII. In 1673 the taking of communion according to the Anglican rite would become the test of suitability for public office.

In drawing up a profit and loss account from the distance of five centuries it is natural to focus on the long-term and easy to overlook what was immediate and obvious at the time. When William Paget, Henry VIII's final secretary, measured the success of the reign, he judged by the primary obligation on a 16th-century monarch – maintaining peace, law and order. '*Kept not he his subjects, from the highest to the lowest, in due obedience and how? By the only maintenance of justice in due course*'.[5] When Henry came to the throne many of his subjects could remember, indeed had taken part in the final battles of the Wars of the Roses and Paget knew that it had been no small achievement for Henry to rule for nearly 38 years, die in his bed and have the Crown pass unchallenged to a boy of nine. Apart from limited disturbances which were dealt with locally, Henry faced large-scale popular protest on two occasions. In 1525 what he saw as a favourable opportunity to make gains in France led to an attempt to raise an 'Amicable Grant'. However, this followed on three years of heavy taxation and people had had enough. They refused to pay. Henry backed down and diverted the blame to his chief minister, Cardinal Wolsey. In 1536 came a more serious crisis but this time Henry was able to surmount the threat without surrendering. First Lincolnshire rebelled, and then the whole of the country north of the Trent in what became known as the Pilgrimage of Grace. A number of grievances fuelled this massive protest but religious discontent was at the heart – notably opposition to the act passed earlier in the year dissolving the smaller monasteries. Henry initially temporised and the 30,000 protesters went home, but this time he had no intention of making real concessions. Within months further minor trouble gave him the pretext he had been waiting for and the Duke of Norfolk proceeded to exact punishment, often at random.

The reason why losing effective control over the North for several months did not mark a return to the royal weakness characteristic of the previous century is the synergy which Henry VIII, following in the footsteps of his father, had built up with the landed elite. As both the Lincolnshire Rising and the Pilgrimage ran their course the gentry of the region had been able to reassert a traditional control over the commons, and the gentry were more concerned to secure the King's pardon than continue to press the region's anxieties even though they shared them. Fundamental synergy between king and the landed elite also explains Henry's success in dealing with opposition from individual magnates – real or imagined. During his reign he executed more notables than any king before or since, but he was able to do this because he only targeted individuals and was able to count on support from the rest. The notion that Henry – or indeed any of the Tudors – was hostile to the aristocracy is simply not true. Effectively he and his father made it into a service nobility and the first line of support.

The roots of this synergy between the king and the elite lay in a fundamental shift in the power structure of the country. The days were gone when disgruntled magnates were able to mount an armed challenge to the Crown. Ever since the reign of Edward IV the king's landed estate had been growing and the dissolution of the monasteries added massively to that. Land did not only mean income but lordship, tenants who would do the king's bidding. Furthermore, properties had to be managed, and the posts which this required provided a supply of patronage for which the gentry competed. Consequently the king's affinity – men sworn to serve him – grew and Henry insisted that no king's man must take service with anyone else. By the end of his reign, royal influence had entirely eclipsed its earlier rivals, the nobility and the Church. The aristocracy and the Church continued to matter, but they now existed to serve the sovereign lord and the supreme head.

The visible embodiment of this authority was the person of the King, and here nature had given Henry huge advantages. At 1.85 m (6ft 2 in) he towered over all but a handful of his subjects. He was an outstanding athlete and enjoyed showing this off, especially in the tiltyard. He had been well educated; he was musical; he was intellectually curious, though with a low boredom threshold; he was an inveterate builder and an architect *manqué*. Henry was also very engaging when it suited him – the 1966 film of *A Man for All Seasons*, based on the play by Robert Bolt, vividly illustrated this with the shot of Henry walking along with his arm round Thomas More's shoulder. Throughout his reign Henry made the most of these gifts, spending lavishly on dress, furniture and decoration. When money was short his servants had to keep him in ignorance of any desirable jewel coming up for sale. How extravagantly he spent we have only realised since the publication of the inventories taken of his possessions in 1542 and after his death. Henry's gold and silver candlesticks alone weighed a quarter of a ton; he had hundreds of tapestries, and thousands of yards of cloth of gold were in store, ready to make into his elaborately ornamented costumes. His palaces were among the most magnificent in Europe and he built on a scale which provided the English Crown with real estate which would prove adequate for many generations.

To 21st-century eyes this can appear as useless conspicuous consumption, but not to Henry's subjects. A king had to be magnificent, and magnificent Henry was. There was first the European dimension – showing that he was in the same league as the King of France and the Holy Roman Emperor. The most remarkable instance of this was the summit meeting of Henry and Francis outside Calais in the summer of 1520 which is known as the Field of Cloth of Gold because of the lavish costumes worn by participants. Magnificence was, of course, not directed only at the other monarchs of Europe. Its immediate function was to dominate his English subjects. Hence the great public occasions of the reign. The coronation of Anne Boleyn is a particularly good example. Many of those involved were certainly not fans of Anne, but the court turned up and the nobility, all behaving as if they were Boleyn enthusiasts. It told the lower orders that the elite was enthusiastically behind what the King had done. Tournaments brought the same message. These were open to spectators and were held on the great occasions of the court year. There, as well as seeing the King display his prowess, the crowd saw the leading nobles and courtiers of the day, disporting themselves at the King's bidding.

All in all, from becoming supreme head of the Church to dominating the country by his personality, Henry realised the strength of the English Crown as no ruler before or since. There was, of course a price to pay. Henry was the most covetous of men. He was also totally self-centred. The bonhomie which allowed the well-attested royal arm round More's shoulders did not keep More's head on those shoulders when he ceased to keep in step with Henry. The bonhomie and the magnificence alike served Henry and Henry alone. The most amiable company, he was also the most unforgiving, and that was accentuated by his being intensely suspicious. As Thomas Wolsey said, an idea once planted in Henry's head was almost impossible to eradicate. This failing grew worse over the years. Among William Paget's reflection on his late master is the comment *'that in our old majesty's time all things were too straight [severe]. Then it was dangerous to do or speak though the meaning were not evil'*.[6] The result was that although serving Henry was the path of opportunity, it was equally strewn with pitfalls. Sir Anthony Denny, Henry's most intimate servant in his latter years, described his court as *'a place so slippery that duty never so well done is not a staff stiff enough to stand by always very surely'*.[7] Sir Thomas Wyatt, like Denny a life-long courtier, wrote *'Around the throne, thunder rolls'*.[8]

History, however, does well to avoid moral judgements. Henry can undoubtedly be accused of gross self-promotion and a concern for himself rather than his subjects. Nevertheless, the ultimate legacy of his reign was the exaltation of the status of the English monarchy as never before. Henceforward the English monarch would be without rivals at home and potentially respected abroad. The events and decisions of his reign fundamentally shaped the years which followed. It can even be argued that Henry VIII's rejection of papal authority massively accentuated the insularity of England, committing it to an identity defined against Europe. If so, his legacy may still have life in it.

Notes and references page 335.

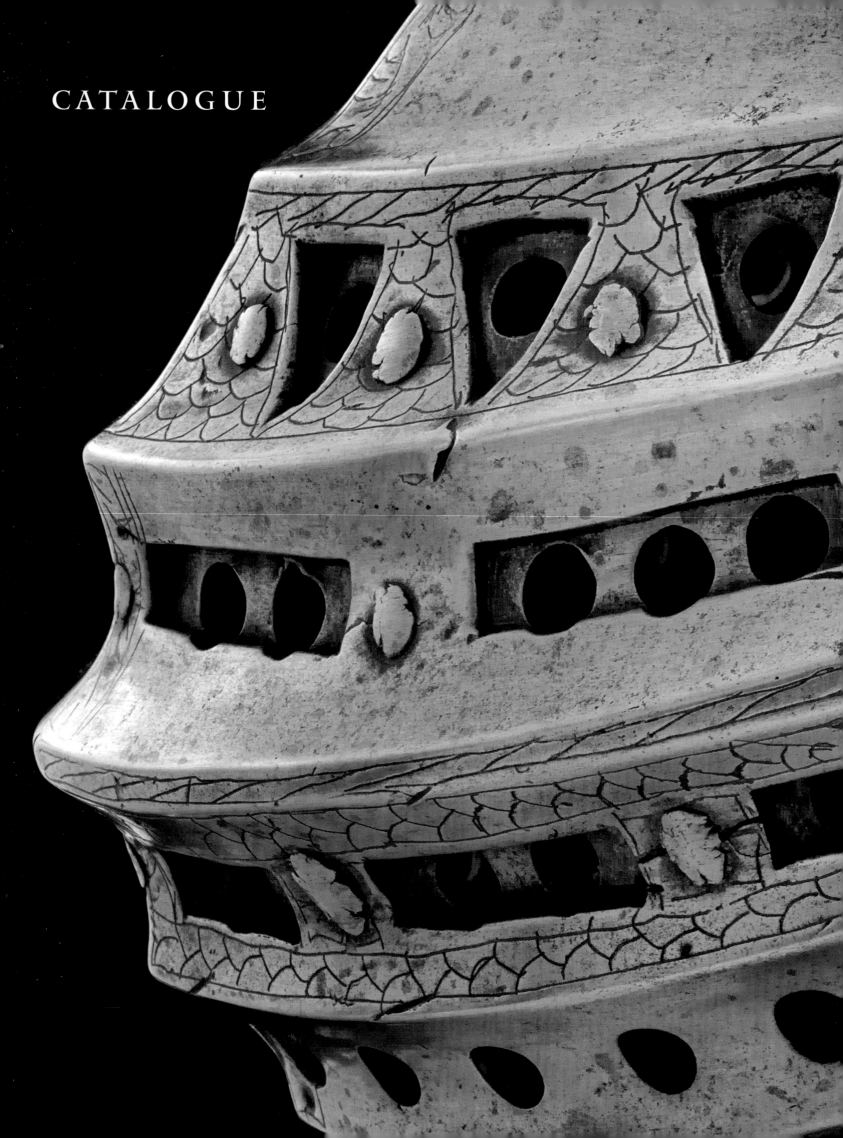

CATALOGUE

{ I }

THE TOURNAMENT
AND HENRY'S
SPORTING INTERESTS

TOURNAMENTS AT THE
COURT OF KING HENRY VIII

KAREN WATTS

King Henry VIII was a good all-round sportsman. He held many tournaments, undoubtedly to a large extent simply because he liked them. However tournaments were not just good sporting occasions: they had political importance and above all were splendid opportunities to impress foreign ambassadors who were likely to write glowing reports of the King's evident wealth and power.[1] This was an important consideration. Henry was playing a political game in Europe against opponents with greater resources. He was also displaying his physical dominance. The combats showed a physically powerful man; the pageantry projected an image of a politically powerful potentate.

The impersonation of allegorical roles was a major feature of the Tudor tournament. The costumes were also often likened to the allegorical framework within which many jousts were set, presenting the jousters as the knights-errant of medieval romantic fiction and the tournament as the response to an heroic challenge.

The Westminster Tournament was held on 12 and 13 February in 1511. The tournament celebrated the birth of a short-lived son to Henry VIII. The event was recorded for posterity in the vast illuminated vellum roll preserved at the College of Arms (fig. 1).[2] The four main jousters at this tournament all adopted chivalric names:

Henry VIII: *Noble Cueur Loyal*

Lord Devon (Courtenay): *Bon Vouloir*

Sir Thomas Knyvet: *Vaillant Desyr*

Edward Neville: *Joyeulx Penser*

The names were derived from the greatest love allegory of the Middle Ages, the *Roman de la Rose*, and they personify the psychological forces in the conquest of love. The elaborate pageantry and allegory shows the influence of the Burgundian court. This habit of externalising qualities and making them visible was important to the court society.

The manuscript only shows the second day of the tournament. However, the results of the first day of jousts at the Westminster Tournament are known through a herald's score sheet, or cheque, preserved in the Bodleian Library, Oxford (Ashmolean MS 1116) which shows that Cueur Loyal (Henry VIII) performed best. A score cheque of very similar form, for a tournament staged by Henry at Greenwich in 1516, preserved in the archives of the College of Arms (cat. no. 11), illustrates the system of scoring which had become accepted by this date, with columns listing the names of the 'challengers' and 'defenders', and next to each

name a rectangular box, marks upon which recorded the individual outcome of each joust. A mark on one part of a line would indicate a strike to the head of an opponent, on another to the body, while another type of mark would indicate a lance successfully broken.

Of Henry's other tournaments, three are noteworthy. A typical tournament was that held in 1517 when Henry VIII held '*costly Justes*' at Greenwich for the '*solace*' of the ambassadors at his court. The whole event was meant to be awe-inspiring. The chronicler Edward Hall described the tournament.[3] Most of Hall's description was concerned with the triumphal entry of King Henry followed by a brief but laudatory description of the actual tilting. The King, gorgeously dressed, headed the procession with his band of eleven challengers and was followed by no less than 125 attendants. Charles Brandon, the Duke of Suffolk, with his band of eleven answerers brought up the rear. The origins of this type of procession came from the Middle Ages and continued on through the Renaissance and into the Baroque period. It refers back to a ruler formally taking possession of a city, making a solemn entrance. This medieval theme was reinforced in the Renaissance with the concept of a Roman triumph. This is exactly how the chronicler Edward Hall saw the tournament of 1517, for he continues; '*after this great triumphe, the king appointed his gestes for his pastime this sommer…*'

Large crowds watched Henry fight and they must have been impressed both by the King's prowess and by the evident wealth, splendour and, by implication, power of the monarchy. Hall certainly was, for his chronicle, first printed in 1548, dwelt on Henry's tournaments in awe-struck detail at the expense of perhaps more significant aspects of his reign. Foreign ambassadors were also impressed, and many of Henry's tournaments were specially arranged for diplomatic purposes, like those held at Greenwich in 1517 and 1527.

The greatest example of tiltyard diplomacy came at the Field of Cloth of Gold in 1520, where more than 150 French and English courtiers, including Henry VIII and Francis I, jousted, tourneyed and fought, on foot on and off for eleven days.[4] The Field of Cloth of Gold was named after the magnificent (and very costly) cloth of gold pavilions embellishing an otherwise drab setting in the Pale of Calais. The 'field' was one of the most extraordinary paradoxes of the period. Even today it is a byword for chivalry and extravagance.

The lists, the area to contain the event, were about 275 metres by 98 metres (900 x 320 feet) and surrounded by a ditch. Around the field were stands for spectators, tents for each king and a triumphal arch at each end. But it was the 'tree of honour' that excited the most contemporary comment, for it epitomised the chivalrous nature of the tournament. An artificial hawthorn tree and a raspberry bush were entwined to form the tree. The hawthorn was symbolic of Henry and the raspberry of Francis. It was on this tree that the challengers hung their shields in the traditional way to declare their intention to take part.

The three main forms of combat were the tilt, the tourney and the foot combat at the barrier. Other sports took place during inclement weather. On one such day there was wrestling and archery. Henry had great success with the bow, while Francis took little or no part in the archery. Afterwards, Henry, rather surprisingly, challenged Francis himself to a wrestling match, but he was quickly thrown by the French king and suffered a subsequent loss of face. The challenge was surprising, as the carefully planned rules of the tournament had agreed that the two kings would fight as brothers-in-arms. As 'brothers' they would not actually fight one another and so would avoid the embarrassment of a defeat.

Tilting was the predominant form of combat, lasting over a week. The object of the course was to break a lance on an opponent, and for this purpose rebated (blunted) lances were used. This did not, however, prevent injury; one French knight died tilting against his brother. Each day's events were formalised according to chivalric ideals. The queens and spectators arrived and were seated, then a knight entered with a band of about ten men as challengers. They paraded around the lists and gave reverence to the queens. The answerers entered and did likewise. The individual jousts then began, with heralds and judges keeping order. The two kings took a full and active part in the tilting, breaking many lances. On one occasion, Francis is said to have received a black eye.

The tourney and tourney course followed the tilt and lasted two days. The tourney was a contest between two groups of mounted combatants who normally first charged with lances and then fought with swords. According to Edward Hall however, the combatants at the Field of Cloth of Gold only fought with swords. The two kings also fought a tourney course between two single contestants. It was in this combat that Henry VIII encountered Robert III de la Marck, Seigneur de Fleuranges. Henry drove him back and disarmed him, breaking a pauldron. In the Musée de l'Armée, Paris is an armour made in Henry's workshop at Greenwich, which according to a tradition already current in the 17th century, belonged to Fleuranges (Musée de l'Armée, G46, H57) (cat. no. 24).[5] It is datable to about 1525 as it was possibly given by King Henry to Fleuranges in recompense.

The pageantry of the tournament was augmented by magnificent banquets and masked balls, with much music and dancing. Each Sunday was devoted to such festivities. At the Field of Cloth of Gold, as on many other occasions, the combats were part of a wide range of revels which included feasting, pageants, plays and masques. The courtiers who danced in the masques were often the same men who had earlier competed in the tiltyard, and the King was frequently among them.

Edward Hall describes the concluding pageantry of the tournament: *After this challenge honourably performed, the Kynges prepared divers maskers, and especially of the King of England....*[6] There was a stunning display of elaborately dressed men representing various heroes of the past, both historical and mythological.

A tournament was held in 1527 to impress the French in the guise of the French ambassador, François de la Tour d'Auvergne, Vicomte de Turenne.[7] In May, a 'Peace and League' was concluded between France and England. This was followed by magnificent celebrations, which included a tournament, a play, a banquet and a masked ball.

The tournaments of Henry VIII were not just good spectator sports: they gave Henry a chance to show off what he excelled at, to appear physically and politically powerful and all within a complex allegory, seen not only in the combats themselves but in the wider aspects of the tournament pageantry.

Notes and references page 335.

Fig. 1 Detail from the Westminster Tournament Roll showing Henry VIII jousting. © The College of Arms

{ I }

FOOT COMBAT
ARMOUR

*Armour of Henry VIII for
foot combat at the barriers*

English, Southwark, 1520

This armour is most probably the earliest surviving product of Henry's Almain armourers, under the master armourer Martin van Royne, who were still in 1520 in temporary accommodation at Southwark while permanent premises were being prepared for them at the palace at Greenwich. The original armour specified for the foot combat at the Field of Cloth of Gold was a '*field armour with pieces of advantage … with an armet without … helm, demi-helm nor basnet*'. The surviving armour has a close helmet designed to turn on the collar, and the gorget, formed of a single plate at front and rear, has a flange at its upper edges for this purpose. The visor is made in one piece, and in addition to its single sight is pierced with a fretwork of quadrangular breaths at either side. The cuirass fits over the collar, and is bolted to it at front and rear. At the waist are two waist lames at the front and rear, the lower of which has a flange over which the thigh defences fit, originally on a stud at the right, now lost. The pauldrons are formed of seven upward-overlapping lames of full width, articulated by internal leathers alone in what would become a characteristic Greenwich style. The vambraces have upper sections articulated on horizontal slots, a style found on contemporary Flemish vambraces, and are fitted inside the elbow joints with sets of articulated lames. Inside the shoulder joint are fitted further sets of twelve lames, articulated by sliding rivets at the rear and four internal leathers, and providing complete plate protection for the usually vulnerable areas in the joints of the arms. The gauntlets are of mitten type, with short tubular cuffs enclosed by flanges at the cuff of the vambraces, an unusual arrangement intended further to protect the wrists. The right gauntlet is a locking gauntlet, the terminal finger plate designed to fasten to the inner wrist plate with a turning pin and keyhole slot. The legs are protected by conventional cuisses on the lower thighs, poleyns at the knees, greaves on the lower legs and sabatons on the feet, the latter articulated with modern rivets only. The plates are coded internally with punched dots at the left and Roman numerals at the right. The defence for the upper thighs and rump is highly unconventional. A large cod-piece with five articulated lames protecting either inner thigh is attached by a pierced stud and pin at the front, and supports another set of internal plates protecting the rear part of the inner thighs and groin, articulated with sliding rivets at either side and internal leathers at the centre to allow for maximum mobility and comfort. The codpiece, but not apparently the defence for the rear of the inner thighs, was fitted with a padded lining, now lost, originally sewn to a lining band whose rivet holes surround the defence. Over the inner thigh defences fits a tasset and culet assembly formed of a series of upward overlapping lames at the front and rear, hinged together at the left, fastened with pierced studs and pins, none original or in their original locations, at the right. The sections covering the inner thighs are hinged also at the outside, and fastened on the inside by their original pierced studs and swivel hooks. One haute-piece, the additional standing guard at the left shoulder, is fitted, but that for the right shoulder, though it has holes for its studs, was either never made or is lost.

Some three months before the tournament at the Field of Cloth of Gold a different type of armour was specified for the event. Henry's agent in France, Sir Richard Wingfield, wrote on 16 March '*as touchyng the combatt at the barrier, ther is left out these words ffollowing "with pieces of advantage". And in stede thereof is sett "in Tonnelett and bacinett."*' Work on the extraordinary Foot Combat armour ceased, and it remained unfinished and undecorated. In the 17th century the armour was still '*rough from the hammer*' and though centuries of polishing by soldiers at the Tower with brick dust and rangoon oil have made it bright today, one small portion of the gorget, hidden below the breastplate, preserves the original surface. The armour is technically quite remarkable. Few similar armours exist; one notable comparison is the foot combat armour by the Milanese master Niccolò Silva, made about 1510–15 presumably for François I, preserved in the Musée de l' Armée, Paris, no. G.178.[1] Together these foot combat armours are among the most remarkable surviving examples of the armourer's craft.   TR

PROV. Transferred to the Tower from the Palace at Greenwich in 1649

Height 1850 mm (73 in), chest outside 1115 mm (44 in), waist outside 960 mm (37.9 in), weight 42.68 kg (94 lb)

PUB. Eaves 1993: 6–8

REF. (1) Pyhrr 1984

{II.6}

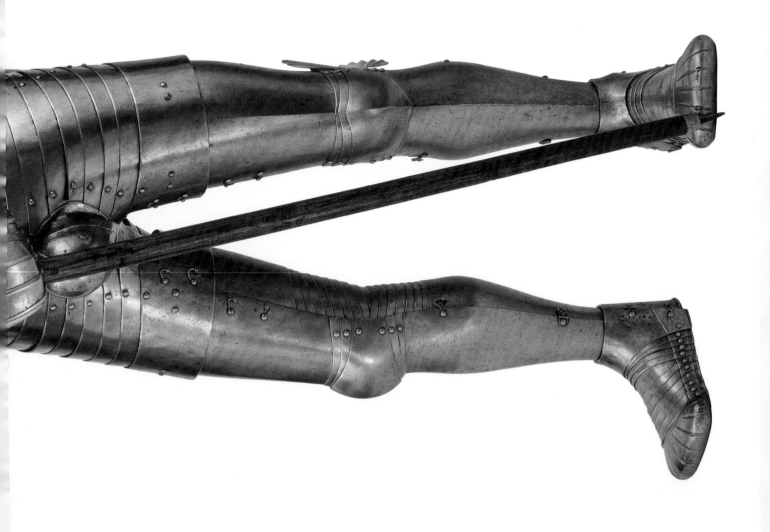

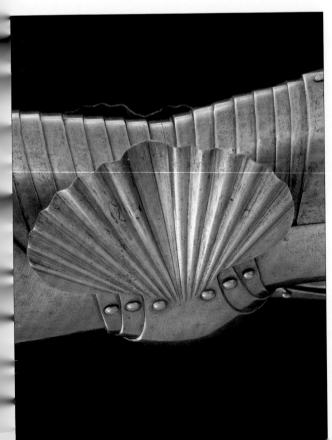

Detail of poleyn and articulated lames defending the back of the knee.

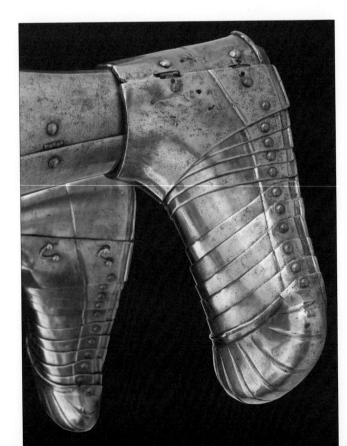

Detail of 'bear's paw' type articulated sabatons.

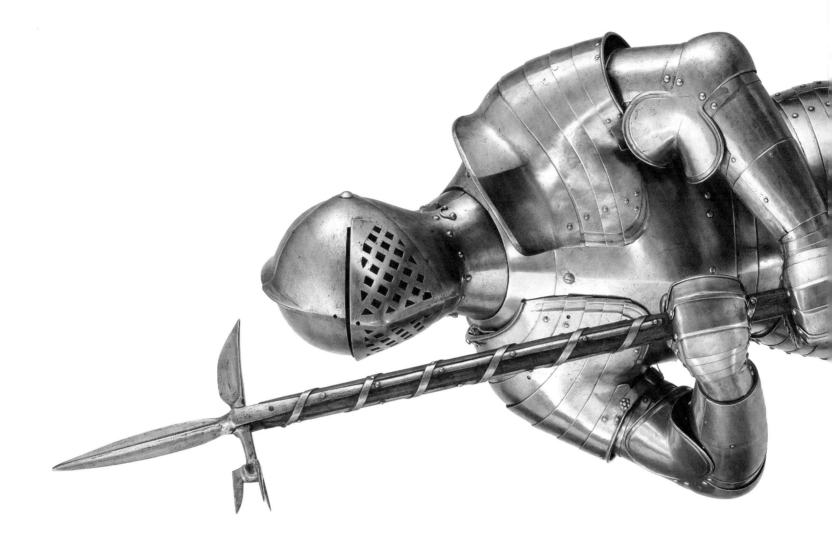

{2}

POLLAXE

Probably English, about 1530; haft modern

Head of steel consisting of a broad, leaf-shaped vertical top spike with a pronounced medial ridge. From the square base of the spike two long langets extend down the wooden haft. Wedged between the spike and the iron cap to the haft is a hammer-head consisting of three knife-like claws set on a long neck, and, in one with it, a heavy counterbalancing back-spike in the form of a hollow-ground triangular-sectioned, slightly downturning fluke.

The upper part of the haft is reinforced by longitudinal strips of iron between the langets of the spike and by a spiral binding of iron. The ferrule at the butt is in the form of an iron spike.

Weapons such as this, sometimes called a pole-hammer (a modern term), were used for battle and tournament. This particular example was almost certainly for use in the tournament, in foot combat at the barriers. The *faux*-combat was fought using the whole of the pollaxe, and moves included hooking or jabbing, the blows being parried by the opponent. Although there is no evidence that this particular pollaxe formed part of Henry VIII's extensive arsenal it dates from the period of his reign. It is also of the type which he could have used with his foot combat armour of about 1520 (Royal Armouries VI.6; cat. no.1) had that armour been worn at the Field of Cloth of Gold and pollaxes used, but Henry's last recorded axe combat was in October 1510 (Though it is not clear whether or not pollaxes or battle axes were used).

It has been suggested that such pollaxes, issued by the Crown, were also carried by the 50 members of Henry's royal bodyguard, the Band of Gentleman Pensioners, who went before the King bearing pollaxes. This was established in 1539 to guard the king's person on the battlefield and in the palace waited upon the king in the presence chamber.[1] The same type of plain pollaxe is depicted in the portrait painting of William (?) Palmer, a Gentleman Pensioner, of about 1540 (Royal Armouries I.1548; cat. no. 90). RCWS

PROV. Acquired 1950; presented by Major H D Barnes

Overall length 2375 mm (93.5 in), head length 286 mm (11.3 in), weight 3.49 kg (7 lb 7 oz)

PUB. Norman & Wilson 1982: 64-5 (illus.); Rangström 1992: 94 (illus.), 95, 348-9; Starkey 1991: 36, no. X.1

REF. (1) Nevinson 1958: 1-13

{VII.1510}

{3}

TWO-HANDED SWORD

Probably English, about 1500
Wooden grip and leather binding modern

Steel hilt comprising a large, roughly spherical pommel and straight quillons which flare out immediately before the hemispherical terminals. The quillon block has a wide, shallow medial ridge. The tapering double-edged blade is of flattened diamond section and ends in a slightly acute tip.

Two-handed swords, like this example, were one of several types of weapon used in tournaments for fighting on foot at the barriers. Often with rebated (blunted) edges they were used to display the strength and agility of the *faux*-combatants. Edward Hall describes how in 1510 Henry VIII

'with two other... chalenged all commers, to fighte with theim at the barriers... xii. strokes with twohanded swords... where the kyng behaved hymselfe so valiauntly by his hardy prowes and great strength...'.[1]

Fighting with these swords involved the use of the whole sword and points were awarded according to where blows were struck. They could be used in either single or group combat to deliver a set number of blows, although at the Field of Cloth of Gold of 1520 the number of strokes was decided by what the heralds and judges thought fit. This sport was regarded as a comparatively hazardous one and Sir Richard Wingfield, English ambassador at the French court, noted that the two-handed sword was *'a whepon daungerous'* whose *'grete strokes'* few gauntlets could survive without *'perisshyng'*. Because of this fighting with two-handed swords at the barriers became an optional event during the Field of Cloth of Gold. However the English, indeed Henry himself, were partial to this form of foot combat and at that event on Friday 22 June, they fought with two-handed swords, presumably with some of the 600 supplied for the event at *'7s. 6d apiece'*.

This particular sword appears to belong to a small group of existing swords that may be classified as English. A very similar example, 1,600 mm in length, reputedly part of a funerary achievement in a *'West Country church'* can be found in the York Castle Museum collection (CA700 [Timperley 33]). That sword and the present sword are listed as part of a group of two-handed swords dating to the late 15th and early 16th centuries which was identified tentatively by Ewart Oakeshott as English owing to their provenance.[2] This group has since been extended and refined and three sub-groups have been identified.[3] Within this framework the present sword belongs to group II and is dated to the later 15th century. However a similar, though decorated, two-handed sword is also depicted as being borne by various members of the King's retinue shown between the Archcliff and Black Bulwark forts in the harbour at Dover in the painting of *The Embarkation at Dover*, of about 1545–50 (The Royal Collection Inventory No. 405793 [Hampton Court; Redgrave: 515] (see p.18–19) which indicates that such swords may have had a long period of use. RCWS

PROV. Acquired 1927; Presented by the officers of the Royal Regiment of Artillery (transferred from the Rotunda Museum of Artillery, Woolwich)

Overall length 1620 mm (63.8 in), blade length 1130 mm (44.5 in), weight 3.15 kg (6 lb 9 oz)

PUB. Museum of Artillery 1873: 125, no. 1798; Rangström 1992: no. 77, 95 (illus.), 349; Starkey 1991: 52

REF. (1) Ellis 1809: 515; (2) Oakeshott 1980: 46; (3) Melville 2001: 22 (illus.), 24 (illus.)

{IX. 633}

4

TONLET ARMOUR

*Armour of Henry VIII for
foot combat at the barriers*

*English, Southwark, 1520, with Italian
and Flemish components*

Some three months before the tournament at the Field of Cloth of Gold was to take place a different type of armour was specified for the foot combat in which Henry VIII and Francis I of France were to compete as part of the same 'band' or team; an armour with '*Tonnelett and bacinet*'. The tournament at the Field of Cloth of Gold lasted from 11–23 June 1520, and on the last two days, Friday and Saturday 22 and 23 June, the foot combats at the barriers were held. The first round of combat was with 'Punchion spears' and single-handed swords, which were given to the combatants when the spears were 'spent'. In these events the '*two valyaunte kynges*' fought '*with such force that the fier sprang out of their armure*'. The second round of combats were with throwing spears ('casting dartes') and two-handed swords. The two kings competed on both days, the second of which was followed by a masque and brought the tournament to a close. Henry's Almain armourers had a very short time to make ready a new armour for the King to wear at the tournament. They succeeded in preparing this armour, now known as the Tonlet armour, by adapting a number of existing pieces, manufacturing additional pieces from new, and decorating the armour.

The armour has a great bacinet, the type of helmet traditionally used in the foot combat, originally made in Milan (the MY under a crown and M under a split cross marks of the Missaglia workshop appear on the rear of the skull) but with a modified visor. The skull has a rear section extended over the nape of the neck, at the centre of which is a large hole for the screw by which it is fastened to the backplate. The bevor is pivoted by modern screws to the skull, and is similarly extended, with two screw holes. Round the neck on both plates is a row of modern lining rivets, and a series of original flush lining rivets with heads stamped with stars surrounded by pellets in the Milanese fashion survives around the face opening. The bellows visor is attached by hinged pivots from which it can be detached by removing the hinge pins. Inside the sights is a plate pierced with smaller holes than the original. The cuirass, probably of Italian or Flemish production, is worn without a gorget, and is hinged at the left and fastened with a strap and buckle at the right. Though it is etched with flutes it is not embossed with them in the fashion popular in Germany and Austria during this period. The skirt (or tonlet) is made of nine lames front and rear, also joined by hinges at the left and straps and buckles at the right. Both are decorated with an even spray of nine flutes, which spread over the whole surface of the tonlet. The pauldrons are formed of seven lames, full length and overlapping upwards, the upper three articulated by rivets, the lower four by six internal leathers, all modern. The vambraces and leg defences were also adapted from existing field armours, and probably were made in Italy or Flanders. The vambraces have the narrow articulated lames protecting the insides of the elbow joints characteristic of foot combat armours

added, while the greaves of the leg defences have slots for the attachment of spurs, essential for a field harness but quite unnecessary for a foot combat armour. The sabatons are detachable, fastened by studs at either side to the greaves.

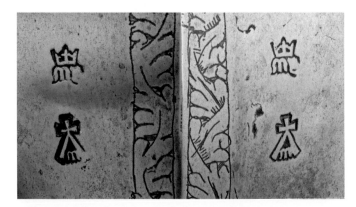

Detail of maker's marks on the skull of the bacinet.

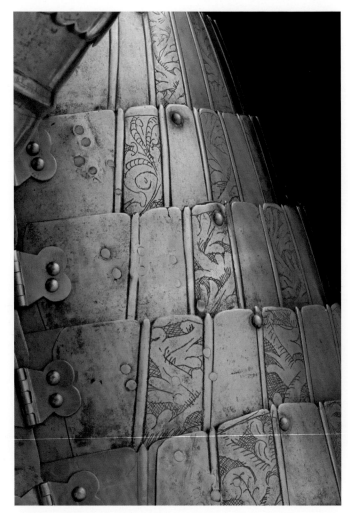

Detail of the skirt (or tonlet), showing evidence of hastily executed etched decoration.

Right: The great bacinet. Iron plates with circular holes were riveted inside the visor to reduce the size of the vision slits.

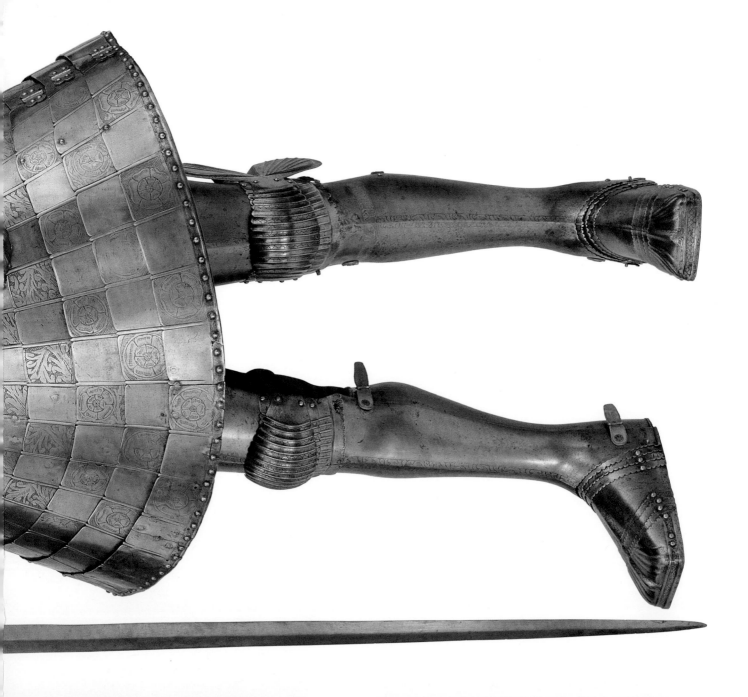

Detail of left couter.

Detail of left poleyn.

The figure of St George etched on the left side of the great bacinet.

The Virgin and Child etched on the left pauldron.

The figure of the Virgin and Child etched on the bacinet.

Order of the Garter etched on the left greave.

Detail of the tonlet. A section was etched in error then left incomplete.

The etched decoration retains traces of gilding, and includes figures of St George and the Virgin and Child in roundels at either side of the bacinet skull and on the pauldrons, the collar of the Order of the Garter around the neck of the bacinet and, around the top of the left greave, the garter itself. The tonlet is etched and was originally gilded in alternate flutes, in checkerboard formation, with stylised foliage and scales on the upper rows, and Tudor roses on the lower rows. Several different hands can be identified in the decoration, and there is an error at the rear (see lower left image). The nature of the decoration suggests that the original finish of the armour was black, producing a striking black and gold effect in checkers and bands. The armour is most probably recorded in the 1547 inventory at Greenwich in the '*bigger of the litle howses*' as '*one Tunlett parcel guilte with A Basenett complete. Lacking one gauntlett*'.[1] The leg defences were separated from this armour at some point, and were reunited with the rest of the armour in 1947, initially on loan, having been in the collection of the Dymoke family, the hereditary Royal Champions, at Scrivelsby Court in Lincolnshire. Few armours of this type survive today; the only other complete examples are preserved in the the Hofjagd- und Rüstkammer of the Kunsthistorisches Museum in Vienna, nos B.33, a Milanese armour made for Claude de Vaudrey, and B.71, a Flemish armour made for Maximilian I.[2] TR

PROV. Transferred to the Tower from the Palace at Greenwich in 1649. Leg defences purchased in 1971 with the aid of the National Art Collections Fund

Height 1850 mm (73 in), chest outside 1060 mm (41.8 in), waist outside 917 mm (36.1 in), weight 29.26 kg (64 lb 7 oz)

PUB. Blair 1995; Eaves 1993: 2–45; Starkey 1991: 52

REF. (1) Starkey 1998: 162;
(2) Thomas & Gamber 1976: 183, 194, Taf 88–9

{11.7}

5

COMPOSITE ARMOUR FOR
THE JOUST OF PEACE (STECHZEUG)

Austrian, Innsbruck, and south German, late 15th century

The type of joust for which this form of helm was used was called the *Gestech*, or in English the Joust of Peace or Joust Royal, in which heavily armoured knights rode against each other in single combat on horseback with lances that were fitted with a coronel or rebated tip rather than a sharp pointed one. The course was run at either side of a tilt, or barrier, and the object of the joust was to score points by striking targets on the opponent such as the head or shield, and ideally shattering the lance upon the opponent. A series of armours of this type is preserved in the collection of the Hofjagd- und Rüstkammer of the Kunsthistorisches Museum in Vienna, together with the quilted fabric lining caps that were worn with the helms (cat. no. 8). They were made for the courts of Sigismund, Archduke of Austria, and Maximilian I the Holy Roman Emperor, by master armourers from Augsburg, Nuremberg and Innsbruck.

The helm is composed of three plates: front, back and skull, fastened together by large, brass-capped iron rivets. The back and skull plates are pierced with pairs of holes for the laces of the lining cap. The front and rear plates spread outwards over the back and chest, and have iron charnels (hasps) for securing the helm in position. The front charnel is a strong, hinged plate pierced with twelve oblong holes in pairs, arranged to fit over staples on the breastplate. The rear charnel is a large, rectangular buckle with three bars of descending thickness through which the strap from the backplate was passed. The magnificent sculptural quality of these helms was evident to the contemporary artist Albrecht Dürer, whose famous pen study of one is in the Musée du Louvre, Paris.

The right pauldron, along with the vambrace (polder mitten) and breastplate are attributed to Klaus Wagner of Innsbruck, parts of a series of armours made for the Archduke Sigismund about 1485 (attribution by Dr Orwin Gamber, compare Innsbruck 1954:

56, no. 19, from Ambras). Its main plate is decorated with sprays of flutes, and the five lames below it have a tight group of scalloped flutes at the centre and chevrons of flutes on the lower lame. The lame at the top is missing. The right vambrace or polder mitten (from the French *épaule de mouton*, named after its shape) has a large flange protecting the bend of the arm, also embossed with a spray of flutes. The left pauldron is attributed to Jorg Helmschmied of Augsburg, and exhibits small differences in detail from the other in the broader panel of flutes running up the centre and the roped rib at the top, a feature also found on some Nuremberg armours in the series. Its upper edge has a boxed outward turn filed with characteristic triple grooves. The manifer, also fitted with a reinforce at the elbow attached by screws, and embossed to protect the bridle hand while allowing the reins of the horse to be held easily, is stamped with the mark of the armourers' guild of Nuremberg. The breastplate is constructed from an upper plate pierced with sets of holes for the helm charnel, or staple, at the centre, the lance rest at the right, the queue, a long bracket which helped support the weight of the lance, at the right and the shoulder shield at the upper left. Fastened by a bolt at the centre is a lower breastplate which has three fauld lames below the waist. The backplate is formed of three plates riveted together with cusped seams, and decorated with panels of fluting. Thia and the breastplate have the same construction mark, three V-shaped nicks in the edges of the plates only visible inside. The back was separated until recently from the breastplate

Various pieces of jousting armour were recorded in the 1547 inventory at Greenwich in the '*lesser of the twoo little howses*' including '*A curette for the Tilte that hath no Basenett…three Manufiers…three paier of Vambrases with ii Polder muttons*' which might well include the pieces assembled here.[1] TR

PROV. The Brocas helm was transferred from the Rotunda Museum of Artillery, Woolwich, 1927. Originally from the collection of Bernard Brocas, Wokefield Park, Stratfield Mortimer, Berkshire, it was sold at auction by George Robins, London 19–21 March 1834 lot 439, to a Norfolk gentleman, presented to Henry Harrod FSA, passed to Mr Bayfield of Norwich, and purchased in 1853 by Sir John Lefroy for the Rotunda Museum. All the other pieces are from the old Tower collection. Though not assembled together until the 1960s, the individual pieces can be traced back to the 1850s, and the lack of additional provenance together with the way in which they are described in the early inventories suggests they may be pieces which have survived in the Tower armoury since the early 16th century

Helm: height 605 mm (23.9 in), width 300 mm (11.8 in), depth 415 mm (16.4 in), weight 10.45 kg (23 lb); Breastplate: height 535 mm (21.1 in), width 310 mm (12.2 in), weight 83 kg (18 lb 4 oz); Backplate: height 355 mm (14 in), width 320 mm (12.6 in), weight 1.57 kg (3 lb 7 oz); Left pauldron: height 340 mm (13.4 in), width 282 mm (11.1 in), weight 1.68 kg (3 lb 11 oz); Right pauldron: height 335 mm (13.2 in), width 285 mm (11.2 in), weight 1.51 kg (3 lb 5 oz); Manifer: length 625 mm (24.7 in), height 200 mm (7.9 in), weight 3.31 kg (7 lb 4 oz); Vambrace: length 290 mm (11.4 in), height 230 mm (9.1 in), weight 1.79 kg (3 lb 15 oz)

PUB. Hewitt 1864 REF. (1) Starkey 1998: 162

{III.96, 731-2, 864, 1366, IV.411}

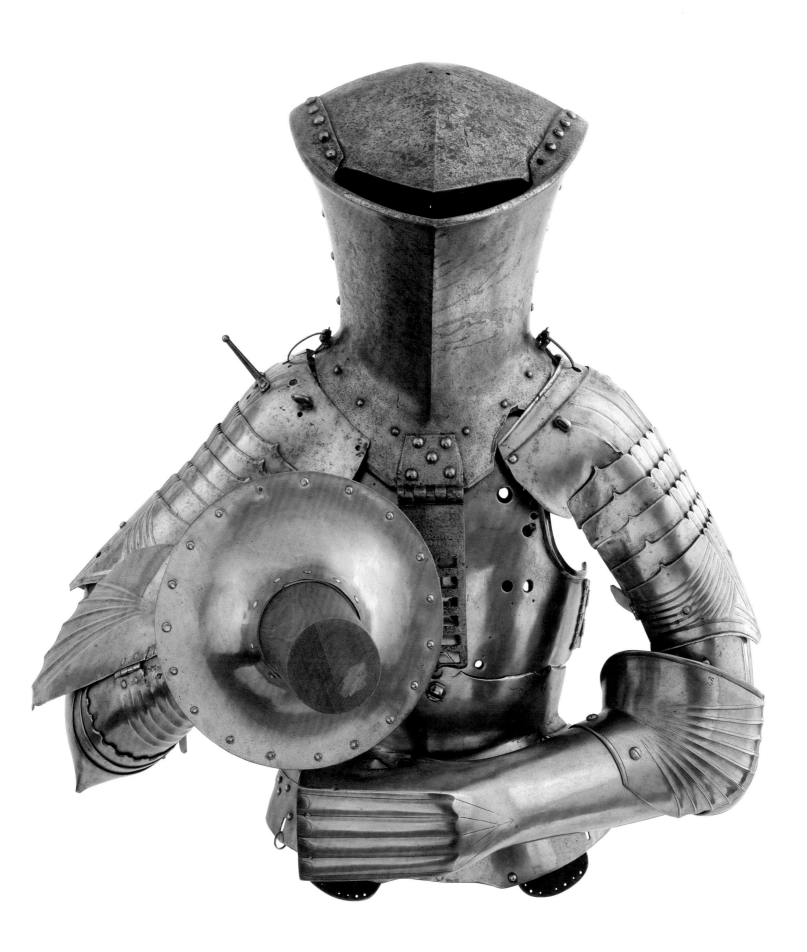

{ 6 }

GREAT BACINET FOR
FOOT COMBAT

Possibly for Henry VIII
European, about 1510

The helmet has a tall, well-shaped skull with a low comb, and extends over the nape of the neck. The bevor is pivoted at either side, also extending over the chest with a large hole at either side for securing the helmet to the breastplate with screws. At either side of the bevor extension is an L-shaped slot for the attachment of the pauldrons. The visor has a central medial ridge, is embossed to simulate sights but not actually pierced for them, and pierced with a group of 45 holes at the left which provided ventilation as well as vision. The lower edge is bordered with a double incised line. The visor was originally attached by terminals with hinge pins at either side, but later modified with simple pivots. Around the lower edges and the narrowest part of the neck are series of lining rivets for attachment of the now lost lining band and lining. It is probable that this bacinet was brought to the Tower from Greenwich having survived among the various pieces of tournament armour described there in the 1547 inventory, such as the 'twoo *Tunelettes with twoo basenettes*' and '*ij Curettes to fight with one fote with Basenettes and breches*'.[1] By the 17th century it had become known as the '*hearse or long head of John of Gaunt*', valued in 1688 at £10. TR

PROV. Old Tower collection, probably brought from Greenwich in 1649

Height 455 mm (18 in), width 260 mm (11 in), depth 340 mm (13.4 in),
weight 5.22 kg (11 lb 8 oz)

PUB. Dillon 1910: 118, no. IV.8; Hewitt 1859: 27, no. IV.16;
Mann 1951: no. 37

REF. (1) Starkey 1998: 162

{ IV.2 }

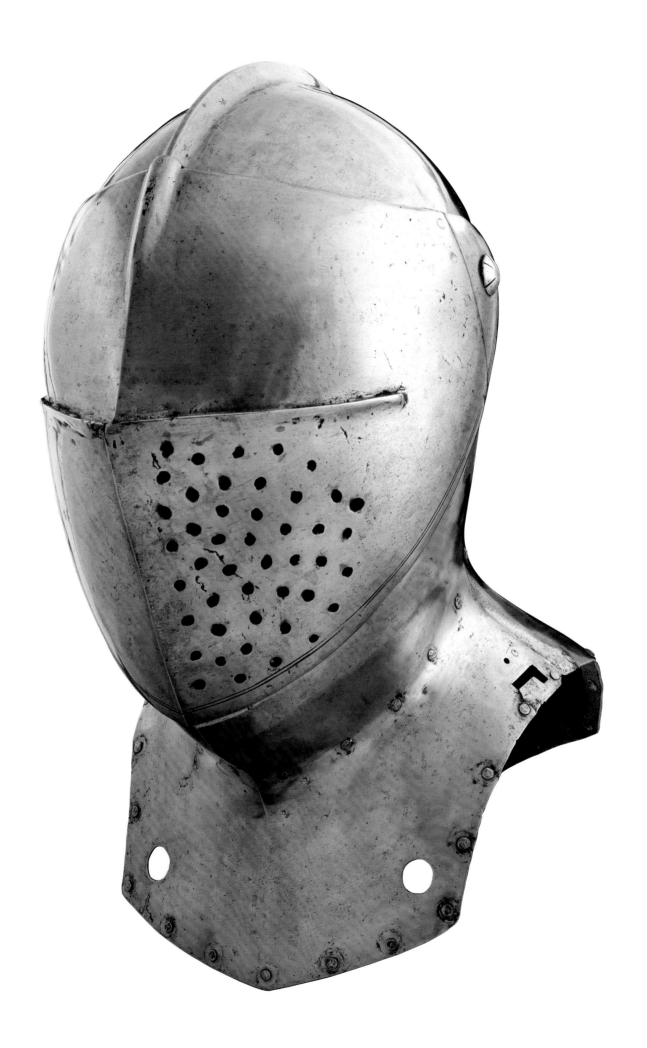

HELM FOR THE JOUST ROYAL

The Stowe helm, Flemish, about 1500

This helm for the Joust Royal, as the Joust of Peace or *Gestech* was known in England, did not belong to Henry VIII but is typical of those used in tournaments at his court. It is made in three parts, a tall, finely shaped skull with a slight medial ridge pierced at the top with a hole for attachment of a crest, a brow plate with holes for attachment of a reinforce and a front plate, the upper edge of which is splayed out to form the sight. The front plate is riveted to the brow plate, and the whole is pivoted to the skull by a pair of hinged pivots, and secured by a turning peg at the right. There is a large rectangular ventilation hole at the right of the front plate, protected by having the front edge flared outwards. The lower part of the front plate is flared to fit over the chest, has been fitted with a reinforcing plate, both pierced with holes for the securing bolts, while a thin, triangular plate was riveted to the lower rear of the skull. The differential corrosion of the surface indicates that the helm was painted and gilded as part of a funerary achievement. It is stamped with a Gothic letter h under a crown at either side of the front. A complete example of a *Stechzeug* armour by the 'Master h', made for Maximilian I or Philip the Handsome, is in the Hofjagd- und Rüstkammer of the Kunsthistorisches Museum, Vienna, no S.II.[1] This form of armour was popular for jousting in England; exactly the same type of helm is illustrated in the Westminster Tournament Roll. Claude Blair has identified another helm marked by the same maker, in Lullingstone Church, Kent, and identified another, in Birling Church, also in Kent, which can be attributed to him, and Blair tentatively suggested that the mark might be identified with the armourer Jacob (Copyn) de Watte who became one of the armourers in Henry VIII's employ at Greenwich. As Blair has pointed out, these helms were called 'bacinets' in the 16th century just like the great bacinets for the foot combat (1998 note 2). At least two remained at Greenwich in 1547, '*Item ij Curettes with twoo bassenettes…Item A curette for the Tilte that hathe no basenett*'.[2] TR

PROV. Purchased most probably from Samuel Luke Pratt of Bond Street in London, see Victoria & Albert Museum Prints and Drawings nos 93.A.38 p. 84, and D.498-1904 drawing inscribed '*at Pratt's*'. From the collection of the Dukes of Buckingham and Chandos, sold at Christie and Manson, London, 15 August–7 October 1848. probably part of Part II lot 251, which was bought by Pratt and included '*a visor helmet, a coat of chain mail; 2 spears; an oriental shield; and 3 swords*'[3]

Height 460 mm (18.1 in), weight 6.95 kg (15 lb 5 oz)

PUB. Blair 1998; Dillon 1910: 118, no. IV.7; Hewitt 1859: 27, no. IV.15

REF. (1) Thomas & Gamber 1976: 149–50; (2) Starkey 1998: 162; (3) Forster 1848: 172

{IV.I}

{ 8 }

HELM LINING (HELMHAUBE)

Austrian, Innsbruck, about 1484

A particular difficulty in the study of historical armour is the understanding of what is lost. Almost all armours were fitted, in whole or in part, with linings of textile, but few of these linings survive today even in a fragmentary state. An example of a piece that does is a small part of the lining of an armet included in this exhibition (cat. no. 20). Often the surviving fittings, holes for points (fastening laces), lining rivets or even the fabric or leather lining bands to which the lost linings were sewn, give us an idea of what is lost. In the case of the helms used for the Jousts Royal or *Gestech* in the late 15th and early 16th century the existence of the linings is indicated by the pairs of holes for the points by which the helms were attached to the linings.

In Vienna, however, a unique series of helm linings survives. These linings were made of linen quilted with wadding, in the form of a hood with a flap covering the chin, fastened closed with a leather strap and iron buckle. Another leather band is riveted or sewn round the brow, and along the medial line is a series of leather points intended to tie the lining into the helm. This arrangement held the wearer's head in a central position within the helm to minimize the risk of injury when struck by a lance or in a fall from a horse.

Some of the eight surviving linings can be identified with individual jousting helms, and the series is associated with the armours for the *Gestech* made for the court of Archduke Sigismund in the 1480s and 90s.[1] TR

Height 400 mm (15.8 in)

REF. (1) Thomas & Gamber 1976: 152 Taf. 72

Hofjagd- und Rüstkammer of the Kunsthistorisches Museum, Vienna

{ B.45 }

{9}

JOUSTING LANCE

Perhaps belonging to Henry VIII
Probably English, early 16th century

Long, fluted and painted wooden lance, made of softwood, probably of the genus *abies* (fir). The shaft is hollow to the tip and it is made up of one piece of wood, which has probably been cut in half lengthways and hollowed out, leaving the grip and butt solid, it was then glued back together again.

The lance shaft swells from the tip towards the handgrip reaching its maximum diameter in front of the grip. Its surface has eight flutes running towards the grip. The grip widens to form a tapering solid wood butt. Behind the grip a thin leather band is wrapped around the butt and secured with nails.

Traces of gilded decoration with coloured glazes remain on the butt and the fluting. In the grooves of the fluting traces of painted patterns in black and red can be seen, such as latticework and organic scrolls. The top edges of the fluting have punch-work decoration of scrolling tendrils. Each top edge also has three fine holes which run around its circumference, next to the grip, the function of these holes is unclear but it could have been from nails used to secure a decorative band. The shaft (from the tip to the beginning of the fluting) has been repainted several times but the original colour scheme was red, it is now black with a red band towards the tip.

Lances, such as this example, are very elaborate and were made for great, prestigious sporting events. The leather band on the butt was designed to press against the lance rest on the breastplate to prevent the lance being driven back on impact. The lances were fluted to reduce weight and designed to dramatically shatter on impact when an opponent was struck correctly.

On 7 July 1517 Nicholas Carew ran a course as '*the blew knyght*' with a tilting lance called a '*greet boordon*', a *bourdannasse* being a richly decorated hollow tilting lance.

This tournament lance might well be one of two '*Great Lances … said to be King Henry VIIIths*' (the other is Royal Armouries VII.634) in the inventories of the Royal Armouries, Tower of London, from 1660. ES/RCWS

PROV: Old Tower collection, listed in the Inventory of the
Tower Armouries taken in 1660

Overall length 2815 mm (9 ft 2 in), weight 4.7 kg (10 lb 4 oz)

REF: ffoulkes 1916: 233, Hammond 1986: 13

{VII.551}

Right: VII.551 and VII.550.

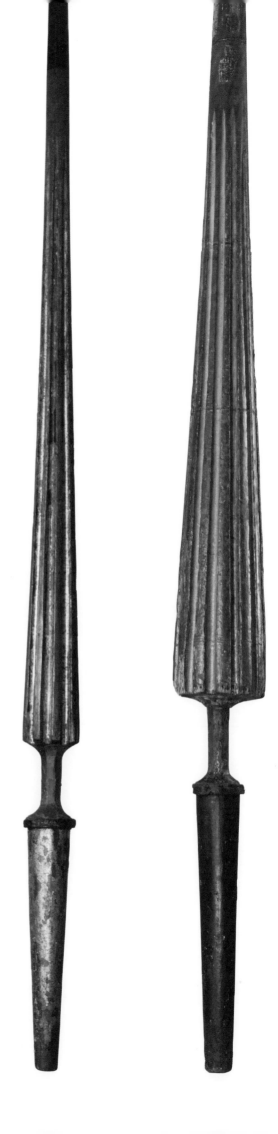

{10}

'BRANDON'S LANCE'

English, early 16th century

Large hollow wooden tournament lance, designed to shatter on impact when an opponent was struck correctly.

It is fitted with a tapered iron head nailed to the wooden shaft. The head has eight shallow flutes, and a blunted four faced tip. Traces of gilded decoration remain. Next to the head a leather band decorated with worn red woollen fringing (much discoloured) is secured to the lance shaft by pyramid headed studs.

The lance shaft swells from the tip towards the handgrip reaching its maximum diameter of 20 cm (8 in) in front of the hand. Its surface is fluted for the latter 139 cm (54.75 in) towards the grip. The haft is painted (tip – grip) black/yellow/red/black – the wood in this area has been largely stripped bare/red/white with broad longitudinal stripes/red with yellow flutes/red grip and black butt. Three transverse unpainted scars run around the fluting 34 cm (13.5 in), 73 cm (28.75 in) and 126 cm (49.5 in) from tip of the fluting. These may be all that remain of an original binding.[1]

The handgrip extends for 18 cm (7 in) and then widens to form a 62 cm (24.5 in) solid wood butt which tapers from 10 cm (4 in) diameter to 6 cm (2.25 in). A leather band is attached to the butt next to the handgrip which is designed to press against the lance rest on the breastplate to prevent the lance being driven back on impact. There is evidence of some repair work to the lance shaft, most visibly to the underside of the fluting next to the grip with remains of glue.

Charles Brandon, Duke of Suffolk (d.1545) was an accomplished sportsman and favourite of Henry VIII, becoming his brother-in-law in 1515 when he married Mary Tudor, widow of King Louis XII of France. In a joust in March 1524 Brandon's lance shattered against Henry's helm. Unfortunately Henry had failed to lower his visor properly and was lucky to escape serious injury.

This lance was first associated with Brandon in 1598, and again in the Tower inventory of 1660 '*Great lances, two said to be King Henry VIIIths and one Charles Brandon Duke of Suffolke's*'.

In the interim, Henry Peacham asked in '*The truth of our times revealed out of one man's experience by way of essay*' (1638) '*who can wield that launce which Charles Brandon D. of Suffolke tilted withal, yet to be seen in the Tower?*'.

Oscar Wilde in his essay '*The truth of masks – A note on illusion*'(1885) notes '*A good deal was of course preserved in the Tower, and even in Elizabeth's day tourists were brought there to see such curious relics of the past as Charles Brandon's huge lance, which is still, I believe, the admiration of our country visitors…*'. BC

PROV. Old Tower collection. First associated with Brandon in 1598, and again in the Inventory of the Tower Armouries taken in 1660

Overall length 4360 mm (172 in); maximum diameter 200 mm (8 in), weight 9.1 kg (20 lb)

PUB. Rangström 1992: 81, 82, 341; Royal Armouries 2000: 9; Starkey 1991: 45

REF. (1) ffoulkes 1916

{VII.550}

the kyng		
the duke of Suff		lorde Herbert
the marques of Exssex		lorde Clynton
Syr Carew		S edward nevell
the kyng		S wyllm kyngston
the duke of Suff		Fraunces bryan
the marques of Exssex		thomas chene
Nycholas Carew		Syr Norres
the kyng		S henry gard
the duke of Suff		S henry capell
the marques of Exssex Carew		S wyllm syd
Syr Carew		Syr compton

3/2 H8

{II}

TOURNAMENT
SCORE CHEQUE

For a tournament at Greenwich, 19-20 May, 1516
Manuscript on paper

In Europe in the 14th and 15th centuries efforts had been made to create a consistent form of accounting for points won during jousts, and in 1466 the rules by which knightly activities in the tournament might be judged and recorded had been formulated by John Tiptoft, Earl of Worcester.[1] This jousting cheque follows the model established by Tiptoft.

It shows in the left column the 'challengers', led by Henry VIII himself and Charles Brandon, the Duke of Suffolk, while the column on the right is that of the 'defenders'.

The scores were recorded in the rectangular boxes; a short stroke through the topmost line meant a strike to the head and one through the middle line a strike to the body. A line right across the box recorded a broken lance – the mark of a successful and strong impact. Strokes made through the line to the right of each box recorded the number of runs each jouster made.

The jousting at this tournament was mentioned in a letter from Thomas Alen to the Earl of Shrewsbury: '*Great jousting at Greenwich on Monday and Tuesday last. The King, the Lords of Suffolk and Essex, Sir Geo.Carewe, were challengers; Sir Will. Kingston, Sir Giles Capell, [John] Sedley and others, defenders*'.[2]

Alen also said that; '*The King hath promised never to joust again except it be with as good a man as himself*'. This has led some to interpret this comment as suggesting that Henry was unhappy with the quality of his opponents on that occasion. The tone of the letter, however, and the use of the term '*great jousting*' suggests that Henry was only keen to ensure that he would in future only take part in events where the jousting was of such high quality.

The Duke of Suffolk, the King's brother-in-law and for many years his counterpart in his outstanding ability in tournament activities, was one of the few people in England who could offer the King an equal competition. A jousting lance traditionally believed to have been one used by Brandon is cat. no.10. GR

Height 437 mm (17.2 in), width 307 mm (12.1 in)

REF. (1) Anglo 1968: 154; (2) Brewer 1864: no. 1935; ffoulkes 1912: 31–50; Gunn 1991: 47

College of Arms, London

{MS, TOURNAMENT CHEQUE IC}

HENRY VIII'S HUNTING INTERESTS

GRAEME RIMER

Manhoood I am, therefore I me delight
To hunt and hawk, to nourish up and feed.
The greyhound to the course, the hawk to the flight,
And to bestride a good and lusty steed –
These things become a very man indeed...

So wrote Sir Thomas More of his perception of the manly and noble act of hunting, eloquently also summarising the attitude of Henry VIII to it.[1] Henry's enthusiasm for hunting was genuine and in harmony with the prevailing view of the time that it was an activity in which a prince should take active participation. Although Henry's father, Henry VII, had been a keen sportsman his son's passion for the hunt and ability as a hunter was greater, and his fondness for it brought about a significant change in the attitude towards hunting in the English court.

In part this new enthusiasm may have been influenced by a translation, made widely available by William Caxton, of a 13th-century work by Ramon Llull, *Libro del ordre de cavalleria*, which became a guide to those who saw hunting as a knightly activity. Llull saw hunting, indeed, as vital *'for to mayntene thordre of knighthode'*, and also that it provided valuable experience in the use of weapons in hazardous situations.[2] Indeed he said that *'Knyghtes ougt to....hunte at hertes, at bores and other wyld bestes, for in doynge these thynges the Knyghtes exercyse them to armes'*.

Henry VIII's passion for hunting became well recorded in songs and poems, and in letters from foreign ambassadors to his court. Perhaps the best known of these is that from Sebastian Giustiniani, the Venetian ambassador at Henry's court early in his reign:

'He is very accomplished; a good musician; composes well; is a most capital horseman; a fine jouster; speaks good French, Latin and Spanish; is very religious; hears three masses daily when he hunts and sometimes five on other days...He is very fond indeed of hunting, and never take his diversion without tiring eight or ten horses...he is extremely fond of tennis'.[3]

Hunting created opportunities for Henry to impress visiting foreign dignitaries but it also provided a release from the pressures and tensions of life at court. Henry spent increasingly large sums of money creating hunting parks around each of his palaces, a process of emparkment which was greatest in the

1530s and 1540s. His enthusiasm extended to the development of special establishments to breed and maintain the animals needed to hunt the different types of game; these included buckhounds for deer, harriers for hares and otter hounds for otters.[4]

Clearly Henry greatly enjoyed hunting, indeed he recorded his views of it in perhaps one of his most famous songs:

Pastime with good company I love and shall until I die
Grudge to lust, but none deny
So God be pleased, thus live will I
For my pastance,
Hunt sing and dance,
My heart is set,
All goodly sport
For my comfort:
Who shall me let?

Despite this innate love of hunting, as a monarch well aware of his developing role on the international scene he was also aware of its political value as an accomplishment expected of a modern prince. Hunting was one of the many attractions offered to visiting monarchs and their courtiers. When Charles V came to England in 1522, and when Frederick of Bavaria was in London in 1539, both were treated to hunting followed by lavish feasts.

While doubtless a thrilling and absorbing passion for the King, the members of his court and for visiting dignitaries it was not, of course, without real danger. The pursuit of wild boar had its obvious dangers; the boar was a formidable animal if cornered when its sharp tusks could cause serious injury to man or horse, but other dangers lurked too. One accident almost cost Henry his life. In 1525, while out hawking near Hitchin in Hertfordshire he attempted to pole-vault over a water-filled ditch. The pole broke and the King was pitched head-first into soft mud. Only the quick action of his hunt servant, Edward Mody, saved him from asphyxiation.

Although he kept mews for hunting falcons and hawks from early in his reign it seems that Henry became truly absorbed by hawking only later in his life. He had, however, been aware throughout his reign that a carefully organised mews containing a large number of fine birds was a visible enhancement of his image as king. As with his other hunting animals he kept different birds to pursue different prey species. Good falcons and hawks were also important diplomatic gifts, and Henry received fine birds from a number of European monarchs (fig. 1).

Fig. 1 Portrait by Hans Holbein of Robert Cheseman, royal falconer to Henry VIII. Mauritshuis, the Hague. Digital Image 2009 © Photo Scala, Firenze

Henry VIII had a true and genuine passion for hunting, as he did with so many other active and often dangerous activities, and certainly he used them to escape the pressures of political life. He also, however, appreciated their importance as a means to demonstrate his physical prowess but perhaps to reinforce his image as a monarch of significance on the European stage. As James Williams has demonstrated so well in his excellent article on this subject, Henry used hunting and hawking to demonstrate to the world at large his legitimacy and authority as King of England.

Notes and references page 335.

LONGBOW

English, mid 16th century

Of yew, of rounded D-section, the original horn nocks now lost, the ends of the bow damaged by long immersion in seawater.

This bow represents the type which would have been familiar to Henry. Although created in England this bow was almost certainly made from imported wood. Yew did not grow straight and true in the temperate climate of England, so for centuries before Henry VIII came to the throne suitable timber was imported into England from the parts of Europe which had high mountainous regions in which the yew there grew slowly, but straight and with few imperfections in the grain. Such was the need for a reliable supply of good-quality bow timber to be maintained, in order that the population of England could acquire bows and practice in their use, that a succession of later medieval English monarchs ordered merchants bringing in certain types of high-value cargo, such as wine, to pay a form of tax by also importing a certain number of billets of wood from which good bows might be made. Agents at the ports of entry monitored both the number and quality of the bow-staves imported in this way.

The price of bows was also controlled by royal order so that they might remain affordable to those within the population of England who were required to provide themselves with bows and arrows so that they would be useful military archers in times of war.

Henry VIII was an archer of great strength and ability, which he often demonstrated in shooting competitions, for example at the Field of Cloth of Gold in 1520, when contemporary accounts record that he '*shot repeatedly into the centre of the white at twelve score yards*'. Despite Henry's interest in archery, however, its use in warfare began to decline during his reign. *(Not illustrated)*. GR

Length: 1850 mm (72.8 in)

PROV: This bow was one of eight recovered in the 19th century from the wreck of Henry VIII's flagship, the *Mary Rose*, lost off Spithead, Portsmouth, in July 1545. Two salvage divers, Charles and John Deane, located the wreck when clearing the remains of a late 18th-century ship, the *Royal George*, which had sunk while at its moorings, and recovered a number of items, including these few bow-staves, which were subsequently sold at auction in London. This and another similar bow (XI.1), still in the Royal Armouries' collection, together with some artillery-related items, were evidently purchased before 1845 since they were mentioned in the Guide to the Tower of London in that year as being on display

REF. Hardy 1976: 21, 32, 54, 56, 130;
Norman & Wilson 1982: 106, no.94

{XI.2}

{13}

HAWKING BELL

English, 15th century

Henry VIII spent much of his time hunting and hawking. When he died his private apartments were found to be full of falconry equipment.

Bells such as this one were tied to the hunting bird's legs with special leather straps called bewits. They were made in different sizes and served to reveal the bird's position to the falconer when hunting, especially after killing in cover. They also served to warn the falconer if the bird had bated off her perch in the mews. Pairing bells for pitch was important, and it was suggested that one should be alto and the other bass. The final choice of bells ultimately depended upon the ear of the individual falconer.

These types of bell are made from brass with an iron pea. It was produced from four components; a hollow body made in two halves by hammering a piece of sheet brass into form, a suspension loop and a round iron pea. The loop was inserted upwards through a hole cut in the upper half of the body and the ends were bent outwards then inwards, in the manner of a staple, so it remained rigid rather than swivelling, and an aperture was cut in the lower half of the body. A lead/tin solder was used to join the two halves together, leaving a flanged seam line. Making them was a specialized craft; in the 14th and 15th centuries Milan was celebrated all over Europe for exporting hawking bells.

This bell was found in excavations in the city of London during re-development. ACS

Diameter 16 mm (0.63 in)

REF. Egan 1991: 338-9

Museum of London. From the River Thames foreshore, Bankside, 1980

{80.447/9}

{14}

TENNIS BALL

English, 17th century

This tennis ball (opposite, top) was found in the roof of Westminster Hall and given to the Museum of London by H M Ministry of Works in 1920. The tennis ball is made from leather and is stuffed with dog hair. Balls were sometimes made of a core of cork wrapped in fabric tape and bound with woollen cloth.

Henry VIII was a particularly keen player of the sport of real tennis – so much so that he had courts built at many of his palaces – including Hampton Court and the sport is still played around the world today with 35 courts still in existence. Henry's wardrobe roll included *'tenes-cotes, tennis-drawers and tennis-slippers for the king'.*

Real tennis required a specially built court, similar to a modern squash court; enclosed by walls on all four sides, three of which had galleries with sloping roofs. Players used rackets made of wood with small, slightly angled heads strung tightly with string. The rules and scoring were similar to those of the modern game of lawn tennis. Players won points by hitting the ball around the walls and into netted windows beneath the roofs.

Henry wanted to make tennis, and other favourite pastimes of his such as jousting, elite royal sports so he banned ordinary people from taking part. The costs involved in such sports excluded all but the very wealthy and thus tennis become known as the 'Game of Kings'.

Anne Boleyn, Henry VIII's second wife, was arrested while watching a game of real tennis at Whitehall Palace and it is said that Henry was also playing tennis at Hampton Court when the news of her execution arrived. ACS

Diameter 40 mm (1.6 in), weight 45 g (1.6 oz)

REF. Inglis, 2005

Museum of London

{A23502}

{15}

FOOTBALL

Traditionally associated with Mary, Queen of Scots
English, between 1540 and 1570

This sporting relic was discovered by workmen inside Stirling Castle in the 1970s. They uncovered the small leather ball in the rafters of the oak-panelled bedchamber once used by Mary, Queen of Scots. The ball was dated between 1540 and 1570, making it the oldest football in the world.

The ball, slightly smaller than a modern football, is of a type known as a 'bladder ball'. It consists of an inflated bladder, generally of pig, with a strong leather cover. It is stitched on the inside to make the exterior kicking surface smoother for better bounce and roll. The ball is remarkably well preserved despite its age.

Early games of football do not seem to have had a limit to the number of players on each side, even extending to whole towns and villages being matched against each other with the goals miles apart. The ball could even be picked up, thrown and run with until wrestled for by an opponent. It was a rough and violent game and could result in riots, which caused the game to be condemned.

In 1365, Edward III ordered men to spend their leisure time practicing archery instead of many games including *'...handball, football, club ball...or other vain games of no value.'* This ban on ordinary citizens playing football continued through Henry VIII's reign; although the ban did not apply to those of noble birth.

Henry enjoyed playing a Tudor version of football, even commissioning a pair of football boots at a cost of 4 shillings (about £100 today). The ban on football would have been hard to enforce as unlike some royal pursuits such as tennis that requiring a purpose-built venue, football could be played in any location, albeit under pain of imprisonment if caught. ACS

160 mm x 150 mm x 140 mm

REF. Dunning 1963: 838–47

The Stirling Smith Art Gallery and Museum, Stirling, Scotland

{15905}

{2}

ARMOURS OF
HENRY VIII

THE ROYAL ARMOUR WORKSHOPS AT GREENWICH

THOM RICHARDSON

Soon after he came to the throne in 1509 Henry VIII established a royal armour workshop that was to survive him by about 100 years. Thom Richardson examines the records that show armourers from Italy and Flanders were at work at Greenwich by 1511 and that by 1515 'Almain' (German) armourers had also been recruited. He reviews the evidence regarding the making of some of Henry's armours that survive in the Royal Armouries collection, including the 'silvered and engraved', foot combat and tonlet armours and the 1540 garniture. His survey concludes by showing the important contribution of the Greenwich workshop during the Elizabethan era and well into the Stuart period. The impact of Henry's Greenwich initiative on the development of armour in England was clearly immense.

The Holy Roman Emperor, Maximilian I, established a royal armour workshop at Innsbruck, and in general the royal, ducal and electoral courts of Europe had attracted the makers of the finest armour (fig. 1). It therefore comes as no surprise to find Henry VIII establishing an armour workshop of his own, based for most of its life in the palace at Greenwich, a workshop which would survive the King for nearly a century (fig. 2).

Armourers worked in England throughout the Middle Ages; a Company of Helmers was formed in London by 1347, and this was transformed by 1453 into the Armourers' Company, which survives to the present day as The Worshipful Company of Armourers and Brasiers. Although there are numerous pieces of armour, especially the great helms such as that of Edward the Black Prince at Canterbury and of Henry V at Westminster Abbey, that were probably made in England, not a single piece of English-made armour can be positively identified before the early 16th century.[1] By the time Henry VIII came to the throne in 1509 it is clear that most of the munition armour needed for the English army, and any fine armour for the nobility, had to be imported from Italy, Flanders or Germany. Evidence of imports of armour early in Henry VIII's reign can be seen in receipts to Guido Portenary, merchant of Florence, for £1,600 paid for 2,000 harnesses for footmen, dated 28 May 1513, and another to the same merchant for £80 for 100 Milan harnesses for footmen.[2]

Long before Maximilian's gift of armour was delivered, Henry was setting up his own armour workshop at Greenwich.[3] John Blewbury, Yeoman of the King's Armoury, provided the armourers of Milan with £6 13s. 4d. wages (as well as two hogsheads of wine and their carriage to Greenwich) in July 1511.[4]

Also paid by our fond Commandment to John Blewbery the

Fig. 1 An armourer's workshop in the early 16th century: Maximilian I visits his armourer Konrad Seusenhofer, from the *Weisskunig*, 1514 illustrated by Hans Burgkmair (1473–1531)

parcellys ensuynge. First for the wages of the armorers of myllene vj li. xiij s. iiij d. Item for ij hogge hedde of wyne for the said armorers liij s. iiij d. Item for Caryage of the sayd wyne to Grenewych viij d. Item for the rewarde of the same armerers iiij li. Item for the glasyers of the same mylle and one spyndelle to the same glasyers iiij li. Item for a gryndestone and the beme to the same mylle xx s. Item for Caryage of thye same mylle and the glasyers to Grenewych ij s. In all xviij li. ix s. iiij d.

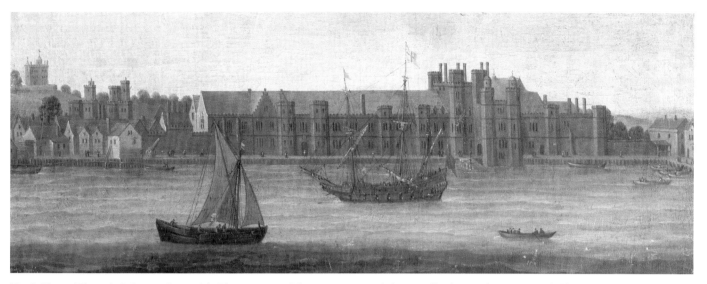

Fig. 2 View of Placentia Palace at Greenwich. The exact site of the armourers' workshop is still unknown, but it was probably in the complex of buildings just to the west of the palace © The Bridgeman Art Library

These particular Milanese armourers, who were under contract for two years from March 1511, are not mentioned again, though the payment records are incomplete, and other Milanese armourers are recorded later. There are further particulars about the mill and the armourers' gear. On 11 July 1511 John Blewbury was paid for:

A '*mill wheel with standard, two beams and bracys belonging thereto and two small wheels to drive the glasys 40 s.... for the wages of John Mylwryght for 12 days at 8 d. a day... 28 lb of soap for tempering the said mill at 2 d. a lb, 500 gauntlet nails [rivets] 8 d. ... three riveting hammers, 2 s., a pair of pynsors 2 s. 8 d., four crest files 4 s., two great files 5 s*[5]. In September 1511 Blewbury equipped the new forge at Greenwich with £13 worth of tools, vices, bicorns, bellows, stakes, shears, hammers, pincers, tongs, chisels, punches, a tool rack, water trough and tempering barrel, for the armourers of Brussels.'[6]

These armourers, Peter Fevers and Jacob 'Copyn' de Watte, certainly made armour for Henry VIII, for in the same month they delivered one to the King in Nottingham. They are recorded as armourers to the King at a half-yearly salary of £10 each in 1512, and this rose to £24 for Copyn and £30 for Peter Fevers in 1516. Peter died in 1518, and in October of that year his widow Joan was paid £117 6s. 8d. for harness made by him, comprising three complete harness '*with pieces of advantage for the tilt*', thirteen 'crynis' and three shaffrons – he had certainly been busy. Copyn continued to work after Peter's death, and was paid his £20 in September 1520 and 1524.[7]

Belonging to the earliest phase of Henry's new workshop, though whether or not it was made there is disputed, is the famous 'silvered and engraved' armour, made in 1514–17 (Royal Armouries no. II.5, VI.6–12).[8] The armour is silvered overall, formerly gilded and engraved through the silvering. The decoration includes scenes from the lives of saints George and Barbara and letters H and K joined by lovers' knots, and is thought to commemorate the marriage of Henry VIII and Katherine of Aragon. The maker's mark stamped on the back of the helmet, a crowned helmet, is similar to a mark used by Peter Fevers as a signature on a document, while on the bard is the same 'M' and crescent mark found on the Burgundian bard, now thought to have been made by one of Maximilian's armourers in Flanders, Guillem Margot;[9] the mark was attributed by Helmut Nickel to Martin van Royne, but recent research by Pierre Terjanian has changed the attribution of this mark.[10] The decoration was certainly the work of Paul van Vrelant of Brussels, who held the appointment of the King's 'harness gilder' with quarterly wages of 25s.[11] Paul was paid £66 13s. 4d. for '*graving harness*' in June 1516, part of a contract for £200 in three instalments for the making, engraving, gilding and silvering of a bard '*like sample according to a complete harness which of late he made for our body*', first contracted in 1514.[12] Vrelant was to provide the gold and silver, wages of workmen, coal and quicksilver, but not the '*barb, saddle, neckpiece and all in stele*'. This bard is clearly that of the 'silvered and engraved' armour, which was listed among the bards in the custody of George Lovekyn clerk of the stables in 1519: '*gilt with a trail of roses and pomegranates with the story of St George and St Barbara, and a crynny and shaffron wrought by Powle*'.[13] Both the armour and bard are Flemish in style, the bard being identical to plain ones for the battlefield also by Margot preserved in the Real Armeria in Madrid, the man's armour close to other plain Flemish pieces, which in turn bear close comparison to the work of the best contemporary Milanese makers, such as Niccolò Silva.[14]

The 'Almain' armourers at Greenwich first appear in 1515, and it is unclear whether they were entirely separate from or included Peter Fevers and Jacob 'Copyn' de Watte. Certainly they wore the same livery: John Blewbury (King's Armourer), John Crochet (Clerk of the Stable), Peter Fevers, Jacob 'Copyn' de Watte, and six master armourers (Dericke, Hans, Albert, Berengar (Berengar Gosse), Cons (probably Kunz Lochner senior) and Yesper), were all given green and yellow damask jackets, as recorded in the revel accounts of May 1515.[15] The first known list of the Almains is dated to the same month, Martin (van Royne), Dericke Hunger, Hans Mery, Hans Clinkdegell, Cons van Nuremberg, Hans Webler, Powlys Mer and Hans Drost the polishers, and Giles the apprentice. By June 1515 they were being paid by Blewbury £16 12s. 6d. each half year.[16]

In October 1516 a mill house in Southwark was hired at 6s. 8d. a week, and the royal armourers set up their workshop there. In July 1517 Henry Smith was paid for making the armoury house at Greenwich, between the palace and stables, to the north of the Grey Friars Church, and the following January George Lovekyn had the task of looking after the workmen there. The project, which also included a new mill house, would take until March 1520 to complete. In January and February 1520 the Almains were still working at Southwark, and Asmus (Erasmus Kirkenar) is first recorded in the account in February of that year, at a salary of £6 16s. 3d. per annum.[17] The Almains were soon joined by Dionys Hotzman of Augsburg, Anthony Schweizer and Wolfgang Grosschedel of Landshut, who returned home in 1521 and made royal armour until 1562, while Derick the Hungarian and Hans Mery disappeared.[18]

The Almains moved back into Greenwich in 1520, but it is not until the early 17th century that a clear picture emerges of the buildings which they occupied at Greenwich. By that time the bulk of the armours, 145 lances and 144 Flanders corselets as well as twelve Greenwich and other royal armours, mounted on horses of wood, were kept in the 'Green Gallery', presumably beside the tiltyard. Mr Pickering's 'Great Chamber' housed sixteen Greenwich armours and numerous parts of armours, the 'Workehouse' (or 'Mr Pickering's Workehouse') contained in 1611 seventeen armours, mostly unfinished, and most of the tongs, vices, hammers, chisels, stakes, anvils, shears, bellows, rasps and the 'panne of iron for fire with four wheels' that made up the tool kit of the workshop, while the Cutting House contained a few hammers, bicorns, grinding stones and old shears, and the Locksmiths Office contained just a few anvils, vices and bellows, 'Remayne of his Maties Armor and other municions in the several Armories at the Towre of London, Greenwich and Woolwiche now within the Chardge of Sir Thomas Monson knight Master of his highness Armory made in June 1611', and 'Remaine of the Armory taken at Sir Thomas Jay his coming to be Master of the Armory', February 1628/9.[19] The accession of Francis I to the throne of France brought a new entente between France and England, and this was embodied in the great tournament, the Field of Cloth of Gold, held between Calais and Guisnes, in 1520. The tournament would culminate in the signing of a peace treaty between the two powers, but also gave the two young kings ample opportunity to show off their chivalric skill. Complex negotiations preceded the event, and in the course of these a small but critical change in the rules for the armour worn in the foot combat event, in which Francis and Henry would fight in the same team, occurred. The original armour specified for the foot combat was 'field armour with pieces of advantage ... with an armet without ... helm, demi-helm nor basnet'. It is most probably that this unfinished armour survives as the Foot Combat armour of Henry VIII (Royal Armouries no. II.6 cat. no. 1). Some three months before the event, a different type of armour was specified for the event. Henry's agent in France, Sir Richard Wingfield, wrote on 16 March: 'touchyng the combatt at the barrier, ther is left out these words ffollowing "with pieces of advantage". And in stede thereof is sett "in Tonnelett and bacinett."'[20]

With this late change, the armourers at Southwark or Greenwich had only a very short time to make ready the new armour for the King to wear at the Field of Cloth of Gold. They succeeded in preparing an armour, now usually called the Tonlet armour, by adapting a number of existing pieces, manufacturing additional pieces from new, and decorating the armour. The armour has a great bacinet – the type of helmet traditionally used in the foot combat, originally made in Milan (marks of the Missaglia workshop of that city appear on the rear of the skull) but with a modified visor. The vambraces and leg defences were also adapted from existing field armours. Only the pauldrons and the hooped skirt or tonlet, were made new. The etched decoration includes figures of St George and the Virgin and child, Tudor roses, the collar of the Order of the Garter and, around top of the left greave, the garter itself. Erasmus Kirkenar went out with the royal entourage, and seems to have made his reputation as the king's armourer there. The armour survived in the palace at Greenwich until 1644 when it was transferred to the Tower of London. The leg defences, however, escaped, and were only reunited with the rest of the armour in 1947, having been in the collection of the Dymoke family, the hereditary Royal Champions, at Scrivelsby in Lincolnshire (Royal Armouries no. II.7).[21] The marks on the bacinet are crowned letters MY and a split cross over the letter M, a combination used by Tommaso Missaglia in 1450–2, and by his son Antonio Missaglia in partnership with his brothers Ambrogio and Filippo, 1452–92.[22]

At the jousts held on Shrove Tuesday (5 March) 1527 Henry appeared in a 'newe harness all gilte of a strange fashion that had not bene sene'.[23] His team, wearing cloth of gold embroidered with knots of silver, tilted before the French ambassadors with a team of nine led by the Marquis of Exeter in blue velvet and white satin like the waves of the sea. On 5 May that year another party of ambassadors from France, led by Francis II de la Tour d'Auvergne, Viscomte de Turenne, were entertained with jousts and an elaborate masque on the theme of the combined joy of the English and French peoples at the peace between their nations, the Alliance of Amiens, which had been signed on 30 April of that year. Turenne and Henry both took part in the masque, and the ambassadors departed bearing '*greate rewards*'.

The armour, if this identification is correct, survives in the collections of the Metropolitan Museum of Art in New York (fig. 3). It is dated 1527 in no less than five places, however, and Claude Blair has pointed out that when Henry first appeared in the armour the year (old style) was still 1526, and would not change until Lady Day 25 March.[24] It can, of course, be suggested that the armour was *intended* for use in 1527, and so dated, and might still, therefore, be identified as the armour worn first by the King at the start of the month. It is etched and gilded overall, the themes of the decoration including, on the leg defences, the labours of Hercules, and on the upper half a merknight and mermaid, supplemented with elephants and castles, and various putti and animals. It has been variously argued that the decoration was executed by the Florentine artist Giovanni da Maiano, who produced a similar scheme at Hampton Court, or by Hans Holbein, who is first recorded working for the King during his first stay in England in 1527–8 (though it could have been the work of both men as two hands seem to be responsible for the two types of decoration). The armour was made up by the Almain armourers at Greenwich, working under Martin van Royne. It includes a locking gauntlet for the tourney, and had a set of reinforces for the tilt, as its manifer survives though its grandguard and pasguard do not. It also includes saddle steels and the shaffron and crinet from its bard, but whether or not it had the other parts of the bard is unclear. It has the earlier example of two features known to be unique to the Greenwich workshop. This is an inner breastplate or ventral plate strapped to the body and designed to lift the weight of the cuirass and arm defences from the shoulders by means of the central bolt to which the breastplate and plackart ware secured. It is recorded that Francis I disclosed a secret device to Henry in 1520, offering to instruct his armourers to make one for Henry if he sent one of his arming doublets for a pattern, and it is likely the ventral plate was the secret device in question. If this was indeed made for Henry VIII, it is interesting to note that his waist measurement was a good deal less than 40 inches. The armour was purchased directly from the French family of Crussol, ducs d'Uzes, and it now bears a modern escutcheon with the arms of Jacques de Genouilhac, known as Galiot, Grand Master of the Artillery under Francis I, a relative of Turenne and ancestor of the Crussols.[25]

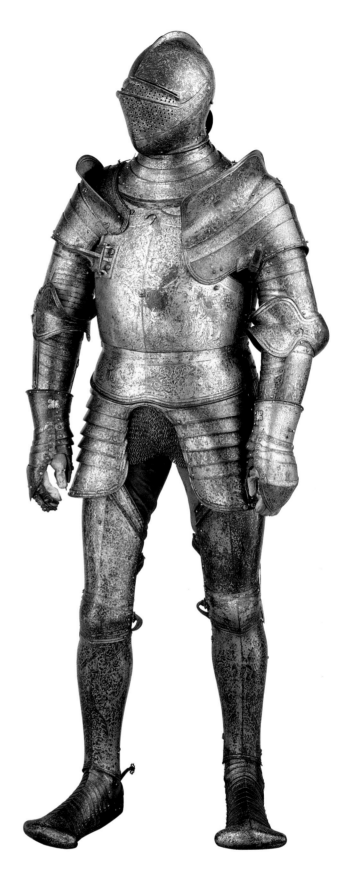

Fig. 3 The 'Genouilhac' armour for field and tournament made in Greenwich, dated 1527 and decorated with an overall etched and gilded design. The Metropolitan Museum of Art, New York. William H Riggs Gift and Rogers Fund, 1919 (19.131.1,2)

As Claude Blair has shown, the order of names in a Kent Subsidy Roll indicates that Erasmus Kirkenar had taken over from Martin van Royne as Master Workman by 1535. In the earliest of the lists of Almain armourers in which Erasmus Kirkenar appears as Master Workman in place of Martin van Royne (probably made in 1539), van Royne continued to be paid £25 5s. 10d., while Kirkenar was paid just £17 6s. 8d. and all the others £14 15s. The list of armourers of 1539 shows that the establishment was divided into two parts, a *'Kinges own armorie'* staffed by Erasmus Kirkenar, the chief armourer, 'Old Martin', Matthew Dethyke, Hans Clinkdegell and Jasper Kemp, and the main armoury, divided into two *'Shoppes'*, staffed by twelve armourers, two locksmiths, four apprentices and two millmen. Old Martin, who became known as 'de Prone' later in his life, was still working in 1549 and eventually died in 1552.[26] The armoury certainly both planned to sell armours at £12 each to the nobility at this time and succeeded, though at lower prices, as payments in 1536–7 for *'harness bothe for Tylte and felde with all manor of pyces be longing to the same'* at £8 from Mr Bartley and at £10 from Lord Matravers, Mr Carew, *'my lorde Parre'*, *Mr Poynynges*, Mr Knowelles, Mr Wyet, *'my Lorde of Surrey'* and *'my Lorde Makes Dosset'*, and for *'complete harness for the felde'* at £8 from *'Lorde Saynte Jones'*, Mr Lister and *'my lorde Comerland'*.[27] The account of 1544–5 lists armours, mostly *'blacke Complyt harness'* made for Henry Howard, Earl of Surrey, Thomas Howard, Duke of Norfolk, Lord Nevell, Mr Bellyngham and Mr Blunte.[28]

The greatest of the Greenwich garnitures created for Henry VIII was made in 1540, as is shown by that date etched in a panel on the collar. It is possible that is was intended for the King to wear at the tournament held during 1–5 May of that year, a *'royal Justes, Tornay and Barriers, whiche wer in white velvet barded and based. The Justes began the first daie of May, the Tornay the third daie, and the Barriers the fifth daie,'*[29] and is readily identifiable with the *'Complete harness parcell grauen and gilte with all manner of peces of advantage for the felde Tilte Turney and fote'* inventoried at Greenwich in 1547.[30] Not only does the armour have all the requisite extra pieces, but it has a double set of them. In addition it has the only other example of the ventral plate, first seen on the 'Genouilhac' armour. Unfortunately the breastplate for the field, tilt and tourney is lost. The decoration is at least in part by Hans Holbein, for a drawing by him of the tritons on the grandguard and breastplate is preserved in Basel. The two tournaments of 1540 were the last Henry VIII is known to have staged, though there is no record that he actually participated in them. Perhaps his advancing age, he was by this time 49, and increasing bulk prevailed against such physical exercise.[31]

Alan Williams and Tony de Reuck have shown that 'Old Martin' [van Royne or de Prone] was content to make armour of air-cooled medium carbon steel, but that this practice changed under Erasmus Kirkenar. From 1545 martensite starts to appear in the steel alongside pearlite and ferrite, and the hardness rises from 250–70 to 290–320 [Vickers hardness scale], probably by slack quenching, that is, leaving the heated metal to cool briefly in the air before quenching it.[32]

The Almain workshop developed a style of its own, which incorporated elements of Italian, Flemish and German armour. During the century of its serious production of armour fashions for both male dress and armour changed, and like all the makers of fashionable armour in Europe, the Almains at Greenwich followed it, while retaining their own distinctiveness. Much of this characteristic style is only visible from the inside of the armour, for example in the use of internal leathers rather than simple rivets for the articulation of shoulder and leg defences. In the 1550s a series of armours made with anime cuirasses appears, formed of articulated horizontal lames which gave the appearance of the *lorica segmentata* of Classical antiquity, following the Italian fashion of the mid 1540s. After 1560 the cut of the waist of the male doublet changed rapidly, acquiring a deep point at the lower front called a peascod, and the armourers followed this fashionable feature in steel. From Henry's reign onwards the form of extended armour or 'garniture', with extra interchangeable pieces usually for the different events of the tournament, became the standard product at Greenwich, but in times of war, such as the period of the Armada campaign, garnitures and single armours for the battlefield were produced in the same distinctive style. Etching and gilding, of borders and bands or complete overall schemes, was a characteristic skill of the Greenwich workshop, and the watercolour album by Jacob Halder, as well as the few surviving portraits including Greenwich armours, illustrate how these decorative features were combined with surface finishes of blues, blacks and russets as well as bright steel to make spectacular works of the armourer's art.

Erasmus Kirkenar died in 1567, and was replaced by the first English master workman, John Kelte, a London armourer who was one of four to join the armoury about 1539 and would serve as Master Workman until 1576. He had been apprenticed to John Lindsey, twice master of the Armourers Company, who is the subject of a melancholy note in the minute book of the Armourers Company that on 16 March 1563 *'he did most ungodly hang himself in his privy house'*; the contemporary London diarist Henry Machyn adds that he had done this because *'he had ys offes taken away from hym by on that he had browth up'*. Possibly he had hoped to succeed Erasmus Kirkenar as master of the Almain armoury.[33]

Under John Kelte Greenwich steel was fully tempered and quenched, raising its hardness to 325–380. One example of a decorated armour of about 1570 was that made for William Somerset, 3rd Earl of Worcester. Somerset's armour is a field garniture with the heaviest set of field reinforces known. A German from Landshut, Jacob Halder is first recorded in the 1558 list of the Almain armourers.[34] He was the compiler of what is known as the *Jacob Album* or the '*Almain armourer's album*', a vividly-illustrated volume, now unbound and in the Victoria and Albert Museum.[35] The artist is identified by inscriptions on several of the armours: '*these pieces were made by me Jacob*', on garnitures where other parts were made '*beyond sea*'. The first two in the series of illustrations, showing small field garnitures for the earls of Rutland and Bedford, are marked 'MR' and can be dated to 1553–8, the remainder, with 'ER', are from Elizabeth's reign and run in sequence up to about 1587. The first two thirds of the collection were originally kept as single sheets, but were bound with the illustrations of later field armours presumably around 1585. Claude Blair has established that the drawings were preliminary ones, intended to show to clients who would pay up to £500 for the privilege of buying such an armour, what they might expect in terms of decoration and garniture composition. There is no reason to assume, therefore, that all the designs in the album were ever executed, although they most probably all were.[36]

Robert Dudley, the Queen's favourite, had at least two armours made at Greenwich. Portraits of him wearing a lost armour are known, the armour that survives in the Royal Armouries also appears in a portrait of his brother-in-law, Henry Hastings, 3rd Earl of Huntingdon, dated 1588, and the first appears as no. 3 in the *Album*, the first marked ER (no. II.81).[37]

Sir Henry Lee (1523–1611) served Elizabeth I as the Queen's Champion at the Accession Day tilts from 1570 to 1590 and in that year was made Master of the Armouries.[38] The album contains designs for three armours for him, of which one complete armour and parts of another survive. George Clifford, 3rd Earl of Cumberland, succeeded Lee as Queen's Champion, and his armour survived at Appleby Castle until 1924 when it was bought by the American collector Clarence Mackay, and subsequently acquired by the Metropolitan Museum of Art, New York, in 1931 (no. 32.130.6). Best preserved of all the later Almain armours, it even retains its original blued and gilt finish. The light field armour of the military leader Sir John Smythe was given to King James I, and was with the other royal armours at Greenwich until being brought to the Tower in 1649 (Royal Armouries no. II.84) (fig. 4 and 5). It certainly included pieces made '*beyond sea*', such as the circular shield or target, which escaped via the collection of the Duc de Dino to the Metropolitan Museum is stamped with the pearled 'A' mark of Augsburg.

All but one of the last nine illustrations in the Album are for field armours or field garnitures of various sizes, and analysis of their owners suggests they date from 1585–7. The armour of Lord Buckhurst, preserved at the Wallace Collection, typifies this group (no. A62).[39] Only two decorated Greenwich armours from Halder's period in charge that post-date the Armada are known: a much restored second field armour of Sir James Scudamore of about 1590 in the Metropolitan Museum of Art, and an incomplete armour of about 1595 in the Art Institute of Chicago. Both are decorated just like the Buckhurst armour. In addition there were numerous plain Greenwich armours made, which went unrecorded in Halder's album. It is also most likely that just before his death he made two superb armours decorated with recessed etched and gilded bands, roses and thistles. One, now in the Royal Collection at Windsor Castle, made at a price of £340 for Henry Prince of Wales, the eldest son of King James I, who died in 1613, and another for £450 for Prince Friedrich Ulrich of Brunswick, now in an American private collection. It is possible, alternatively, that these were made by his successor.[40]

Jacob Halder died in 1608 and was succeeded by an Englishman, William Pickering, a member of the Armourers' Company. He served as the company's Upper Warden in 1603, and in 1608 was its Master as well as becoming Master Workman at Greenwich.[41] He was responsible for a large series of small tournament garnitures, of which no less than five survive in the Royal Armouries, including number II.73 which is probably the armour (or at least parts of it) depicted in the portrait by Mytens of Charles I as Prince of Wales about 1615 (Royal Armouries no. AL.15.4, on loan from the Government Art Collection, no. 2176).

Pickering died in 1618 and was succeeded by another London armourer, Thomas Stevens.[42] The armoury, already in decline, started to deteriorate rapidly, with quarrels among the Almains about who should lead them. Payments fell into arrears, and the tournaments for which they made armour ceased in England after the Whitehall joust of 1626 to celebrate the marriage of Charles I and Henrietta Maria. In 1625 there were complaints of financial impropriety, and a counter petition in which no less than 36 armours made by the workshop were listed. Stevens resigned in 1628 and died the next year, to be succeeded by Nicholas Sherman, a former apprentice of Jacob Halder.[43] He was probably responsible for the last Greenwich armour, the little harquebus armour of Charles II as prince. Internal examination shows this was made from an unfinished rose and thistle armour, and its punched and chiselled decoration shows the influence of Dutch armour in England (Royal Armouries no. II.92).[44]

In 1642 Edward Ansley, a London armourer and Almain Clerk, was commissioned to recover the royal armour from Greenwich, and in 1644 it was brought *en masse* to the Tower of London. Ansley rose up through the Armourers Company, as Renter Warden in 1645, Upper Warden in 1646–7 and Master in

1648–9, and in 1647 he became Surveyor of Works at Greenwich. In 1650 he was appointed Clerk of the Armoury at the Tower, with a salary of £65 8s. 8d. and would be the very last Master Armourer at the (formerly Royal) Armoury at Greenwich at £108 per annum. He most probably died in 1654.[45]

Despite the demise of the establishment that created them, and though the royal armoury would produce its last royal armour in 1686, the remaining Greenwich armours were to have a distinguished future.[46] With the restoration of Charles II in 1660 came a need to emphasise the continuity of the monarchy after the troubled times of the Civil War and Commonwealth. To this end a display known as the 'Line of Kings' was mounted at the Tower of London, depicting the good kings of England from William the Conqueror (wearing a plain Greenwich armour of about 1590, no. II.40) to the then present monarch.[47] This exhibition, made up largely of the pieces brought from Greenwich, was the beginning of the historical displays at the Tower which, in time, developed into the national museum of arms and armour as it is today.

Notes and references page 335.

Above: Fig. 4 Field armour of Sir John Smythe, part made in Augsburg, the rest made and all decorated with etching and gilding in Greenwich, about 1585. Royal Armouries II.84, III.1430–1

Above left: Fig. 5 Pen and watercolour illustration of the armour of Sir John Smythe from the Jacob Album by Jacob Halder. Victoria & Albert Museum, D.585–607.94

THE KING AND THE
ARMOURERS OF FLANDERS[1]

PIERRE TERJANIAN

*One of Henry VIII's undoubted achievements was to attract some of the finest armourers from
mainland Europe to work for him in London. Pierre Terjanian explores the roles of craftsmen
like Martin van Royne and Paul van Vrelant. He analyses the extant artefacts in the context
of the archival evidence allowing him to argue for a new identification of the armourer who
used the mark of a Roman M under a crescent, shedding light on some of the Royal Armouries'
most important Henrician armours. The author suggests that attracting migrant armourers
was only one way Henry was able to obtain fine armour; exploiting a network of contacts
gave him access to some of the best craftsmen working in Flanders.*

Henry VIII began his reign with the ambition of installing in his lands the best craftsmen that could be
had on the Continent to make fine armour for his
royal person, since none in his realms it seems, possessed the
requisite skills. Little is known about how the search was
conducted, but it was evidently carried out diligently, for within
two years following Henry's accession to the throne two groups
of armourers were recruited, one in Milan and the other one in
Brussels. This was seemingly not quite enough, however, for in
1515 a third group of foreign armourers drawn from Germany
and apparently also from the Low Countries, and collectively
known as the 'Almains', was also installed at Greenwich.[2]

The workshop of the Almains (known as the 'Almain
Armoury') was structured very much like the court workshop
that the Emperor Maximilian had founded in Innsbruck, at the
heart of the Austrian hereditary lands, in 1505. It was headed by
a chief armourer, also known as 'Master Workman'. This man
and the remainder of the staff earned wages paid by the King.
The shops and polishing mills in which the Almains worked
belonged to the King; the raw materials, combustibles, and tools
that they needed were also paid for by him. In return, during
Henry VIII's reign at least, the King paid nothing else for the
armour that they made, as it was deemed his property.

MARTIN VAN ROYNE: A FORMER ARMOURER TO
THE HAPSBURGS?

The first Master Workman of the Almains was Martin van
Royne, an armourer thought to have originated from the Low
Countries in view of the fact that the suffix 'van' in his name was
a common one there. Although van Royne must have had strong
credentials to be chosen to head the King's Almains, we do not
know what these were. Nothing at all is known of his career

before 1515, when he is first recorded in England.[3] However,
because the major part of the Low Countries were at the time
under the domination of the Hapsburgs (these territories will
henceforth be called 'Burgundian Low Countries'), and because
the Hapsburgs used the services of skilled armourers there, it has
been suggested that van Royne had perhaps acquired and
perfected his skills in their service, under the assumption that an
armourer of note in the Low Countries is likely to have attracted
their attention.[4]

Van Royne's past is of great interest because it was under his
leadership that many of the features that distinguish the original
style of armour produced by the Almains were introduced. While
some of these were perhaps adopted at the suggestion of staff
members, as Master Workman, van Royne was ultimately
responsible for the design and the quality of the armours
produced in the Almain Armoury. Because there can be little
doubt that he had the authority to decide how the armours
should be built and formed, as long as these met the
specifications laid out by the King, he should be regarded as the
principal architect of the distinctive suits that the Almains made
during his tenure – including the remarkable foot combat armour
of Henry VIII in the Royal Armouries (II.6 cat. no. 1) and the so-
called 'Fleuranges' armour in the Musée de l'Armée, Paris (inv.
G46, H57 cat. no. 24).

Van Royne's past is also intriguing because, following a
suggestion put forward by Helmut Nickel in 1982, he is
commonly suspected to be the author of two spectacular horse
bards of silvered, engraved, and formerly gilded steel in the Royal
Armouries (VI.6–12, cat. no. 18 and VI.1–5, cat no. 21), which
belonged to Henry VIII, and of other remarkable pieces in other
collections, all struck on some of their elements with an
armourer's mark, a Roman M under a crescent.[5] This mark, as

Claude Blair noted in 1965, belonged to an armourer who had ties to the Hapsburgs, since one of Henry's bards was a present from the Emperor Maximilian I of Austria, and since additional pieces struck with it mark are associated with the Hapsburgs. Blair argued that its owner (henceforth the 'M and crescent' Master) is likely to have been one of the armourers working in the Low Countries for Archduke Philip of Austria, or his son and successor Charles, on the grounds that the pieces bearing the mark are Flemish in style, and that one, the bard presented by Maximilian, was most likely decorated in the Low Countries.[6]

Nickel suggested that the mark was probably that which Martin van Royne used to sign his works before the time he became Master Workman of the Almains. In support of this attribution, Nickel argued that the pieces bearing the M and crescent mark share features that characterizes the very distinctive style of armour produced by the Almains during van Royne's tenure, and further noted that the mark could be easily explained as combining the initial for van Royne's first name (Martin) with an element from his family coat of arms, a half-moon between three stars.[7]

Although Nickel's attribution of the mark to van Royne provides an elegant solution to the origin of the style of armour that characterizes the works of Henry's Almains, it is fraught with difficulties. As was mentioned earlier, nothing is known about van Royne's life before 1515, thus there is not the slightest evidence in support of the supposition that he had worked for the Hapsburgs. Van Royne might have been a Netherlander, but he can conceivably also have been a German, as the suffix 'van' was also a common one in German territories adjacent to the Low Countries (as in Cologne).[8] More importantly, as Claude Blair pointed out in 2002, there is no certainty that the first Master Workman of the Almain Armoury belonged to the van Royen family whose coat of arms includes a crescent emblem. This prospect seems rather doubtful in light of the fact that his real name was perhaps 'Martin de Prone', since it is the one under which he is recorded in some of the lists of Almains, and that which he used in his last will.[9]

Conclusive proof that Martin van Royne did not ever own the M and crescent mark, however, is the evidence, noted by Blair, that the owner of this mark had ties to the Hapsburgs, and in all probability worked in their dominions in the Low Countries.[10] There is no mention, however, of a Martin van Royne, or Martin de Prone, in the accounts of the treasurers of the Hapsburgs in the Low Countries. These, particularly the accounts of their chief treasurer, The Receiver General of All Finances,[11] record in great detail the identity of the craftsmen who worked for them, the nature of the weapons and armour that they made, and the places in which these had been deposited. A consultation of these documents establishes that van Royne was not one of the armourers that they employed. If, as is probable, he was a Netherlander, the Hapsburgs do not seem to have ever been among his clients.

THE OWNER OF THE M AND CRESCENT MARK

In the light of this knowledge it is thus clear that the first Master Workman of the Almains was not an armourer that Henry had succeeded in taking away from the Hapsburgs, and that the King's magnificent two bards were the work of another armourer. The mark of this anonymous armourer is known to occur on a total of nine armours: (1) on the crupper of the so-called 'Burgundian bard' of silvered, engraved, and formerly gilded steel in the Royal Armouries (VI.6–12 cat. no. 18; the crinet is associated);[12] (2) on the peytral of the so-called 'silvered and engraved' bard of Henry VIII in the Royal Armouries (VI.1–5 cat. no. 21; the shaffron and crinet are associated);[13] (3 and 4) on the peytrals and cruppers of two bards of plain steel in the Real Armería, Madrid (inv. A.3 and A.4; their shaffrons and crinets are probably associated),[14] (5) on the breastplate, backplate, lance-rest, and the haute-pieces of both pauldrons of a fragmentary armour of plain steel in the Hungarian National Museum, Budapest (inv. 55.3260; the gorget is associated; the fastenings of the cuirass are restored);[15] (6) on the rear right side of an incomplete armet of plain steel formed of a bowl with brow plate riveted at the front, and cheekpieces hinged at the sides in the Metropolitan Museum of Art, New York (Bashford Dean Memorial Collection, Funds from various donors; acc. 1929.158.52; the visor is associated and the hinges are restorations);[16] (7) on the left side of the front portion of a jousting helm of plain steel in the same museum (Gift of Williams H. Riggs, 1913; acc. 14.25.572; the unmarked rear portion appears to be associated);[17] (8) on the rear right side of a foot-combat helm of plain steel formed of a bowl with visor and bevor both secured by hinge and pin to pivots at the sides, and a brass plume-holder riveted at the rear, also in the Metropolitan Museum (Bashford Dean Memorial Collection, Funds from various donors; acc. 1929.158.38; the mark is much rubbed: only the tips of the crescent are visible);[18] and (9) on each side of a couter of plain steel in the same museum (Bashford Dean Memorial Collection, Funds from various donors; acc. 1929.158.1h).[19]

The 'M and crescent' Master had ties to the Hapsburgs since four of his surviving works are connected to them. The most spectacular of these, the Burgundian bard, was a present from the Emperor Maximilian, as is specified in an inventory (1 May 1519) of items in the care of George Lovekyn, Clerk of the King's Stables, in the armoury in the tiltyard at Greenwich, in which the bard and its saddle are clearly recognizable.[20] Similarly, the two bards of plain steel bearing his mark in the Real Armería, Madrid are recorded in the earliest surviving inventory (1594) of the armoury of King Philip II of Spain, and one is illustrated in the pictorial inventory (about 1542) of the armoury of his father, the Emperor Charles V, at Valladolid.[21] Finally, the fragmentary armour in the Hungarian National Museum belongs to a group of objects originally from the collections of the Kunsthistorisches Museum, Vienna, that were ceded by Austria to Hungary in 1932/3, by virtue of an international treaty concluded in 1932.[22] Records at the Kunsthistorisches Museum suggest that the armour was in the imperial armoury of the Hapsburgs in Vienna, or in the collections of Schloss Laxemburg before it entered its own.[23] It thus appears to have been an old Hapsburg heirloom.

However, this armourer is likely to also have had ties to Henry VIII's court, since there are no indications that Henry received the silvered and engraved bard in the Royal Armouries as a present, and since the helm for the joust in the Metropolitan Museum appears to have hung over the tomb of Sir Anthony Browne (died 1548), Henry's Master of the Horse and Standard-Bearer, as it is believed to come from Battle Church, where Browne was buried with great pomp.[24]

One reason that Blair argued in favour of the view that this master probably worked in the Low Countries is the fact that the Burgundian bard was almost certainly decorated there by the goldsmith Paul van Vrelant. Van Vrelant entered Henry VIII's service in 1514 and was appointed as his harness gilder. Before that time, however, he appears to have resided in Brussels, where he worked for the Hapsburgs. In 1505 he was certainly living there, when he received from The Receiver General of All Finances a sum of 100 *livres* (the currency of Flanders) in payment of a gilded crinet that he had decorated at the orders of Archduke Philip of Austria, then also King of Castile.[25]

Once in England van Vrelant decorated armour for Henry. He silvered, engraved, and gilded an armour for the King's person in 1514, and immediately after that a bard to match that armour. Shortly thereafter, in 1515, he silvered, engraved, and gilded '*certan harness for the kinges grace*', thus unspecified pieces that perhaps were a second armour for the King in view of the fact that the sum he received for that task was more than that which he had received for the King's suit but much less than that which he had received for the bard.[26] The 'silvered and engraved' armour in the Royal Armouries is one of these armours or, more probably, a combination of both. The silvered and engraved bard in the Royal Armouries is naturally the bard engraved by van Vrelant to match that armour.

The Burgundian bard's engraved decoration is similar in execution to that of the silvered and engraved armour and bard, so much so that there can be little doubt that it is also van Vrelant's work. Since it is highly improbable, as Blair has argued, that Maximilian would have sent his gift to England for decoration by a craftsman employed by the recipient, there can be little doubt that it was decorated by van Vrelant in the Low Countries during the period he still resided there (thus before February 1514), from which it follows that it is likely to have been made by an armourer there.[27]

Blair's suggestion is fully supported by iconographic evidence that the pieces bearing the M and crescent mark are of types favoured in the Low Countries. His bards are all constructed with pieces individually formed in the manner of the caparisoned bards represented in the 'Tournament' tapestry panel, woven in Brussels for the Elector Frederic the Wise of Saxony, about 1495, and perhaps commemorating the tourneys held in celebration of the beginning of Philip the Handsome's personal rule (1494), in the Musée des Beaux-Arts, Valenciennes (inv. O.A. 87.19).[28]

Similarly, the fragmentary armour in the Hungarian National Museum, made about 1510–15, compares closely in construction and form to that on the figure of St George in a panel from a Netherlandish altar, painted about 1510, in the Germanisches National Museum, Nuremberg (inv. Gm 69) (fig. 1); and to that worn by another figure of St George, in the left wing of an altar painted by Joos van Cleef the Elder, about 1530, in the Kunsthistorisches Museum, Vienna (Gemäldegalerie, inv. GG 938) (fig. 2). Incidentally, the couter in the Metropolitan Museum of Art is quite similar to those of the armour worn by St George in the first of these two panels.

Finally, the front portion of the jousting helm in the Metropolitan Museum of Art is constructed in the manner of examples made by Flemish armourers, including a helm in the Royal Armouries believed to come from Stowe Church and bearing the much abraded marks of the Master of the crowned 'h' (IV.1 cat. no. 7), a piece that is further related in having a rectangular opening at the right side, for ventilation, protected by an integral flange.[29] The Metropolitan Museum's piece was never meant to be permanently riveted to the piece that protected the wearer's skull and the nape, in the manner of German examples, but was presumably secured to it by strap and buckle, or perhaps by pivots at the temples in the manner of the helm from Stowe, and another helm by the same Flemish armourer in the Kunsthistorisches Museum, Vienna (Hofjagd- und Rüstkammer, inv. B. 141).[30]

GUILLEM MARGOT

Since it can be established beyond reasonable doubt that the 'M and crescent' Master was an armourer active in the Low Countries, it seems likely that the some of the armour that he made for the Hapsburgs should be recorded in the detailed accounts of their chief treasurer there, i.e. The Receiver General of All Finances, as this particular treasurer was the one who normally paid for the arms and armour that they commissioned. His accounts record many payments to craftsmen who supplied, embellished, and maintained swords, hafted weapons, crossbows, spurs, horse bits, saddles, horse bards, shaffrons, and armour for the bodies of the sovereigns and their armouries in Brussels.

The receiver general's accounts indicate that, while a number of armourers made shaffrons at the sovereigns' request, only one supplied bards during the entire period 1494–1530, i.e. during the time the bards bearing the M and crescent mark were certainly made. His name was Guillem Margot.

Margot was one of the Hapsburgs' favourite armourers in the Low Countries. He is first recorded in the accounts of the receiver general in 1505, when he was paid for a man's armour and a horse bard that he had made for Archduke Philip's use in his forthcoming military campaign against the Duke of Guelders.[31] It is clear that by that time he was already a seasoned armourer. Almost all the items that he delivered on that occasion are expressly identified as being for the sovereign's personal use. In view of the fact that his pieces were to be worn in an actual military campaign, it is probable that Philip had already used his services or at the very least had heard the best things about his abilities. Philip actually presented one of the armours made by Margot to an Italian nobleman in the retinue of Bianca Maria Sforza, his father's second wife.

The bard that Margot made for Philip in 1505 was a full bard comprising collar and crinet. The sum of 144 livres, which he received for it, was an enormous one, equivalent to three times the price that the receiver general customarily paid for a complete armour made for the sovereign's body. In this light the bard appears to have been of the highest quality, hardly the kind of item that one would order from a novice.

Over the following years Margot periodically delivered armour and bards to the Hapsburg court. He was particularly active during the period preceding Charles's accession to the thrones of Castile and Aragon (1515) though he kept working for Charles thereafter, particularly just before Charles' trip to Aachen in 1520, to be crowned King of the Romans. The accounts show that Margot made armours for Charles on numerous occasions; i.e. in 1508, 1509, 1511, 1515 and 1517, when Charles was about eight, nine, eleven, fifteen, and seventeen years old. Margot also made armours in 1518 and 1520 for Charles's younger brother, Archduke Ferdinand, who briefly governed the Burgundian Low Countries while Charles was in Spain. After 1520, Margot's name is no longer mentioned in the accounts.

Margot appears to have excelled at making bards. In addition to the bard that he made for Philip in 1505, Margot made three bards of plain steel for Charles, for which he received 100 livres a piece. He delivered two of these in 1512 and the last in 1515. These three bards were in all probability the ones that Charles took with him to Spain, along with a large retinue and a large portion of his armoury, when he left the Low Countries for the

Fig. 1 (left) St George in a panel from a Netherlandish altar, painted about 1510 (Gm 69) © Germanisches National Museum, Nuremberg

Fig 2 St George, in the left wing of an altar painting by Joos van Cleef the Elder, about 1530 (GG 938) © Kunsthistorisches Museum, Vienna

first time in June 1517 to meet his new subjects, following his accession to the thrones of Castile and Aragon in 1516.[32] The two bards bearing the 'M and crescent' mark in the Real Armería are likely to be their remains, not only because Charles established his Spanish armoury at Valladolid and at least one of the Real Armería's bards was in that armoury by about 1542, but also because, upon close examination, it becomes clear that the two bards in question are the remains of originally three nearly identical bards of plain steel. Indeed, one of them (inv. A. 3) consists of elements from originally two distinct bards, as the turned edges of its peytral (chest piece) (struck with the 'M and crescent' mark) are plain whereas the turned edges of its flanchards (side panels) (unmarked) and crupper (rump defence) (struck with the same mark) are roped exactly in the same manner as the turned edges of the peytral (marked), flanchards, and crupper (marked) of the other bard, which is thus homogeneous. From this it follows that the Real Armería possesses the remains of originally three bards by the 'M and crescent' Master, two of which seem to have formed a pair.

In view of the fact that he appears to have been the sole maker of bards of steel for the court of the Hapsburgs from 1494 through 1530, and considering that the letter 'M' in the 'M and crescent' mark matches the initial of his family name, there can be little doubt that Margot is the author of the bards bearing this mark and, by extension, of all the other pieces known to be struck with the same mark.

Final proof that Margot and the 'M and crescent' Master were a same person is provided by the record of the armour that he made for the Hapsburgs, as the accounts of the receiver general show that he made all the kinds of pieces known to bear this mark. Margot made armour for the field, the joust, the foot tourney, and the foot combat. Margot's repertoire also comprised garnitures. In 1520 he was paid for four harnesses with '*double pieces*' for the joust and the tourney that he had made for Ferdinand's personal use and his armoury.[33] These documented deliveries are absolutely consistent with the corpus of pieces struck with the 'M and crescent' mark, especially with the nature of the three helmets in the Metropolitan Museum of Art.

The two splendid bards of Henry VIII in the Royal Armouries were thus made by one of the most important armourers in Brussels. It is not known when Margot made the spectacular Burgundian bard because, from the time Philip began his personal rule (1494), the treasurers in the Burgundian Low Countries no longer took any orders from Maximilian. Consequently, there is no mention of any armour commissioned by him after that date.

Since with Peter Fevers and Jacob de Watt, two armourers recruited in 1511 in Brussels and thereafter working for the King's body at Greenwich through the time of their deaths (1517/8 and 1533/40, respectively)[34], and van Vrelant, his harness-gilder, Henry had in his service craftsmen specializing in the manufacture and decoration of armour, who originated from the very city in which Margot was active, he lacked no expert intermediaries to secure a bard made by Margot. As was noted earlier, the Burgundian bard made by Margot and presented by Maximilian to Henry was almost certainly decorated by van Vrelant in Brussels. Van Vrelant and Margot are thus likely to have known each other, at least in a professional capacity. Since in 1505 Margot made an expensive bard for Philip's use in his military campaign in Guelders, and since in the same year van Vrelant was paid for having enriched a crinet for Philip's use in the same campaign, it is possible that van Vrelant was already decorating horse armour made by Margot by that time. Therefore because when it came to crafting horse bards Margot appears to have had no match in the Low Countries; van Vrelant would have certainly thought of him when Henry resolved to have a bard that would complement his silvered and engraved armour.

Whether working in their homeland or at his court, the armourers of the former Low Countries thus played an important part in the provision of fine quality armour in the early part of Henry's reign. The identification of the 'M and crescent' Master confirms that Henry's silvered and engraved bard and his Burgundian bard were made in the Burgundian Low Countries, by an armourer closely connected to the Hapsburgs. Like earlier Flemish colleagues known to have worked for the Valois and Hapsburg sovereigns of their homeland, such as Martin Rondelle in Bruges, Lazare de St Augustin in Valenciennes, or the anonymous 'Master of the crowned h',[35] Margot made armour for clients in England. Henry certainly seems to have thought quite highly of the armourers active in the Low Countries. Aside from the fact that he took several craftsmen from Brussels in his service, and the possibility that the first two men chosen to head his Almain Armoury, Martin van Royne and Erasmus Kirkenar, were perhaps Netherlanders, there is a report that the King sought to recruit additional armourers in Brussels in 1515, when the Almains were already in Greenwich. According to a source that could not be verified, Charles of Austria apparently instructed his chief chamberlain, sent to England on a mission, to inform Henry of the probability that the magistrate of Brussels would use every means in its power to prevent the further emigration of skilled armourers to England.[36] If this account is true, Charles' response is likely to have been a tactful way of letting Henry know that he was depleting the Low Countries of men whose skills were much valued at home, and which he also very much required.

Notes and references page 336.

{16}

PORTRAIT OF HENRY VIII

After Hans Holbein the Younger
Oil on panel, English school, late 16th century

In this three-quarter length portrait the King is depicted in at the age of 46, facing and looking to the front, wearing a jewelled cap, grey slashed doublet, scarlet gown or gaudekin trimmed with brown fur, his right hand holding gloves, wearing on his left index finger a ring enamelled with the royal arms. He wears a jewelled collar and a second collar with initial H's on it, from which is suspended the St George of the Order of the Garter. The painting was latterly preserved in an English country house, the Tudor-Gothic Butleigh Court near Glastonbury built in 1845 by J C Buckler for Henry Neville-Grenville. It was cleaned in 1957: *'when they got it, it was quite black, the jewels in the cap and the pillar behind the king's right shoulder were invisible. The cleaning revealed the baldric of pearls across the tunic from the left shoulder'* which passes curiously under the slashing of the doublet.

This is one of the standard, late portraits derived from the Whitehall Palace Privy Chamber wall-painting of 1537 by Hans Holbein. The original painting, which included portraits of Henry VII, Elizabeth of York and Jane Seymour, was destroyed by fire in 1698, but its form is known from the ink and water-colour cartoon which is preserved in the National Portrait Gallery (NPG 4027) and a copy of the entire painting by Remigius van Leemput in the Royal Collection (RICN 405750) painted in 1667, as well as numerous later versions in full, three-quarter and half-length forms. The first full-length portrait of a reigning English monarch, it was commissioned and officially endorsed by the king to communicate his power and majesty to his people, in a deliberate act of state propaganda. Other versions after Holbein include the full-length portrait in the Walker Art Gallery, Liverpool, another at Parham Park, and two attributed to Holbein's contemporary Hans Eworth at Trinity College Cambridge and Chatsworth House. There are several later examples dating to the later 16th and early 17th centuries, including examples in the Royal Collection (RICN 404438), St Bartholomew's Hospital and Belvoir Castle. The small half-length portrait by Holbein, probably painted in 1534–6, in the Thyssen-Bornemisza Museum, Madrid, is similar in form. TR

PROV. Presented by Rupert L Joseph, October, 1957. Formerly at Butleigh Court, Glastonbury, Somerset, sold by Captain Richard Neville, Christies, 5 April 1946

1130 x 900 mm (44.5 x 35.5 in)

REF. (1) Downman 1865

{1.51}

{17}

PARADE ARMOUR
FOR A YOUTH

Armour of the future Charles V made by Konrad Seusenhofer
Austrian, Innsbruck, 1512–14

Henry's first foreign enterprise, alliance with the Holy Roman Emperor Maximilian I (reigned 1493–1519) against the French, culminated in victory in the battle of the Spurs (named after the rapidity of the French knights in retreat) on 16 August 1513. They met before the battle '*in the fowlest wether that lightly have been seen since*' and formed a cordial understanding. Maximilian himself with 30 of his men-at-arms took part in the battle. The victim of the battle was the town of Tournai, into which Henry rode in triumph. Beside him rode his nephew the young Archduke Charles, later King Charles V of Spain. Naturally Henry immediately held a tournament there, in the market square, taking up all the paving slabs to prepare the surface for the horses.

Maximilian celebrated the alliance between England and the Empire with the presentation of the celebrated gift armour to Henry. At the same time he commissioned from Konrad Seusenhofer, his court armourer in Innsbruck, a similarly decorated armour for the young Archduke Charles.

The armour, made for the Archduke Charles (1500–58) when aged between twelve and fourteen years old, is made in the 'puffed and slashed' style most fashionable for armour in the second decade of the 16th century. It has an armet, a cuirass with a fluted plate base or skirt fastened over the waist flange, tubular pauldrons imitating textile over-sleeves, and conventional vambraces embossed with puffed and slashed ornament in imitation of fashionable textile garments of the period. The gauntlets are short cuffed, and turn on the cuffs of the vambraces. The leg harness are of conventional form, embossed with puffed and slashed ornament, with full plate sabatons. The base, cuirass, shoulder defences and the wings of the poleyns are constructed with recessed borders and vertical bands designed to accommodate fretted silver-gilt panels, many of which survive. These are decorated with the ragged staves, firesteels (shaped like the Lombardic letter B for Burgundy) and suspended sheepskin badges of the Order of the Golden Fleece, the order of knights founded by Philip III of Burgundy in 1430 in imitation of the English Order of the Garter. It was headed subsequently by Charles's grandfather Maximilian, his father, Philip the Handsome and himself, and Charles was invested in 1501. Much of the silver-gilt decoraton is missing, and is thought to have been removed during the reign of Maria Theresa for the manufacture of currency. The components decorated with the silver panels are otherwise plain, but the other parts of the armour are richly decorated with etched and gilded floral ornament following the edges and the puffs and slashes imitating fashionable garments.   TR

REF. Capucci 1990: 128–31; Innsbruck 1954: 66–7, no.62; Richardson 2004: 9; Thomas & Gamber 1976: 206, taf 110

Hofjagd- und Rüstkammer of the Kunsthistorisches Museum, Vienna

{A109}

18

THE BURGUNDIAN BARD

Horse armour of Henry VIII by Guillem Margot, decorated by Paul van Vrelant

Flemish, about 1511–14

This bard, or horse armour, of steel consists of a shaffron for the horse's head, crinet for his neck, peytral for the front of the horse's body, crupper for the rear and flanchards for the sides, together with a set of saddle-steels and decorated plates for the reins. It is decorated with the firesteels and crossed ragged staves, intervening spaces being filled with scrolling tendrils bearing pomegranates, the ornament being embossed in high relief with details rendered by engraving. The entire surface was silvered and at least partly gilded, though little silver and none of the gilding has survived.

It formed another part of the gift of armour to Henry VIII from the Holy Roman Emperor Maximilian I. Unlike the personal armour the Emperor gave him, which was made at Innsbruck, this part of the gift was made in one of Maximilian's provinces, Flanders. Unlike the armour of the court armourer, Konrad Seusenhofer, whose maker's mark is unknown, the maker of this piece stamped his mark, an M and crescent, on the horse armour. The mark was formerly identified by family heraldry as that of Martin van Royne or de Prone of Brussels, who was to be found in Henry's own employ as master armourer in his newly formed royal armour workshop at Greenwich, but identified recently as Guillem Margot, an armourer of Brussels commissioned by Maximilian I to make numerous important armours including horse bards.[1] Examples of the same maker's plain bards survive in the Real Armería, Madrid. The etching and gilding is also attributed to a master who was subsequently found working in London for the king, Paul van Vrelant. The bard was still with Maximilian's gift armour at Greenwich in the 1547 inventory, '*A barde of stele with a Burgonion Crosse and the fusye* (firesteel)'.[2]   TR

PROV. Transferred to the Tower from the Palace at Greenwich 1644

As mounted height 1940 mm (76.6 in), width 1010 mm (39.8 in), length 2400 mm (94.7 in), total weight 32.46 kg (71 lb 8 oz); Crupper: height 630 mm (24.9 in), width 1010 mm (39.9 in), length 890 mm (35.1 in); Flanchard: height 315 mm (12.4 in), length 685 mm (27 in); Peytral: height 670 mm (26.4 in), width 695 mm (27.4 in), length 595 mm (23.5 in); Crinet: length 640 mm (25.3 in); Shaffron: height 610 mm (24 in), width 330 mm (13 in), depth 300 mm (12 in); Rein plates: length 685 mm (27 in), saddle height 670 mm (26.4 in), width 760 mm (30.0 in), length 480 mm (18.9 in)

PUB. Blair 1965a; Richardson 2004: 11

REF. (1) Terjanian 2006; (2) Dillon 1888: 279

{VI.6-12}

19

PARADE ARMET OF HENRY VIII

Horned helmet by Konrad Seusenhofer

Austrian, Innsbruck, 1511–14

This extraordinary helmet is all that remains of what was probably the finest armour ever seen in England.

The skull is in the form of an armet, with cheekpieces hinged at either side. It is embossed with recessed panels bordered by small rivet holes for the attachment of the original silver-gilt decorative panels. The lower edge is flanged to turn on the collar, and the main edges are bordered with brass-capped iron lining rivets with circular washers, some retaining fragments of the original leather lining band. At either side is a slot through which a realistically embossed and formerly gilded steel ram's horn is inserted, and attached rather crudely by rivets. The cheekpieces follow the shape of the skull, are similarly bordered with original lining rivets, and have half hinges in raised notches low at either side, for the attachment of an additional face defence. They do not meet under the chin, and both have rather broken out regions at that point. At either ear is a rosette of six pierced holes etched with a rosette of flowers centred on each hole. The lining rivets on the cheekpieces are etched around with four-petalled flowers with sepals, probably intended to be roses. Each side hinge has an etched dragon, and the borders are etched with narrow bands of hatching. Traces of gilding remain on these on the right cheekpiece, and it is likely that all the etched areas were originally gilded. At the centre front of the skull is a restored hinge, which engages the apparently original hinge at the top of the mask. The mask is embossed with a full face, with a long, hooked nose complete with dewdrop, and many of the features including the eyes and mouth are fretted. Under the chin are two studs of some age (but probably not original) for some earlier attachment to the cheekpieces. High at either side are crude slots where the mask was forced over the cheekpieces. Across the brow is a narrow recessed band bordered by small rivet holes for a silver-gilt fretted band matching those of the skull. Over the eyes are bolted a pair of brass spectacle frames, the right eyepiece mended with rivets at either side (with iron patches at the back) and at the join of the frame. The mask is etched with a similar border to that of the skull, though slightly cruder in execution, and is humorously etched with stubble, eyebrows, shading on the lips and creases at the corners of the eyes.

The presentation armour from which this is the only surviving element was commissioned by the Holy Roman Emperor Maximilian I in 1511 from Konrad Seusenhofer, the master workman of the Emperor's imperial armour workshop at Innsbruck, as a gift for the young King Henry VIII, who was already an ally of the emperor's against the French. After long delays and wrangling over expenses, the armour was delivered in 1514 by the master's brother Hans, who was also an armourer, together with another armour that Henry had commissioned privately. Seusenhofer manufactured at the same time a similar armour for Henry's companion at the triumph at Tournai, the Archduke Charles V, and this armour survives in the Kunsthistorisches Museum in Vienna (cat. no. 17). Comparison between the two shows that Henry's armour too was decorated with the same silver-gilt fretted panels laid over velvet which survive on Charles' armour, as well as being etched with further decoration and partially gilded. The main part of the armour is identifiable from the 1547 inventory of Henry's possessions as the '*Harnesse given unto the kings Majestie by Themperor Maximilian wth a base of stele and goldesmythe worke Silver and guilte with A border abowt the same silver and guilte of Goldesmythes work*' in the first house at Greenwich.[1] This armour was apparently sold off as scrap in 1649 at the end of the English Civil Wars and the establishment of the Commonwealth. The helmet was separated in 1547, for it was with a '*playne harness*' on the third horse in the second house at Greenwich, '*a hedde pece with a Rammes horne silver parcell guilte*'.[2] The surviving helmet was used in 17th-century displays at the Tower of London as part of the '*armour of Will Somers*', Henry VIII's court jester. One hundred and fifty years after its manufacture its original ownership had been completely forgotten.

In more recent years huge academic arguments have raged over the authenticity of the helmet. Whether, for example, the ram's horns and spectacles were originally part of it, or added later, and above all why such an unflattering object should have been given by one monarch to another. These arguments have never been completely resolved, and the helmet remains an enigmatic survival of an extraordinary work of art.　TR

PROV. Transferred to the Tower from the Palace at Greenwich 1644

Height 335 mm (13.2 in), width 485 mm (19.1 in), depth 370 mm (14.6 in), weight 2.89 kg (6 lb 6 oz)

PUB. Blair 1974; Borg 1974; Richardson 2004: 8

REF. (1) Dillon 1888: 279; (2) Dillon 1888: 279

{IV.22}

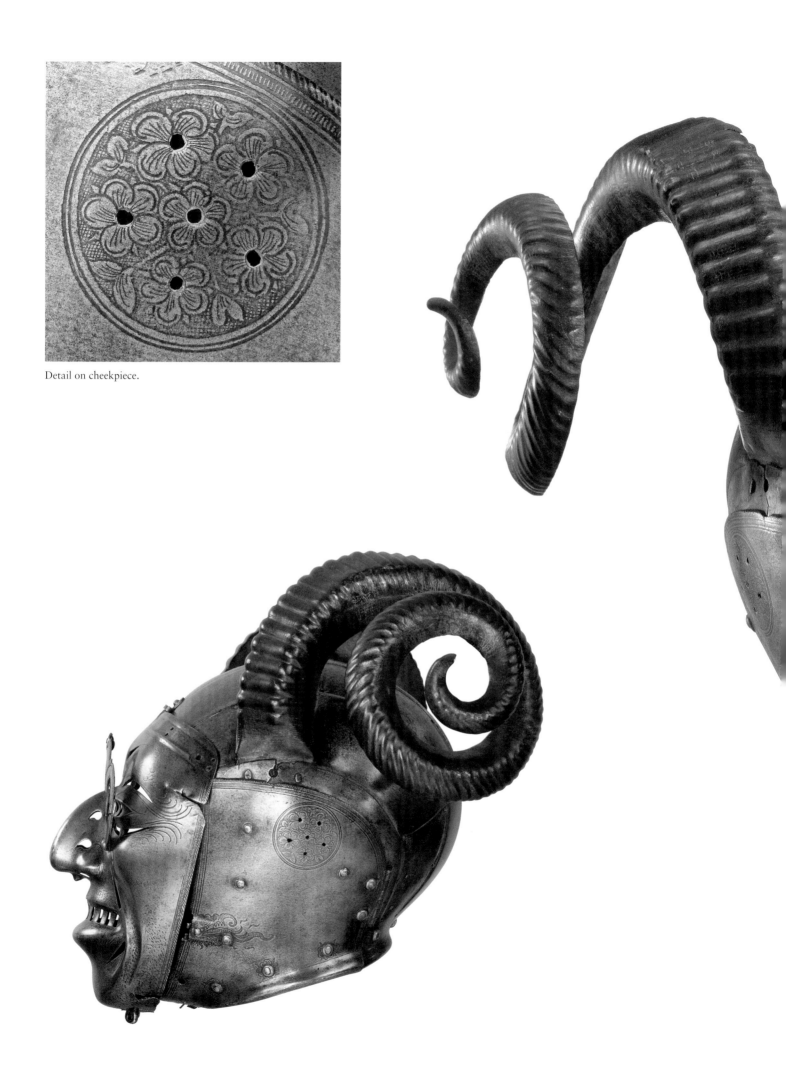

Detail on cheekpiece.

{20}

ARMET

Armet possibly for Henry VIII, attributed to Konrad Seusenhofer

Austrian, Innsbruck, about 1510–15

The Holy Roman Emperor Maximilian I reigned from 1493–1519. He was an important patron of armourers, particularly Konrad Seusenhofer (1450/60–1517), an armourer of Augsburg whom he established as master armourer in his royal workshop in Innsbruck, to the outrage of the Innsbruck armourers. So influential was Maximilian that a whole style of armour, in which the rounded forms of the Italian style was merged with the fluted German style, is now named after him. Seusenhofer was probably the greatest armourer of his day, and all his surviving products are now regarded as masterpieces.

The helmet is formed of steel, with a long and elegant skull embossed with fluting, and large, hinged cheekpieces, all forged with a flange at the lower edge so when close the helmet turned on the upper edge of the gorget. The visor is of the 'bellows' form popular in Germany in the early 16th century. The etched and gilded decoration is now rubbed but still clear. Above the sights on the visor a band of decoration includes a putto riding a goat and a human figure emerging from a dragon's mouth, all amongst foliage, while around the neck is a band of roses, one around each lining rivet. Similar roses appear on a jousting armour preserved at Vienna, and there are two other armets very close to this one in form and detail, also preserved in Vienna, all attributed to Konrad Seusenhofer (nos B 16, A 244 on the armour of Matthais Lang de Wellenberg of 1511, and A 295). The lining rivets retain leather lining bands to which the original quilted linings survive on the cheekpieces.

Although the famous armour given by Maximilian I to Henry is known to be by Konrad Seusenhofer, contemporary documents reveal that the King had earlier ordered two armours from the imperial workshop, probably in 1510, and these were delivered together with the gift armour, by Konrad's brother Hans, in 1514. Certainly there were three armours by the great master in the King's collection, and it is just possible that this helmet formed part of one of those armours. This helmet is one of the finest armets of the Renaissance in England, is etched with Tudor roses around the lining rivets that surround its lower edge, and physically fits other elements of Henry's head defences. Thus it is possible that this helmet was part of the armour commissioned from Konrad Seusenhofer by the King.   TR

PROV. Probably old Tower collectionl, transferred to the Rotunda Museum of Artillery, Woolwich and returned in 1927

Height 148 mm (5.83 in), width 240 mm (9.45 in), depth 350 mm (13.78 in), weight 3.49 kg (7 lb 7 oz)

REF. Blair 1965a; Blair 1974: 175; Dufty & Reid 1968: pl.xc; ffoulkes 1928: 63–4, pl. x, fig. 2; Richardson 2004: 10; Woolwich 1889: 147, no. xvi.21; Woolwich 1874: 135, no. 2085

{IV.412}

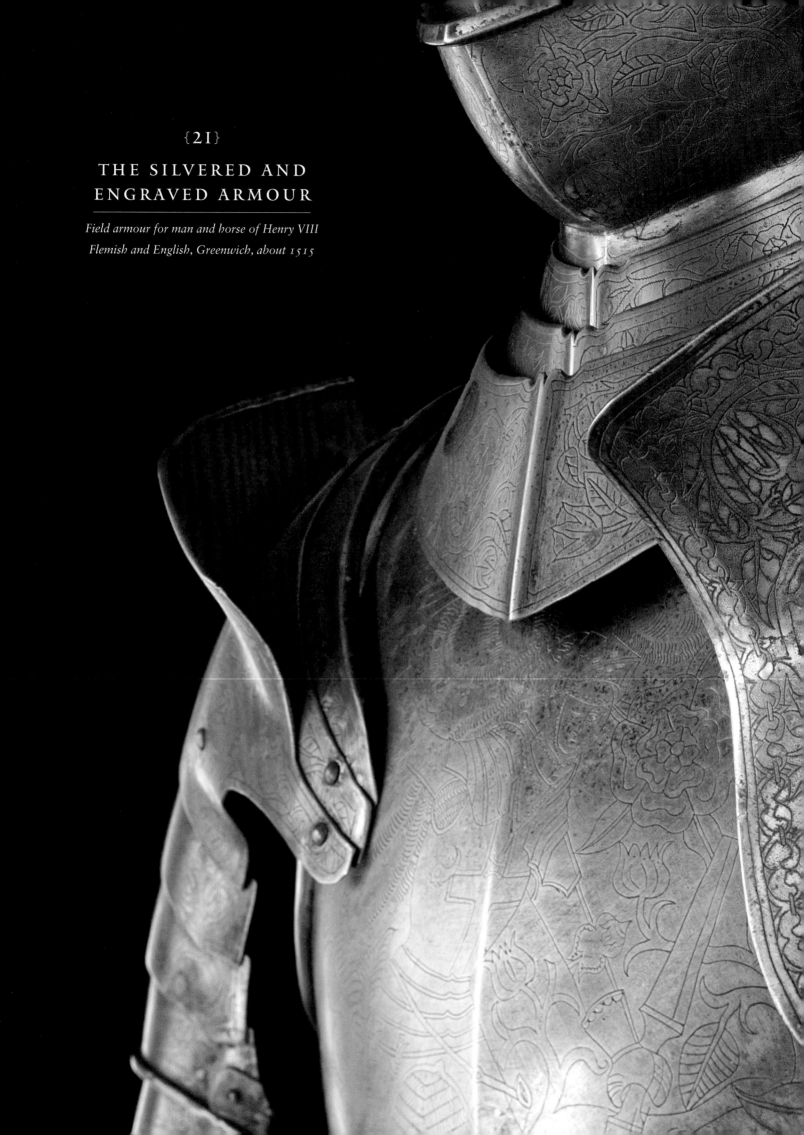

{21}

THE SILVERED AND ENGRAVED ARMOUR

Field armour for man and horse of Henry VIII

Flemish and English, Greenwich, about 1515

The first known product of Henry's new workshop is the famous 'silvered and engraved' armour, made about 1515. The armour is silvered overall and formerly gilded, and engraved through the silvering. The decoration commemorates the marriage of Henry VIII and Katherine of Aragon. On the breastplate is a figure of St George and on the backplate one of St Barbara. The rest of the armour is decorated with an all-over pattern of scrolling foliage flowering with the Tudor rose and fruiting with the pomegranates of Aragon. On the back of each greave is a female figure emerging from the calyx of a flower; the neck-band of the figure on the left greave is inscribed *glvck* ('good fortune'). The wings of the poleyns bear the sheaf of arrows badge of Ferdinand II of Aragon and the combined Tudor rose and Katherine's pomegranate badge, while the toecaps of the sabatons have the castle badge of Castile and the Tudor portcullis. The base or skirt has an applied copper alloy border incorporating the repeated intertwined letters H and K for Henry and Katherine.

The decoration of the horse armour matches that of the man's armour, and is based around scenes from the lives of the two saints. On the left boss of the peytral, Saint George is brought before the procurator Dacian and refuses to recant his Christianity. On the left side of the crupper are three more scenes from the life of Saint George. At the front he is tortured in a bull-shaped cauldron of molten lead, but is protected by the Lord. At the rear the saint is tortured on two wheels fitted with swords, but is undamaged by them. On the upper panel is his execution. On the right side of the peytral Saint Barbara talks to masons about building a third window, representing the trinity, into a tower they are constructing. On the right front of the crupper Saint Barbara is driven through a gateway by her father Dioscorus and at the rear she is escorted by men with bundles of twigs for whipping, while a bagpiper plays in the background (see page 175). On the upper panel she is executed by her father Dioscorus for refusing to recant her Christianity, and in the same scene, her father is shown dead after being struck by lightning. At the front of the peytral is a scene of Saint George slaying the dragon, and at the rear of the crupper the initials H and K, with a rose, are supported by putti. The side panels or flanchards are decorated with winged mermen holding shields with combined rose and pomegranate badges, flanked by portcullis and sheaf of arrows badges for the king and his queen. The lower border of the bard is decorated with the King's motto *'Dieu et mon droit'*, interspersed with roses and pomegranates.

The maker's mark, a crowned helmet stamped on the back of the skull, is similar to the mark used by Peter Fevers, one of the Flemings working for the king at Greenwich. This identification is not certain however, and it is quite possible that the armour

Maker's mark on the helmet.

was made by the Italians Filippo de Grampis and Giovanni Angelo de Littis who were working at Greenwich from 1512–15, as it bears considerable stylistic similarity to contemporary Italian armours such as those made by Niccolò Silva. It is equally possible the man's armour was made in Flanders by an unidentified armourer. The bard was certainly made in Brussels as it bears the 'M and crescent' mark now attributed to Guillem Margot. The armour is known to have been acquired as a plain harness and decorated in England. The decoration is the work of Paul van Vrelant, originally from Brussels, who held the appointment of the King's 'harness gilder' from 1514 until at least 1520. He was paid £66 13s. 4d. for *'graving harness'* in June 1516, part of a contract for £200 in three instalments for the making, engraving, gilding and silvering of a bard *'like sample according to a complete harness which of late he made for our body'*, first contracted in 1514.[1] Vrelant was to provide the gold and silver, wages of workmen, coal and quicksilver, but not the *'barb, saddle, neckpiece and all in stele'*. This bard is clearly that of the silvered and engraved armour, which was listed among the bards in the custody of George Lovekyn clerk of the stables in 1519: *'gilt with a trail of roses and pomegranates with the story of St George and St Barbara, and a crynny and shaffron wrought by Powle'*.[2] TR

PROV. Transferred to the Tower from the Palace at Greenwich 1644

Height of man's armour as mounted 1850 mm (73.2 in); Cuirass: height shoulder to waist 355 mm (14 in), external waist 880 mm (34.7 in), chest 1055 mm (41.7 in), weight 30.11 kg (66 lb 6 oz)

PUB. Blair1965a; Richardson 2004: 12–15; Terjanian 2006a

REF. (1) Brewer 1864: 566; (2) Brewer 1864 1548–9

(II.5, VI.1–5)

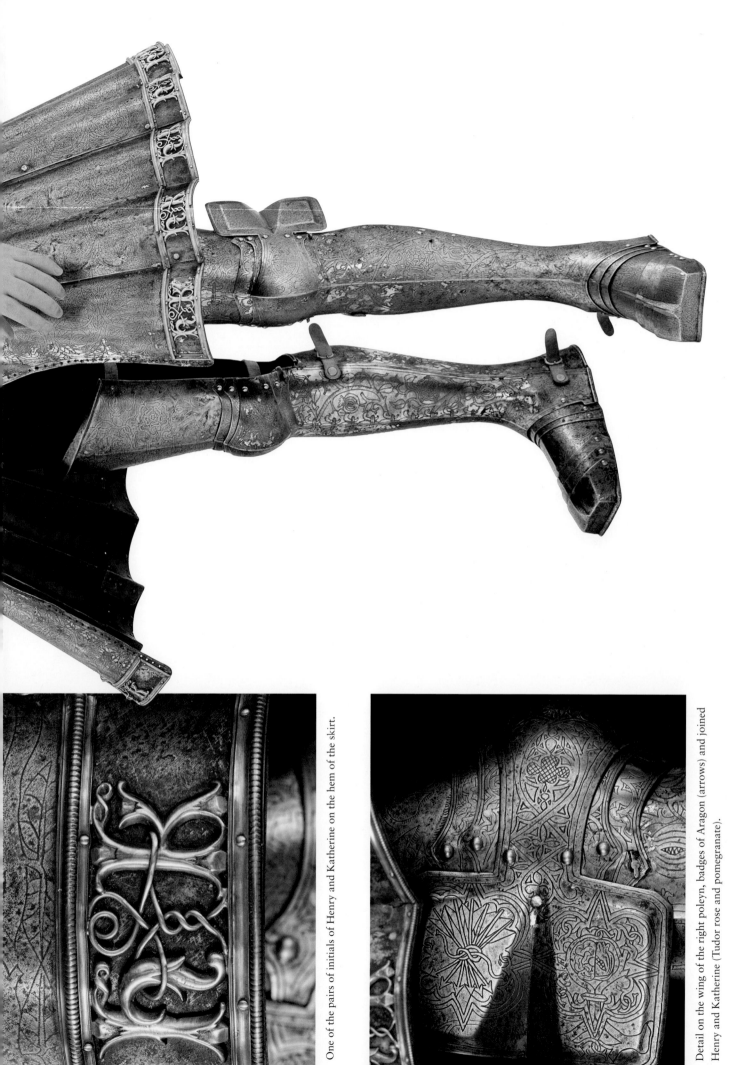

One of the pairs of initials of Henry and Katherine on the hem of the skirt.

Detail on the wing of the right poleyn, badges of Aragon (arrows) and joined Henry and Katherine (Tudor rose and pomegranate).

Detail of helmet.

Detail of right vambrace.

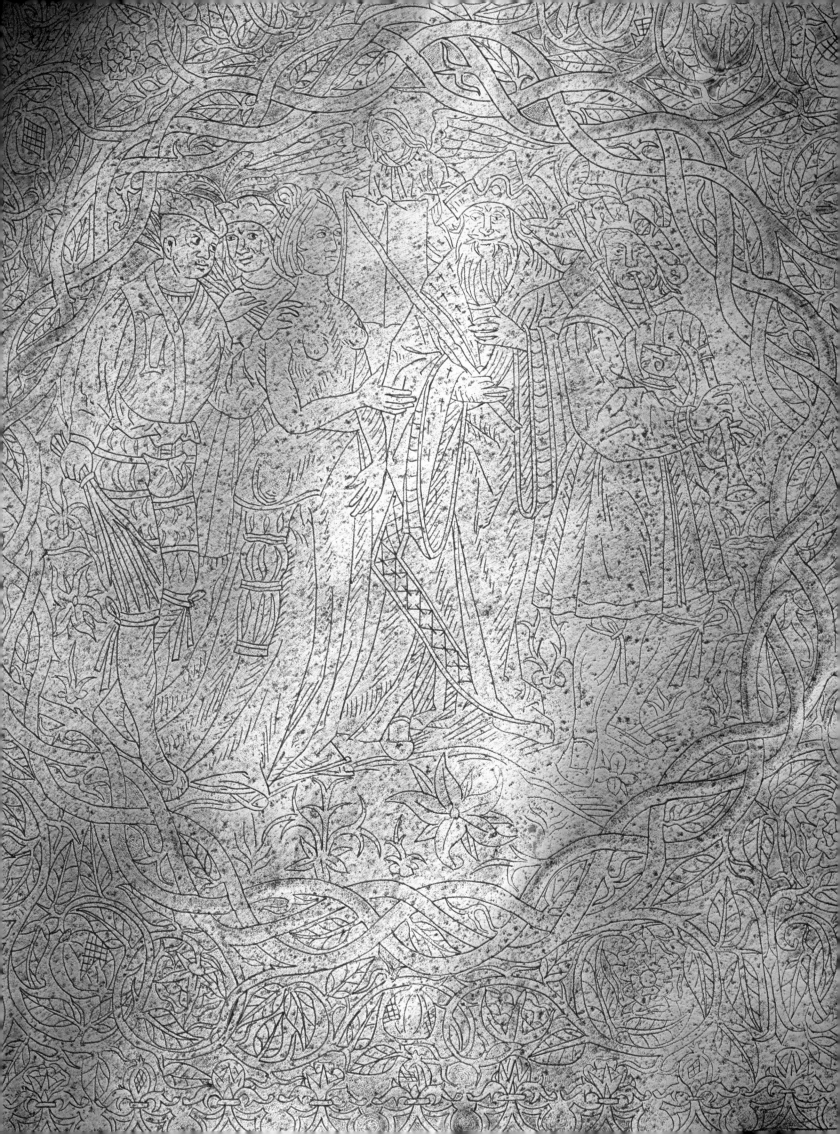

CUIRASS OF HENRY VIII

Flemish or English, Greenwich, about 1515

The breastplate is made in one piece with a shallow medial ridge and strong, boxed turns at the neck and arms. Riveted to the right are four lance rest studs. Riveted to the waist flange is a fauld of three lames, embossed with medial ribs. Riveted to either shoulder is a buckle, the one at the right a modern restoration, the one at the left probably original. It is fastened to the backplate by an external hinge at the left side and a later turning pin and keyholes slot at the right replacing the original strap and buckle. The hinge is a replacement, and evidence of rivet holes shows the original was smaller and fitted internally. The backplate is shaped to the shoulders with a low neck and a narrow flange at the waist to which is riveted a culet of two lames. The main edges have plain inward turns. At the left side is half a hinge, riveted to the outside, for fastening it to its breastplate; this is a replacement, and evidence of rivet holes shows the original was smaller and fitted inside. They were fastened at the right with a strap and buckle, later replaced with a turning pin and keyhole slot. At either shoulder is a rivet for a shoulder strap. Both pieces are stamped at either side of the neck with a 'crowned W' mark. It is possible that this mark belonged to Jacob 'Copyn' de Watte, who was in Henry VIII's employ from 1511 and in 1516 made for the king *'iiij complete harness for the Kinges Grace of diverse faccones'*.[1] TR

PROV. Transferred to the Tower from the Palace at Greenwich 1644.

Breastplate height 480 mm (18.9 in), width 358 mm (14.1 in), weight 3.66 kg (8 lb 1 oz); Backplate: height 394 mm (15.5 in), width 362 mm (14.3 in), weight 1.75 kg (3 lb 14 oz); Assembled cuirass: external waist 940 mm (37 in), external chest 1085 mm (43 in), waist to shoulder 355 mm (14 in)

REF. (1) Cripps-Day 1944: 11–12, note 1

{III.71-2}

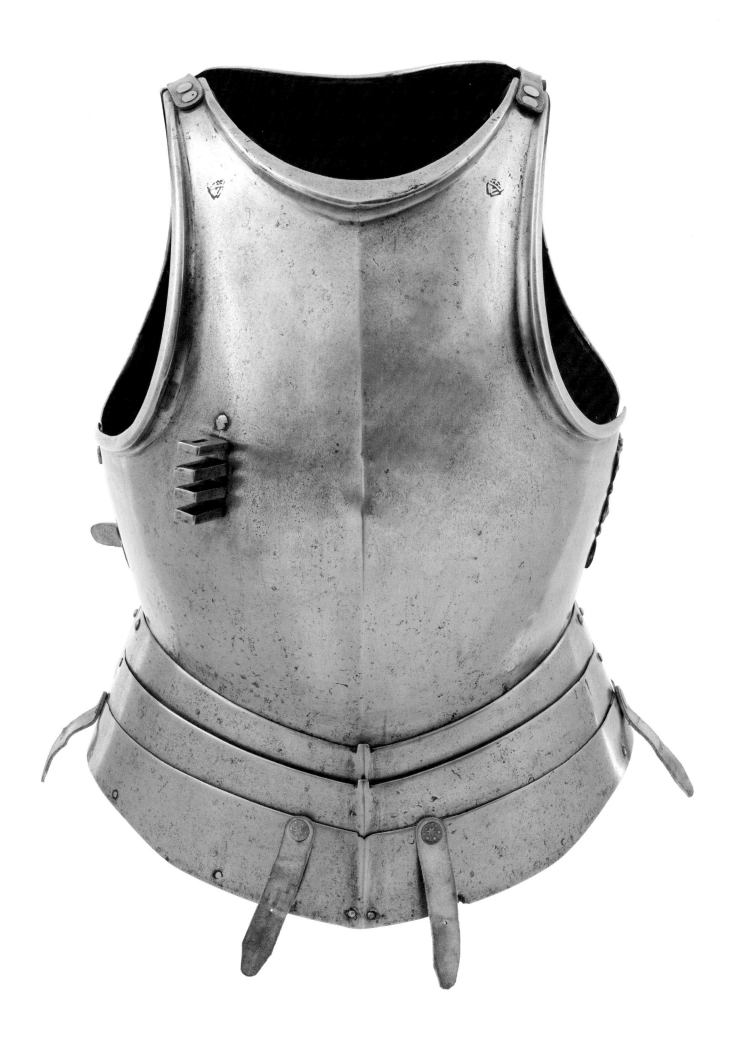

THE 'ITALIAN' BARD

Horse armour of Henry VIII

English, Greenwich or Southwark, about 1515

By 1515 Henry had a workshop staffed with eleven German and Flemish armourers, collectively termed 'Almains'. From late 1515 or early 1516 the workshop was moved from Greenwich to Southwark where they stayed while improvements were made to their facilities. There they stayed for at least six years before returning to Greenwich. This bard, which Mann dated about 1530, comprises a peytral, crupper, one flanchard and a pair of stirrups. The crinet formerly displayed with is was a modern restoration and the shaffron associated, while the saddle and steels are original but associated, as their decoration does not match. It is decorated with sprays of embossed flutes and bands of etched and gilt foliage on a hatched ground, with the king's badges, the rose and portcullis, repeated at intervals. It is on account of the 'Italianate' nature of its decoration that the bard is associated with the Italian craftsmen working for the king.

The saddle displayed with it has one of a set of four saddle steels for the king, mentioned in Erasmus Kirkenar's accounts for 1544/5. The bow is made in three plates, pierced with holes at either end and at either side of the pommel for attachment with screws to the saddle frame, the cantle in four plates, attached together by the screws fixing them to the saddle frame. The main edges have plain flanges with etched and gilded borders decorated with thin scrolling foliage. Bands at the centre of the bow and at the ridges running across either side of the cantle are etched and gilded with bands of arabesques. The surfaces are bright, and may originally have been so. The decoration is like that by Hans Holbein on the field armour, and may also be by him. TR

PROV. Transferred to the Tower from the Palace at Greenwich 1644

As mounted height 2080 mm (82.1 in), width 870 mm (34.3 in),
length 2350 mm (92.8 in); Peytral: height 655 mm (25.8 in),
width 615 mm (24.3 in), length 552 mm (21.8 in);
Crupper: height 620 mm (24.5 in), width 870 mm (34.3 in),
length 910 mm (35.9 in); Flanchard: height 330 mm (13 in),
length 605 mm (23.9 in)

REF. Mann 1951: 12 no. 4a; Richardson 2004: 16

{VI.14–16, VI.99 A–B}

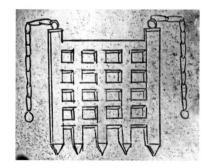

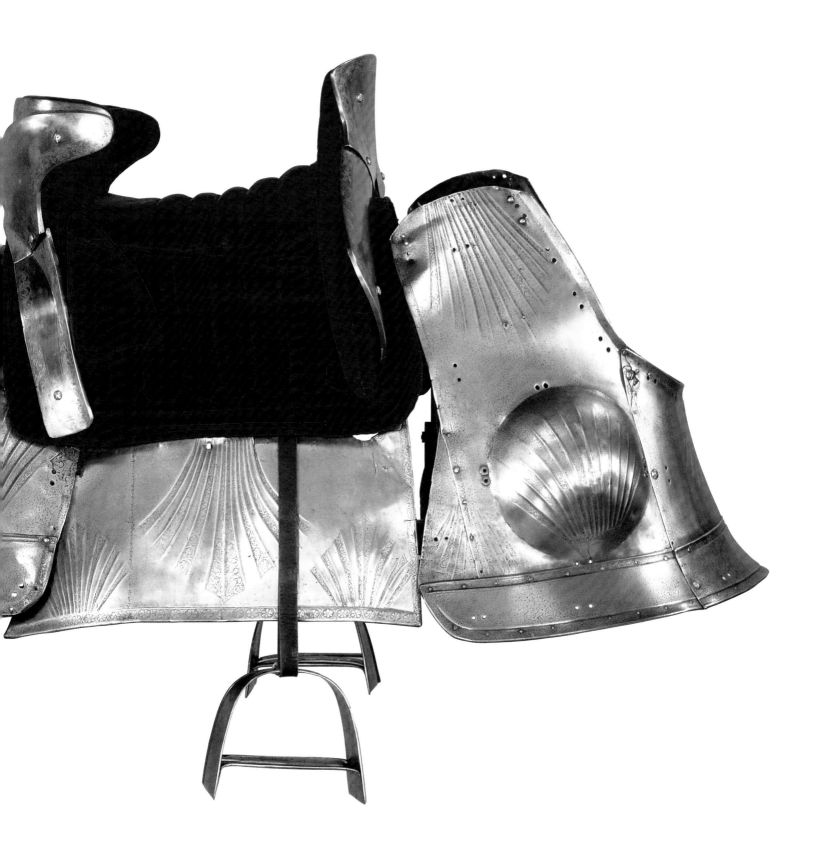

{24}

THE FLEURANGES ARMOUR

Field armour

English, Greenwich, about 1525

The armour is plain, the main edges finished either with plain, boxed inward turns or with partial turns accompanied by double recessed borders. The breastplate is pierced at the right with three holes for the attachment of a missing lance rest. The tassets, attached by modern straps and buckles, are of five lames overlapping upwards, and articulated by three internal leathers. The backplate is fitted with an associated culet plate at the waist. These are worn over a gorget with sharply flanged upper edges. The pauldrons are asymmetrical, with a cut-out at the right armpit for the lance, and each formed of six lames overlapping upwards, in characteristic Greenwich style. The vambraces have flush turning joints with two lames above at the outside of the arm, bracelet couters with single articulating lames above and below, and small articulating lames at the tops of the inner plates of the lower cannons, to increase the freedom of movement at the elbows. The cuisses both lack their upper plates, and are joined to poleyns with heart-shaped wings with two articulating lames above and below. The lowest of these are fastened by turning pins in keyhole slots to three-quarter greaves, the plates of which are hinged at the outside and fastened by two straps and buckles at the inside rear. The lower edges have plain, boxed turns above the ankle. The armet has a deep, scalloped brow reinforce, a single plate 'sparrow's beak' visor with a prow-shaped point stepped below the sight, and is pierced with numerous breaths at either side. The cheekpieces extend to the rear, and are hinged to the skull on their upper edges.

The Field of Cloth of Gold tournament of 1520 included two tourneys, on Wednesday 20 and Thursday 21 June, between bands of 10–13 men-at-arms using lances and single-handed swords. On the last of these days one of the bands of challengers was headed by Robert III de la Marck, Maréchal de Fleuranges, the hero of the battle of Novara (where he is said to have received 46 wounds) in the Italian Wars. Henry fought with Fleuranges with such vigour that he '*bare back M Florenges and brake his Poldron* (shoulder defence) *and him disarmed*'. This armour is thought to have been presented by Henry to Fleuranges, either to commemorate this event, or in October 1532 when Fleuranges attended a meeting of Henry and Francis I at Calais and Boulogne. The helmet is one of a number which have been associated with this armour; the one numbered with the armour is a close helmet with a visor similar in shape to those of the How armet, Foot Combat armour and Lord Mordaunt portrait; Charles Beard identified another close helmet, lacking a visor, as the correct one (no. H 85)[1], and Jean-Pierre Reverseau subsequently found a better match in this possibly Greenwich armet, with which the armour is currently displayed. TR

PROV. From the arsenal of Sedan, removed to Paris by Napoleon in 1804

PUB. Beard 1934; Cripps-Day 1934: 18; Mann 1951: 9, no. 2; Reverseau 1982: 136; Richardson 2004: 22;

REF. (1) Robert 1890 II: 54, no. G 46, 157 no. H 57 182 no. H 85

Musée de l'Armée, Paris

{G46, H57}

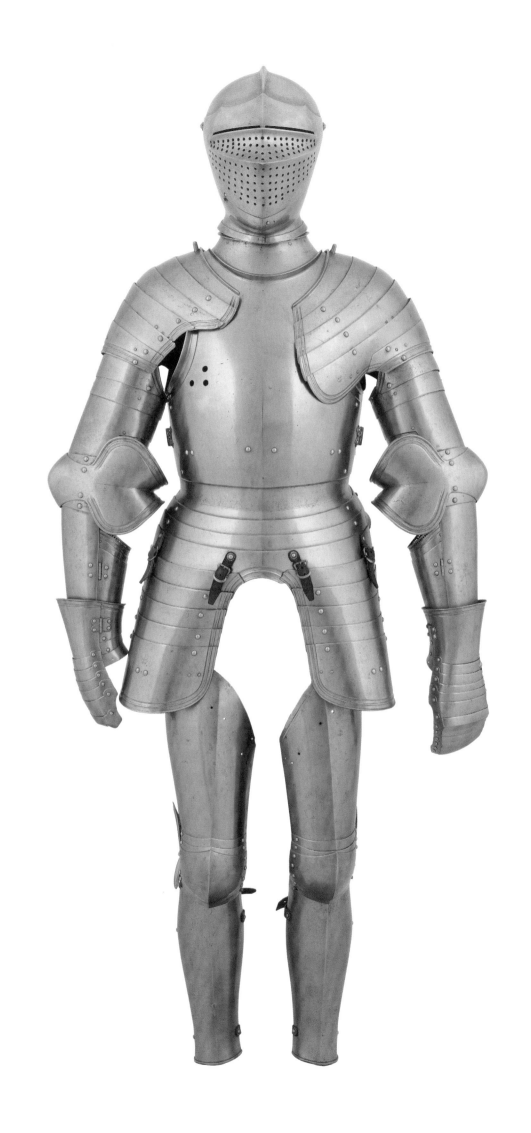

{25}

ARMET

English, Greenwich, about 1530

The skull is formed in one piece with a low comb and a flange at the bottom for the collar. Riveted to the comb to the rear of centre is an iron disc with serrated edge and a small hole at the centre. At the right front is a rectangular slot for a now lost sprung stud designed to support the visor in the raised position; the rivet by which this was attached can be seen just below the visor pivot. The main edge has a plain outward turn with a recessed border containing five original flush lining rivets, and a sprung stud at either side for the cheekpieces. These are hinged low at either side of the skull, and fastened with an original pierced stud and swivel hook at the front. The main edges have plain inward turns with recessed borders containing two remaining flush lining rivets at the right and four at the left. Inside the right cheekpiece is riveted a spring, missing its terminal stud, designed to fasten the visor closed. The surface is bright but patinated, and has been heavily corroded. The front of the right cheekpiece is missing, and replaced with a riveted repair. Holes are pierced at either side on the cheekpieces, and at the top of the skull at either side of the comb, probably for securing the helmet to a mount.

This armet is the only known example of a Greenwich armet of the reign of Henry VIII designed to 'turn on the collar', that is to be fastened directly to the collar or throat defence of its armour. Stylistically it should be dated about 1530. Another Greenwich example of about 1535, from the church of St George at Southacre, Norfolk, is of the same shape and date as the present armet, but is also made as a close helmet. Another close helmet from the reign of Henry VIII is illustrated in the mid 16th-century portrait of Lord Mordaunt of Turvey (Royal Armouries I.55, cat. no. 38) but the original armour does not survive.[1] The visors of this portrait, the present armet and the Southacre church close helmet are particularly similar. Another example of a lost Greenwich armour of exactly this period is depicted in the portrait of Sir Nicholas Carew attributed to Hans Holbein or his workshop, in the collection of the Duke of Buccleuch and Queensberry, usually at Drumlanrig Castle.[2] In this the helmet is not included; both portraits illustrate clearly that Greenwich armour in these early years tended, like so much north European armour, to be blackened in its original state. This explains the Greenwich fashion for gilded fittings and rivets of iron with gilded brass heads, which stood out against the blackened ground but are lost in the bright finish of most of the armours today. TR

PROV. Assigned to the Royal Armouries by HM Government 2007, accepted in Lieu of Inheritance Tax. Formerly in the collection of E J Brett, sold Christie's 1895 lot 131 for £17 to S J Whawell, and in the collection of H G Radford, sold Sotheby's 1946 lot 329, £30

Height 230 mm (9.1 in), width 202 mm (8 in), depth 337 mm (13.3 in), weight 2.47 kg (5 lb 7 oz)

PUB. Mann 1951: 35, no. 40, pl. XXXII; Richardson 2009

REF. (1) Mann 1951: 42, no.71, pl. V; (2) Beard 1931, pl. V; Foister 2006: 122–3, no.135

{IV.2061}

{26}

SABATON

From a plain Greenwich armour of Henry VIII

English, Greenwich, about 1527

This plate sabaton is the only surviving fragment of a plain Greenwich armour probably made for Henry VIII. It is formed of a toe cap, shaped in the fashionable 'bear's paw' form, with a series of seven articulating lames, the rearmost with a boxed plain turn on its main edge and a series of pierced holes for points. It is most probably from a field armour as the King does not seem to have participated in the tournaments that had been such a part of his life hitherto. In form it is closely comparable to that of the sabatons of the 'Genouilhac' armour in the Metropolitan Museum of Art, New York (no. 19.131.1,2) which is dated 1527. It is interesting that Henry does not appear to have taken part in any jousts after 1527, and the May Day jousts of 1534 are the only ones he is recorded as even attending (if only to leave early). Perhaps the King was, at the age of 36, getting too old for the tournament, but it is noteworthy that, if the identification of the 'Genouilhac' armour as his is correct, he had certainly not attained the great girth to which his later armours attest. TR

PROV. Transferred to the Tower from the Palace at Greenwich 1644

Height 95 mm (3.74 in), width 154 mm (6 in),
depth 140 mm (5.5 in), weight 264 g (9 oz)

REF. Richardson 2004: 24

{II.8T}

{27}

GORGET PLATES

From a lost close helmet of Henry VIII

English, Greenwich, about 1535

This defence is composed of three lames front and rear, articulated together by internal leathers only in the characteristic Greenwich style. The lower two of these are gorget plates, fastened at either side at the lower edge with studs and keyhole slots, the main edges with plain inward turns and recessed borders containing the lining rivets, and traces of gilding. The subsidiary edges are bordered by double incised lines. The upper plate at front and rear form lower skull and bevor plates respectively. This fragment was until 1964 riveted to the modified lower edge of the close helmet of Henry's 1540 armour (cat. no. 39). Its leathers are modern replacements, and many of its rivets have been substituted with screws. It is an excellent fit to the close helmet of the 1540 armour, suggesting that it did form part of a helmet made for the king, but it does not match the armour, having only gilded decoration without etching. Since no example of an armour so described can be traced in the king's inventory of 1547, the fragment remains enigmatic. TR

PROV. Probably brought from Greenwich to the Tower in 1649

Height 120 mm (4.7 in), width 265 mm (10.5 in),
depth 305 mm (12 in), weight 775 g (1 lb 7 oz)

{II.8W}

{28}

SADDLE STEELS,
BUFFE AND TOE CAP
FROM A LOST ARMOUR
OF HENRY VIII

Greenwich, about 1544

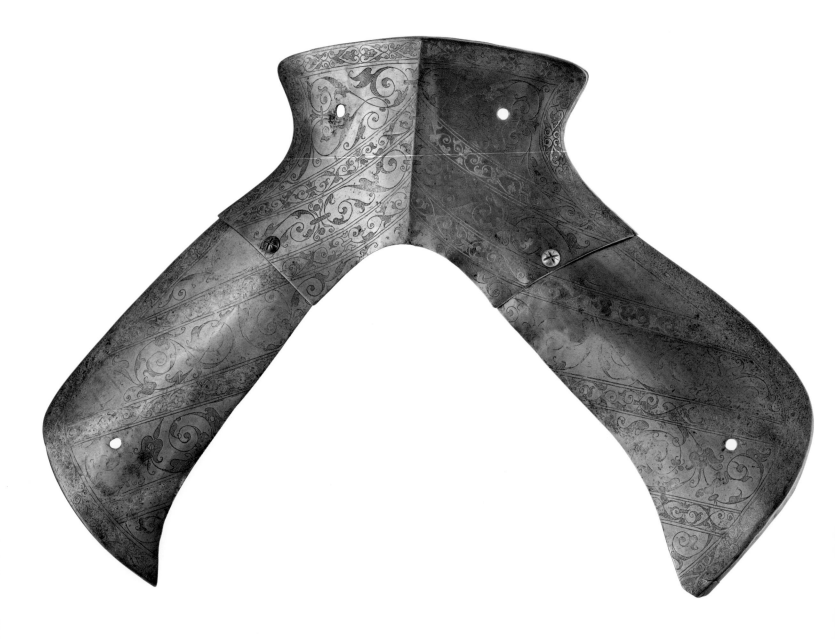

Henry had at least two armours made for him in 1544 for the Boulogne campaign. From a field armour made by Erasmus Kirkenar at Greenwich all that survives is a buffe (the face defence of the burgonet, the standard light field helmet of the period), together with the toe cap of one of the sabatons and the saddle steels. The buffe is formed of three articulated plates pierced at the right with breaths, and secured in the closed position by sprung studs. All of these are articulated by rivets to a lower bevor with holes at either upper corner where it was secured to the skull of its helmet. The main edges have plain inward turns with recessed borders bounded on the inside with ribs; the border on the upper buffe plate contains a series of slots, for additional vision as well as for ventilation. The toe cap is designed to be worn with mail sabatons, and has a series of

pierced holes around its main edges. The saddle bow is made of three plates and the cantle of four, the central plates embossed with deep curving ridges at either side, each set with six holes for screws fixing the plates to the saddle frame, those at the joins also fastening the plates together. The armour was decorated overall with narrow bands and borders etched and gilt with arabesques, the ground between these is covered with a widely spaced etched design of scrolling foliage. The decoration is probably based on designs by Hans Holbein the Younger as it is reminiscent of, but not identical to, some of the designs in the *Englischen Skizzenbuch* in the Kunstmuseum, Basel (inv. 1662.165.11). It is possible that this is the armour '*one harnesse for the kinges Majestie all graven and parcel guilte bothe for the felde and Tilte complete which was commanded to be translated at the kinges*

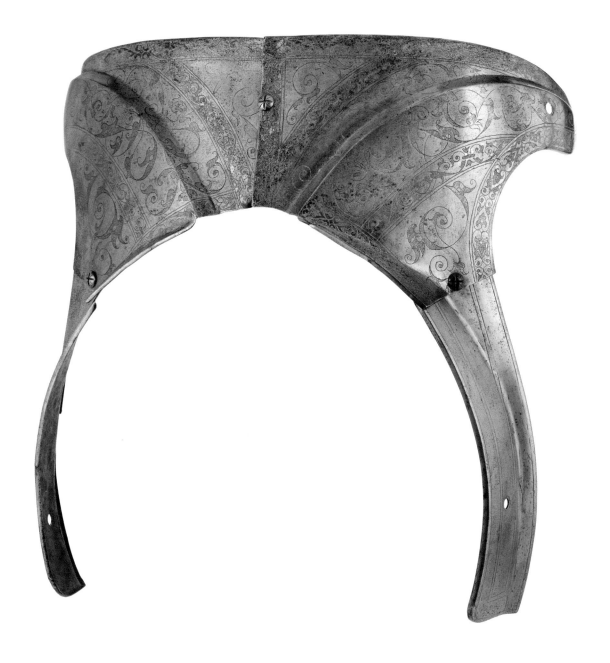

goinge over to Bulloigne whiche lieth in peces parte translated and patre untranslated by A contrarie comaundement by the kinges Majestie' at Greenwich in the 1547 inventory.[1] TR

PROV. Transferred to the Tower from the Palace at Greenwich 1644

Saddle bow: height 505 mm (20 in), width 745 mm (29.5 in), weight 1.62 kg (3 lb 9 oz); Saddle cantle: height 560 mm (22 in), width 550 mm (21.7 in), weight 1.4 kg (3 lb 12 oz); Buffe: height 270 mm (10.7 in), width 258 mm (10.2 in), depth 317 mm (12.5 in), weight 1.36 kg (3 lb); Toe cap: width 105 mm (4.1 in), weight 113 g (4 oz)

PUB. Mann 1951: no.53; Richardson 2004: 41

REF. (1) Starkey 1998: 161

{11.9, VI.96-7}

{29}

SADDLE STEEL OF HENRY VIII

Italian, about 1545

Cantle steel of two plates, overlapped left to right and pierced for connection by a modern bolt. The steel is decorated with alternately raised and sunken vertical bands, the raised bands etched with sprays of flowers and foliage, classical vases, cornucopiae and entwined dolphins on a plain gilded ground, the latter with scrolling floral ornament ending at the base in dolphin-like monsters on a stippled ground and originally gilded overall. The main edges have roped inward turns and a wide recessed border. An attachment hole is pierced through each side of the cantle. It is possible that these pieces may have formed part of the diplomatic gifts accompanying the negotiations for the peace which was concluded between England and France in 1546. TR

PROV. Transferred to the Tower from the Palace at Greenwich 1644

Width 660 mm (26 in), height 198 mm (7.8 in), weight 0.95 kg (2 lb 10 oz)

REF. Richardson 2004: 45

{VI.114}

{30}

FRETTED SADDLE STEEL
OF HENRY VIII

Italian, about 1545

The right plate of a two-piece cantle steel. The main edges have roped inward turns. The plate is pierced with a design of scrolling floral ornament incorporating a central bearded head amongst foliage with a bird above left, a winged wyvern on the left, and double profiled heads on the right. Both the wyvern and profiled heads are pierced with an attachment hole. Detail is rendered by etching of fine quality and the whole exterior was originally entirely gilded. The bird and upper edges of the plate have repairs to the inner surfaces. It is most probably the '*tree of A Saddell covered with stele plate cutte owte with braunches graven and guilte*' recorded at Greenwich in the charge of Erasmus Kirkenar in the 1547 inventory.[1] By the early 17th century they were probably detached from the saddle, and identifiable in the Green Gallery at Greenwich, recorded as '*steeles for saddles viz … another of cutworke guilt*' in Sir Thomas Jay's Remaine of the Armory of 1629.[2] TR

PROV. Transferred to the Tower from the Palace at Greenwich 1644

Height 197 mm (7.7 in), width 462 mm (18.2 in), weight 540 g (1 lb 3 oz)

PUB. Richardson 2004: 45

REF. (1) Starkey 1998: 161; (2) SP Dom Chas I vol. 139, pt 94

{VI.III}

A FIELD GARNITURE

Field armour of Henry VIII
North Italian, about 1544

The armour comprises a burgonet and buffe, a cuirass of anime type formed of articulated lames, short tassets with tasset extensions, cuisses and poleyns, pauldrons, vambraces and gauntlets. The alternative set of vambraces with smaller spaudlers at the shoulders, in the Royal Collection at Windsor Castle, is polished bright, but the remaining pieces have their original black from the hammer finish and bands of etched and gilded decoration. New research by Blair and Pyhrr shows that the armour was modified, probably at the king's behest and by his armourers at Greenwich, by the removal of at least three lames from the cuirass and the provision of new gussets at the arms, extension plates at the shoulders, one of which has a stud decorated in the form of a Tudor rose, new plates at the neck of the burgonet and lowest lames of the tassets, all decorated to match the decoration of the original.[1]

Until recently the armour was known as the armour of the French nobleman Anne de Montmorency (1493–1567), constable of France, who was taken prisoner at the battle of Saint Quentin in 1557 at which William Herbert, 1st Earl of Pembroke, commanded the English contingent.[2]

Blair and Pyhrr's new research has shown that the armour is identifiable with one belonging to Henry VIII at Greenwich in 1547, '*one Complete harnesse of Italion makinge with Lambes blacke and parcel guilte for the feilde lacking greves and Sabbetters*'[3], and that by 1555 it was still in Greenwich but on a horse with '*A stele Saddle parcel guilte covered the half with clothe of golde and the other half with clothe of silver with a Crinit and Shafron parcel guilte and a bitte*'. They show that it was one of three new armours provided for the King for the French campaign, the others being the fragmentary Greenwich armours with scales and arabesques respectively (cat. no. 33 and 28). By 1558 it was at Wilton House, the new home of William Herbert, the '*felde armor graven and gilte that was Kinge Henry theights*'. It continued to be known as an armour of Henry VIII in 17th-century descriptions of the Wilton armoury, but subsequently lost its association with the King. The armour was offered for sale in London in 1917 (Sotheby's lot 540) but withdrawn after failing to reach its reserve following the publication of a damaging letter by Charles ffoulkes, curator of the Tower Armouries, published in the *Burlington Magazine* shortly before the sale which cast doubts on its date and attribution. The extra vambraces, which enable the armour to be regarded as a 'small garniture' for the field, are identified by Blair and Pyhrr as those transferred from the Tower to Windsor in 1688.[4] They have turning joints in the upper cannons, articulating lames above and below the couters and a series of articulated lames protecting the inside of the elbow joints, while the New York vambraces are articulated by leathers joining the upper and lower cannons to the couters, thus providing examples of the two current types of Italian vambraces of the period. Among the many decorative elements represented on the armour are a series of running dogs on the buffe, third lame of the breastplate, fifth lame of the backplate and gauntlet cuffs. These are closely comparable to those on Henry's Italian saddle steels (cat no. 32) leading Blair and Pyhrr to suggest that these might be the steels of the saddle associated with the armour in 1555, and also supplied by Francis Albert of Milan, the only purveyor of Italian armour to the English court at this time.[5] TR

PROV. Purchased privately from Clarence H Mackay, 1932. From the armoury of the Earls of Pembroke at Wilton House by 1558, offered for sale in 1917 but withdrawn, sold privately to Clarence Mackay 10 December 1929
Extra vambraces brought from Greenwich to the Tower in 1649, transferred to Windsor castle in 1688

Height as mounted 1816 mm (71.5 in)

REF. (1) Blair & Pyhrr 2003; (2) London 1890: 1249, no. 575; (3) Starkey 1998: 159, no. 8262; (4) Blair & Pyhrr 2003: 117–20; (5) Blair & Pyhrr 2003: 101, 126, figs 24, 44

Metropolitan Museum of Art, New York, Harris Brisbane Dick Fund

{32.130.7}

Extra vambraces Royal Collection, Windsor Castle

{67399}

Pages 196-97: The alternative set of vambraces.

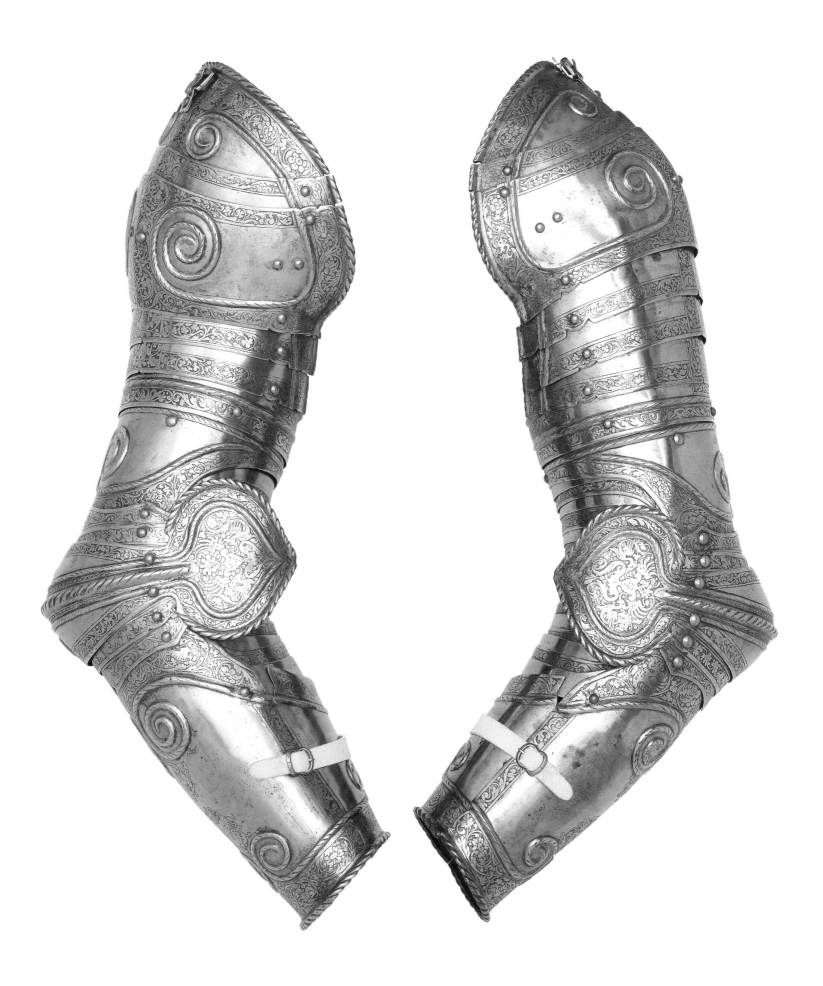

{32}

SADDLE STEELS

From a saddle belonging to Henry VIII

Italian, about 1544

Associated with the '*Complete harness of Italion makinge wth Lambes (lames) blacke and pcell guilte for the felde lackinge greves and sabbetters* (sabatons)' recorded at Greenwich in the 1547 inventory,[1] the Wilton armour of King Henry VIII is a set of saddle steels, of the same manufacture and similar, but not identical decoration. The saddle steels remained in London, and are possibly the partly gilt and etched steels in the Green Gallery at Greenwich, recorded as '*steeles for saddles viz one guilte and graven another parcel guilt and graven another of cutworke guilt in all iii*' in Sir Thomas Jay's *Remaine of the Armory* of 1629.[2] The saddle steels seem to have been brought to the Tower with the rest of the contents of the Greenwich workshop in 1644.

The steels for the saddle-bow originally comprised three plates, but the central plate is lost. The cantle is made of two plates. The main edges have roped inward turns with recessed borders. Each plate is pierced with a hole for attaching it by screws to the wooden frame of the saddle. The steels are decorated with vertical sunken bands etched and formerly gilded with running foliage interspersed with animals, birds and classical figures. The upper and side edges are roped, with sunken borders whose decoration includes dogs in form similar to greyhounds or whippets. TR

PROV. Transferred to the Tower from the Palace at Greenwich 1644

Right bow plate: width 295 mm (11.6 in); Left bow plate: 293 mm (11.5 in); Cantle: height 155 mm (6.2 in), width 515 mm (20.25 cm), weight 675 g (1 lb 5 oz)

PUB. Blair & Pyhrr 2003; Richardson 2004: 44

REF. (1) Starkey 1998: 159; (2) SP Dom Chas 1 vol. 139, pt 94

{VI.121-2}

CRINET AND GAUNTLET

From a lost armour of Henry VIII
English, Greenwich, probably 1545

Another armour made at Greenwich under Erasmus Kirkenar in the mid 1540s was decorated with embossed, etched and gilded scales. All that remains of it are the crinet (the defence for the horse's neck), formed of nine plates embossed to imitate the shape of the vertebrae in the horse's neck, and the right gauntlet, a mitten gauntlet with seven metacarpal plates and a set of six carpal plates which are detachable, fastened by turning pins to the knuckle plate. The decoration of this armour includes Tudor roses, on the knuckle plate of the gauntlet. A close helmet from this armour was formerly preserved at the church of St Botulph at Lullingstone, Kent, but is no longer there.[1] Erasmus Kirkenar's accounts for 1544/5 record the *'gyldyng of a harnysh made with Skalles for the Kynges maieste with 2 hede pyces. Item for Gylding of the same harnysh and the 2 hede pyce. Summa 19 li'*, which almost certainly refers to this armour.[2] The crinet at least is identifiable in the 1547 inventory at Greenwich, *'as a 'Crenet with Skales percell graven and guilte'*.[3] It had by then become separated from the rest of the armour, as it was included in *'a Complete Harnesse for the felde all doble pieces longinge thereto graven and parcell guilte'* together with saddle steels and a *'steel Barbe'*. TR

PROV. Crinet transferred to the Tower from the Palace at Greenwich 1644. Gauntlet formerly in the collection of Lord Astor of Hever Castle, sold Sotheby's 5 May 1983, lot 43

Crinet: length 769 mm (30.5 in), width at top 190 mm (7.5 in), at bottom 327 mm (12.8 in), weight 2.55 kg (5 lb 10 oz); Gauntlet: length 298 mm (11.8 in), cuff diameter 129 mm (5.1 in), weight 510 g (1 lb 2 oz)

PUB. Mann 1951: 4a; Richardson 2004: 42

REF. (1) Mann 1932; (2) Cripps-Day 1945: 58; (3) Cripps-Day 1945: 14

{III.1788, VI.69}

{34}

SADDLE STEELS

From a saddle belonging to Henry VIII

English, Greenwich, about 1545

Erasmus Kirkenar's accounts for 1544/5 also mention set of four saddle steels for the king, '*Yett Gyldyng of 4 stele saddelles for the Kynges maieste*'.[1] The bow is made in three plates, pierced with holes at either end and at either side of the pommel for attachment with screws to the saddle frame, the cantle in four plates, attached together by the screws fixing them to the saddle frame. The main edges have plain flanges with etched and gilded borders decorated with thin scrolling foliage.

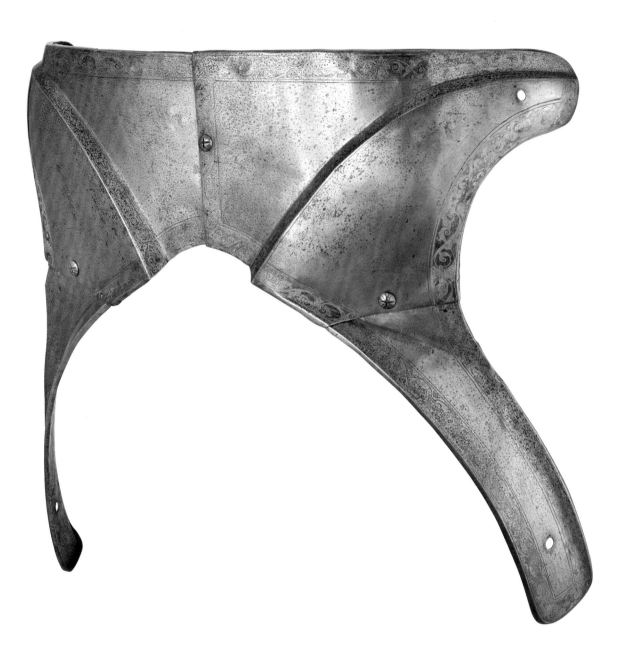

Bands at the centre of the bow and at the ridges running across either side of the cantle are etched and gilded with bands of arabesques. The surfaces are bright, and may originally have been so. The decoration is like that by Hans Holbein on the field armour, and may also be by him. The other half of the set is probably that displayed on a saddle with the 'Italian' bard (cat. no. 23). TR

PROV. Transferred to the Tower from the Palace at Greenwich 1644

Bow: height 600 mm (23.7 in), width 800 mm (31.6 in), weight 1.86 kg (4 lb 2 oz); Cantle: 600 mm (23.7 in), width 700 mm (31.6 in), weight 2.21 kg (4 lb 14 oz)

PUB. Richardson 2004: 43

REF. (1) Cripps-Day 1944: 57

{VI.98}

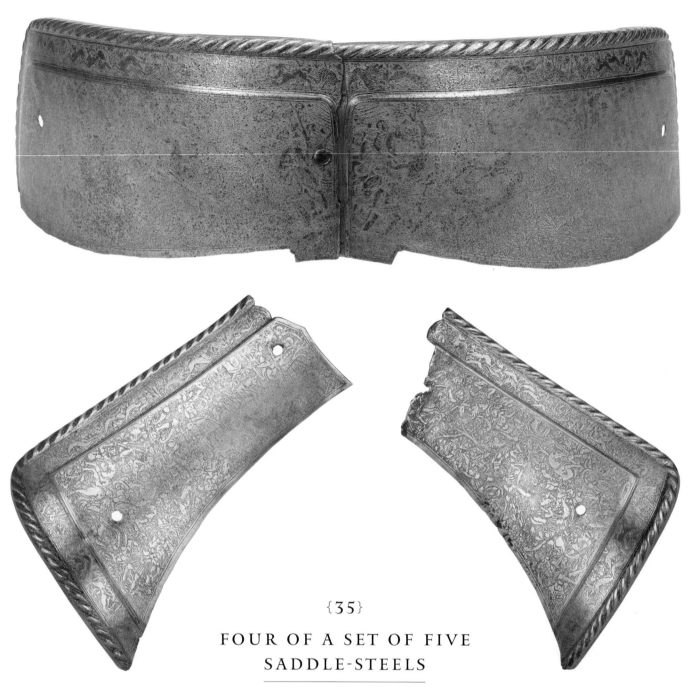

{35}

FOUR OF A SET OF FIVE
SADDLE-STEELS

From a saddle belonging to Henry VIII

*The etched decoration perhaps by Marco da Ravenna
after engravings either by Raphael or Giulio Romano*

Italian, about 1540-45

The iron plates consist of the two side plates for a symmetrical bow whose central plate is now missing and two plates for the cantle. The outer edges of each plate are raised and turned back with the ridge roped, followed on the inside edge by a recessed border. The fore plates are pierced by two holes originally to secure them to the saddle. The top edge of the left plate is partly broken away.

The left rear plate had a decorated flange which has been cut away; this overlapped a plain flange on the right plate. Both rear plates were pierced with a pair of holes, the centre ones designed to overlap, for three retaining bolts to the main saddle.

Overall the plates were originally covered completely in etched relief and fire-gilding. The recessed border is etched against a densely dotted ground with hounds chasing deer, hares and wild boar through a wooded countryside. The main areas are etched all over with battle scenes between cavalry and infantry in classical armour or in quasi-Oriental dress, in a lightly wooded landscape. The same figures are repeated, some reversed and with alterations of equipment.

The source of many of the figures is an engraving possibly by Marco da Ravenna, possibly after Giulio Romano, or from the repetition of it by Agostino Veneziano. Others come from an engraving by Marco da Ravenna, possibly after either Raphael or Giulio Romano.[1]

The saddle steels have recently been identified by Claude Blair and Ian Eaves as belonging to Henry VIII. They are listed in an unpublished 1555 inventory of the Royal Armouries.[2] In the First House of The Green Gallery at Greenwich: *'The fforeparte and hinderp[ar]te of a guilte Saddle graven and guilte'*. It is possible that the fore plates were the *'Saddle Bow, imperfect, highly Engraved in 2 Pieces'* supplied from the Tower for the Windsor Castle refurbishment of 1831.[3] SM

PROV. From Henry VIII's Armoury. 1555 inventory Royal Armouries. The fore plates transferred from The Tower to Windsor Castle in 1831 Nos.1868-9 in the Superintendent's Inventory of Windsor Castle & Laking No.792; The rear plates Class 6.63 in 1859 then VI.116–7 in 1910 and then No.VI.115 in the Tower Armouries. Transferred to Windsor Castle in 1914 No.1870 in the Superintendent's Inventory of Windsor Castle

Right fore plate: height 322 mm (12.7 in), width 210 mm (8.3 in), weight 394 g (13.9 oz); Left fore plate: height 290 mm (11.4 in), width 210 mm (8.3 in), weight 374 g (13.2 oz); Right rear plate: height 185 mm (7.3 in), width 370 mm (14.6 in), weight 538 g (1 lb 2 oz); Left rear plate: height 185 mm (7.3 in), width 395 mm (15.5 in), weight 506 g (1 lb 1 oz)

PUB. Dillon 1910; ffoulkes 1916; Hewitt 1859; Laking 1900–22

REF. (1) Bartsch 1803–21; (2) Fo. 76v; (3) From an unpublished Royal Collection Catalogue entry by A V B Norman, with acknowledgements to S W Pyhrr

Royal Collection

{RCIN 67652.A–D}

{36}

SHAFFRON

From a horse armour belonging to Henry VIII
English, Greenwich, about 1540

The shaffron is made in two parts overlapping upwards and joined by pierced studs and swivel hooks. The upper section had detachable extension plates, fastened by a pierced stud and swivel hook and a turning pin and keyhole slot; the right one is now missing. The edges of the lower plate are plain and have keyhole slots showing that there were originally side plates there also. At the top is the poll plate, attached by modern internal leathers. The main edges have plain inward turns with recessed borders containing the lining rivets. A medial ridge runs up from the nose, becoming a rib swelling between the nose and a fluted roundel and continuing beyond to the rear, where it is decorated with an etched rope design. The etched and gilded rondel is secured to the upper plate by a modern screw through an internal rectangular brass bar itself secured inside the upper main plate by a rivet either side of the screw. The shaffron is decorated with radiating bands alternately raised and sunken, the former bright and etched with masks, urns and foliage on a hatched ground, the latter with similar decoration, gilded on a plain ground. The rondel and poll plate are similarly decorated.

It is possible that this shaffron might be the '*Shaffron all graven and pcell guilt*' which was at Greenwich in 1547 in the charge of Erasmus Kirkenar, mounted with the scaled crinet (VI.69) and a bard '*pcell graven and guilte*'.[1] ffoulkes suggested this might be the '*Shanfron sanguined and partly damascined 1@ 15s*' in the Tower inventory of 1691–3, and if this identification is correct the areas which are now bright were originally russet.[2] TR

PROV. Transferred to the Tower from the Palace at Greenwich 1644

Length including poll plate 690 mm (27.2 in), width 292 mm (11.5 in),
weight 1.91 kg (4 lb 3 oz)

PUB. Dufty & Reid 1968: pl. CLXVIII

REF. (1) Dillon 1888: 276; (2) ffoulkes 1916 I: 204

{VI.55}

{37}

MODEL OF ST GEORGE
SLAYING THE DRAGON

In steel on a wooden figure, presented to the Armourers'
Company of London in 1527 and probably made by William
Vynyard (alias Segar), Master of the Company.

An example of the armourer's art that gives a very clear
impression of the of harness of men-at-arms in the early
16th century is the exquisite model of St George riding down a
lizard-like dragon, preserved in the hall of the Worshipful
Company of Armourers and Brasiers in London. The saint wears
complete armour, certainly of the style favoured in England about
the turn of the 16th century. It was almost certainly presented to
the Company in 1527 by William Vynyard or Vynzard (alias
Segar), Master of the Company in 1503–4, 1513–14 and 1531–2,
and was most probably made by him. Arms and armour had been
made in England throughout the Middle Ages. The London guild
of armourers, which survives to this day as the Armourers and
Brasiers Company, evolved from the Guild of Heaumers (helmet-
makers) in the 14th century, received its Royal Charter in 1453
and continued to make armour until the end of the 17th century.
Unfortunately it is not currently possible to identify their works
with any certainty. Two groups of helms, one of the late 14th
century and another of the early 15th, are almost certainly of
English manufacture, but few other pieces can be identified.
Certainly by the middle of the 15th century the nobility of
England bought armour from abroad, occasionally from Italy,
where Milan was recognized as the leading production centre, but
mostly from Flanders, where many Milanese had migrated to
take advantage of the north west European market. TR

PROV. In the collection of the Worshipful Company of
Armourers and Brasiers

Height 860 mm (34 in), length 660 mm (26 in)

REF. Richardson 2004: 7

{38}

PORTRAIT OF JOHN
LORD MORDAUNT OF TURVEY

Oil on panel, English, mid-late 16th century

The sitter is shown half length, leaning on one elbow over a balustrade, the other hand resting on a helmet, wearing a black but burnished Greenwich field armour with gilded bands and borders. Another version of the same portrait is in the possession of the Stopford-Sackvilles of Drayton, Northamptonshire, inscribed later and erroneously '*John Earl of Peterborow*'[1] The break in the line of gilding at the top of the visor in this version, which does not occur in the Drayton version, has led to the suggestion that this is a copy of the Drayton version, rather than the other way round, but both portraits seem near contemporary. The armour shown gives a good impression of the appearance of Greenwich armours during the reign of Henry VIII, and adds evidence that many of them originally had blackened finishes, which showed off the gilded fittings to advantage.

The sitter was identified by Charles Beard (1931) as Lord Mordaunt, being a common ancestor and a man high enough in Henry VIII's favour to have been granted the right to order an armour from the Greenwich workshops. His father was Sir John Mordaunt of Turvey, Bedfordshire, a commander under Henry Tudor at the battle of Bosworth in 1485 and at Stoke in 1487, who became King's Serjeant in 1495 and Chief Justice of Chester and Chancellor of the Duchy of Lancaster in 1504. John Mordaunt (1485–1562) was admitted to his father's inn, the

Middle Temple, in 1503, and appointed sheriff of Bedfordshire and Buckingham-shire by 1509. He married Elizabeth de Vere, heiress to a con-siderable fortune, and in 1520 he was knighted after attending the queen at the meeting with Francis I at The Field of Cloth of Gold. In 1522 he attended on the king at the meeting with Charles V at Canterbury. In 1530 he was one of the committee who investigated the landed possessions of Cardinal Wolsey, and from 1532–58 summoned to Parliament as a baron. Both their funerary monuments are in All Saints Church, Turvey. The first Baron was not a military man, unlike his father who was both a soldier and a lawyer, but the culture at the early Tudor court seems to have encouraged a martial appearance among the new gentry. The armour is similar to that depicted in the portrait of Sir Nicholas Carew attributed to Hans Holbein or his studio, in the collection of The Duke of Buccleuch and Queensberry, usually at Drumlanrig Castle[2], and Sir Nicholas is recorded as paying Erasmus Kirkenar £10 for a '*Complet harnesh bothe for Tylte and felde with all manor of double pyces be longyng to the same*' in 1536.[3] Unfortunately none of the other names recorded buying Greenwich armours in this and the following account of Erasmus Kirkenar for 1544 appears to have any direct connection with Lord Mordaunt. TR

PROV. Purchased at Sotheby's, 15 November, 1961, lot 4, catalogued as 'English School, Portrait of Edward Osborne' (for the cloth worker and Lord Mayor of London, 1530-91). From the collection of the Duke of Leeds, formerly at Hornby Castle

902 x 686 mm (35.5 x 27 in)

PUB. Mann 1951: 42, no. 71, pl. V

REF. (1) Collins Baker 1928: pl. Iia; (2) Beard 1931: pl. V, Foister 2006: 122–3, no. 135; (3) Cripps-Day 1934: 32, 53; 1944: 54; British Library MS Royal 7 F XIV f.66

{I.55}

{39}

THE 1540 ARMOUR

Armour garniture for field and tournament
of King Henry VIII by Erasmus Kirkenar

English, Greenwich, dated 1540

This armour is the greatest of the Greenwich garnitures made for King Henry VIII. It is possible that is was intended for wear at the tournament held during 1–5 May 1540 to celebrate May Day, which included tilts, tourneys and foot combats over the barriers. The two tournaments in January and May 1540 were the last Henry is known to have staged, but there is no record that he actually participated in them. No doubt his age (he was by this time 49) and his great bulk made this inappropriate.

The armour is readily identifiable with the 'Complete harness parcell graven and gilte with all manner of peces of advantage for the felde Tilte Turney and fote' at Greenwich in the 1547 inventory of the king's goods. Not only does the armour have all the requisite extra pieces, but it has a double set of them. Also it has the second of only two known examples of a feature unique to the Greenwich workshop. This is an inner breastplate or ventral plate strapped to the body and designed to lift the weight of the cuirass and arm defences from the shoulders by means of the central bolt to which the breastplate and plackart were secured. It is recorded that Francis I in 1520 disclosed this secret device to Henry, offering his armourers to make one for Henry if he sent one of his arming doublets for a pattern. The earlier example is on the 'Genouilhac' armour made for the king in 1527, and now in the Metropolitan Museum of Art, New York. Unfortunately the breastplate for the field, tilt and tourney of the 1540 armour is lost, and only that for the foot combat, which is not fitted for a lance rest, survives. The lance rest itself does survive. It is most likely that the armour had a reinforcing breastplate, like that of the 'Genouilhac' armour also, and a symmetrical right pauldron (without a cutout for the lance) for use in the foot combat. The original foot defences, probably sabatons of plate, are also lost. The groin defence, or codpiece, was intended to be worn for the foot combat together with the articulated culet or rump defence. It is of considerable size, and was reputed to have been used as a charm in the old days at the Tower; young women would stick pins into the lining in order to improve their prospects of conception. Unusually it is fitted with additional articulated plates at either side of the main plate. A substantial part of its original lining bands survive, though none of the original linings do.

Erasmus Kirkenar was the Master Workman at Greenwich responsible for the construction of this armour. We do not know when he took over as master from Martin van Royne, as no lists of the workmen there survive between 1521 and 1540, but in the latter year 'old Martin' was still on the payroll, in second place and with a higher salary than Erasmus, either as a pensioner or some kind of Master Emeritus. The few surviving records of the

works of his armourers from later in his reign show that they were not idle. Erasmus Kirkenar's accounts for the year 1536/7, for example, show that they were making a succession of armours, mostly garnitures for the tilt and field with extra pieces at £10–12, and for the field only at £8, to order for the nobility of England. The armour is decorated with etched and gilded borders throughout. Most of these are narrow, and decorated with conventional scrolling foliage. Those on the two sets of tilt reinforces, however, are broad, and based on designs by Hans Holbein the Younger. His 'Englischen Skizzenbuch' (English sketchbook), executed between 1534–38 and preserved in the collection of the Kunstmuseum, Basel, from the Amerbach-kabinett

The ventral plate or inner breastplate.

Detail of left gauntlet.

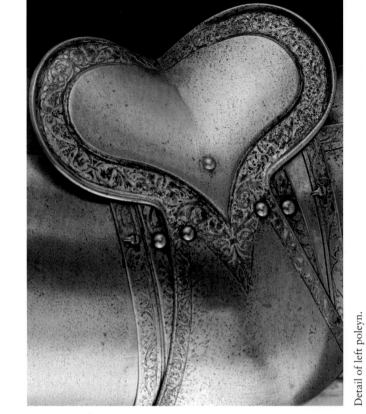

Detail of left poleyn.

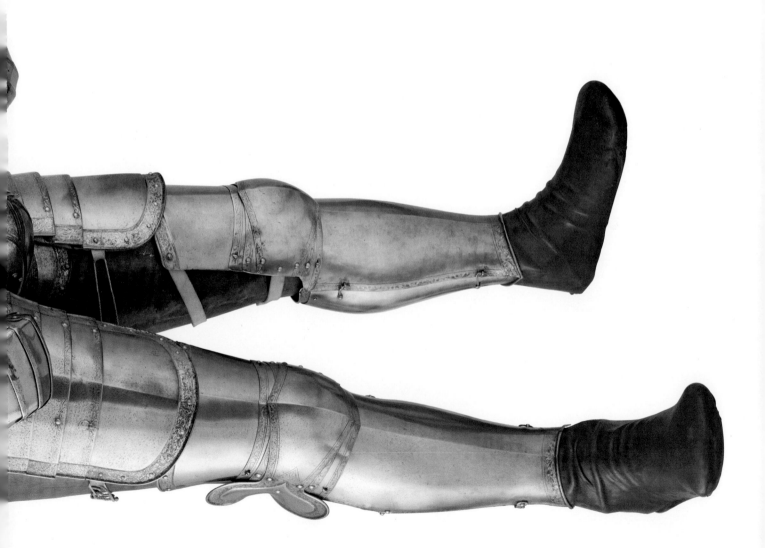

Detail of gorget and left pauldron.

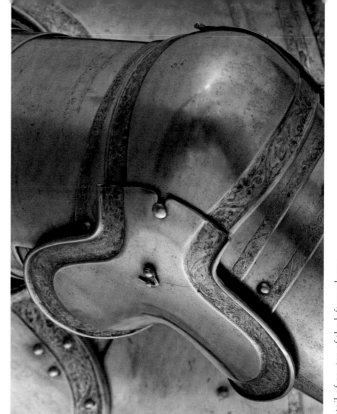

Detail of couter of the left vambrace.

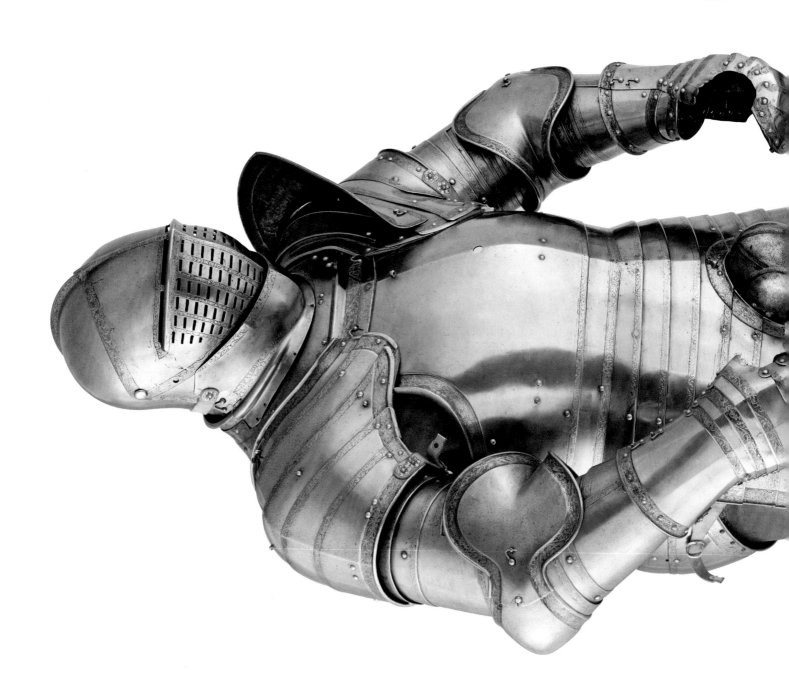

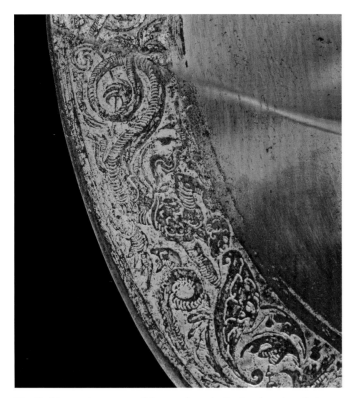

The date 1540 etched on the neck of the breastplate.

Detail of decoration on one of the grandguards: A triton based on design by Hans Holbein.

(formed in the 16th century by Bonifacius and Basilius Amerbach, both professors of the University of Basel), contains several motifs which appear on the armour. No. 1662.165.23 shows a foliage scroll with a merman holding a shield, found on the border of the grandguard.[1] Another similar merman is found on the other grandguard. No. 1662.165.24 has a foliage scroll with sphinxes at either side of the floral spray shown next to the triton on the grandguard, and the winged cherub's head found next to the floral spray and at intervals around the borders is close to those in no. 1662.165.11. No. 1662.165.28–9 illustrate cherubs like those found cavorting around the side edge of the grandguard. At the upper centre of one of the grandguards are the arms of England, supported by a merman, the sketch by Holbein for which is no. 1662.165.43, and a mermaid, while on the other one are the arms of the king with similar supporters.

The etching and gilding could have been carried out by Giovanni di Maiano, still in the king's employ in 1542, or by Francis Quelblaunce, appointed in 1539 as '*gilter and graver of the Kinges harnis*'.[2] The date, 1540, is etched at the front of the collar.

It is perhaps the later of the two great Greenwich armours made for the king during this late period of his reign. The other is that formerly in the Tower collection but since 1916 in the Royal Collection at Windsor Castle. This armour was made for the tilt, with the reinforces for the left side of the body, the grandguard, pasguard and manifer, and may have been made for the jousts held on 11 January 1539/40 to celebrate his marriage to Anne of Cleves. It is decorated with etched borders, most probably to designs by Holbein. An interesting feature of the decoration appears on the sabatons, where the edges of each lame are given a different border, one of which was chosen by the king for the rest of the armour. The armour has been modified during its lifetime, and for this reason has always been regarded as the armour '*all graven and parcell gilt both for the field and tilt*' that was modified for the king to wear at Boulogne in 1544. However recent examinations suggest that it was never gilded, and the main recorded modification to the armour for Boulogne was the cutting away of the legs defences for Henry's still-poorly legs. For these reasons, it is probably best identified as the '*Complete harnesse parcell graven with all doble peces longing to the Tylte and the felde*' at Greenwich in the 1547 inventory, the only one of the king's decorated armours which is not recorded as gilded in the inventory. TR

PROV. Transferred from the Palace at Greenwich 1644

Height as mounted, assembled for foot combat, 1880 mm (74.2 in), weight 35.33 kg (77 lb 13 oz); Grandguard: height 522 mm (20.6 in), width 590 mm (23.3 in), depth 265 mm (10.5 in), weight 5.65 kg (12 lb 7 oz); Pasguard: height 518 mm (20.4 in), width 406 mm (16.0 in), weight 2.65 kg (5 lb 13 oz); Manifer: length 428 mm (16.9 in), weight 1.7 kg (3 lb 8 oz); Right Cuisse: height 375 mm (14.8 in), width 230 mm (9.1 in), weight 1.24 kg (2 lb 12 oz); Left cuisse: height 365 mm (14.4 in), width 230 mm (91. in), weight 1.05 kg (2 lb 5 oz); Left fauld and tasset: width 450 mm (17.8 in), height (left) 360 mm (14.2 in), Right fauld and tasset: height 320 mm (12.6 in), weight 2.75 kg (6 lb 2 oz); Right vambrace: length 560 mm (22.1 in), weight 2.76 kg (5 lb 11 oz) Left vambrace: length 560 mm (22.1 in), 2.52 kg (5 lb 4 oz); Lance-rest: 140 x 78 mm (5.5 x 3.1 in), weight 840 g (1 lb 15 oz); Ventral plate: height 420 mm (16.6 in), width 228 mm (9.0 in), weight 690 g (1 lb 7 oz); Culet width 530 mm (20.9 in), height 150 mm (5.9 in), weight 1.78 kg (3 lb 15 oz)

PUB. Eaves 1993: 2–45; Richardson 2004: 34–39

REF. (1) Mann 1951: 8, fig 2; (2) Cripps-Day 1934: 66

{II.8, VI.13}

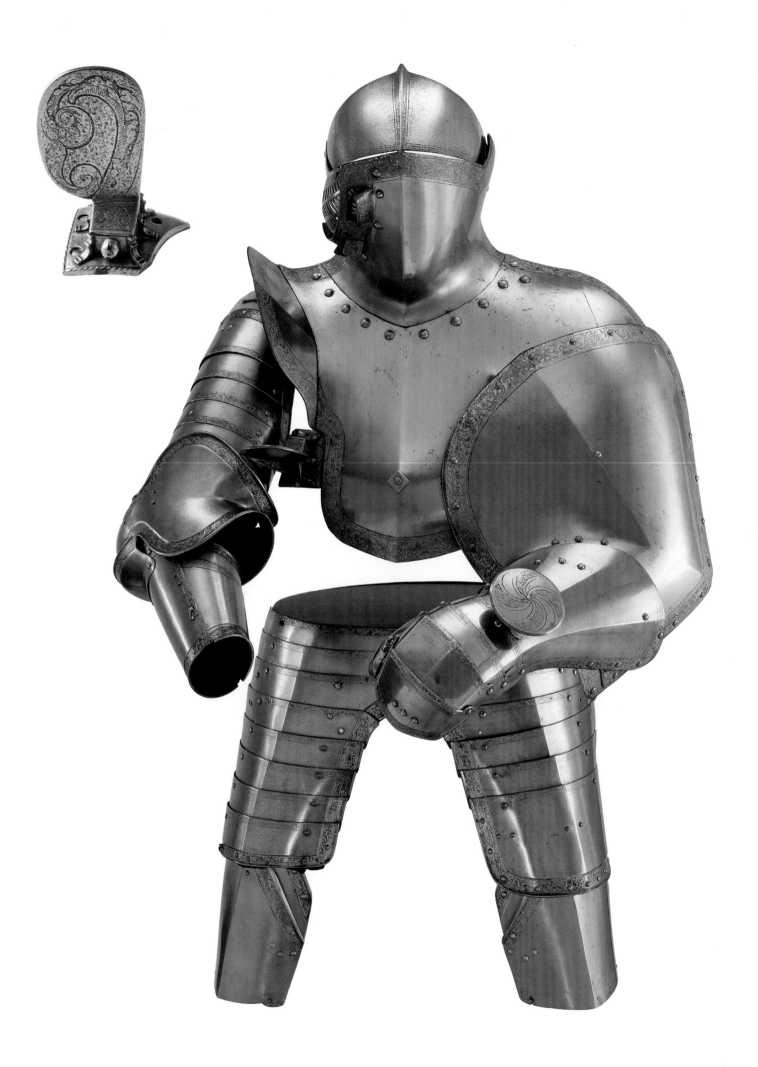

Far left: Lance rest and pieces of exchange for the tilt.

Left: Shaffron: The only surviving element of horse armour from the 1540 armour is this shaffron. It was for use in the tilt and tourney as well as the field. It is made in two sections: the lower one can be detached by undoing the three swivel hooks (only one survives) leaving the upper section as a half-shaffron.

Below: Locking gauntlet: Worn on the right hand for the tourney, this has a finger defence formed of three articulating plates, the end one embossed with fingers and extended to fasten with a pierced stud and swivel hook to the inside of the cuff. The opening at the top and bottom of the hand is shaped to fit the hilt of a sword.

{40}

DAGGER, WITH
ETCHED BLADE

Traditionally belonged to Henry VIII

Probably English, about 1510–20; the wooden grip with steel pommel and ferrule 1960

The short, acorn-shaped quillons are made in one with a shell-guard which is slightly inclined towards the blade. The blade is long, hollow ground and single-edged. It is etched near the hilt with roses, pomegranates and foliage. The blade is marked, near the hilt, with two V-shaped maker's marks inlaid in copper.

The rose and pomegranate (the heraldic device of Granada in Andalucia, Spain) were badges of King Henry VIII and Katherine of Aragon. It has been stated that the presence of Katherine's badge dates it to within the first two decades of Henry's reign but given the rapidity of the deteriorating relationship between Henry and Katherine during this period the dagger probably dates from between 1509-19.[1] RCWS

Overall length 465 mm (18.3 in), blade length 384 mm (15.1 in), weight 227 g (8 oz)

REF. (1) Starkey 1991: 164, no. XI.34; Richardson 2002: 40

{X.39}

{41}

SABRE

Possibly Flemish, about 1500

The hilt consists of a slightly curved hand-and-a-half grip formed from two pieces (scales) of wood, riveted on either side of the tang. The tang remains the same width for its whole length and does not taper. The wooden grip was originally bound in leather, some traces of which still remain. The wooden scales of the grip curve round to form a 'beaked' pommel, the tip of which is now broken off. This was once covered by a cap. The scales are held to the tang by three large rivets, the circular heads of which are engraved with a five-petalled flower (three of the original six rivet heads are now missing). There is one additional large possibly later rivet which shows evidence of having had a circular head. The quillons and quillon block are forged in one piece and attached to the blade by a single rivet passing through the centre of the quillon block. The forward quillon curves upwards to form a knuckle-guard, becoming flattened and spatulate in the plane of the blade edge, and terminating in a single-turn scroll. The rear quillon curves down and makes a short S-bend before terminating in a tongued serpent's head. The entire surface of the quillon is etched and gilded with foliate scrolls which spring from what appear to be Tudor roses at the centre of the quillon block.

The curved single-edged blade bears a shallow fuller which runs two-thirds of its length along the back edge. The forte of the blade bears two crudely etched and gilded panels of decoration at the hilt; on one face is the image of St Katherine, complete with sword and wheel relating to her martyrdom, and on the other St Barbara, with palm and tower.

The blade is stamped on one face three times with an unidentified maker's mark of a punched circle within a cross. This mark was one seemingly used by a number of swordssmiths, including some in Solingen. It has also been stated that the blade bears the maker's mark of 'three-double headed eagles' but this appears to be the result of a confused reading of the above marks.[1]

Weapons of this type are illustrated in Flemish and South German manuscripts of between about 1490–1520. The style of the engraving on the blade may also be compared with Flemish work of the period and is similar to that found on the 'silvered and engraved' armour of Henry VIII (Royal Armouries II.5) although the sword has been described as 'Italian'.[2]

The two saints represented have martial links, St Katherine being the patron saint of knife grinders and sharpeners and St Barbara the patron saint of artillerymen as well as of armourers, military engineers, and soldiers in general.

St Barbara is also represented on the backplate of the 'silvered and engraved' armour mentioned above. Interestingly the bard of this armour also bears the engraving of a falchion, borne by Dioscorus, father and executioner of St Barbara, with a similar form of hilt, the end of one of the quillons terminating in a beaked and tongued head. RCWS

PROV. Transferred from the Rotunda, Woolwich, 1927; Probably taken from the Musée d'Artillerie, Paris, in 1815

Overall length 1219 mm (47.9 in), blade length 991 mm (39 in)

PUB. Blair 1962: pl. 158; Carré 1795: pl. VF; Dufty 1974: 21, pls 35a, 108 (marks); Hewitt 1862: 318-322; Museum of Artillery 1906: 136 (class XIV.8)

REF. (1) Hewitt 1862, Blair 1962; (2) Dufty 1974

{IX.634}

{42}

BIT

Curb bit, probably from the armoury of Henry VIII
Possibly English, about 1515

The S-shaped branches are etched and gilded on both sides with stylized foliage on a hatched ground. Ported mouth with a fluted, melon-shaped roller on either side of the curved port, the latter fitted with a narrow roller to bear on the roof of the mouth, from which depends a three-lobed dangle. A heavy curb chain is attached below the loops for the headstall straps, the branches being connected below centre by a pair of linked bars on which the gilding is preserved. Each branch terminates in a loop pierced by a short bar terminating in a loop that holds a rein-ring. This bar also pierces the terminal loop of one of a pair of linked bars, which connects the branches together in the same way as the pair further up. This bit whose decoration is reminiscent of that of the 'Italian Bard' (cat. no.23) has been ascribed to the ownership of Henry VIII. This association is uncertain as no royal badges are included in the decoration; these might well have appeared on the missing bosses. The 1547 inventory records '*one Bitte of Counterphet Damascene worke with bosses*' at Westminster in the custody of Hans Hunter.[1] WF

PROV. Transferred to the Tower from the Palace at Greenwich 1644

Length 330 mm (13 in), of branches 26.7 cm (10.5 in), width 150 mm (6.0 in), weight 1.22 kg (2 lb 11 oz)

REF. (1) Dillon 1888: 269

{VI.200}

BIT

Curb bit, probably from the armoury of Henry VIII
Possibly English, about 1520

The branches of moderate length, the lower extremities only slightly curved. Ported mouth with a conical hollow roller on either side of the curved port, which is pierced for a missing dangle. Above the mouthpiece is fastened a chain with four roller rings. The curb-chain is formed with a central curved bar of hollow concave section with serrated edges. There are loops for a snaffle rein behind the mouthpiece pivots. Each branch terminates in a loop pierced by a short bar terminating in a loop that holds a rein-ring. This bar also serves to hold a narrow bar that connects the two branches. Each branch is pierced above for a second connecting bar, or for a chain, now missing. Riveted to each branch is a large boss of gilded copper, embossed with a pine-cone in high relief. The branches and curb-chain retain extensive traces of gilding. TR

PROV. Transferred to the Tower from the Palace at Greenwich 1644

Length 250 mm (9.9 in), length of branches 229 mm (9 in),
width 270 mm (10.7 in), weight 1.53 kg (3 lb 6 oz)

{VI.201}

{ 3 }

HENRY VIII: TECHNOLOGY AND INNOVATION

HENRY VIII'S GUN SHIELDS

PETER SMITHURST

These implements which formed part of Henry's armoury were not, of course, intended for the personal use of the King. Their presence in the armoury, and their inclusion in the exhibition are, however, a further reflection of his well-known taste for innovative firearms. Though they may appear somewhat bizarre or even fanciful at first sight, we must assume they were taken seriously at the time since the inventory made at the time of Henry's death in 1547 records 35 'targets steilde wt gonnes' being brought to the Tower from Westminster. A further inventory of 1676 shows that this group had been supplemented and by this time there were 66.[1] Such a quantity is hardly likely to have been accumulated had they been merely fanciful amusements. It has been suggested that they were for use by a royal bodyguard, however, compelling evidence for them having credibility as military weapons arises from the fact that fragments of several have been recovered from the wreck of the *Mary Rose*.[2] This has led to the suggestion that they may have been for naval use, but from their location apparently in storage in the ship's orlop deck it would seem they were not ready for immediate use and therefore were not part of the ship's armament. However, they would not have been there at all unless they were potentially useful additions to the royal arsenal and their compact nature gave them a variety of possible offensive and defensive uses.

Sixteen of these gun shields survive in the Royal Armouries collections and others survive in various public collections around the world, though their origins are a little obscure.[3] Those destined for Henry VIII's armoury may have been produced complete for the King by Giovanbattista of Ravenna around 1544, or, Giovanbattista may have supplied the shields which were subsequently fitted with guns in England.

They are all of the same basic form; circular, approximately 50 cm (20 in) in diameter with the muzzle of the gun protruding through the convex front face. They are constructed of thin strips of wood, possibly oak, ash or elm, laid side-by-side and formed into a dished shape. This first layer is then overlaid with a second layer glued together such that the grains cross at 90°, exactly in the same manner that ordinary plywood is made. By using thin timber strips it would be easier to mould to shape, and layering and crossing the grain would give added strength. The wooden base was then edged and faced with sheet iron or steel cut to the appropriate shape. The inside face appears to have been lined with a woollen cloth, possibly covering a layer of tow or hemp fibre as padding in the region where the arm would rest, and was fitted with leather straps into which the arm could fit. An iron bracket or brace supported the gun.

The guns themselves are of particular interest. Although the matchlock was the simplest of firearms ignition technologies, these particular firearms are of additional technical interest because they were breech-loading and used pre-loaded iron chambers or cartridges tapered on the outside to match the taper of the opening in the breech of the gun. When inserted, they were held in place by a stirrup which pivoted downwards over their rear and locked in position by a spring catch. Not only did this stirrup serve to hold the cartridges in place – it and its fixings also had to resist the full recoil forces when the gun was fired. The creation of matching taper on breech and cartridge so that they are a sufficiently close fit to avoid excessive escape of gas at the moment of firing and yet not so close a fit that the two components 'jammed' together, would have provided a severe technical challenge. But it was a challenge which had to be overcome, otherwise the shooter, taking aim with the gun almost at eye level, would have been at risk of possible serious injury from the hot gases blasting backwards into his face. Although the stirrup which held the cartridge in place would have served to deflect any such gases, the risk of injury would have remained.

The match cord, a length of twine impregnated with saltpetre to promote smooth smouldering, by means of which the gun was fired, was fixed in the jaws of a 'serpentine', a clamp formed at one end of a pivoted shaft carried in a bracket attached to the shield. The opposite end of this shaft was cranked and terminated in a loop to which was secured a short length of cord or twine. With the shield being carried on the left arm, all the preliminary manipulations would have to be carried out using the right hand; the insertion of a loaded chamber into the breech of the gun; the dropping of the stirrup to hold the chamber in place; the priming of the small pan on the chamber with loose powder and the positioning of the smouldering match cord. From that point, the left arm took over; positioning and aiming the gun. It has been generally assumed that the gun was then fired using the thumb of the left hand to pull downwards on the cord of the serpentine to bring the smouldering end of the match into contact with the priming powder. With the shield carried on the left arm and using the right hand to give additional support by grasping one of the guns supporting braces, with the gun mounted above the left arm, at the moment of firing the arm would act as a fulcrum, allowing the recoil forces to attempt to flip the top of the shield back towards the face. At best, these devices can only have been very cumbersome and unwieldy and those factors, coupled with the risk of possible injury to the face, eyes and even the right hand from a blast of hot combustion gases, may have been the causes of their seeming to have had very limited use.

While retaining an overall close similarity, the gun shields can be classified into two basic groups; those in which the barrel protruded through the centre of a conical boss on the shield and those in which the barrel protruded just above the centre of a shallow convex circular boss.

In most of the shields with a centrally mounted gun, there is a small aperture covered by a grille just above the boss, presumably serving as a means of sighting and aiming the gun.

In those which might be referred to as the 'upper gun' type, the outer face is covered with flat plates, some of which are decorated with freehand scrolling gilded ornament though whether this has been added at a later date is uncertain. The central boss is less pronounced and closely follows the contour of the shield. Many are also found with the bosses carrying engraved decoration.

In one (v.39) (cat. no. 44B) Mucius Scaevola is depicted with a hand in a fire. Mucius Scaevola was a hero in Rome's early history. Legend tells that when the Etruscan king, Porsinna, and his army besieged Rome, Mucius entered the enemy camp and attempted to kill Porsinna. He was unsuccessful and when arrested by the guards was brought before Porsinna. Mucius showed no fear and spoke in such a manly way to his enemy that Porsinna was impressed. Then, to show his contempt for pain and torture, Mucius voluntarily placed his right hand in a fire and let it burn without showing the slightest trace of weakness. Even more

impressed with this feat, Porsinna released Mucius. From that time onwards, Mucius was nicknamed Scaevola ('left hand')

Another (v.42) (cat. no. 44D) depicts the mythological character Orion the Hunter with his helmet, a flowing cloak and a sword. He was believed to be the son of the sea-god Poseidon, or Neptune, and the great huntress, Queen Euryale of the Amazons. Poseidon gave Orion the ability to walk on water and he inherited his mother's talents and became the greatest hunter in the world. Unfortunately for him with his immense strength came an immense ego and he boasted that he could outmatch any animal on earth. In response to his vanity a single small scorpion stung and killed him.

A third example (v.99) (cat. no. 44F) shows the biblical character Judith with the head of Holofernes. Judith, a rich and beautiful widow from the Israelites' town of Bethulia, was respected for her devotion to God. Her hometown was besieged by King Nebuchadnezzar's Assyrian army under the command of Holofernes. Judith, invited to a private party with Holofernes in his tent, waited until he was so drunk that he fell asleep on his bed then cut off his head with his sword. She brought the head to Bethulia. Next day Bethulian soldiers, armed with the head of the enemy's commander, managed to drive the Assyrians away.

The rarity of gun shields today might suggest that they did not find widespread military use after their introduction. At best they can perhaps be seen as an experimental diversion which did not quite produce the results expected of them but which, nevertheless, reflect a growing awareness of the potential versatility of firearms in a military context.

Notes and references page 336.

44

GUN SHIELDS (UPPER TYPE)

Probably Italian, about 1540

44ᴬ GUN SHIELD

A gun shield of the type in which the gun projects through the upper portion of the central boss. The main body of the shield is faced with eight segmental thin iron or steel plates, their outer edges held in place by a convex sheet iron rim made up in sections. The junctions between the plates are covered by strips of iron or steel and the inner edges are covered and secured by the central boss. The boss itself is engraved with a scene depicting Mucius Scaevola, a Roman hero, with his hand held in the flames of a fire. The segmental plates are russetted and decorated with gilded scrollwork and there are traces of a fringe on the outer rim.

The gun is typical of its type in this application, being breech-loaded using a pre-loaded removable chamber or cartridge and ignited by a match cord held in a special lever arrangement allowing it to be brought into use by the thumb of the left hand. Its greatest distinguishing feature perhaps is the spiral fluted barrel. PS

PROV. Old Tower collection since 1676

Length of barrel 165 mm (6.5 in), bore approximately 12.7 mm (0.5 in) (36 bore), diameter 483 mm (19 in), weight 4.9 kg (10 lbs 14 oz)

REF. Dufty & Reid 1968: pl. CXL, Norman & Wilson 1982

{V.39}

44ᴮ GUN SHIELD

Similar in general construction to the previous example (V.39). The central plate or boss is octagonal and is decorated with a female figure and windmill in the background. The gun is complete with its restored steel cartridge but lacks the match cord holder. *(Not illustrated)*. PS

PROV. Old Tower collection

Length of barrel 229 mm (9 in), bore approximately 12.7 mm (0.5 in) (36 bore), diameter 483mm (19 in), weight 6.35 g (8 lb 13 oz)

REF. Blair 1958: 182-3

{V.40}

44ᶜ GUN SHIELD

Similar in general construction to V.40 and with a central plate or boss of octagonal form. The gun has a plain muzzle without any mouldings and the sighting aperture is of an outward curving 'V' shape. *(Not illustrated)*. PS

PROV. Old Tower collection

Length of barrel 229 mm (9 in), bore approximately 12.7 mm (0.5 in) (36 bore), diameter 483 mm (19 in), weight 6.34 kg (8 lb 12 oz)

REF. Blair 1958: 182-3

{V.41}

Left and above: Gunshield V.39.

44ᴰ GUN SHIELD

Similar in general construction to V.39 but with a central plate or boss decorated with a representation of Orion the Hunter in a combination of engraving and gold-wash . The segmental facing plates are similarly also decorated with gilded scrollwork but a dis-tinguishing feature is that alternate plates are embossed with a teardrop shape. One of the plates forming the rim is missing and the interior grip has been partly restored. PS

PROV. Old Tower collection

Length of barrel 178 mm (7 in), bore approximately 12.7 mm (0.5 in) (36 bore), diameter 483 mm (19 in), weight 6 kg (8 lb 5 oz)

REF. Blair 1958: 182-3

{V.42}

44ᴱ GUN SHIELD

Closely similar to V.42 but with the absence of decoration on the central boss. The gun lacks its breech lever but the other fittings are complete.*(Not illustrated).* PS

PROV. Transferred from Ordnance Stores, Didcot, 1923

Length of barrel 216 mm (8.5 in), bore approximately 12.7 mm (0.5 in) (36 bore), diameter 495 mm (19.5 in), weight 6.7 kg (9 lb 4 oz)

{V.80}

44ꜰ GUN SHIELD

Similar in general construction to V.39 but with a central plate or boss decorated with engraved representation of the biblical story of Judith and Holofernes, accompanied by a now illegible in-scription. The facing plates are decorated with gilded scrollwork in a manner similar to other shields in this group. The gun lacks the spring lever which holds the breech closed. PS

PROV. Acquired from the United Services Institution, 1958. The remains of a label on the interior of the shield suggest it may have been exhibited at the Art Treasures Exhibition in Manchester, 1857.

Length of barrel 210 mm (8.25 in), bore approximately 12.7 mm (0.5 in) (36 bore), diameter 508 mm (20 in), weight 7.2 kg (9 lb 14 oz)

REF. Dufty and Reid 1968: pl. CXXXVIII

{V.99}

Below and right: Gun shield V.99.

45

GUN SHIELDS (CENTRE TYPE)

Probably Italian, about 1540

45ᴬ GUN SHIELD

The major difference between this item and the preceding group in that the gun projects through the centre of the shield boss which is markedly convex and does not follow the curvature of the shield itself. Also, there is a sighting aperture with a grille immediately above the boss to allow the gun to be aimed. The gun lacks the stirrup which retains the chamber or cartridge, but the match cord holder remains. The facing plates are decorated with gilded scrollwork in a manner similar to some other examples of these shields. *(Illustrated page 226).* PS

PROV. Transferred from Ordnance Office, Tower of London, 1922

Length of barrel 171.5 mm (6.75 in); bore approximately 12.7 mm (0.5 in) (36 bore), diameter 495 mm (19.5 in), weight 6.7 kg (9 lb 4 oz)

{V.79}

45ᴮ GUN SHIELD

As in the previous example, in this shield the gun projects through the centre of the boss which has greater curvature than the shield itself. A sighting aperture with a grille immediately above the boss to allow the gun to be aimed. The segmental plates are embossed to create a medial ridge which branches into two ridges close to the rim, creating a facetted appearance. The gun is complete except that the handle of the shield is missing. PS

PROV. Old Tower collection

Length of barrel 165 mm (6.5 in); bore approximately 12.7 mm (0.5 in) (36 bore), diameter 457 mm (18 in), weight 4 kgs (9 lbs)

REF. Dufty and Reid 1968: pl. CXXXVIII

{V.81}

Right, far right: Gun shield v.81.

45ᶜ GUN SHIELD

Another example of the type in which the gun is placed centrally. It has been extensively restored, including replacement of the supporting bracket for the gun, the handle and the outer central boss through which the barrel protrudes. The gun lacks the stirrup which retains the chamber or cartridge, and the match cord holder. The facing plates are decorated with gilded scrollwork in a manner similar to some other shields. *(Not illustrated).* PS

PROV. Transferred from Ordnance Office, Didcot, 1923

Length of barrel 165 mm (6.5 in), bore approximately 12.7 mm (0.5 in) (36 bore), diameter 457 mm (18 in), weight 3.6 kgs (8 lbs)

{V.82}

HENRY VIII'S FIREARMS

GRAEME RIMER

Henry VIII is known to have had a fascination for many martial sports, among them the shooting of bows, crossbows and firearms, but the first reference to his ownership of a gun does not occur until 1530/31, when he is recorded as having received a *'hand gonne'* from a now unknown ambassador.[1,2] Unfortunately no details of the form or construction of the gun are given, but it is reasonable to assume that at that time, as a piece appropriate for the attention of a king, it would have been of advanced or novel design and probably also decorated. By that date too it was most probably fitted with a wheellock mechanism, the form of ignition system for firearms which appeared in Europe at the very beginning of the 16th century.

Shooting competitions using all manner of projectile weapons had been common in Europe for centuries before Henry's reign, and there are numerous references in the *Book of King's Payments* to losses incurred by the King in shooting matches.[3] These entries, however, do not specify the nature of the weapon used, which could have been a bow, crossbow or handgun. In 1531 a clearer indication that Henry was shooting handguns appears in a record of the purchase of 8,000 pellets while the King was at Woodstock, and later that the King's goods, including handguns, were to be transported back to London.[4] In the following year an entry records that *'Asamus* (Erasmus) *Kirkener'*, the King's Master Workman in the Almain Armoury at Greenwich, was paid *'for trymyng of his graces gonne'*, presumably meaning the reupholstering of the butt (XII.1–2 cat. no. 46–47).[5] In 1536 and 1537 works were carried out at Windsor Castle and at Greenwich Palace to create ranges for the King to use for shooting handguns.[6]

Although clearly Henry must have owned many firearms there is no record until very late in his reign of anyone being appointed specifically to make them for him. One of the two guns surviving known to have belonged to the King (XII.1 cat. no. 46), bears the date 1537 and the initials WH, which were identified by the late Howard Blackmore as perhaps those of William Hunt, who was appointed in 1538 as the first *'Keeper of the King's Handguns and Demi Hawks'* (meaning probably harquebuses) in the Tower of London. This appointment suggests, however, that although Hunt was a gunmaker his role in this post was the supervision of the storage and issue of firearms kept for military use and not those for the personal use of the king. It was not until 1545 that Henry appointed a Royal Gunmaker; Allen Bawdeson. While a gun possibly by William Hunt survives, however, no example of a gun made by Bawdeson for the King is known.

In an article on the subject of Henry VIII's firearms Claude Blair has examined the number remaining at Henry's palaces at the time of his death.[7] Blair estimated that 19 handguns remained at Westminster and 26 at Greenwich, including *'twoo fier Lockes thone grauen thother parcel guilte and grauen'*. This is significant in most clearly indicating the existence of *fier*, ie fire, locks, the term then applied to the wheellock mechanism in preference to the simpler and earlier matchlock.

A high proportion of the handguns listed in Henry's 1547 inventory appear to have been made in Germany, with *'graven and guilte'* decoration and with stocks overlaid or inlaid with staghorn or bone. An idea of the form of the locks and proportions of a German sporting wheellock gun of the mid 1530s can be had from one in the Royal Armouries' collections (fig.1: XII.1566).

Of the firearms recorded in the inventory of 1547 as having belonged to Henry VIII just two survive (XII.1–2 cat. no. 46–47).[8] Although their original wheellocks have not survived, these guns are still remarkable for the sophistication of their construction. Although the guns are significantly different in size they are of a similar design, both being breech-loaders. The inventory mentions no fewer than 139 *'chamber peces'*, so called because they had barrels where a segment of the breech which could be hinged to one side, enabling the insertion of a reloadable iron cartridge, or chamber, containing the main charge and a lead ball or perhaps a charge of shot. Once the cartridge was placed in the breech, the barrel's breech piece was hinged back into place and locked. The lock would be primed and when the trigger was pulled the igniting priming powder would connect with the main charge through a touch-hole drilled through a special locating lug made as part of the cartridge. This design of breech mechanism strongly resembles that of Jacob Snider, whose patent breech mechanism was adopted in 1867 to convert muzzle-loading British military rifles and carbines to breech loading.

While the inventory and the surviving weapons had been a guide to the nature of guns personally owned by Henry VIII there was little firm evidence about the nature of the military firearms he acquired for his forces until the recovery of finds from his flagship *Mary Rose*, which sank in the Solent during an engagement with the French fleet in 1545. Among the material recovered were fragments of the wooden stocks of a particular form of snap matchlock musket, (or more properly *harquebus*). Knowledge of the form of the firearms found on the *Mary Rose* led to the acquisition by the Royal Armouries in 1986 of three examples of

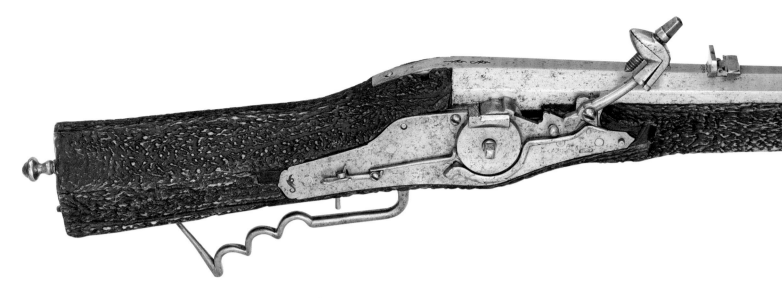

Fig.1 Wheellock sporting gun with a stock veneered with strips of antler, German, about 1535. XII.1566

this type of harquebus (XII.5313–5315, XII.5315 cat. no. 72).[9] One thousand five hundred such harquebuses were sold with a large quantity of other military equipment by the Venetian Republic to Henry VIII in 1544, and it is quite likely that fragments of some of those were recovered from the wreck of the *Mary Rose*.[10]

The discovery of significant numbers of both longbows and harquebuses on the *Mary Rose* led scholars to speculate on the relative power and military efficacy of one compared to the other and on Henry VIII's inclination to have both in active military service. In 1998, therefore, the Royal Armouries conducted a number of comparative ballistic tests, contrasting a modern yew longbow of similar form and draw weight to those recovered from the *Mary Rose* to a careful reconstruction of one of the *Mary Rose* type matchlock harquebuses. These tests showed that although the longbow could be shot more rapidly than the harquebus and with good accuracy it lacked the penetrative capability of the lead ball

of the firearm. Plates of mild steel sheet 2 mm thick were used as penetration targets and at a range of 30 metres these resisted the arrows shot from a 90 lb yew longbow, while with even a light charge of just 50 grains of black powder the matchlock balls easily passed through.[11]

From these tests it was possible to speculate that Henry VIII and his military advisers understood the advantages of the harquebus. Although relatively expensive compared to the longbow, and slower to load, it would not have required the long period of training which effective military archery demanded yet had a much greater ability to penetrate armour. Firearms were clearly the way forward, and research into military equipment later in the 16th century shows why the days of the longbow in war were numbered.[12, 13]

Notes and references page 337.

{46}

BREECH-LOADING GUN

Probably English, dated 1537

Made for Henry VIII and signed with the initials WH

This fine quality gun was originally fitted with a wheellock mechanism but this has been lost and a simpler matchlock has been made to fit the aperture. The date of this lock is uncertain. It has been suggested that it may have been made in the 17th century, but it could be later.

The angular butt of the wooden stock has recesses cut into its outer face and underside. Originally fitted with sliding lids, now lost, these recesses formed boxes to contain shooting necessaries. That on the outer face probably held the winding key which would have been needed to span the wheellock. The left side of the butt has a group of brass nails, which would originally have secured a fabric cheek-pad. Behind the breech tang is an applied leaf-shaped copper alloy plaque, originally gilded, engraved with St George and the Dragon. The left side of the stock opposite the lock aperture is carved with panels of foliage. On the right side of the stock, behind the lock aperture, the letters GT have twice been incised, but no explanation of their meaning has so far been established. Beneath the fore-end the stock has a spherical boss, carved with now much rubbed acanthus foliage, perhaps also incorporating the face of a Green Man. The heavy iron trigger-guard and trigger are later replacements, probably made at the same time as the lock. The partially restored fore-end would originally have extended almost to the muzzle of the barrel but now ends short of it and its tip has been reshaped.

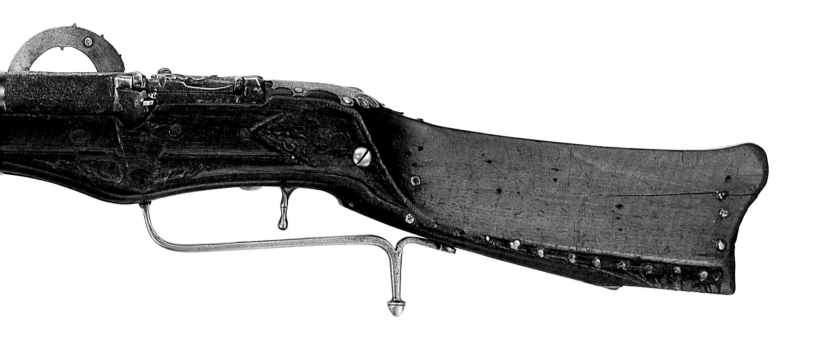

The fine quality iron barrel is formed in the manner of an architectural column but much of its finely executed decoration is now lost through past corrosion and abrasion. The muzzle has a raised circular moulding, behind which is a long section of narrow longitudinal flutes. This section meets a raised band containing the initials HR (Henricus Rex) chiselled in relief, and behind this band is a section containing three slender Corinthian columns, chiselled in relief, between which are two medallion heads. The rearmost element of the barrel is of square section. In the forward end of a framed rectangular panel on top of the breech, chiselled in relief, is a crowned Tudor rose with two supporters, apparently lions, while the foliage engraved on the rest of this panel is now almost obliterated. Behind this panel is an iron breech-block, which, when released after a locking pin is withdrawn to the right, can be hinged to the left to allow the insertion of a reloadable iron cartridge. The lid of the breech-block is strongly chiselled with acanthus foliage and has a small lifting lug on the right side. Its forward end is stamped with the date 1537, and behind that with the initials WH. It has been suggested by the late Howard Blackmore that these were likely to be those of William Hunt, who in 1538 was appointed *'keeper of the king's handguns and demi-hawks'*.

This is one of only two guns surviving which are known to have originally formed part of Henry VIII's personal armoury (cat. no.47 for the other gun, XII.2), and both can be traced back to the 1691 inventory of the pieces then within the collections of the Royal Armouries. In the inventory of the King's effects prepared after his death in 1547 139 'chamber-pieces', that is guns with reloadable cartridges or chambers, to be loaded at the breech, were recorded, and this gun has been identified as most likely to be to one listed in only two possible entries: 8212: *'Item one Chamber pece in a Stocke of woode lyned in the cheke with vellet'*; or 8242: *'Item ij handgun's with fier lockes* (that is wheel locks) *thone with a chamber and percell guilte'*.[1] It is most likely that given its quality and form this gun was intended to be used for target and possibly game shooting by the King. This raises the question of sighting for accuracy. From other even quite modest quality military firearms in use in western Europe in the middle years of the 16th century (see for example the military harquebus XII.5315, cat. no.72) it is clear that there was an understanding of the need for carefully designed sights to assist in accurate aiming.

The maker's initials on top of the breech.

The foresight of this gun is a small iron bead on the muzzle moulding but there is no backsight, at a time when firearms were commonly fitted with a simple but effective tunnel or peep sight at the rear. There is, however, an unexplained metal tongue within a horizontal hole running longitudinally within the copper alloy plaque on the butt. Perhaps this was for the temporary attachment of an aperture sight of some kind, which is now lost. GR

PROV. Old Tower Collection. Recorded in the 1691 Inventory as *'King Henry Eights Carbine'*

Overall length 975 mm (38.4 in), barrel length 650 mm (25.6 in), bore diameter 13 mm (0.54 in), weight 4.22 kg (9 lbs 5 oz)

PUB. Blair 2002b: 22–39; Blackmore 1965: 65, pl. 350-51; ffoulkes 1916: 331, pl. XXXIII; Hayward 1962: 106-10; Hewitt 1859: 67; Norman & Wilson 1982: 73–4, no.60; Reid 1976: 114–15; Rimer 2001: 15; Starkey 1998: 158-9; Starkey 1991: 166, no. XI.39

REF. (1) Blair 2002b: 28

{XII.I}

Far right, top: Inside and outside views of the lock from XII.1566.
Far right: Detail of the recess in the stock of XII.1.

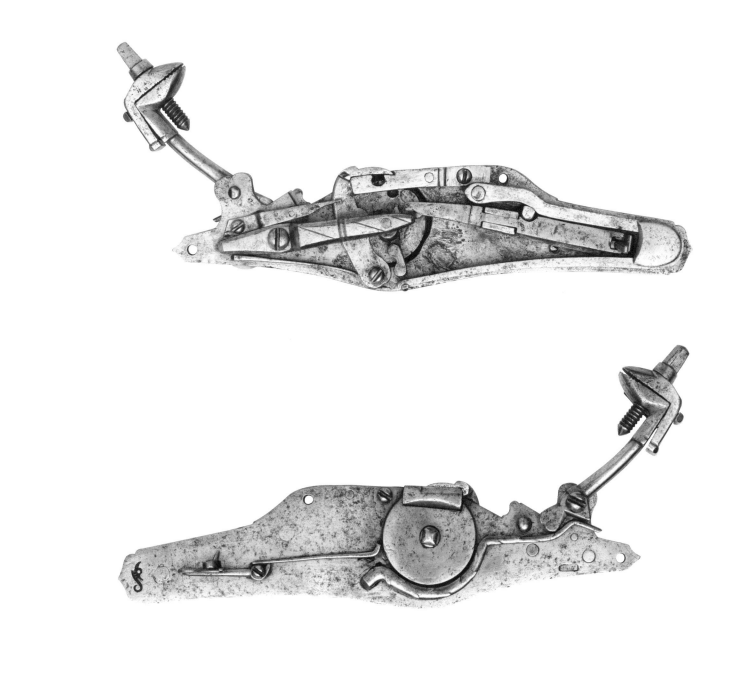

{47}

BREECH-LOADING GUN

Probably German, about 1540
From the armoury of Henry VIII

The wooden stock, perhaps of walnut, is unusual in that it is of two halves glued together longitudinally. The lock is lost, but the form and depth of the recess make it clear that it was originally a wheellock. The angular butt is of a form found on German military firearms of the middle years of the 16th century. It has been shortened and a sheet iron butt plate screwed in place. A substantial fluted mushroom-headed iron peg project outwards from the forward end of the upper right facet of the butt. Initially thought to have been a thumb-rest it is too far back to allow the firer's finger to reach the trigger. Beneath the forward end of the lock aperture the underside of the stock is in the form of a scroll, carved with acanthus leaves on the underside and with a small rosette on each side. Above this on the face opposite the lock is a Tudor rose carved in relief within a raised circular moulding of a form which follows the edges of the forward end of the stock On either side of the fore-end is a lozenge-shaped panel containing a fleur-de-lys carved in relief. Only small fragments of the original copper-alloy trigger-guard survive. The small rounded iron trigger is probably the original.

The substantial iron barrel is decorated on its outer surface in three distinct areas. The bore of the barrel is parallel, but the muzzle flares gently and is fluted for approximately a third of the overall length. The face of the muzzle is engraved with two concentric lines. The centre part of the barrel is of circular section and without surface decoration, while the breech area has flutes of a similar form to those at the muzzle. Carefully and expertly fitted into this section is a breech-block, which hinges to the left to allow the insertion of a reloadable iron cartridge, an example of which is present in this gun and might be original to it. The breech-block is locked in the closed position by a stout internally-mounted spring catch. The large baluster-form knob for this catch is on top of the breech-tang of the barrel and is pierced with a small hole in line with the barrel so that it may also function as an aperture backsight. The breech mechanism is similar to the smaller breech-loading gun XII.1 (cat no.47), but is more refined. Not only does it have a cleverly constructed internal locking mechanism, but the opening of the breech-block is assisted by a spring. Thus when the backsight/breech locking handle is drawn back the breech-block opens automatically.

This gun is much larger than the handgun (XII.1) described above. It is so large and heavy that it is believed it may be an example of a type of gun designed to be mounted on a rest and perhaps fired from a hide.[1] In an article in which these two guns are discussed Claude Blair suggests that such a heavy gun may have been used to shoot large water-fowl, or perhaps deer or boar, by taking a cord or line from the trigger of the gun to shooters concealed from their prey. This would certainly help explain the presence of the mysterious iron peg projecting from the forward upper end of the butt, in a position which suggests it could not really have been for use as a thumb rest.

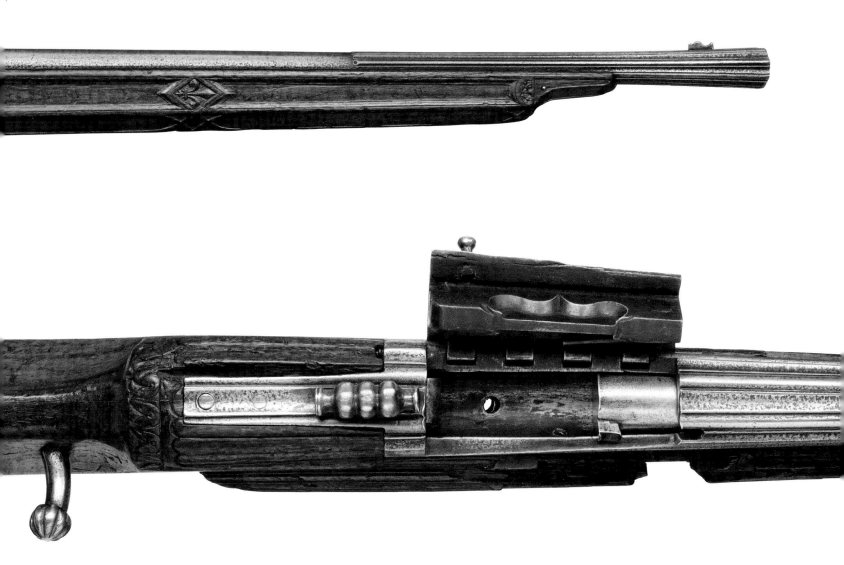

This gun is of less fine quality than the smaller one, and for that reason is less easily identifiable from the 1547 inventory of Henry VIII's effects. Mr Blair has suggested, however that it might be one of those referred to in two possible entries: 8211: *'Item twoo lardge Chamber peces set in Stockes of Walnuttree with fier Lockes'*, or 8213: *'Item one longe chamber pece with a fier locke sett in walnut tree'*.[2] GR

PROV. Old Tower collection. In the 1691 inventory it was described as *'King Henry Eights fowling piece'*

Overall length 1450 mm (57.1 in), barrel length 1105 mm (43.5 in); bore diameter 20 mm (0.7 in); weight 8.16 kg (18 lbs)

PUB. Blair 2002b: 22-39; ffoulkes 1916: 331; Hewitt 1859: 67; Rimer 2001: 15; Starkey 1998

REF. (1) Blair 2002b: 28; (2) Blair 2002: 28; Starkey 1998: 158

{XII.2}

Top: The breech-block in the open position with an iron cartridge partially withdrawn.
Above: A Tudor rose carved on the left side of the stock.

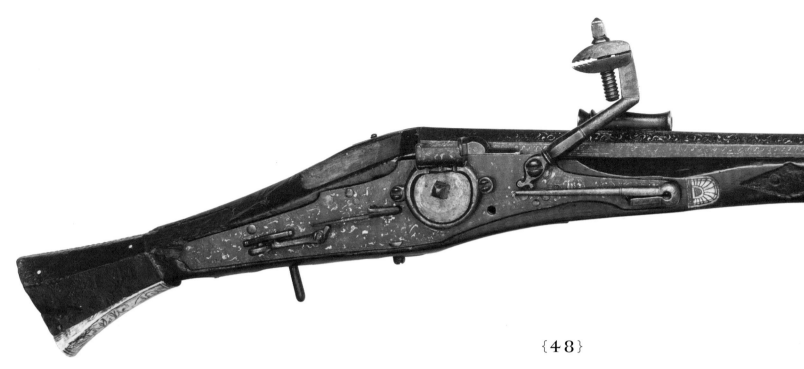

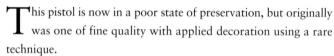

{48}

WHEELLOCK PISTOL

Probably German, about 1550
Decorated by Diego de Çaias or Damianus de Nerve

This pistol is now in a poor state of preservation, but originally was one of fine quality with applied decoration using a rare technique.

The lock is of the form and construction found in the middle years of the 16th century, and is similar to those which would originally have been fitted to the two surviving sporting guns originally owned by Henry VIII (XII.1 and XII.2, cat. nos. 46 and 47). The wheel is mounted on the outer face of the lockplate, held in place by a circular wheelcase. The dog, for holding a piece of iron pyrites to create sparks when in contact with the spinning wheel, is held in its operating positions by an unusual flat v-spring with one short and one long arm. A swivelling safety catch is mounted on the outer face of the rear of the lockplate and operated by preventing the movement of the sear bar, one end of which projects through from the inside of the lock. The outer face of the lockplate retains traces of decoration in false gold damascening in the form of scrolling foliage. The slender and elegant wooden stock extends almost to the muzzle of the barrel, but has lost many of its original engraved bone decorative plaques, including arch-shaped ones which acted as ramrod pipes. The ramrod is therefore missing. One engraved plaque which does survive on the underside of the stock shows a rear three-quarter view of a bearded male figure wearing a Tudor bonnet and a fur-trimmed cape and holding an apple. The long fine

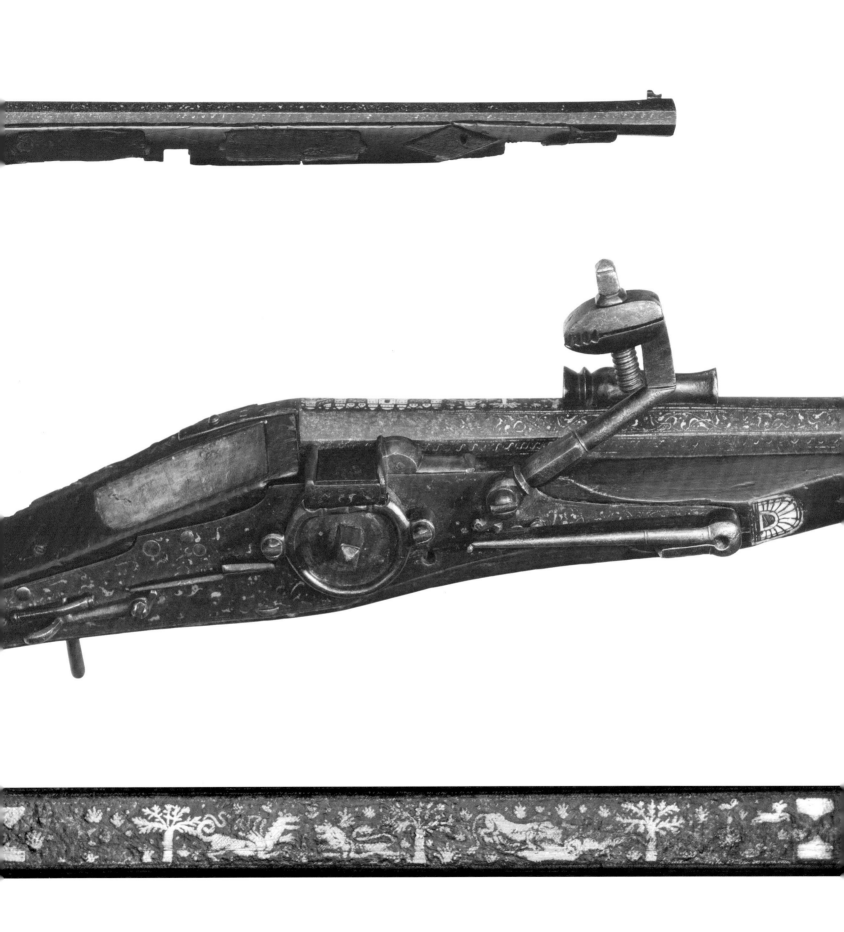

quality barrel is of octagonal section, gently 'swamped' or swelling slightly towards the muzzle. A tall blade foresight is fitted, and at the rear is a tubular iron backsight of baluster form. The visible surfaces of the barrel were originally covered with finely executed decoration in false gold damascening. The vertical and angled facets of the barrel have fine border lines along their edges, and are filled with fine foliate scrolls similar to those on the lockplate. The top surface, however, is decorated with a scene of a townscape, with trees, shrubs and human figures.

While there is no evidence that this pistol was originally in the collections of Henry VIII its most likely date of manufacture and the distinctive nature of its decoration are matters of considerable interest. The form of the pistol would suggest that it was made in Germany in the middle years of the 16th century. The decoration, however, especially the frieze of townscape and country-side features present on the uppermost surface of the barrel, is strongly reminiscent of the work of Diego de Çaias, a Spanish swordmaker and damascener who began working for Henry VIII in 1543 and was still employed by him at the time of his death in 1547, and who worked on in the royal household for Edward VI and appears to have left royal employment between 1549 and 1552.[1] The technique used in applying the decoration is known today as false damascening. True damascening required cutting designs into the surface of a piece of metal, usually iron, with a special tool. Gold or silver was then gently hammered into these grooves and any of this inlay left proud of the surface is then filed off. False damascening is another technique. This did not require the cutting of grooves to form a design, instead the surface of the iron was roughened with a very fine tool to create cross-hatching resembling the cutting surface of a file. Onto this roughened surface tiny carefully shaped pieces of gold or silver were hammered, being held in place by being forced into the irregularities in the surface.

This may have been a less time-consuming method than true damascening but the extraordinary level of skill demonstrated by Diego de Çaias in creating tiny decorative features with remarkable precision and accuracy was exceptional. From known pieces by him surviving in other collections, and from his choice of decorative motifs, commonly town and country scenes involving buildings, trees, horse-drawn vehicles and human and animal figures it is possible that this pistol was decorated by him, or perhaps by his associate or pupil, Damianus de Nerve. A surviving piece known to have been decorated by de Çaias for Henry VIII is a short sword or 'woodknife', whose hilt, scabbard mounts and by-knife bear have gold false damascened decoration, and the blade is similarly decorated with a depiction of the Siege of Boulogne, which took place in 1544. This woodknife is now in the Royal Collection and is on display at Windsor Castle.[2] The provenance of this formerly very fine pistol is regrettably unknown, but its date of manufacture and the nature and quality of its decoration suggest that it must have been made very close to or even before the end of Henry VIII's reign. Several pieces were recorded in the 1547 inventory as having been decorated by de Çaias, but these are all edged weapons. There are just two entries which indicate that the King owned pistols (called 'Tackes' in the inventory) of this type; both recorded as being 'In the Chardge off Erasimus kerkener Armerer'. 8315: 'Item A white Tacke with A fier locke (ie a wheellock) grauen and all the stock white bone…' and 8316: 'Item A Tacke with a fier locke vernisshed locke and all with a Redded stocke set with white bone…'. Clearly Henry VIII would have been familiar with pistols or tackes of the type represented by the pistol shown here, but sadly neither entry refers to either tacke being of 'Dego (sic) his making', which is the way whereby the edged weapon made by Diego de Çaias can so clearly be identified. GR

PROV. Presented to the Royal Armouries by the Metropolitan Police, 1992

Overall length 807 mm (31.75 in), barrel length 584 mm (23 in), bore diameter 11 mm (0.4 in), weight 1.93 kg (4 lbs 5 oz)

PUB. Blair 1970: 149-198; Rimer 2001: 37; Richardson 2002: 40

REF. (1) Blair 1970: 150–1; (2) Richardson 2002

{XII.1025}

COMBINED SWORD (ESTOC)
AND HANDGUN

Country of origin uncertain, probably early 16th century
Traditionally from the armoury of Henry VIII

The blade is of slightly hollow-ground square section, struck on two of its faces with an orb and wolf mark, inlaid in copper. The base of the blade was probably originally bound in leather. The plain square-section iron quillons, which may be a later replacement, taper at their ends to short faceted points, perhaps to allow the sword to be used by grasping the blade and striking with the quillon ends. The plain blackened iron hilt is a muzzle-loading gun barrel.

The estoc, sometimes known as a tuck, was a type of sword designed solely for thrusting, so blades were commonly of triangular or rectangular section, without cutting edges. Estocs could occasionally be found in use in hand-to-hand combat in tournament events, but were also used against dangerous game in the hunting field. After Henry VIII sent the Marquis of Dorset and the Duke of Suffolk on an embassy to France in 1514 the Marquis reported to him later how they had hunted wild boar with the Dauphin: '...*with a wood by the waye as we shulde ride two wild boores of which it was my lord of Suffolks fortune to encountre the fyrst and to give him the furst stroke with his tokke...*'.[1] This example of an estoc is most unusual in having a gun barrel forming the grip. It could have been used conventionally as a thrusting sword of this type, but it would probably have been fitted with a removable pommel acting as a stopper for the muzzle, held in place by a transverse peg or screw, and the vent or touch-hole of the barrel would also have had some form of cover. Both of these are now lost. The barrel was a late example of a small hand-cannon. Once loaded at the muzzle (i.e. pommel) end with powder and ball it would have been primed then fired using a hand-held match cord. This in an unusual combination, and one which brought its own potential hazards. If the sword was used with its barrel charged the muzzle of this loaded weapon would often be pointing at its owner and an accidental discharge would be potentially deadly. GR

PROV. Old Tower collection. Traditionally associated with the contents of the armoury of Henry VIII it may be the estoc referred to in the 1547 Inventory as 14450; '*Item a longe Tocke gilte with gonnes having a locke and a skaberde of blac vellut the crosse and pomell guilte*'[2]

Overall length 1270 mm (50 in), length of grip/barrel 557 mm (21.9 in), bore diameter 13 mm (.50 in), weight 4.1 kg (9 lbs 12 oz)

PUB. Richardson 2002: 32; Williams 2005: 41–59

REF. (1) Williams 2005: 51; (2) Starkey 1998: 362

{XIV.10}

COMBINED MACE AND GUNS

Possibly English, early 16th century

From the armoury of Henry VIII and traditionally known as *Henry VIII's Holy Water Sprinkler*

The stout wooden shaft thickens at the head which is fitted with three short iron gun barrels, between which are set three groups of three short square-section iron spikes. Each barrel was originally fitted with a sliding cover over its vent or touch-hole, perhaps to prevent water or dirt entering but also to help retain priming powder if the barrels were charged ready for shooting. At the top the head has a stout hollow-ground spike which acts as a pivot point for three swivelling sheet iron plates, each shaped to cover the muzzle of one of the barrels.

This weapon could therefore function simply as a long-hafted spiked mace or club, but its user could also choose to fire the guns in its head. This would be done by positioning the mace horizontally, opening the muzzle cover and sliding pan cover of the uppermost barrel, then simply igniting the priming powder with a smouldering match cord, in the manner of a medieval handgun.

There are no makers' marks or other features to help identify the date or country of origin of this piece, however it is recorded as one of a number of spiked maces from Henry VIII's armoury which were given the name of 'Holy Water Sprinklers'. This example was one of only two recorded in the 1547 inventory: Either one listed as being at the Tower; 3775: a *'Holly Water sprincles with thre gonnes in the Topp'*, or one listed as being at Greenwich; 8297: *'Item A holy water sprincle with iij gonnes in thende'*.[1] In 17th century inventories it had become known as *'King Henry ye 8ths Walking Staff'*, and by the 18th century a story had developed among the Yeoman Warders, who gave tours of the arms and armour displays in the Tower of London, that it was the weapon favoured by the King to take with him on nocturnal inspections when he travelled incognito to test the alertness and effectiveness of his guards. Their story suggested that on one occasion a guard, not recognising the King, arrested him for carrying a dangerous weapon at night and threw him in a cell. The unfortunate guard feared for his life when the King's identity was revealed, but was instead congratulated by Henry for carrying out his duties so diligently. GR

PROV. Old Tower collection

Overall length 1829 mm (72 in), barrel length 190 mm (7.5 in), bore diameter 11 mm (.45 in), weight: 3.34 kg (7 lbs 6 oz)

PUB. Borg 1976: 348, pl. XCIIb; Hammond 1993: 35; Richardson 2002: 32; Richardson & Rimer 1997: 44–5; cat. no. 8

REF. (1) Starkey 1998: 103, 160

{XIV.I}

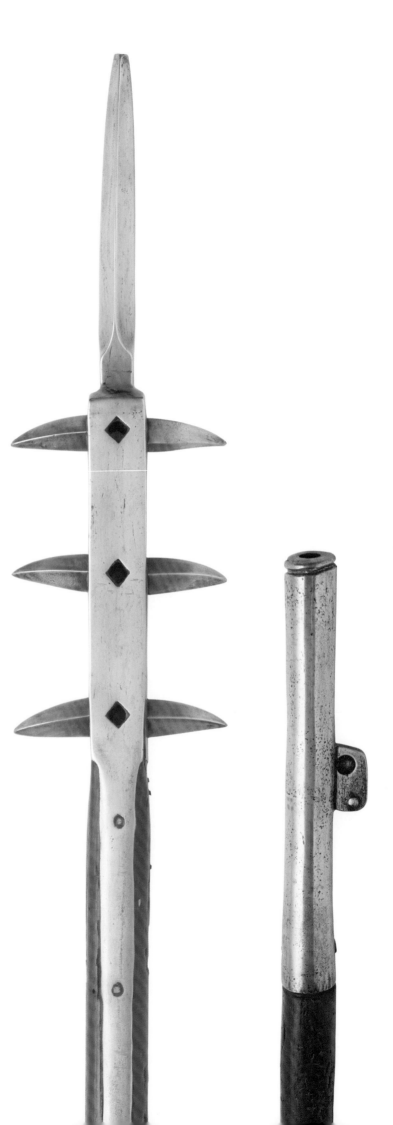

{51}

COMBINED MACE AND GUN

Possibly English, early 16th century
'Holy Water Sprinkler' from the arsenal of Henry VIII

The wooden haft is fitted with a steel head of rectangular section, equipped with a stout top spike and on each of its four sides originally fitted with three shorter spikes. Those from two sides are now missing. The opposite end of the shaft is fitted with a shoe which is in fact a short iron gun barrel. This was originally fitted with an end cap or ferrule which screwed onto the muzzle of the barrel. It was fired in the manner of a small hand-cannon by the use of a hand-held piece of smouldering match cord. The priming pan was originally fitted with a pivoting cover, now lost.

This is one of a number of long-handled maces known as 'Holy Water Sprinklers', fitted with guns which are listed in the 1547 inventory of the effects of Henry VIII as being preserved at the Tower, and is most likely one from a group mentioned under item 3774: *Holly water sprincles with gonnes in thende – vij.*[1] Although it was not one of the pieces clearly described in 17th century and later guides to the Tower it is probably one referred to as a *'Foreign Battle Axe'*, and was probably part of the Spanish Armoury display.[2] GR

PROV. Old Tower collection

Overall length 1765 mm (69.5 in), barrel length: 254 mm (10 in), bore diameter 11 mm (.44 in), weight 3.005 kg (6 lb 10 oz)

PUB. Borg 1976: 317–32

REF. (1) Starkey 1998: 103; (2) Borg 1976: 350, pl. XCIVa

{XIV.2}

{52}

BRONZE BREECH-LOADING
THREE-BARRELLED GUN

English, before 1540

Three bores are contained in the single casting, recessed at the breech to accept three separate powder chambers, now missing. The casting is rectangular in form, resembling the architectural form of a pilaster, much used in Renaissance architecture. At the muzzle is the inscription POUR DEFENDRE 'To defend', the chase being engraved with foliage and candelabrum ornament on a hatched ground. Decoration is confined to the upper surface of the gun, with the exception of low mouldings forming rectangular panels on the sides of the chase. The reinforce bears in high relief a Tudor rose surmounted by a crown supported by two putti (cherub-like figures) indicating plenty, one holding ears of wheat the other a branch, perhaps bearing fruit. Below this is a flat rectangular panel inscribed HENRICUS OCTAVUS DEI GRACIA ANGLIE ET FRANCIE REX FIDEI DEFENSOR DNS HIBER[N]IE '*Henry VIII by the grace of God King of England and France, defender of the faith and Lord of Ireland*'. The founder's name is found in front of the recess for the powder chambers PETRUS BAUDE GALLUS OPERIS ARTIFEX '*Work by craftsman Pierre Baude of France*'. The cascabel button has been fashioned in the form of a dolphin on either side of a central feature now much damaged. There is a transverse slot for the wedge that would have been used to drive the chambers tightly against their breeches.

The gun appears to be that described in the 1540 inventory as: '*a Square pece of brasse with iij halles and vj chambers*'. There was only one, so this must have been a rare piece when cast. It is the only piece in the collection today that can be traced to the 1540 inventory. The entry is not unusual in referring to bronze, an alloy of copper and tin with strong mechanical properties, not brass, which is an alloy of copper and zinc, less strong than bronze. It also indicates the traditional identification of the parts of breech-loading guns in terms of domestic architecture; the component to contain the powder charge at the breech is the *chamber* or smaller private room in a dwelling, while the barrel is

the *hall*, the chief room. As expected for breech-loading guns of this period, the three barrels have two chambers each. The fact that the gun was then in the Mint perhaps indicates it was not part of the main artillery stores. In the famous 1547 inventory the gun has become a '*broad falcon shooting three shot*' (spelling modernised). The *falcon* was a small field gun of about 53 mm calibre [2.1 in] and fairly long in proportion to its bore. It was not usually a breechloader and this description seems somewhat fanciful, although correct for a gun of this calibre.

The decoration, on account of the unusual form of the gun and, it may be surmised, the special circumstances of its production, is more familiar from the decorative arts than artillery, for example on English armour of the period. The royal motif of the Tudor rose with putti as supporters is like that cast on a bronze pollaxe from Cambridge Museum of Archaeology believed to have been made in England for Henry (AL.101.1, cat. no. 93). This kind of decoration was still fairly new in England and the artist may have been one of the Florentine engravers who worked in England, perhaps Giovanni da Maiano or Benedetto da Rovezzano with whom Baude is believed to have been associated.[1]

The gun was mentioned by two 16th-century visitors to the Tower, Paul Hentzner (1598) and Joseph Platter (1599). It was badly damaged in a disastrous fire which destroyed the Grand Storehouse at the Tower of London on 31 October 1841.

Peter Baude, active 1528–46 was a Frenchman apparently of high technical ability. He became one of the King's gunfounders working in Houndsditch, convenient to the Tower of London, where he also cast bells and fine monumental bronzework. He became involved, perhaps at the instigation of the King, with William Levett, the ironmaster priest, and Ralph Hogge, foundry-man, who were working at Buxted in Sussex during the 1540s developing the revolutionary ability of casting large iron guns. He was granted denization in the name of Bawood on the 10 October 1542.

Inscription at the muzzle.

Detail of the decoration on the reinforce.

Gunners and their commanders have always sought to increase the firepower at their disposal. Increasing the rate of fire is one method; it may be taken that the wrought iron breech-loaders in widespread use during the 16th century had a higher rate of fire than contemporary muzzle-loading guns. Therefore this gun can be seen as an attempt to increase further the rapid fire of a breechloader by using three barrels to give six shots in quick succession from one weapon. The King is likely to have encouraged such an experiment even if he did not instigate it. The gun's decoration and the fact that it was cast by Peter Baude links the piece closely to Henry. Another indication that the King was interested in multi-barrelled guns can be found in the inventory of 1547.[2] At the Palace of Westminster, and thus not just forming part of the main stores of arms and armour at the Tower of London, the inventory records several guns with between two and four *halles* (barrels) apiece. These were in a room with some artillery models and so perhaps this was a special collection maintained by Henry and only moved to the Tower after his death.

The difficulty of manipulating the chambers during firing and the weight of the surviving piece must soon have been found to outweigh any advantages. It must quickly have found a place at the Tower as a splendid curiosity, rather as two later three-barrelled guns were to do. Three-barrelled bronze muzzle-loading guns were adopted in the early years of the 18th century by France under King Louis XIV to defeat the Duke of Marlborough; they likewise proved ineffective in combat. NH

Length approximately 2134 mm (7 ft), calibre 53 mm (2.1 in)
PUB. Blackmore 1976: 58
REF. (1) Blair 1959; (2) Starkey 1998: 104
{XIX.17}

{ 4 }

HENRY'S ARMY
AND NAVY

ARMING THE EARLY TUDOR ARMY

THOM RICHARDSON

The army which Henry VIII inherited from his father was essentially a medieval one, equipped similarly to those which had fought the Hundred Years War and the Wars of the Roses in the preceding centuries. The core of the army was of infantry, equipped either with the longbow or the bill; the latter were introduced in the mid 15th century to supplement the men-at-arms in the role of close fighting foot, and eventually replaced them in the role they had so successfully filled since the start of the Hundred Years War. The cavalry were a minority, equipped either as *lances* with complete armour and fighting on horseback, or lighter armed *demilances* used in more mobile roles. The proportions of Henry's 1542 expedition to Scotland were typical; 3,345 horse to 14,407 foot.[1] Although the Tower provided a central arsenal for supply of the army, it was never expected to provide all the equipment for a campaign and the army continued to rely on the armed citizenry. The continuing medieval nature of their equipment is revealed in the military surveys of the counties in 1522 and 1539.[2] The muster rolls taken in Dorset in 1539 and 1542 are particularly rich in detail about the equipment provided. For 7,458 names, 3,503 longbows and 2,147 bills are listed. 648 provide 'harness' (used to cover a wide variety of body armour), and there were 351 sallets, 7 sculls, 238 pairs of splinted arm defences, 12 brigandines, 56 jacks, 144 Almain rivets, 11 doublets of fence, an apron of mail and a buckler. Other weapons included 145 swords, 127 daggers, 5 guns, 12 polaxes, 9 halberds, 8 glaives, only 2 morris pikes, and single examples of the ragged staff, javelin and boar spear.[3]

Towards the end of the 15th century a trend towards equipping the close fighting foot with cheap munition half armours of plate appeared, probably instigated by Maximilian I who ordered a quantity of such armour. Early in Henry's reign we find numerous purchases of these armours, which in England were called 'Almain rivets'. They were, however, not necessarily imported nor necessarily German, though those struck with guild marks inevitably bear those of Nuremberg. The imported armours came at an apparently fixed price of 16 shillings each.

Not all this armour was imported, and the domestic products were substantially cheaper. In 1512 William Gurre, brigandiner of London and addressed by the King as 'our armourer', produced 100 footmen's armours, breast and backplates at 6 shillings and 8 pence a set, the pairs of splints at 3s. a pair, the sallets at 3s. each and the gorgets at 12d. the pieces, a total of £68 6s. 8d. or 13s. 8d. a set; Gurre was in 1516 appointed 'vice Ralph Pontewe brigandiner

during pleasure' at a salary of £10.[4] He was also employed in maintaining the armour, '*making clean of certain harness, bokeling, ledering of cccc Alman rivets*' for the armoury at Eltham in 1517 for £24 7s. 8d., and scouring 1,000 pair of Almain rivets at 12d. a pair in 1520.[5] In July 1516 Godfrey Horne supplied 400 'pair of Almain rivets' for £143 6s. 8d., only 7s. 2d. each.[6]

Large quantities of Almain rivets remained at the end of Henry's reign, as recorded in the 1547 inventory where some 3,700 are recorded in whole or parts in different locations. Although the English army continued to rely on traditional weapons, new firearms technology had been embraced in England since it first became available in the 14th century. Indeed the operation of the arsenal at the Tower, established under the Privy Wardrobe in the 14th century, had become so focused on gunpowder weapons that by 1410 it became the operation of the Office of Ordnance. The proliferation of hand firearms of the early 16th century is illustrated by orders such as that of June 1513 to John de Castro, merchant of Spain, for 80 'handguns with horns' while Leonard Frescobaldi was paid £681 9s. 2d. for halberds, axes and guns.[7] The 1547 inventory itemises in detail the extensive holdings of firearms, both handguns and artillery, in the king's service by the end of the reign.

New types of close combat weapons were also imported from the start of Henry's reign, as a receipt of 1513 for '*maryspikes*' (pikes, or Morris pikes, probably for 'Moorish pikes', as they are called in the 1547 inventory) illustrates.[8] Only small quantities of pikemen, and those mercenary *landsknechts*, are evident in Henry's early campaigns such as the Battle of the Spurs campaign of 1513.[9] Other close combat weapons were homegrown, such as the 260 '*sprynkelles of yron*' purchased in 1513 from Thomas Hert (spiked maces, often called '*holy waters sprinklers*' in the inventories).[10] By the end of the reign there had been a substantial change, and the stock of pikes was substantial. The 1547 inventory gives exact details of these holdings. The Tower of London held 20,100 plain pikes in addition to 785 garnished with velvet, with partly gilded heads, and the separate decorated heads for 476 more; most of the castles and garrisons had a small stock of pikes, the largest being Calais 1,600, Carisbrooke Castle 500, Boulogne 538 and Newhaven 420, a total on land of 24,947 excluding the decorated group.[11] On the ships they were carried in approximately equal numbers with bills, a total of 2,315, making a grand total of 27,262 pikes in the service of the King.

The illustrations in the British Library's MS Cotton Augustus III show how the process of modernising had progressed during

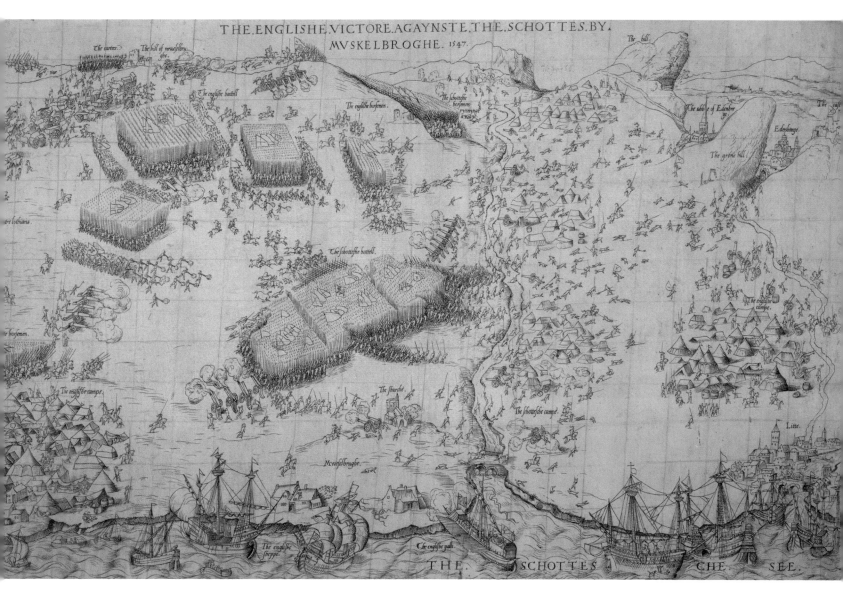

Fig. 1 The battle of Pinkie: 'English victore against the Schottes by Muskelbroghe, 1547' published in 1548. British Library, Maps CC.5.a.409 © The British Library Board

Henry's reign. The foot are now shown as blocks of continental-style pikemen, some eleven ranks deep with three ranks of harquebusiers in front and behind, and groups four ranks deep of longbowmen on either flank,[12] or in a tercio-like formation with three pike blocks nine, 24 and twelve ranks deep respectively, preceded by three, five and four rank lines of harquebusiers, and followed by a further four rank group, and flanked by longbows four, twelve and five ranks deep. The flanks were guarded by blocks of cavalry lances three or eight ranks deep, and small bodies of light horse skirmished in front, while a train of horse-drawn artillery brought up the rear with a few guns advanced on either flank.[13] Nor was this fiction; in a contemporary copper plate print of the battle of Pinkie, the 'English victore against the Schottes by Muskelbroghe, 1547,' published in 1548–9, we see the English army depicted as a textbook continental one, with three pike blocks flanked by harquebusiers, artillery and cavalry on either side (fig. 1).[14] The first appearance of English militia foot

armed with pike and harquebus is recorded in 1539, when the London trained bands paraded before the king at Mile End with harquebusiers preceding bows, pikes and bills.[15] By the end of the reign the English army had been substantially modernised, though affection for the longbow continued for the rest of the century.

Although the troops were not centrally issued with uniforms, the issue of their coats and wages did provide a de facto uniform. Henry's personal troops are recorded at Thérouanne in 1513 in white coats trimmed with green, and this livery is found extensively early in his reign.[16] In 1544, Norfolk's troops were provided with 'a cote of blew clothe garded with redde, after suche ffacon as all fotemen be made at London that shal serve the Kinges Maieste in this journey … Ev'y man to p'vyde a payer of hose for ev'y of his men, the right hose to be all redde and the left hose to be all blewe'.[17] By the end of Henry's reign the former medieval army had been transformed into one recognisable to those who fought in the English Civil wars over a century later.

Notes and references page 337.

ARTILLERY AND FORTIFICATION

NICHOLAS HALL

Henry VIII transformed the place of artillery in warfare on both land and sea. Nicholas Hall examines the change in both the quantity and quality of guns available to English soldiers and sailors. He shows that Henry was not only a big spender on artillery but also interested in fostering developments to make guns fire further, faster and to use heavier projectiles. Similarly, in order to make them more resistant to artillery fire, Henry was personally involved in designing new forts and blockhouses – as well as funding them. As the author shows, recent experiments with replicas have demonstrated the effectiveness of Tudor artillery. Henry clearly did his utmost to bring England up-to-date with the latest designers and makers - for both attack and defence.

And the chiefest cause that English men are thought to be good Gunners is this, for that they are handsome about their Ordnance in ships on the Sea... [1]

If, as David Starkey has observed, the chief princely pastime was killing, either for sport or warfare, artillery promised a spectacular and effective means of execution in battles and sieges. David Starkey also remarked that Henry VIII saw himself as the new Henry V.[2] To prove the similarity meant continuing the Hundred Years War and winning, thus England would once again become powerful on mainland Europe. Before the problem of the succession arose, everything seemed possible to Henry, young and vigorous yet, in terms of power politics naive.

French fortunes during the Hundred Years War had been transformed by artillery. While King Henry VII grasped the value of artillery, in 1496 his ordnance store contained only 63 guns yet vast quantities of longbows and arrows.[3] His neighbour King James IV of Scotland had good reason to indulge '*one of the characteristic enthusiasms of the Renaissance prince: heavy guns*'.[4] James IV built up a powerful artillery inventory for service on land and sea. Henry VIII's ambitions and the example of his powerful neighbours and rivals caused a transformation in English gunnery. The inventory of his possessions taken after the King's death in 1547 contains 52½ pages of lists of guns, with many on each page. For example, at Hull, taking up less than a page of the published inventory, there were 49 guns.[5]

WHAT THEN WERE HENRY'S INNOVATIONS IN GUNNERY?

Henry sought first to increase his arsenal in quantity and second to foster important technical and operational innovations. Finding the home industry wanting he began by importing high-quality bronze muzzle-loading guns from the Low Countries, long established as the centre of an extensive European arms

trade; the fine but damaged falcon in the late Gothic style, cast by Hans Poppenruyter is an example (Royal Armouries XIX.10). And in one case, a culverin was cast for Henry in Fuenterabbia, northern Spain.[6] Gunfounders were amongst the most highly skilled technicians of the day. Henry went on to strengthen the home industry by importing French and Italian gunfounders to work in England.

Field and siege guns were based broadly on the famous French long-barrelled guns firing cast-iron projectiles, universally feared since King Charles VIII's whirlwind campaign in Italy in 1494.[7] Shorter barrelled cannon were produced for siege work where a heavier projectile was required for battering. Muzzle-loading guns had the disadvantage that they required great skill and care in loading, reducing their rate of fire. Henry may also have encouraged therefore the introduction of the port piece – a large wrought-iron breech-loading gun. It seems that the widely-used small breechloaders were redesigned to reach calibres of about 7 or 8 inches in order to fire a substantial stone shot.

Henry encouraged experiment. One of the great challenges for the gun designer was to gain more firepower for a given weight of gun. The use of cast iron instead of stone projectiles in King Charles VIII's guns increased projectile weight without increasing calibre. Another approach is to improve the rate of fire of a given gun. In the close defence of ships or forts, rapidity of fire may exceed other ballistic considerations. This might explain the number of breech-loading guns seen in Henry's ships and forts. Increasing the number of bores in one gun, with the intention of obtaining a high rate of fire, has a long history. Prior to the use of self-contained ammunition during the 19th century, such hopes have foundered on the time taken in reloading. (See Baude gun cat. no. 52). Yet one can imagine the promise of a wonder weapon of devastating firepower and compact dimensions appealing to Henry.

Following the King's death, '...*dyuers and sondry kyndes of*

Munycions and habillements of warre... from the kinges Majesties Palace at westminster' were received at the Tower of London.[8] A group of three guns is described as having three, four and two *'halles'* each. 'Hall' referred to the bore of a gun, on the analogy of the hall and chamber of domestic architecture. Hence 'chamber' to hold the powder charge in a breechloader. Following the multi-barrelled weapons are several *'Little gonnes of brasse mounted uppon cariage....'.* These cannon, demi-cannon and culverin, are described as patrons (patterns) indicating that they were specimen models for full-size guns, presumably presented to the King for approval and retained for reference. If so, it is a delightful piece of evidence of his interest in artillery design.

Henry's success in establishing foreign gunmakers in London created an enduring skilled craft tradition. But copper and tin were expensive and had to be imported. The successful use of cast iron as a cheaper alternative to cast bronze was a significant development. While the raw material and fuel – iron ore and timber – were available in southern England, a degree of technological innovation might be attributed to the naturalised Frenchman Peter Baude (see three-barrel falcon cat. no. 52).[9]

THE GUNPORT

Henry was not alone in facing the problem of the galley in naval warfare. Despite lack of seaworthiness in rough weather, high cost of maintenance and short endurance, the modern galley, in suitable conditions, carrying heavy guns right in the bows, was a threat to any conventional northern ship, unable to close and grapple with a nimble galley while being fired at from a safe range. Some answer had to be found. Warships were adapted to mount heavy armament firing forward. Building galleys was another response. The hybrid galleasse appeared, a conventional northern warship but with the addition of oars, probably more for manoeuvre rather than main propulsion. The real solution to carrying additional heavy guns on board was to mount them low in the hull, firing through gunports, closed when necessary to keep out the sea. Although there must have been some reluctance among shipwrights in cutting large holes in ships' sides, but this major innovation occurred during the first half of the 16th century, possibly in France.[10]

Henry VIII, if not directly responsible for ordering gunports to be provided, must have taken a direct interest in the matter, ensuring his favourite ship, the *Mary Rose* was thus modernised by 1536 at the latest. Perhaps lack of experience in using the new gunports in action contributed to the mournful loss of the *Mary Rose* off Portsmouth in 1545, watched by the King. Henry may not really have been the founder of the modern navy as popularly believed, yet near the end of his reign he created a permanent navy office, vital for continuity and the building up of skills and expertise in warfare at sea.[11]

Was Henry seen as an artillery innovator in his own day? Despite military success that proved limited and very costly, part of his ambition was realised. Henry was able to force his powerful neighbours across the Channel and the Scottish border to acknowledge English power. Henry had both the resolve to engage in European power struggles and the means to wage war, whose costs were inexorably rising. He could lay his hands on phenomenal quantities of cash, first from his father's savings and second his windfall from the dissolution of the monasteries. This cash funded his ambitious policy and covered the cost of defensive measures when it all went wrong.

Henry's reputation abroad is hinted at by the dedication to him of Niccolò Tartaglia's famous book on gunnery and related matters, *Quesiti & inventioni diverse* (1546). The book is written in the form of dialogues, a popular literary device. Castiglione's influential *The Book of the Courtier* (1528) is written in this manner, known in England either in the original or through Sir Thomas Elyot's *Governor* (1531). Italy, although wracked by war and at the mercy of French, Spanish and Imperial troops, had high standing abroad not only in the arts, manners and scholarship, but in gunnery and fortification. Amongst the rival Italian states, Venice lead in gunnery and mechanical matters. Tartaglia, a prominent mathematician, realised that ballistics presented challenging mathematical problems and discovered a deplorable level of knowledge amongst gunners. Tartaglia's work on ballistics was extensively read, and copied, by generations of artillerists; perhaps he is best known for the gunner's arc for fixing gun elevation, with which the book commences, and the first range tables.

Why Niccolò Tartaglia dedicated his book to Henry VIII is unrecorded. But Henry's employment of Italian experts was surely well-known in scientific and technical circles in Northern Italy. Tartaglia, from a humble background, became a lowly mathematics teacher: did he hope for an invitation to England where he would join well-paid Italians already in Henry's service? Tartaglia knew Sir Richard Wentworth, described in Cyprian Lucar's translation as *'gentleman'* to the King.[12] Tartaglia was told that Henry *'delighted much in all manner of warlike devices'.* This gentleman was presumably Sir Richard Wentworth, born between about 1468–75. Knighted in 1512, he was at the battle of the Spurs the following year and attended at the Field of Cloth of Gold in 1520. It is not known if he was ever in Italy; it seems perfectly possible that he was sent on official business or chose to visit Italy some time before his death in 1528. Sir Richard appears, as well as in the dedication of *Quesiti...* , in the fifth book where he discusses surveying techniques. Curiously, Lucar omitted this from his translation title (1588).[13]

Tartaglia might well have admired Henry as a possible check on French power. He had reason to hate the French. Tartaglia, had difficulty speaking and was nicknamed 'estammereri'. At the age of only five, he was taken by his mother for refuge in the cathedral during the sack of Brescia by the French (1512). French soldiers stormed the church and Niccolò suffered vicious sword cuts to his face and was left for dead. Though nursed back to health by his mother, who perhaps could not afford a doctor, his speech remained impaired.

Despite little formal education, he became an original mathematician. He insisted correctly, against the prevailing wisdom, that the path of a projectile was curved from the very muzzle of the gun [unless fired vertically]. The dedication to Henry VIII surely reflects the King's reputation as a mighty prince of Christendom who treated the improvement of military technology with proper importance and lavishly rewarded expert practitioners.

Gifts between heads of state were made primarily for diplomatic reasons. But the magnificent gift from Maximilian van Egmont, Count of Büren and Stadtholder of Friesland of the basilisk long since at Dover Castle, was one surely calculated to appeal to the English King's enthusiasm for artillery. Maximilian had first hand knowledge of this, since he had served with Henry at the seige of Boulogne (1544). This great gun was cast specially for Henry: his arms are prominently displayed. The founder equal to the technical challenge of casting this extraordinary barrel, with its Renaissance decoration, was Jan Tolhuys. Tolhuys served as founder to the city of Utrecht; he supplied many guns to the Emperor Charles V. Henry's basilisk was delivered in 1545. Despite being one of the most impressive guns ever cast, it was far from a mere status symbol; the learned gunner, William Eldred fired the basilisk on several occasions early in the following century, achieving remarkable range and accuracy. Despite its size, it was not just a static piece, somehow being dragged to Cornwall during the English Civil Wars and back to Dover, where it remains.[14]

WHAT OF THE REAL PERFORMANCE OF ARTILLERY DURING HENRY'S REIGN?

The Royal Armouries has long collaborated with The Mary Rose Trust. One of the key questions concerning the *Mary Rose's* main armament was, why did she carry a mixture of wrought-iron breechloaders and bronze muzzleloaders? The question was perhaps unavoidably coloured by the knowledge that later 'broadside' warships had a main armament of lines of similar muzzleloaders, and by the fact that large breechloaders were soon to go out of use. The reasonable suggestion as to why she carried such a mixed armament was that the guns had different tactical purposes. But without data on the performance of the two natures of gun, this remained pure hypothesis. The Royal Armouries and The Mary Rose Trust therefore decided to have

replicas of a port piece and a culverin built in order to fire them with a view to establishing their performance. The author was fortunate to be involved in this programme, starting with the wrought-iron breechloader in 1997 followed by the bronze muzzle-loading culverin in 2001.

Of course, there is far more to the matter of tactical effectiveness than, so to speak, the brute performance of a particular gun. For example, the port piece must have had a higher rate of fire than the culverin. But it seemed necessary to start with ballistic capability as a basis for comparing the two guns. This might lead to some idea of why the port piece went out of use. Perhaps the rising cost of cutting stone shot was a factor, but unlikely to have been the only cause. Although bronze guns were much more expensive than those of cast iron, bronze continued long after the introduction of cheaper iron guns.

The port piece fired stone shot, implying a short-range weapon.[15] It can be light since the powder charge will be smaller than that for an iron shot, since iron is about three times heavier than stone. The culverin usually fired cast-iron shot. Of course, both guns could fire a variety of anti-personnel rounds, such as 'lantern shot' so-called from the resemblance of the casing to the construction of a horn lantern, which was filled with broken stones. Lantern shot fired from the port piece showed that this would have been effective at short range; useful for the close quarters fighting of the early 16th century. But for comparative purposes, round shot of stone and iron were fired. The amount of energy contained in the shot when it issues from the muzzle of the gun, muzzle energy [ME], can be calculated to compare different guns and their possible effects on the target. To test such effects, a target was constructed of oak to resemble a part of the hull of the *Mary Rose*. (The target and the two replica guns are on show at the Royal Armouries, Fort Nelson, Hampshire).

The port piece was constructed from wrought iron using the largely the same blacksmithing skills as those of the 16th century. The staves [strips along the barrel forming the bore] were carefully fitted to each other over a former, held together only by rings like a traditional wooden barrel. The staves were not welded together, as is sometimes stated. The ring and hoops were put on hot, shrinking when cool to bind the staves tightly together – a strong, light construction. The separate powder chamber, two or more per gun were originally provided, makes reloading easier on board ship. Like the barrel, although thicker, it is first made as a tube open at both ends. A plug, in the form of a short cylinder, was welded in place. The construction technique stands as testament to the quality of 16th-century blacksmithing and to that of the 20th-century blacksmiths who forged the replica.

The port piece was impressive on the range. Firing a stone ball weighing about 6.25 kg (15 lb) the maximum velocity achieved was about 338 m/s – approximately the speed of sound.

At short range, the ship-side target was easily pierced, although some shot broke up in flight, a problem noted during the 16th century.[16] No doubt the velocity of the projectile would decrease markedly if fired at long range; our trials only included one longer-range shot. From this limited evidence, it appears that a maximum effective range might be 183 m (200 yards). This was not necessarily a typical fighting range; or evidence of accuracy. Perhaps in good conditions at sea one might hope to hit a target the size of a ship at that distance. Against the ship's side target at short range, the port piece was able easily to pierce it, shattering the stone ball as it did so. This would have caused many lethal fragments of wood and stone to be thrown around the gun deck.

The trials thus confirmed the theory that the port piece was intended for close quarters action at sea. Firing anti-personnel rounds it could be used against boarding parties. In addition, it appeared to be able to penetrate a ship's hull, although unlikely to seriously damage ship structure. No attempt was made at rapid fire, but equipped with two chambers (only one was made for trial) the port piece should have been capable of firing two rounds quickly, much more quickly than the beautiful but cumbersome bronze muzzle-loading guns sharing the gun deck.

One of these, a culverin (MR 81 A1423) was also copied, rather fittingly, in a bell foundry, for it was the technique of casting bells that lead to the production of large cast bronze barrels. If the culverin was the basis of the long-range naval gunnery for which the English were to become renowned by the time of the Spanish Armada (1588), it had to be capable of accurate fire at a greater distance than the port piece. Range tables from a little later credit the culverin with an extreme range of up to a mile, which has been doubted.[17] In fact, our trials showed that this was achievable. Such was not a fighting range; but it was evidence of a more useful ballistic characteristic. Long range was a result of high muzzle velocity: over 500 m/s being achieved. This had an important benefit for the gunner. While it is true, as Tartaglia pointed out, that the projectile in flight, in this case a cast-iron shot, begins to drop towards the ground immediately due to gravity, when the velocity is so high, the amount of drop is negligible for perhaps 185–275 m (200–300 yards). It also means that a target moving at a given rate will have travelled a shorter distance during the time the shot is in flight. This must have made aiming a culverin mainly a matter of judging the movement of the ship nicely, and allowing, probably instinctively, for the slight delay in firing as the priming powder takes fire from the match and ignites the main charge. If the range was not too great, then structural damage was possible, since the smashing effect of a fast-moving shot weighing about 20 lb or more was considerable. It also caused large splinters of wood to fly around the gun deck, causing heavy casualties. Thus in terms of energy contained in the projectile, the culverin proved to be a

much more powerful gun. But the culverin, although more 'powerful' than the port piece, is about twice as heavy – and unnecessary weight was always to be avoided on ships. But comparing the firepower of port piece and culverin per weight of gun the culverin delivers considerably more striking energy. Despite the lack of modern instruments in Henry's time, this effect must have become apparent to keen observers, tending towards the replacement of the port piece type by the cast bronze, and later cast-iron guns. This perhaps justified the muzzleloaders' awkward gun drill and slower rate of fire. Since it could also fire anti-personnel rounds, the muzzle-loading gun supplanted the port piece as main armament by the end of the 16th century.

FORTIFICATION

When Henry VIII came to the throne, the importance of artillery in siege warfare was long established. What was not established was the best way of mounting artillery in the defence. Castles were adapted to mount light guns, as a modern alternative so to speak to archery; rather than real artillery. Purpose-built artillery towers, such as those at Dartmouth, did not mount heavy guns. The problem of the best form of fortification to resist artillery attack was brought rudely to the fore by King Charles VIII's whirlwind campaign in Italy in 1494.[18] Italian engineers, like Michelangelo and Leonardo da Vinci, Renaissance artists and architects, lost no time in responding to the shock of seeing their walled towns falling so rapidly.

Masonry alone was no defence. While height remained useful for look-outs and to command the approaches, high towers were vulnerable. Therefore, low defences using earthworks to protect masonry structures were laid out to plans that gave the maximum effect to the artillery of the defence while avoiding dead ground in front of the works in which an enemy could shelter whilst preparing an assault. This revolution in fortification ensured the high reputation of Italian experts as fortress and seige engineers, leading to their frequent employment by foreign princes, including both Francis I and Henry VIII. Henry offered Girolamo Pennacchi a house and the phenomenal, presumably one-off, sum of £5,000 when employed for the siege of Boulogne [1544], where he was killed. By comparison John Rogers, Henry's trusted English engineer, who had risen from master mason, was awarded an annuity of £36 10s. in 1543, about twice the rate for a master mason.[19]

Fortification from the Middle Ages through to the late 17th century has been seen as the move from masonry to earthworks, from high walls to the low angle bastion, the latter arranged in ever more sophisticated ways. A plan using angle bastions, which gave a platform for artillery to engage the enemy approaches and provided batteries to rake the curtain wall was appealing. Its ability to avoid dead ground and its majestic imposition of geometry on landscape has given the angle bastion an almost magical virtue, perhaps not harmed by its triangular shape. The angle bastion did not spread throughout Europe immediately, and it was not suitable for all situations.

Henry VIII, although undoubtedly genuinely and necessarily interested in fortification design, had the sense to recruit experts, such as John Rogers. Henry frequently made detailed suggestions, as for example for Ambleteuse (1546) where discussion went on for some time about whether the work was to have five bastions (Henry) or four (Rogers and the commanders on site). The latter were clearly worried as to how to put their case to their fierce royal master. Henry might have been trying to emulate his rival Francis I who was building a fortified town of the latest type at Villefranche-sur-Meuse. The design for Ambleteuse using five modern bastions has a similar street plan, suggesting it originated with the King himself.

Yet at Hull, which Henry had visited in 1541, his own scheme was quickly set aside. Instead, across the Humber, Rogers was able to proceed with two large blockhouses connected by a fortified wall almost 760 m (2,500 ft) long (blockhouse is the term used in the inventory of 1547, MS 129, eg folio 365v for those at Hull). Although not according to Henry's plan this was better judged to achieve his aims and the King accepted Roger's proposal. In plan, these blockhouses were cloverleaf or trilobate, similar to those at Guines near Calais. Rogers had been working at Guines when called back by Henry to take charge of the technical side of the re-fortification of Hull. These bastions can be seen as rather provincial compared with the latest Italian designs. Rogers was a competent fortifications designer but as a mason by training, he might not have been completely up-to-date with current Italian ideas. The new angle bastion was only one of the competing theories of the best form for artillery fortification.

One of the greatest recent continental fortresses was Salses in Roussillon [1503; then under Spanish rule], of which something must have been known in England. Salses was traditional in having a high donjon, [tower] but unlike a medieval castle this was surrounded by really massive walls, protected by rounded bastions and a wide dry moat. Despite its lack of angle bastions, it proved impregnable and was considered still very strong over one hundred years later. The blockhouses at Dover depicted by an unknown artist may look exposed compared with an earthwork, yet they were probably well fitted for their purpose (*The Embarkation at Dover*, about 1545, see page 18 and fig. 1). These blockhouses provide substantial mountings for the heavier guns now used, presumably to engage enemy ships, and accommodation and some protection for the gunners, at least from anything except close range bombardment from heavy artillery. This the tower's own armament should prevent. But in the event of close attack, the wrought-iron BL guns could lay down a rapid and destructive fire on waterborne or land assault.

Henry's 'Device Forts', arising from the crisis of 1539, have been discussed extensively.[20] Their cost, about £376,500, was astronomical – royal income was about £250,000 per year. Henry's choice of Stephan von Haschenperg as fort designer was questionable. The forts at Sandown and Camber were over-complicated and he was eventually dismissed for incompetence.[21]

Albrecht Durer's great work on fortification available in England, seems to have influenced English fortification design. Henry, well-informed and well-read, is likely to have been aware of Durer's ideas.[22]

Henry and his advisers sited their castles well. The Earl of Southampton and Lord St John went afloat early in 1539 to work out the siting of Calshot and Cowes Castles.[23] Some were adapted over the years; Sandgate and Hurst Castles became Martello towers during the Napoleonic Wars. Southsea Castle remained in service until the abolition of coast artillery in 1957. Henry's castles would have been stronger if, like the Martello towers of the early 19th century, they had been vaulted in stone. Possibly timber was used for speed of construction. But the continued value of masonry gun towers for coast defence is demonstrated by the construction of Martello towers from 1805 to resist French invasion; one, Tower CC in Suffolk, even shares a henrician-looking quadrilobate (or four-leaf clover) plan.[24]

Camber Castle near Winchelsea, where Stephan von Haschenperg designed the second phase, proved not to be one of the best sited. It was stranded by the harbour silting up. Fortunately this leaves us the castle largely in its Tudor form. Careful excavation has revealed not only its intricate building history but even what the garrison ate.[25] Camber Castle was first a simple artillery tower (1512–14), to which von Haschenperg added an octagonal fort having 'stirrup towers' of unusual design (1540). In plan, the flat part (or tread) was on the outside, projecting enough to mount Italianate flank defence guns. Von Haschenperg's rather weak plan with limited room for artillery prompted a costly rebuild (1542–3) during which more conventional massive semi-circular bastions were added reminding one of Durer's book.[26] Camber altogether cost about three times as much as Pendennis Castle. Henry's castles, essentially functional artillery platforms, needed no lavish ornament. Yet, reminiscent of some of his bronze guns contrasting plain and decorated surfaces, the castles also exhibit decoration, such as carved stone details for fireplaces and coats of arms set against expanses of plain masonry.

Shore installations generally, but not always, had the advantage in a fight against ships. James IV of Scotland, Henry's rival and often superior in military and naval matters, showed in his defeat of the Lord of the Isles (1504) that naval guns could attack fixed defences with success.[27] But this was an unusual case

Fig. 1 Detail from an engraving of *The Embarkation at Dover* showing a blockhouse in the foreground. (In the background Henry VIII is shown aboard ship) I.223

and more often, the difficulties of naval gunnery put ships at a disadvantage against forts and sometimes against field guns. Indeed as late as the 19th century warships using rifled guns could find it hard to hit shore batteries.

Cloverleaf bastions forming part of a carefully considered plan, as at Hull, should then have have proved adequate in wartime. Recent excavations revealed much surviving below ground level and, unusually, found one of the guns of the original armament, removed from the South Blockhouse and laid aside, eventually to dissappear under debris. It must be one of the three port pieces of iron with six chambers listed in 1547.[28] There was an adequate allowance of twenty stone shot per gun.

The combination of heavy bronze guns with breech-loading iron pieces listed for Hull is exactly as shown in *The Embarkation at Dover* (see page 18). Amongst the heavy guns at Hull is, rather surprisingly, a *basilischo*. The term was not precise but always implied large size, in length or in calibre. Here it can hardly have been a very long gun, given the limited space in the blockhouse. Probably it was an especially large cannon, a relatively short gun of heavy calibre, unlike Maximilian's gift. No projectiles are specifically recorded for it; perhaps some of the 60 cannon shot of stone listed were suitable.

At the beginning of Henry's reign, simple square or round towers, accommodating fairly small guns on the lowest floor, to be near sea level to engage enemy ships, were current. Comparison with his last work reveals a remarkable contrast, achieved as a result of the pressures and alarms of the reign. Finally, Yarmouth Castle (1547), on an apparently simple, compact plan uses two angle bastions for landward defence. Yet, for its main tactical purpose, control of the harbour and approaches, Yarmouth relies not on an elaborate plan but on its artillery. Henry's 'castles' – the language had not caught up with the buildings – are evidence of the successful adaptation of European practice to suit local English needs during a period of rapid technological change. In this, fortification development was broadly parallel to that of artillery. Forty years after Henry's death, his reputation for improving gunnery still shone:

We Englishmen have not beene considered but of late daies to become good Gunners... but that for the knowledge in it, other nations and countries have tasted better thereof as the Italians French and Spaniardes, for that English men have had but littel instructions but that they have learned of the Dutchmen or Flemings in the time of King Henry the eight.[29]

Henry, '*rich, fierce and greedy for glory*' may have squandered the royal treasury on his dream of glory.[30] But from his lust for conquest and bulwark against invasion, England gained modern artillery, powerful ships and the greatest system of coast defence since the departure of the Roman legions in 410. His monumental expenditure was matched only by his reputation, illustrated for us by his magnificent legacy of artefacts and buildings.

Notes and references page 337.

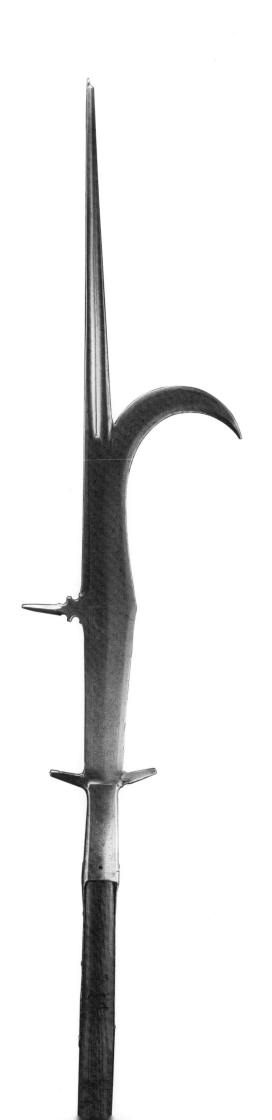

{ 53 }

BILL

For the guard of Henry VIII
Italian, early 16th century

The head is iron, consisting of a long cutting edge that slopes outward to a point opposite the diamond section fluke. Above the fluke the blade becomes double-edged and rises to a large hook. It is topped with a spike reinforced with a medial rib. At the base, just above the socket, are two upturned squared-ended lugs. There is *pointillé* (punched) decoration on both sides up to the middle of the blade. On one side is the image of St Katherine, and on the other St Barbara. Each side also bears a head in profile with an oval cartouche and, composed differently on each side, an oblong cartouche with the cipher HENRY. The socket is decorated with matching floral scrollwork. The haft is modern.

This example is probably one of a small group made in Italy for the personal guard of Henry VIII. This guard eventually evolved into the Yeoman Warders that guard the Tower of London to this day. Records describe these special bills as being gilded, with silk and velvet trim in the Tudor colours of green and white.

The bill is a staff weapon that originated as an agricultural implement. Bills are depicted in many illustrations as being used for pruning or harvesting fruit from high branches. Over time, its power as a weapon was recognized, and military bills are recorded as early as the 13th century. Wielded by large blocks of tightly formed infantry, it was a formidable cutting and thrusting weapon. It was a particular favourite of English infantry by the later 15th and 16th centuries, used most notably at the battle of Flodden in 1513. Henry was said to have stored over 6,700 of his own bills in the Tower and more elsewhere. Although it saw wide use on the medieval battlefield, in the 16th century the bill became more commonly carried as a ceremonial weapon. JH

PROV. Transferred from Rotunda Museum, Woolwich in 1927. Thought to be presented by King George IV (source for this theory unknown).

Overall length 2172 mm (85.5 in), length of head 813 mm (32 in), weight 4.51 kg (9 lb 15 oz)

PUB. ffoulkes 1928: 64, 78; Lankester 2000: 27–43;
Woolwich 1889: 121–2, inv. no. XII.8;
Woolwich 1864: 88, inv. no. XII.14; Norman & Wilson 1982: 68–70;
Richardson 2002: 30; Wilson 1985: 18

{ VII.1341 }

{54}

PARTIZAN

For the guard of Henry VIII
Italian, first half of the 16th century

The long tapering head is made of steel. It has a substantial medial rib with a fuller on either side, making it a powerful thrusting weapon. Two small wings curve out from the base of the head. The head is secured to the modern haft by two small langets. The haft is shorter than the original one would have been. *Pointillé* (punched) decoration depicts the Tudor royal arms, but with the quarters reversed. The arms are supported by a lion to the right and a dragon to the left. On the other side is a helmeted head in profile. The octagonal socket is decorated with rope-work.

The presence of the Tudor arms marks this partizan as one intended for use by Henry VIII's Guard. Though the arms are reversed, this does not appear to have been a mistake, as ceramics have been found that depict the arms in the same fashion. The decoration is consistent with the style of those staff weapons purchased from Italian merchants such as Leonard Frescobaldi of Florence in the early years of Henry's reign. Fifteen hundred decorated partizans are recorded in the 1547 inventory of Henry's possessions. From the 17th century onwards, it was on display at the Tower of London's Spanish Armoury under the label 'Spanish Officers' Lance'. The Spanish Armoury was supposed to have exhibited weapons and torture equipment taken from the Spanish Armada of 1588. In reality, most of the items on display were originally part of Henry VIII's arsenal.

The partizan developed in Italy in the 15th century. It evolved from a simple spear head into its more exaggerated triangular blade design flanked with small wings. It has been thought that the corseque, another staff-weapon, was an off-shoot from the partizan that evolved into a separate type. Though it saw use on the battlefield, by the later middle ages it had become a popular parade weapon. JH

PROV. Old Tower collection

Overall length: 2112 mm (83.1 in), length of Head
(excluding langets) 938 mm (36.9 in)

PUB. ffoulkes 1916 II: 223; Hammond 1993: 35; Lankester 2000: 27–43;
Norman & Wilson 1982: 65, no. 47 (illus.), pl. XII; Richardson 2002:
30 (illus.), 31 (illus.); Richardson & Rimer 1997: 53–3 (illus.);
Royal Armouries 2000: 10

{VII.147}

{55}

HALBERD HEAD

Probably Italian, second quarter of the 16th century.

Steel, with a top-spike of hollow-ground diamond section which tapers evenly to a point. The top-spike is decorated in gilded *pointillé* work with a helmeted male head in profile within a double-line border. Below the top-spike is a separate bulbous moulding which bears incised vertical lines. The axe blade has a straight cutting edge angled down towards the haft. The upper and lower edges of the blade are cusped twice. The downturned fluke terminates in a reinforced spike of diamond section. The flat-sided socket has broad langets, one of which is now broken away. Both socket and langets also bear considerable traces of gilded *pointillé* decoration, again, within a double-edged border.

The form and decoration of the halberd head imply an Italian origin and it is therefore likely to have been one of the staff weapons bought by Henry VIII from Italian merchants and which still survive in large numbers in the Royal Armouries.[1] An almost identical helmeted head, for instance, also appears on a Henrician corséque (Royal Armouries VII. 389) and the 'slashed' pattern on the collar is also found on the mouldings of a number of Henrician pikes (Royal Armouries VII.767 for example – cat. no. 56). However there appear to be very few surviving examples of such halberds, there being perhaps only two other Henrician halberds in the Royal Armouries (VII.962 and 970). The 1547 inventory lists some 940 halberds in possession of the King at his death.[2] Many of these are likely to have been used by the various bodyguards of the King and in particular the Yeoman of the Guard. This suggestion is supported by references such as that in the *King's Book of Payments* for April 1520 which includes the payment of £91. 6s. 8d. (£91. 03) to Sir William Skevington, Master of the Ordnance, who was paid for supplying '*gilt halberds and javelins for the Guard*'.[3] Similar halberds, also with gilt decoration, are depicted as being borne by various members of the King's retinue shown between the Archcliff and Black Bulwark forts in the harbour at Dover in the painting of *The Embarkation at Dover*, of about 1545–50 (The Royal Collection Inventory No. 405793 [Hampton Court; Redgrave: 515]) and also in the companion painting *The Field of Cloth of Gold* (The Royal Collection Inventory No. 405794 [Hampton Court; Redgrave: 520]) also of about the same date. RCWS

PROV. Excavated from the bed of the River Thames at Queenhithe dock in 1977; Acquired in 1978

Overall length 650 mm (25.6 in) (incomplete), weight 995 g (0.99 kg)

REF. (1) Wilson 1985: 16–17; (2) Starkey 1998: 103, nos 3746, 3783, 3784; 104, 3840, 3841; 120, 5094; 132, 6620; 133, 6297; 160, 8286, 8289; 346, 13864; (3) Brewer 1867: 1540; Richardson 2002: 31 (illus. centre); Starkey 1998; Wilson 1985: 15–20

{VII.1717}

{56}

PIKES

English and Italian, mid 16th century

Pikes such as the example shown here are of a style known today as 'Henrician' from their original association with the military arsenal assembled during the reign of King Henry VIII. The narrow leaf-shaped blades are of diamond section and have a spherical moulding just above the socket. The head is attached to the haft by two langets and three nails. Though some of the hafts are thought to be of considerable age, not many are likely to be contemporary with the heads and probably date from the 17th century. Some hafts have remnants of fabric, particularly velvet or leather. Many are drastically shortened, probably at a later time for ease of display. Some *pointillé* decoration, mainly foliage, remains visible. Two of the pikes (VII.2301 and 2302) still have traces of gold wash on the studs that secure the head to the haft.

The pike shown here was probably made for Henry VIII's arsenal to be stored at the Tower of London. Much of the surviving *pointillé* decoration matches the style of that on other staff weapons commissioned for Henry. The 1547 inventory of Henry's possessions list 20,100 *'Morris Picks'* held at the Tower. The name 'Morris' may come from 'Moorish', indicating a possible Spanish origin of the weapon. Later in the 16th century, they were referred to simply as 'pikes'.

Pikes saw much use in the 15th to 17th centuries. Used by blocks of well-formed infantry, they were very effective against cavalry charges. Swiss, German and Italian troops were amongst the first to organize pike units. From there, the trend spread throughout the rest of Europe. Early on in his reign, Henry VIII had to hire mercenaries, particularly German *Landsknechts*, to fill the ranks of his pikemen during campaigns to the continent. Henry eventually encouraged the use of pikes in England, resulting in the later formation of units such as the London Trained Bands in 1572. JH

PROV. Old Tower collection

Average overall length 4570 mm (180 in), average length of head 216 mm (8.5 in), average length of langets 330 mm (13 in)

PUB. ffoulkes 1916: 235; Lankester 2000: 27-43; Richardson 2002: 30 (illus.)

{VII.767, 737, 793, 722, 727, 732, 744, 782, 791, 773, 802, 729, 746, 768, 734, 779, 736, 781, 725, 735, 799, 748, 775, 2301, 2302}

{57}

SPEARS (JAVELINS)

Italian, early 16th century

Spears such as the example shown here are known generally today as 'Henrician' from their association with the arsenal assembled by Henry VIII. The head is hollow and attaches to the haft by a short socket and two rivets. The medial rib extends from the socket to the tip of the blade. The haft is modern. One haft, on VII.31, could be original as it still contains some traces of leather and fabric. Each is decorated with an etched or engraved shield-shaped frame encompassing a Tudor rose on top of two leaves and sprigs. On some of the heads, this design is placed over a hatched background. One spear (VII.44) still retains some of its original gilding. Each also bears a stamped maker's mark of either a seven or eight-toothed cogwheel.

They were commissioned from Italian merchants by Henry VIII, probably for his Guard known as the *'King's Speres'*. This unit of bodyguards later became the Gentleman Pensioners. The 1916 catalogue of the Armouries at the Tower of London has them labelled as 'Military Boar Spears'.

Spears are one of the most basic infantry weapons. They have existed in some form for millennia, and the principle of the spear has lived on in subsequent weapons such as the pike and the bayonet. Spears were still a popular infantry weapon in Henry VIII's armies, particularly amongst the Welsh. The muster list of Denbighshire in 1539 records even more spearmen than billmen. Decorated spears also served as marks of rank for infantry officers. JH

PROV. Old Tower collection

Average length of head 432 mm (17 in)

PUB. ffoulkes 1916: 221; Hammond 1993: 23 (illus.)

{VII.15, 23, 27, 31, 33, 37, 39, 43, 44, 45, 47, 48}

CORSEQUE

From Henry VIII's arsenal
Italian, early 16th century

The head is steel, consisting of a large triangular blade with two flat-ended lugs at its base. Two wings extend diagonally out from the base, each with two downward-facing points. All three blades are reinforced with medial ridges for enhanced thrusting capability. The decagonal section socket has two langets that extend down the modern haft. The base of the central blade, the two wings and the socket are decorated with etchings depicting putti, centaurs, grotesques, foliage and scroll-work. This whole area was also fire-gilded, of which significant portions have survived. On each side of the central blade is an I-shaped maker's mark that is found on many Italian-made weapons.

This is most likely one of the '*three-grayned staves*' mentioned in the 1547 inventory of the possessions of Henry VIII. The Middle English word '*grayne*' often referred to a blade. Hence, '*three-grayned*' likely refers to a three-bladed weapon. There were 279 of these listed on the inventory, of which 25 were recorded as being gilded. This piece is almost certainly one of that set, presumably intended for use by Henry VIII's Guards.

Weapons such as these were popular in the 16th and 17th centuries. They could have evolved from the medieval lugged spear. These began as hunting spears, the two lugs at the base of the blade serving to prevent a strong thrust from bringing dangerous game, such as a boar, too close to the hunter. Gradually these spears were adopted as weapons of war. Another theory is that the corseque evolved from another staff weapon, the partizan, growing a wider central blade and less pronounced wings. JH

PROV. Transferred from Rotunda Museum, Woolwich. Thought to have been presented by King George IV (source for theory unknown)

Overall length 1931 mm (76 in), length of head 559 mm (22 in), weight 1.45 kg (3 lb 3 oz)

PUB. Lankester 2000: 27–43; Woolwich 1889: 121, inv. no. XII.1; Woolwich 1864: 88, inv. no. XII.10; Norman & Wilson 1982: 67–8, no. 50 (illus. 66); Richardson 2002: 31 (illus.)

{VII.1340}

MUNITIONS ARMOUR
FROM HENRY'S ARMOURY

English or Flemish, about 1510-30

This group gives a good impression of the type of munition armour that was issued to men-at-arms from the king's armoury in the early 16th century. During that period men-at-arms continued to fight as 'lances' wearing full plate armour and often riding barded horses. The English heavy cavalry of Henry's army are nicely illustrated in the painting of the meeting of Henry and Maximilian at the battle of the Spurs (Guinegate, 1513) in the Royal Collection (no. RICN 405800), where the style of their armour is contrasted accurately with that of their Imperialist counterparts. A small number of components for these armours is recorded at Greenwich in 1547, '*iiij white harnesses complete for the felde lackinge iiij paier of legge harnesses and iij paier of cushes, Item vj blacke harnesses complete for the felde lacking v paier of cushes and vj paier of greves*'.[1] Far more were issued for service; at Bridewell there were '*Demilaunces brests and backs iiij*[XX], *collers lx, Vambraces lxxviij paier, Cushes iiij*[XX] *paier, Gauntlettes iiij*[XX] *paier, Poldernes iiij*[XX] *paier, Hedpeces xl*' as well as among '*Thodde harnesse remayninge for horsemen, Cusshes lxij paier*'.[2] At Hampton Court there were 68 cuirasses for demilances together with 52 headpieces and 68 pairs of cuisses, and among '*Thodde harnesse for horsemen, Cusshes iiij*[XX] *xj paier*.[3] There were also '*great Shaffrons cccxvj, demi Shaffrons xiij*' in the inventory of 1547, and several of these survived in the Tower arsenal.[4] The group of these pieces in the Royal Armouries are among the earliest surviving pieces from the working arsenal. None of them is struck with a maker's mark, and it is impossible to be certain whether they were imported from Flanders or made in England in imitation of the Flemish style. TR

REF. (1) Dillon 1888: 278, Starkey 1998: 161; (2) Starkey 1998: 162; (3) Starkey 1998: 163; (4) Starkey 1998: 163

59A CLOSE HELMET

The skull has a low comb and a deep reinforcing plate on the brow, with a cusped rear edge. The visor is solid, of 'sparrow's beak' form with a point at the front and a step above it to the sight. The right side is pierced with breaths, and there is a single sight. The bevor has a square cut-out at the centre of its upper edge, and is secured to the skull by a swivel hook and pierced stud at the right. There are single gorget plates at the front and rear, both associated. The surface of the brow reinforce and the front right of the visor are damaged. *(Not illustrated)*. TR

PROV. Old Tower collection

Height 295 mm (11.6 in), width 188 mm (7.4 in), weight 2.93 kg (6 lb 7 oz)

PUB. Blair 1958: 202-3; Dufty & Reid 1968: pl. LXXXIX

{IV.23}

59B CLOSE HELMET

The skull has a low comb and a deep reinforcing plate on the brow, with a cusped rear edge. The visor is solid, of 'sparrow's beak' form with a point at the front and a slope above it to the sight. Both sides are pierced with breaths, and there is a single sight. The lower edge of the sight is roped, and the upper edge of the visor is cusped. The bevor has a square cut-out at the centre of its upper edge, and is secured to the skull by a swivel hook and pierced stud at the right. It has a reinforce riveted to the upper centre, with a roped upper edge, designed so that the lower edge of the visor fits inside it when closed. There are double gorget plates at the front and rear, those at the rear restored, those at the front probably original. The flange of the skull is pierced with holes for lining rivets. TR

PROV. Old Tower collection

Height 300 mm (11.9 in), width 190 mm (7.5 in), weight 2.8 kg (6 lb 3 oz)

{IV.24}

Right: IV.24

59ᶜ CLOSE HELMET

It comprises a skull made of one piece, with a medial ridge. There is a deep skull-reinforce, cusped at the rear, and with a boxed outward turn at the front forming the upper edge of the sight. At the rear are three holes for a plume holder. The visor is of 'sparrow's beak' form, with a central point and a slope above. The lower right side is pierced with breaths. The bevor is shaped to the chin, and fastened closed by a swivel hook and pierced stud at the right. The visor and bevor are secured by a pivot at either side of the brow. The flanges retain their original flush lining rivets. There is a single gorget plate at front and rear, both associated and of mid- to late 16th-century date, with roped main edges and a recessed border with holes for lining rivets. TR

PROV. Old Tower collection

Height 285 mm (11.3 in), width 172 mm (6.8 in), weight 3.52 kg (7 lb 12 oz)

REF. Dufty & Reid 1968: pl. LXXXIX
Rimer & Richardson 1997: 176 no. 16

{IV.26}

59ᴰ CLOSE HELMET

The skull is of one piece, with a medial ridge decorated with roping formed with double incised lines. It has a deep reinforce cusped at the rear. The visor is of one piece, of 'sparrow's beak' form pierced with series of breaths at the right. The bevor is weakly shaped to the chin, with three holes at the right and two at the left for the missing fastenings. The original flush lining rivets survive. There are two gorget plates at the rear and one at the front. Inside the plates construction marks of two stamped wedges can be seen. *(Not illustrated).* TR

PROV. Transferred to the Tower from the Ordnance Store, Didcot, 1923; originally from Royal Hospital, Kilmainham, Dublin.

Height 290 mm (11.4 in), width 186 mm (7.3 in), weight 3.25 kg (7 lb 3 oz)

{IV.388}

59ᴱ CLOSE HELMET

The skull is made in two pieces, joined in a horizontal riveted seam below the visor pivots. At the centre is a low comb, and either side is embossed with a spray of low flutes. These continue on the brow reinforce, which is deep and cusped at either side. The visor has a substantial additional brow reinforce, and a two-piece sight across the centre with a step below it. The upper bevor is prow shaped at the front, narrowing at the sides to the pivots, with a roped upper edge. The lower bevor is shaped to the chin. There are two gorget plates at the front and rear, those at the front restored, the main edges with roped inward turns and narrow recessed borders, the subsidiary edges cusped and scalloped. Construction marks in the form of incised Roman numbers can be seen inside the plates. TR

Height 340 mm (13.3 in), width 205 mm (8 in), weight 3.41 kg (7 lb 8 oz)

REF. Dufty & Reid 1968: pl. LXXXIX

{IV.521}

Right: IV.521

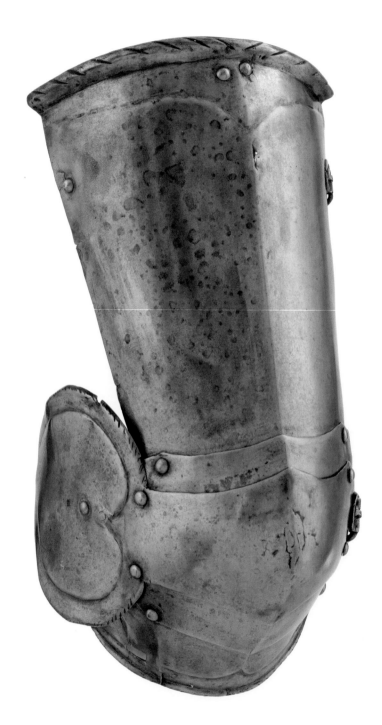

60ᴬ PAIR OF CUISSES AND POLEYNS

The main plate, poleyn and the lames above and below it are embossed with three vertical file roped ribs. The upper edge has a roped inward turn. The poleyn has a side wing with two embossed ribs. TR

Right: length 418 mm (16.5 in), width 201 mm (7.9 in), weight 910 g (2 lb); Left: length 418 mm (16.5 in), width 202 mm (7.9 in), weight 915 g (2 lb)

{III.829–30}

60ᴮ RIGHT CUISSE AND POLEYN

For the right leg. The upper edge of the main plate has a bold, roped inward turn. The poleyn has a rectangular side wing with a roped edge and recessed border. Below the poleyn are two articulating lames, the lower of which is pierced with two keyhole slots for the attachment of the greave. *(Not illustrated)* TR

Height 350 mm (13.8 in), width 187 mm (7.4 in), weight 700 g (1 lb 9 oz)

{III.932}

60ᶜ PAIR OF CUISSES AND POLEYNS

Right: height 400 mm (15.8 in), width 165 mm (6.5 in), depth 150 mm (5.9 in), weight 800 g (1 lb 12 oz); Left: height 400 mm (15.8 in), width 166 mm (6.6 in), depth 5.9 in), weight 955 g (2 lb 1 oz) *(Not illustrated)* TR

{III.951A–B}

60ᴰ PAIR OF CUISSES AND POLEYNS

Right: height 365 mm (14.4 in), width 184 mm (7.3 in), weight 705 g (1 lb 9 oz); Left: height 365 mm (14.4 in), width 182 mm (7.2 in), weight 820 g (1 lb 13 oz) TR

{III.4665–6}

Left: Right cuisse and poleyn III.4665.
Right: Right cuisse and poleyn III.829.

61ᴬ SHAFFRON

The main plate is embossed with a roped rib at the nose, and with fluted facets at either side. The eye defences are forged from the main plate while the ears are attached with rivets. At the centre of the brow is one large and three small holes for the attachment of a roundel and threaded spike and a plume holder. The edges are bordered with round headed lining rivets, all modern. *(Not illustrated).* TR

Height 620 mm (24.5 in), width 242 mm (9.6 in), weight 950 g (2 lb 2 oz)

{VI.23}

61ᴮ SHAFFRON

The single main plate is embossed with a bulge at the nose and a medial ridge. The ear and eye defences are all forged in one with the main plate. The main edges have roped inward turns with double recessed borders, and all the edges retain their original flush lining rivets. At the centre of the brow is riveted inside a threaded bracket to which the faceted roundel and threaded spike, both apparently original, are attached. TR

Height 615 mm (22 in), width 230 mm (9 in), weight 1,790 g (3 lb 15 oz)

{VI.36}

61ᶜ SHAFFRON

The main plate is shaped over the nose, with a medial ridge and fluted facets at either side. The ear defences are made separately and riveted on. The main edges have roped inward turns with recessed borders. The edges are bordered with round headed lining rivets with square washers, all probably original, and retaining inside the nose the original lining band. At the top is a hole and a keyhole slot for a detachable poll plate. At the centre of the brow is a hole through which a later threaded spike of square section, probably not original, retains a contemporary faceted roundel. TR

Height 560 mm (24 in), width 253 mm (10 in), weight 1435 g (3 lb 2 oz)

{VI.40}

61ᴰ SHAFFRON

The main plate is made in one piece with separate ears attached by rivets. The main edges have roped inward turns with recessed borders. The edges all retain their original flush lining rivets. The shaffron has broken at the top where the original poll plate was attached, and has a modern welded repair at that point. It has a large faceted roundel attached by a modern nut and bolt. *(Not illustrated).* TR

Height 630 mm (24.7 in), width 258 mm (10.1 in), weight 1,535 g (3 lb 6 oz)

{VI.45}

61ᴱ SHAFFRON

The main plate is embossed for the nose, with embossed ribs at the centre and at either side of the brow and is made with a separate nose and ear defences and side pieces below the eyes, all attached by rivets in cusps and scallops. The main edges have roped inward turns. At the centre of the brow is a small rosette roundel attached by a short threaded spike. At the top is a poll plate, attached by its original hinges. The rear of the plate is pierced with a keyhole slot at either side and a central hole for a peg, for the attachment of the crinet. The rivets attaching the components together also serve as lining rivets, with circular washers. Traces of the original leather straps survive. The original eye defences have broken off and riveted repairs fitted. The knurled roping is found on a substantial group of munition armour of the mid 16th century. *(Not illustrated).* TR

Height 750 mm (29.6 in), width 240 mm (9.5 in), weight 965 g (2 lb 2 oz)

{VI.35}

Top right: VI.36   Right: VI.40

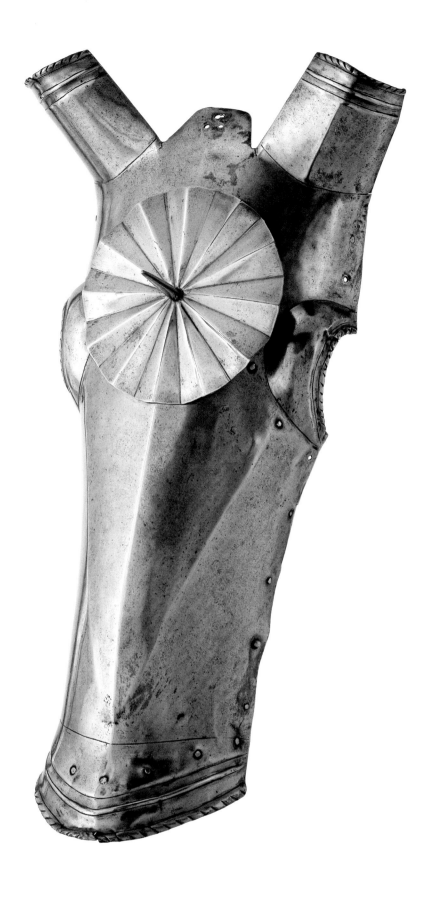

62ᴬ SADDLE STEELS

The bow is made in three plates, the cantle in a single piece. The main edges have roped partial turns with recessed borders. The ground is decorated with sprays of triple flutes. The lower section of the pommel plate has been broken off, and replaced with a modern plate which joins the two side panels. All the plates are secured together with modern nuts and bolts. TR

Bow height 420 mm (16.6 in), width 615 mm (24.3 in), pommel height 195 mm (7.7 in), width 198 mm (7.8 in), weight 850 g (1 lb 14 oz); cantle height 455 mm (18 in), height 145 mm (5.7 in), weight 655 g (1 lb 7 oz)

{VI.100-1}

Above: VI.100

Right above: VI.101

Right below: VI.103

62ᴮ SADDLE STEELS

The bow is made in three plates, a central pommel and two side plates; of the cantle only the central plate survives, and the narrow side sections are lost. The main edges have roped partial turns with double recessed borders. The ground is decorated with sprays of triple flutes. All the plates are secured together with modern nuts and bolts. ᴛʀ

Bow height 430 mm (17 in), width 700 mm (27.6 in), weight 1210 g (2 lb 10 oz); cantle height 155 mm (6.1 in), width 435 mm (17.2 in), weight 490 g (1 lb 1 oz)

{VI.IO2-3}

62ᶜ SADDLE STEELS

The bow is made of three plates, the cantle of two, all joined by modern nuts and bolts. The main edges are plain and flanged. The inner corner of the right plate and a section around the bolt hole is damaged and reinforced with a riveted repair. Inside the plates are stamped with the broad Arrow mark of the Board of Ordnance *(Not illustrated)*. ᴛʀ

Bow height 515 mm (20.3 in), width 682 mm (26.9 in), weight 1730 g (3 lb 13 oz); cantle height 300 mm (11.8 in), width 620 mm (24.5 in), weight 965 g (2 lb 2 oz)

{VI.I27A-B}

FRAGMENTS OF A FIELD ARMOUR

English or Flemish, about 1500

Examples of armour used in England in the late 15th and early 16th centuries are exceedingly rare, and only fragments of the latter survive in the Royal Armouries. One highly unusual survival is a group of fragments of armour preserved in the Church of St Lawrence, Hatfield, in Yorkshire. Originally comprising a complete field armour, all that is left now is the visor from the armet, parts of both arm defences, comprising both couters, the inner plate from the left lower cannon, the greave and poleyn from the left leg defence and part of the right foot defence. The main edges have boxed outward turns. The couters and poleyn have the broad, heart-shaped wings characteristic of north west European armour of the period. The greave has a keyhole slot at the front for the attachment of the plate sabaton.

Helmets of the 15th and early 16th centuries in English churches, while not exactly commonplace, are at least fairly numerous. However, the limb defences preserved at Hatfield are quite possibly a unique survival. The only substantial comparable group of components from a complete armour preserved in England is that now at Helmingham Hall in Suffolk, which was also said to have come from a church. The fragments of armour preserved at Hatfield bear close comparison to a number of important armours made around the turn of the 16th century in England and Flanders. The 'silvered and engraved' armour of King Henry VIII, for example, provides a good impression of a complete version of the Hatfield fragments, albeit a highly decorated and royal one, and many detailed features are common to both, such as the form of flat-seamed turner used on the upper cannons of the vambraces. Most closely comparable to the Hatfield fragments is the so-called 'man in the cupboard', the armour associated with the tomb of Karel von Egmond, Duke of Gelre, in the church of St Eusebius, Arnhem.[1] This armour, which is complete, almost exactly matches the Hatfield fragments, and is stamped with two makers' marks which are regarded as Flemish, one including the letters WG under a star in a shield, the other with the letters WE over a star in a shield. The latter mark is also found on the right rear of one of the close helmets formerly at St Mary's Church, Warwick, and on a couter in the Royal Armouries which matches closely the Hatfield and Arnhem couters (no. III.1353, from the collection of Sir Edward Barry, sold Sotheby's 5 June 1965 lot 63). The Flemish collection is reinforced by comparison with the couters and flat turners of the armour of King Philip the Fair of Spain by the Master of the Orb and Cross in the Real Armería, Madrid.[2] TR

Visor: height 115 mm (4.5 in), width 210 mm (8.3 in), depth 220 mm (8.7 in), weight 675 g (1 lb 8 oz); Lower cannon: length 198 mm (7.7 in), weight 150 g (5 oz); Right couter and upper cannon fragment: height 193 mm (7.6 in), width 125 mm (4.9 in), weight 458 g (1 lb); Left couter: height 174 mm (6.8 in), width 100 mm (4.0 in), weight 342 g (12 oz); Left upper cannon: height 215 mm (8.4 in), weight 505 g (1 lb 2 oz); Poleyn: height 174 mm (6.9 in), width 131 mm (5.1 in), weight 364 g (13 oz); Greave: height 480 mm (18.9 in), width 132 mm (5.1 in), weight 1075 g (2 lb 6 oz); Sabaton fragment: height 90 mm (3.5 in), width 115 mm (4.5 in), weight 166 g (6 oz)

PUB. Richardson 2000

REF. (1) van der Sloot 1985; (2) No. A11, Ortiz et ql 1991: 114–7, no. 17

Church of St Lawrence, Hatfield

{AL.288/1-8}

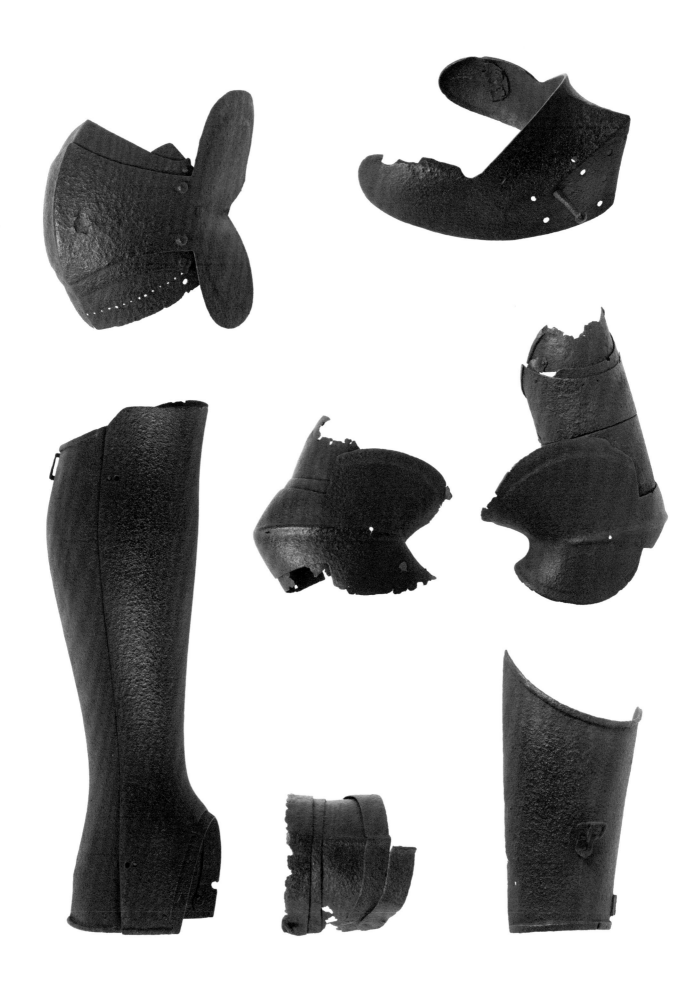

{64}

JACK OF PLATE

English, mid 16th century

Made in the form of a doublet, composed of small iron plates about 30.5 mm square each with a central hole and cropped corners, between two layers of coarse canvas and a covering layer of fine linen, possibly fustian. These plates are secured by a net pattern of cords through the central holes, with diagonal cords only beside the front opening. The plates within the rows overlap towards the centre, while the rows overlap downwards at the left front and upwards at the right front. The cords are knotted where they pass though the fabric and plates, each knot being covered originally by a tuft of green silk. Inside the jack is lined with a layer of fine canvas. The jack opens at the front, where it is five columns of plates wide at either side, and is fastened by modern laces in original eyelet holes. It is of deep-bellied form without the distinct peascod found on the later 16th-century group of jacks of plate. There is a low standing collar also formed of a single row of plates, and a short skirt divided into four trapezoid panels, six rows of plates deep. The textiles are quite worn and fragile, and a few plates are missing in the skirts.

The jack of plate is a, or perhaps the, characteristic English body defence of the middle and later years of the 16th century. It was developed from the earlier, quilted jack which is first recorded in the late 14th century, and provided the mainstay of armour for the English infantry in the 15th century.[1] Jacks lined with mail are known from at least the early 15th century[2] and these continued in small numbers into the early 17th century. Jacks lined with plates appeared for certain by about 1532, and in the 1547 inventory of Henry VIII there were '*iij Northern jackes made of canvas and plate*' at Greenwich.[3] An order for 1500 '*Jackes of plates for the furniture of the quenes shippes*' was placed in 1557 and delivered in 1560,[4] and that this jack of plate and the other of the same type in the Royal Armouries, no. II.26, were from this batch. During Henry's reign jacks were used by extensively by archers and light horse, though none survive from this period. In Ireland in 1515 for archers it was '*ordeyned at lengyth, that every man shall have his jakke; and*

because a man cannot shoote easye with a brest, archers of Ingland will bere no brest*'; for the horse '*to have his horsse and his harnoyse, and his speres, after the maner of Welsh speres... and hit be at his election to ryde in whyt (white) harnoyse, after the maner of England orelles to ryde in his jakke, with his halbryk and his gorgete*'.[5] TR

PROV. Old Tower collection

Height 625 mm (24.7 in), width 420 mm (16.6 in), depth 310 mm (12.2 in) as mounted

REF. (1) Richardson 1997; (2) Eaves 1989: 142–3, notes 44-5; (3) Dillon 1888: 275; (4) Eaves 1989: 135, note 21; Cripps-Day 1944: 73-4; (5) Eaves 1989: 140, note 39

{II.27}

{65}

ALMAIN RIVET

Probably German, Nuremberg, about 1510

Early in Henry's reign we find numerous purchases of half armours for infantry, which in England were called 'Almain rivets'. They comprised simple head defences, called a '*Salette*' or '*Skulle*', breastplates, occasionally with tassets, backs, sometimes a gorget of plate or a mail collar, often neither, and simple vambraces called '*Splintes*' which had gutter-shaped upper and lower cannons joined by a single internal leather to a shell-like couter, a simple spaudler with articulating lames at the shoulder and plates for the back of the hand and cuff articulated by rivets sliding in slots. Despite their name, they were not necessarily imported nor necessarily German, though those struck with marks inevitably bear those of the Nuremberg guild. The imported armours came at an apparently fixed price of 16s. each: in May 1513 1,700 such '*complete harness for footmen*' were purchased for £1,360 from John Cavolcaute through Robert Bolte, grocer, followed in the same month by 1,300 more for £1,040 from the same source, from Guido Portenary, a merchant of Florence, for 2,000 more for £1,600, and in June 1513 for 4,500 more from Leonard Frescobaldi, another Florentine merchant for £3,600.[1] Some of these armours at least were Italian, as the warrant to John Daunce to pay Guido Portenary of Florence £80 for 100 '*Milleyn harness for footmen*' in 1514 illustrates.[2]

Large quantities of Almain rivets remained at the end of Henry's reign, as recorded in the 1547 inventory. At Westminster there were 544, comprising breastplates, backs, splints, collars and sallets, and at Windsor 384 breastplates, 382 backs, 380 pairs of splints, 357 sallets and skulls, 377 gorgets of mail and 369 codpieces of steel, while at Bridewell there were '*Fotemens harnesse, Allmayne Revettes brests and backes clx, Splentes clx paier, wantinge the salettes and gorgettes*' as well as among '*Thodde harnesse remayninge for fotemen, Brestes cxxvij, Splintes ccvij paier*'.[3] At Deptford there were '*Allmayne reuet brestes viij*ᶜ *xlviij, Backes viij*ᶜ*, Splintes viij*ᶜ *xlviij paier, Salettes ccccvj, Thodde harnesse being good, Splintes lxvj paier, Refuse harnesse being litell worthe, Brestes and backes for Allmayne Revettes m*ᶦ*m*ᶦ *paier, Salettes iiij*ᵐᶦ*, Splintes m*ᶦ*m*ᶦ *paier, Gorgettes j*', and at Hampton Court 433 breast and backplates, 358 collars, 298 pairs of '*Arme skynnes*' and 200 '*Hufkines*'.[4] In the armoury at Portsmouth there were 526 '*Almayne ryvettes with splentes and salettes vnuto them for the moost parte*' and 20 more in the south castle, 300 at Boulogne, 123 with tassets and 69 without in Pontefract Castle, 200 at Alnwick Castle with 90 sallets and 10 extra breastplates, 20 in Hull and 99 pair in the garderobe at the House of St John's.[5] TR

PROV. Old Tower collection

Breastplate: height 450 mm (17.8 in), width 315 mm (12.5 in), weight 2200 g (4 lb 13 oz); Right vambrace: length 735 mm (29 in), weight 1005 g (2 lb 3 oz); Left vambrace: length 705 mm (27.8 in), weight 1115 g (2 lb 7 oz); Sallet: height 135 mm (5.3 in), width 185 mm (7.3 in), depth 214 mm (8.4 in), weight 920 g (2 lb)

REF. (1) Brewer et al 1920: 1.2, 872–3, 876, 897; (2) Brewer et al 1920: 1285; (3) Starkey 1998: 162; (4) Starkey 1998: 163; (5) Starkey 1998: 111, 131, 133, 135, 141, 345

{III.78, II65A-B, IV.276}

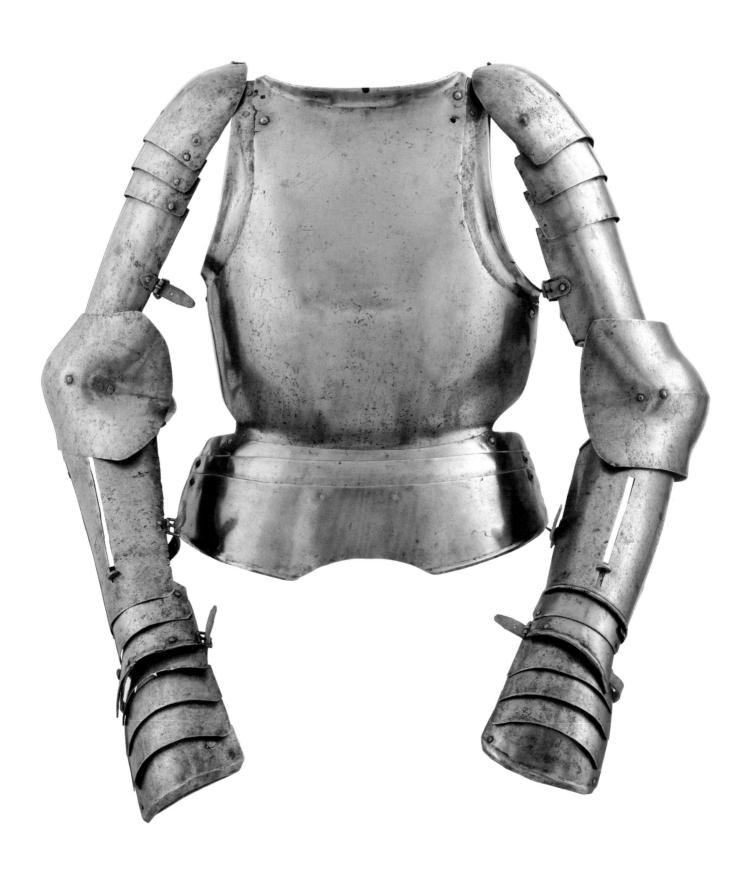

{66}

BRIGANDINE

North West European, 1540–50

The brigandine is formed in two parts, a front and a back panel, sewn together at the right and over the right shoulder, and closed at the left side and left shoulder with laces which passed through eyelet holes in the edge of the fabric. The front section has a slightly curved profile and dips down at the centre of the waist. The defence is formed of small, overlapping, tinned iron plates riveted inside a canvas coat. The rivets are of brass, probably gilded. They are arranged in single straight lines, one row per plate, except at the lower edge where they are arranged in rosettes, and round the neck where they form a wavy line. Those round the arms and neck are decorative, riveted only through the fabric. The front section has fourteen columns of plates, all overlapping downwards (viewed from inside). Separate rows of plates run round the arms and neck, and those round the neck have decorative scalloped edges. The rear section has twelve columns of plates, overlapping upwards above the waist and downwards below it. The canvas is covered with crimson velvet of which substantial traces survive, particularly round the rivets. The brigandine is sleeveless and has an upstanding collar and a short skirt indented over the fork. On either side of the skirt are three rivets and rosette washers of brass with retain fragments of the velvet covered canvas straps by which the missing tassets were originally attached.

The brigandine evolved from the type of body defence known as a pair of plates of the 14th century, and the term is first found in England in the 1390s.[1] Throughout the 15th century the brigandine was a lighter alternative to the plate cuirass, and though it is usually associated with well-armed retinue infantry was often used by men-at-arms. Retinue archers of John Howard Duke of Norfolk in 1464 were mostly equipped like John Strawenge '*on his hauen horse. And my master lent hym a payr of briganarys cueryd wyth blak ledyr and a standard off mayll and a bowe and a salat wyth a vesere of meleyn*', the brigandines bought at '*xij s vj d apece*'.[2] The inventory of Henry VIII of 1547 records at Westminster '*Briggendines covered with black fustian and white lynnen Clothe called Millen cootes ccx, Item Briggendines covered with lynnen clothe havynge longe Taces ij*' and '*x Blacke Briggendines*' at Westminster, At Greenwich '*one Briggendine complete having sleves covered with Crymson clothe of golde*', '*one Briggendine covered with blewe Satten*' and '*one Briggendine covered with Crimsem Satten and sett with guilte Nailles*'.[3] These last three were clearly the King's personal brigandines, and it is tempting to identify the last with the present brigandine. Five hundred more were purchased by the Armouries Office in 1560,[4] of which 200 were issued to the Guards at Greenwich in 1558, but after about 1570 the brigandine became redundant. In the early 17th century 142 brigandines survived in the Tower, and a brigandiner was still on the staff of the armoury in the early 17th century though no brigandines were made. TR

PROV. Old Tower collection

Height 635 mm (25.1 in), width 1025 mm (40.5 in),
waist circumference 990 mm (39 in), weight

PUB. Dufty & Reid 1968: pl. CXXIII; Eaves 1989: 99–101, note 7;
Grosea, 1786, pl.26; Laking 1920 II: 179, fig 544

REF. (1) Eaves 1989: 102, note 13; (2) Crawford 1992 I: 194, II: 33;
(3) Dillon 1888: 270-1, 273, 276; (4) Eaves 1989: 105, note 16;

{III.47}

BRIGANDINE OF CLOTH OF GOLD

Possibly for Henry VIII

Possibly English, mid 16th century

The brigandine is formed of small, overlapping tinned iron plates, or lames, riveted inside a canvas doublet. The rivets are of gilded brass with small, round heads, and are arranged in straight rows, one per lame, except round the lower edge where they are in double rows. The canvas is faced with a richer material which Hewitt (1859) identified as silk, ffoulkes (1916) as velvet, but Eaves as cloth of gold. Two fine, silver-gilt strands are woven between the horizontal threads of the silk. Traces of this facing survive, especially round the rivets. There are hints of a purple or maroon colour in some areas, which may have been crimson as suggested by ffoulkes. The brigandine is made in two parts, a front and rear panel, laced together through pairs of holes at the edges of the left side and shoulder, and probably sewn together originally at the right. The back panel is preserved almost complete. Two of the lace holes at the shoulder retain iron reinforcing rings, originally stitched in place. The original canvas lace survives in this position, and another, with its conical iron termainals, at the side. The back panel is made of twelve columns of horizontal lames, overlapping upwards above the waist and

downwards below it. The fabric at either side of the back is decorated with rivets simulating another column of lames. The fabric along the lower edge of the short skirt is scalloped. Each pendant scallop is decorated with a rosette of seven rivets backed by rough octagonal washers. The two central columns and the separate row of lames running round the neck are scalloped, and each lobe of the scallops is stamped with a six-petalled flower. The outer edge of each lame in the columns bordering the arms is stuck with a dot. Of the front panel only the lower right portion survives. The bottom four lames of the skirt are missing, and the remaining portion is six of the original columns above the waist and eight of fifteen below it. Three separate rows of lames run round the arms. Those in the outer row of the arms and the central column of the front have scalloped edges, also punched with flowers. The outer edge of the fabric above the waist has a column of decorative rivets backed by square washers. Fragments of green edging material occur at the left side and left shoulder of the back panel. KW

Front height 259 mm (10.25 in), width 234 mm (9.25 in), back height 488 mm (19.25 in), width 494 mm (19.5 in),
skirt depth 108 mm (4.25 in), estimated waist 810 mm (32 in), estimated chest 937 mm (37 in)

REF. ffoulkes 1916; Hewitt 1859

{III.48}

Details showing front and back of lame.

{68}

WREXHAM BUCKLER

Probably Welsh, Wrexham, 1520-40

This circular concave buckler is constructed of a series of thirteen closely set concentric steel rings riveted together by fourteen rows of numerous small brass rivets, the prominent rounded heads of which also create a decorative 'beading' effect. These rings and rows encircle the central conical iron boss which is prolonged into an onion-shaped finial from which projects a short, blunt, spike. The boss is hollow on the inside to allow the hand to hold the transverse wooden grip, which is bound to the shield by steel bands. The inside of the buckler is lined with pigskin tooled with a cross-hatched pattern.

A buckler is a type of small shield held in the fist, with a grip at the back, used extensively by English infantrymen from about 1440–1580 in conjunction with a weapon such as sword. These bucklers are plain and are strongly functional. Interestingly, all of them are distinctly British and of a type unknown in any other country. It is of a characteristic Welsh type manufactured in the area around the town of Wrexham, in the English-Welsh borders.

Others have been found near neighbouring English border towns, such as Oswestry and Shrewsbury, both in Shropshire. That they were associated with Wrexham is clearly shown by the entry in the inventory of 1547 which lists: *'Item twoo wreckesham Buckelers'*.[1]

Such bucklers are depicted as being carried by members of Henry's retinue, including a man in a rowing boat and a page of one of the Yeoman of the Guard, between the Archcliff and Black Bulwark forts in the harbour at Dover in the painting of *The Embarkation at Dover*, of about 1545–50 (The Royal Collection Inventory No. 405793 [Hampton Court; Redgrave: 515] see page 18). In the companion painting *The Field of Cloth of Gold* (The Royal Collection Inventory No. 405794 [Hampton Court; Redgrave: 520]), also of about the same date, another page is also depicted with a buckler suspended from a sword-hilt and slung over the forearm. The paintings also show that when not in use bucklers could be carried, presumably by a strap or thong looped around the grip, suspended from the hilt of a sword or a belt at the hip. RCWS

PROV. Purchased from Samuel Luke Pratt, 1859. From the Bernal collection, sold Christie's, 27 March 1855, lot 2395. In the Armouries by 1859

Overall diameter 362 mm (14.25 in), weight 2.44 kg (5 lb 4 oz)

REF. (1) Starkey 1998: 364, no. 14526; Dufty & Reid 1968: CXXXIX; Edwards & Blair 1982: 74–115; ffoulkes 1916: no. V.21; Hewitt 1859: no. V.17; Laking, 1900–22: 244 (illus.615), 245; Richardson & Rimer 1997: cat. no. 14, 54–5, 175 (illus.); Starkey 1998

{V.21}

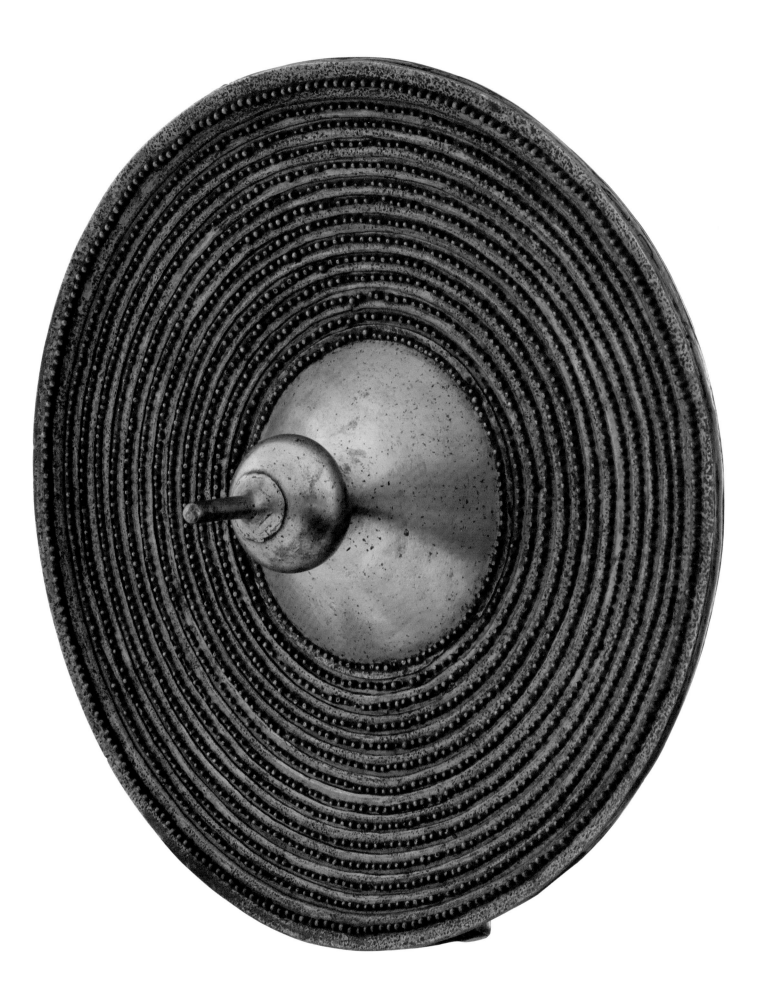

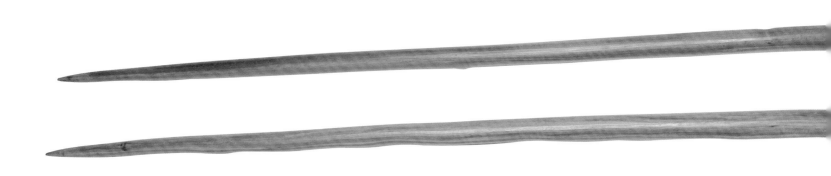

{69}

ARROWS

Recovered from wreck of the Mary Rose
English, mid 16th century

The shafts are of poplar. White poplar, also known as aspen, was one of several types of British timber used for making arrows. The small nocks for the bowstring are still visible on the rear end of each arrow, but the fletchings have not survived. The nocks were reinforced with a small piece of horn set at right angles to the notch. This prevented the impact of the bowstring from splitting the arrow when it was shot. The tips have been worked to a point in order to accommodate the arrowhead. Traces of the copper-based glue used to secure the fletchings to the shaft have survived, visible as a membrane due to shrinkage of the shafts. Trace amounts of an unknown wax-like substance were found in this area as well. No arrowheads had survived, but iron staining indicates that these arrows were furnished with them when the ship sank.

Only half of the arrows listed in the *Anthony Roll* as being aboard *Mary Rose* have been recovered. The inventory suggests around 9,600 arrows stored on board, usually 50 sheaves per chest, with 24 arrows per sheaf. This would mean that there were approximately 10 chests on board to store all the arrows. This tally would allow for approximately 36–48 arrows per bow.

Whereas bows were crafted from materials imported from the Continent, arrow components were made entirely of English materials. Feathers would be gathered from domestic geese for fletchings. Unique to military arrows was the presence of silk thread, in addition to the usual glue, to secure the fletchings to the shaft. This prevented their loss if the arrow became damp while in storage. JH

PROV. The Mary Rose Trust

Average length 800 mm (31.5 in), diameter 12.8 mm (0.5 in)

{80A764/53, 80A764/107, 80A764/197, 80A764/169, 80A764/142}

{70}

LEATHER ARROW SPACER

Recovered from the wreck of the Mary Rose
English, mid 16th century

This leather fragment was part of a disc, originally pierced with 24 holes, that was sewn into the centre of a canvas tube to store arrows for transport and for issue to archers. An arrow would be pushed through each hole in the spacer in order to separate it from others to keep the fletchings from being damaged. The tips of the arrows would be pushed into a disc of woven straw and the canvas tube would then be tied top and bottom to cover the arrows.

It was common for arrows to be distributed to archers in 'sheaves'. Once the arrows were required, the bag would be opened at the end where the heads were lodged in the straw disc. That would have been discarded then each arrow could be removed by pulling them down through the leather disc. ASC

PROV. The Mary Rose Trust

Length 87 mm (3.4 in), width 70 mm (2.8 in)

{MR 80A1376}

Top: Longbows *Above*: Arrows

{71}

CHEST OF LONGBOWS

Recovered from wreck of the Mary Rose
English, mid 16th century

The chest is made of elm. There are two holes drilled in to each of the ends to allow rope carrying-handles to be threaded through. The nails and ropes have decayed, reducing the chest to its component planks. Although no chests are recorded in the *Anthony Roll*, later inventories mention them often enough that we can infer that they were a common method of storing and transporting bowstaves. Four identical chests were also recovered on the upper and orlop decks, each capable of holding 50 longbows.

The bows are made of yew. Self-bows, made of a single piece of wood, use a piece of yew incorporating both the outer layer, or sapwood, and the innermost layer, the heartwood. The sapwood resists tension while the heartwood resists compression when the bow is drawn. These qualities made yew the most highly prized wood for bow-making. The wood for these bows was probably imported from the continent, where straighter and better-quality yew could be found than in the British Isles. The tips of the longbows show that they would have been fitted with horn nocks to accommodate the string, but these have dissolved while immersed in sea-water. Some of the bows have other marks including crosses and five-pointed chevrons. These could be guild marks, maker's marks, or indicators for arrow placement. Draw weights for the *Mary Rose* bows have been estimated to range from 50–84 kg (110–185 lb), with most in the area of 68–72 kg (150–60 lb). 172 longbows were recovered from *Mary Rose*, of which 138 are undamaged.

The archery equipment recovered from *Mary Rose* remains the only precisely dated equipment of its kind. Archery was a crucial aspect of late medieval and early Tudor warfare. At sea, volleys of arrows would be used to clear decks and cover assaults launched by men-at-arms. On land, the supremacy of the English archer in the later Middle Ages is undisputed. Though guns were growing in popularity throughout 16th-century Europe, English armies still valued longbowmen until the 1590s. All men over sixteen were required to practice shooting the longbow, and over 24 they were required to qualify for military service by being able to hit a target at 200 m (220 yards). This practice was necessary to condition the body for the strenuous work of repeatedly drawing bows in excess of 45 kg (100 lb) with accuracy. JH

PROV. The Mary Rose Trust

Chest: length 1935 mm (76.2 in), width 385 mm (15.2 in), height 340 mm (13.4 in);
Longbows: average length 1950 mm (76.8 in), average diameter 35 mm (1.4 in)

{MR 81A2398, 81A3942, 81A3969, 81A3946, 81A3975, 81A1604,
81A1639, 81A3940, 81A3933, 81A1647, 81A3928}

72

SNAP MATCHLOCK HARQUEBUS

Italian (Gardone and Brescia), about 1544

The small lock of this fine quality military musket, or harquebus, is of forward-acting snap-matchlock type. The match-holder or serpentine was brought back against pressure from an internal mainspring until its tail engaged with a small laterally moving spur emerging through the lockplate. This spur was attached to the small acorn-shaped trigger which, when pulled, withdrew the spur and allowed the serpentine to fall forward. This brought the smouldering end of the match cord down onto the pan and into the priming powder. The serpentine is in the form of a monster's head and is fitted with a small thumb-screw to adjust the jaws needed to hold the match cord. The head of the screw is pierced with two circular holes. The narrow iron lockplate is held into its recess in the wooden stock by two square-headed iron woodscrews. The stock is of angular outline but the facets of the butt are gently scalloped. There are three on the outer face, underside and end of the butt, while the left side has a broad scalloped upper facet forming a cheek-rest. The small acorn-shaped trigger is protected by a sheet-iron trigger guard which is decorated with a series of closely placed diagonal notches cut in its edges. The stock extends to the muzzle and in a narrow channel is a thin wooden ramrod tipped with a scourer - a spring-steel device with curved outer blades to scrape clean the bore and a flat blade reminiscent of a screwdriver to clean the face of the breech-plug. The barrel is of unusual form, but one known to have been used in Italian harquebuses of this type. It is of quite small calibre but with thick barrel walls. In cross-section the barrel is of irregular octagonal section, in effect one which is square but set corner-ways in the stock, with narrow flats formed on the points of the square. The outer surface of the barrel is also 'swamped', in which it tapers from the breech towards the muzzle, then gently and subtly flares again. The bore, however, remains parallel. A small blade foresight is fitted, and at the breech is a tapered tubular iron aperture backsight, decorated with bands of simple but well-executed chiselled foliate decoration. A small iron priming pan, shaped rather like the body of a waisted stringed musical instrument, is attached to the right side of the breech. The swivelling pan cover is broken off near to its pivot point. The topmost facet of the barrel, just forward of the backsight, has an inlaid shield-shaped copper alloy mark bearing the letters GARDO. In front of and behind this mark are stamped crude trefoils, and on the facets to left and right of it is an inlaid copper alloy panel, each one bearing an embossed representation of St Barbara. The rear edge of the barrel is punched and chiselled with large trefoils and border lines containing smaller transverse lines resembling the rungs of a ladder. The barrel tang is decorated with two pairs of incised border lines.

Harquebuses of this type were positively identified as those used by the troops of Henry VIII after fragments of many examples were recovered from the wreck of Henry's flagship the *Mary Rose*. No complete stocks were recovered, and almost all the iron barrels had corroded away, but sufficient numbers of fragments confirmed the overall form. This harquebus was one of three acquired by the Royal Armouries in 1985 when they became available through a well-known arms and armour dealer in London. There is no evidence that these belonged to Henry's armoury, but they are precisely of the type known to have been bought in quantity from the Venetian Republic by several of the major monarchs in Europe in the 1540s. In June 1544 Henry VIII

bought 1,500 such harquebuses,[1] and it may be that some of those were the ones lost on board the *Mary Rose* in the following year. The identification of the source of these firearms lies in the small mark of GARDO. An identical mark has survived on a badly corroded gun barrel fragment recovered from the *Mary Rose*, and this mark was later identified as being the abbreviation for the name of the town of Gardone, in the Via Trompia, Italy. In the 1540s Gardone held the monopoly for gun barrel making for the Venetian Republic, sending its products to the nearby town of Brescia to be made up into complete weapons which were then sold out through the acceptance of an order by the Venetian Senate. The discovery of this harquebus and two others (XII.5313 and 5314), gave confirmation of what a *Mary Rose* musket in good condition would have looked like and therefore a precise idea for the first time of the true nature of the military harquebuses issued to Henry's forces at that late period in his reign. GR

PROV. Purchased with XII.5313 and 5314 by the Royal Armouries in 1985

Overall length 1295 mm (51 in), barrel length 973 mm (38.3 in), bore diameter 12 mm (.460 in), weight 3.44 kg (7 lb 6 oz)

REF. (1) Morin & Held 1980: 27; Richardson & Rimer 1997: 175, cat. no. 15; Wilson 1988: 3–10

{XII.5315}

73

BALLOCK DAGGER HILTS

Recovered from wreck of the Mary Rose
English, early 16th century

The hilts are of boxwood, a popular material for knife handles in the Middle Ages. The pommel is decorated with raised ridges, and the hilts bear a characteristic low medial ridge on both sides of the grip. Though the blades have not survived, after studying X-ray images of daggers in concretion, archaeologists determined that most on board the *Mary Rose* would have been single-edged, probably of wedge-shaped section to make the blade stronger for thrusting. An intact ballock dagger of this type (X.1705) is given for comparison. This particular style was found to have been popular elsewhere in England in the 16th century, leading them to suppose that most daggers carried by the crew would conform to this design.

Sixty-five ballock daggers were found on *Mary Rose*. Many of these were found in the ship's hold or on the main deck. All of the daggers except one (found in a locked chest outside the carpenter's quarters) were associated with human remains. This indicates that they were being worn when the ship sank. Under new regulations for equipping garrisons in 1540, all crew were responsible for supplying their own swords and daggers. This would allow for each crewman to select weapons that best suited his size and personal preferences. Daggers would have been kept in a leather sheath and fastened to the belt by leather cords. Many of these ballock daggers would have had by-knives, for eating and other non-military uses, held in front pockets on the sheath. Some have been found in the vicinity of hilts, indicating a probable association.

Most people in medieval and Tudor society carried some form of knife or dagger at all times, both for self-defence and as a tool for daily tasks. Ballock daggers were so named because of the resemblance of their hilts to male genitalia. Some sources alternatively label them as kidney daggers. Such daggers were popular throughout Europe from the late 14th century, being a popular accessory both in military and civilian life. JH

PROV. The Mary Rose Trust

81A1304: length 120 mm (4.7 in), width 63 mm (2.5 in), diameter 37 mm (1.5 in); 81A0073: length 123 mm (4.8 in), width 59 mm (2.3 in), diameter 32 mm (1.25 in)

{MR 81A1304, 81A0073}

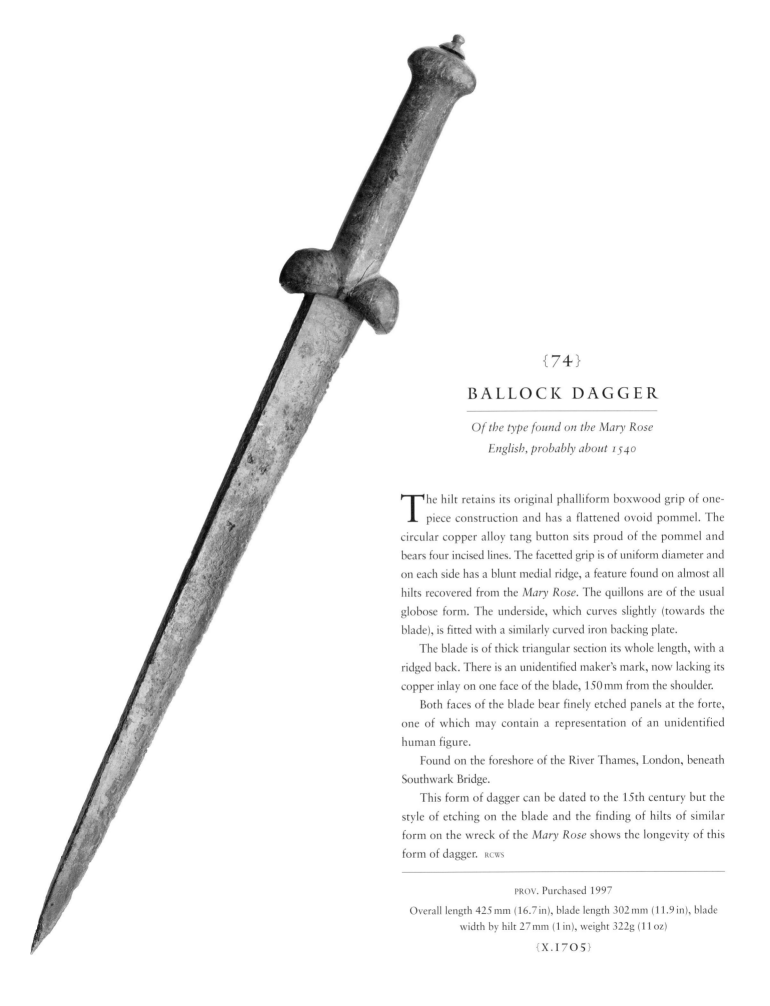

{74}

BALLOCK DAGGER

Of the type found on the Mary Rose
English, probably about 1540

The hilt retains its original phalliform boxwood grip of one-piece construction and has a flattened ovoid pommel. The circular copper alloy tang button sits proud of the pommel and bears four incised lines. The facetted grip is of uniform diameter and on each side has a blunt medial ridge, a feature found on almost all hilts recovered from the *Mary Rose*. The quillons are of the usual globose form. The underside, which curves slightly (towards the blade), is fitted with a similarly curved iron backing plate.

The blade is of thick triangular section its whole length, with a ridged back. There is an unidentified maker's mark, now lacking its copper inlay on one face of the blade, 150 mm from the shoulder.

Both faces of the blade bear finely etched panels at the forte, one of which may contain a representation of an unidentified human figure.

Found on the foreshore of the River Thames, London, beneath Southwark Bridge.

This form of dagger can be dated to the 15th century but the style of etching on the blade and the finding of hilts of similar form on the wreck of the *Mary Rose* shows the longevity of this form of dagger. RCWS

PROV. Purchased 1997

Overall length 425 mm (16.7 in), blade length 302 mm (11.9 in), blade width by hilt 27 mm (1 in), weight 322g (11 oz)

{X.1705}

BASKET-HILTED SWORD

Of a type found on the Mary Rose
Hilt English, blade possibly German, about 1540

The hilt is frontally asymmetrical and has a two-piece brazed hollow spherical pommel. This is decorated with eight applied, longitudinal, decorative ribs. The end of the tang is covered by a decorative washer, in the form of a six-petalled flower. The guard is composed of round-section fire-welded bars and has a pair of straight quillons with domed terminals. Outside the hand the main knuckle-guard is joined to a side knuckle by two bars crossing in saltire with a small lozenge at the junction. On the outside the lozenge is decorated with two diagonal incised lines which form a cross and on each edge with a split double cusp. A rear-guard joins the end of the side knuckle-guard with the rear quillon. A thumb-guard curves from the side knuckle-guard before joining the root of the forward quillon. Inside the hand, a diagonal bar joins the end of the main knuckle-guard nearest the pommel with the rear quillon, opposite the junction to the rear-guard. A short bar joins the centre of the diagonal bar with the thumb-guard. The flattened oval-sectioned wooden grip swells slightly towards the centre. The original grip binding is lost.

The straight, two-edged blade has a ricasso which extends for approximately 70 mm from the hilt. The ricasso has two narrow fullers (one at either edge of the blade). Two wide, shallow fullers run from the end of the ricasso to the point. The blade has the black patination associated with river finds and there are nicks on both edges. Traces of an inlaid mark (possibly a running wolf) in copper alloy remain on the inside of blade, 229 mm from the hilt.

This sword was found on the northern foreshore of the River Thames, under Southwark Bridge, in 1979.

It is by far one of the best-preserved examples from a small important group of basket-hilted swords which have been positively identified as English. The type is also found in mid 16th-century paintings and portraits, such as that of one of the Gentleman Pensioners, (Henry VIII's royal bodyguard) William (?) Palmer (cat. no.90).

One was also found on the wreck of the *Mary Rose* (No. MR 82/A 3589). Other examples of the group in the collection of the Royal Armouries include IX.1120, IX.1404 (found in the moat of Pembridge Castle), IX.2574, IX.3688, and IX.5517. RCWS

PROV. Purchased by private treaty 1993

Overall length 1105 mm (43.5 in), blade length 950 mm (37.4 in), width of blade at hilt 40 mm (1.57 in), weight 1.5 kg (3 lb 3 oz)

PUB. Blair 1981; Wilson 1986

{IX.4427}

THE ENCAMPMENT OF THE ENGLI
TOGETHER WITH A VIEW OF THE ENGLISH AND FRENCH FLEETS AT
ENGRAVED FROM A COEVAL PAINTING AT COWDRY IN SUSSEX THE S

{76}

'THE ENCAMPMENT OF THE ENGLISH FORCES NEAR PORTSMOUTH, TOGETHER WITH A VIEW OF THE ENGLISH AND FRENCH FLEETS AT COMMENCEMENT OF THE ACTION BETWEEN THEM ON THE XIXTH JULY MDXLV'

By James Basire, engraver, Great Queen Street, London

Engraving, English, London. Published 1778

ORCES NEAR PORTSMOUTH,
MMENCEMENT OF THE ACTION BETWEEN THEM ON THE XIX.TH OF JULY MDXLV.
RIGHT HONOURABLE ANTHONY BROWNE LORD VISCOUNT MONTAGUE

Often called 'The Cowdray engraving' this picture is one of a set of five. It describes the attempt by the forces of the French King, Francis I, to invade England in 1545 and shows the events of 19 July that year.

The loss of King Henry VIII's flagship, the *Mary Rose* is clearly shown. The image presents a birds-eye view looking from north to south across the southern part of Portsea Island towards the Solent and to the Isle of Wight beyond. On the left-hand side of the image is the French invasion fleet represented as a mass of ships drawn up in St Helen's Roads around the eastern end of the Isle of Wight. In the central upper right-hand area of the image are the ships of the English fleet, which are occupying the anchorage of Spithead to oppose the French invasion. The town of Portsmouth is shown in the lower right-hand side and South-sea castle is the large building in the centre of the image.

The original paintings from which the engravings were derived decorated the walls of the dining hall at Cowdray House in Midhurst, Sussex, and were probably painted between 1545

and 1548 for Sir Anthony Browne, Master of the King's Horse. Browne inherited Cowdray House from his half-brother in 1543, and it remained one of his principal residences until his death in 1548.

Sir Anthony is shown prominently in the centre of the image riding a white horse immediately behind King Henry VIII. Next to Browne is Sir Charles Brandon, Duke of Suffolk, who at that time was commanding the English land forces at Portsmouth.[1]

The image is in the form of a printed reproduction from hand-engraved copper printing plates. The Society of Antiquaries of London commissioned the Sherwin brothers to make a water-colour copy of the original painting and this was completed by 1775. In 1773 Sir Joseph Ayloffe (c. 1708–81) read a paper to the Society about the wall paintings at Cowdray House and suggested that they should be recorded.[2] There was some opposition to the project within the Society because of the likely cost, however the picture was engraved and distributed to members. It is over 1.8m (6ft) wide and was engraved onto two separate copper plates.

The engravings were made by James Basire of Great Queen Street, London. Basire specialized in antiquarian subjects and used a painstaking, carefully drawn and, even for the time, rather old-fashioned style of engraving. William Blake, painter and poet, was apprenticed to Basire in 1772 and lived in his household until 1778 when he completed his apprenticeship. He is likely to have been involved in the engraving of this image.

Cowdray House was largely destroyed by fire in 1793 and the original wall paintings were lost. Consequently we only have Basire's monochrome engravings as a record of what they represented. A few notes were made by Sir Joseph Ayloffe (1775) recording some of the colours used in the original paintings but beyond this we have no further information. A few copies of the engravings were hand coloured at some time, possibly when newly printed in 1778 or shortly afterwards, but it is not known if the colours chosen were based on the original images. At least two coloured examples of the engraving are known to exist.

There is considerable topographic detail within the picture which can be identified. Portsmouth Harbour's narrow entrance is accurately drawn and there are some English ships passing through the passage to join the rest of the English fleet at Spithead. The implied seabed configuration is exactly as it exists today with some of the ships using the Swashway, a slightly deeper channel across Spitbank, as a route to Spithead.

The built environment too depicts many identifiable features. On the Portsmouth side of the Harbour entrance is the Round Tower, a circular stone structure originating from the 1530s–40s. On the Gosport shore opposite the Round Tower is Fort Block-house. Adjacent to the Round Tower is the capstan for raising a defensive boom chain across the harbour entrance. This is also shown on a 1552 map of Portsmouth fortifications[3] and referred to in John Leland's itinerary (written about 1535–43). Williams suggests that the chain was not available for the 1545 battle which could explain why the capstan is shown but the chain itself is not evident. Also identifiable are the Square Tower, (about 1495) rebuilt in stone during Henry VIII's reign and the structures of the southeast corner of Portsmouth including the Saluting Platform, Long Curtain and King's Bastion. Further along the Southsea shoreline the smaller defences of Lumps Fort and Eastney Fort are also clearly shown. The half-timbered building in the lower left-hand side of the picture is Eastney Farm which was the only substantial building in that part of Portsea Island at the time. Within the town walls there is also considerable detail shown which can be compared with the 1552 map of Portsmouth.[4] The four Brewhouses: Dragon, Lion, White Hart and The Rose are clearly shown on the map as being located around a pond, probably a freshwater spring providing the water essential for brewing. The engraving shows them as timber framed buildings located above a pond.

The appearance of the *Mary Rose* herself presents what is likely to be an accurate depiction of the ship resting on the seabed. Only the highest parts of two of the ship's masts protrude above the surface of the sea complete with their fighting tops. The foremast mainsail can be seen floating on the surface of the water surrounded by a number of drowned sailors. The image shows one man clinging to the underside of the fighting top of the main mast with two men on the foremast, one clinging to the mast itself and the other standing on the fighting top waving animatedly. The depiction of the masts would suggest that the *Mary Rose* had been proceeding in a northerly direction at that time that she sank which accords with her archaeological position and that she was rigged with the mainsail on the foremast. There is no suggestion of the mainsail on the main mast which may imply that this was reefed at the time of the sinking and is a similar sail configuration to a number of the English vessels shown with bowsprit sails and lateen sails set.

In the centre of the image an advance party of four French galleys is seen exchanging fire with the largest of the English ships, the *Great Harry*. Towards the front of the French main fleet can be seen a galley flying the crossed keys of St Peter and just behind it is a galley which appears to be partially sunken. To the left of the sunken galley a large ship may be seen with its masts sloping markedly towards the left. It is possible that this represents the second French flagship. This ran aground shortly after leaving harbour in France and was reported to have damaged its keel which could cause displacement of its masts. The French army is shown as making landings on that the Eastern coast of the Isle of Wight at Bembridge and Sandown Bay. The bridge at Yarbridge is shown as being defended by the English with two cannons and part of the bridge structure has been demolished as a defensive measure keeping the French constrained to the eastern end of the island. DF

REF. (1) Ayloffe 1775; (2) Ayloffe 1775; (3) British Library Cotton MS Augustus I II 117; (4) British Library Cotton MS Augustus I II 117

Society of Antiquaries

Right: At bottom right is Henry VIII on horseback by Southsea Castle. Immediately above this the tops of two of the *Mary Rose's* masts are just visible above the water.

{77}

BRONZE SAKER BY
FRANCESCO ARCANA

English, dated 1529

The tapered barrel is divided into two main sections by a prominent moulding in front of the trunnions. The muzzle terminates in a bold moulding. Inscribed in a band adjacent to this is the founder's name

FRANCISCUS • ARCANUS

and behind this is a band of foliage decoration moulded in relief. The reinforce bears the Tudor badge in relief consisting of a crowned rose surrounded by the Garter, below which is inscribed

POUR • DEFENDRE and then
HENRICUS VIII • ANGLIE
ET • FRANCIE • REX • FIDEI
DEFENSOR • ET • DNS • HIBERNIE
• A • D M • CCCCCXXIX

To Defend, Henry VIII by the grace of God King of England and France, defender of the faith and Lord of Ireland in the year of our Lord 1529.

In front of the base-ring moulding is a panel, within which the vent is located, containing foliate scroll decoration in relief incorporating Tudor roses and fleurs-de-lys. The cascabel button is of a plain cylindrical form sometimes seen on earlier guns. In the 16th century it was still common to name different sizes and natures of artillery after birds of prey. This gun is a saker, named after a species of large falcon, and is a member of the culverin family of guns, characterised by having a long barrel in relation to their bore diameter. Sakers were widely used on land and sea but displayed considerable variations of length, weight and calibre. This example is a smaller version of the type but its calibre corresponds to that of the ordinary saker listed later in the 16th century.[1]

Francesco Arcana was a member of the Italian gunfounding family from Cesena who came to England in 1523. The family established a foundry in London at Salisbury Place. Henry VIII found it necessary to import foreign craftsmen to satisfy his requirements for large quantities of good quality arms and armour. As in the case of armour making, the settling of foreign founders had a beneficial effect on English gunfounding.

This saker would have fired a cast-iron ball of about 89 mm (3.5 in) diameter, weighing about 2.7 kg (6 lb). Its effective range would have been about 330 m (360 yards).

The saker is mounted on a field carriage of wood and iron, resembling the kind of carriage indicated for this kind of gun in 16th-century art. For example, the funerary monument of King Francis I of France, Henry's contemporary and rival, and in particular, the sculptured frieze on the church of Genouilhac give a great deal of detail. The latter is especially likely to be accurate since the church was built to the order of the distinguished soldier Galiot de Genouilhac (died 1546) Master of the Artillery to Francis I. Similar carriages are also visible in the so-called Cowdray engraving (cat. no. 76).

For preservation and appearance, gun carriages were painted or, as in this case, treated with linseed oil.

The carriage was built in the workshops at the Royal Armouries, Fort Nelson. It is usually seen with a replica barrel, used for historical firing demonstrations at the museum. The iron hoop [one-piece] tyres adopted for ease of construction are not historically correct; until the middle of the 19th century, *strake* tyres, made of separate, usually six, segments, were used. These were secured by nails and clasps around the fellies (the wooden segments forming the rim) of each wheel. NH

PROV. Transferred in 1930 from the Rotunda Museum, Woolwich

Length 2083 mm (6 ft 10 in), calibre 95 mm (3.73 in)

REF. (1) Blackmore 1976: 393;

PUB. Blackmore 1976: 58

{XIX.165}

{78}

GUNNER'S LINSTOCK

Recovered from the wreck of the Mary Rose
English, mid 16th century

A range of equipment was used in conjunction with the variety of artillery onboard ship to enable effective loading and firing.

One such item was a linstock. This was a length of wood with a forked end designed to hold a length of smouldering match cord. The cord was used to ignite the priming powder in the touch hole of cannon. This linstock is made of ash and is nearly 70 cm long enabling the gunner to stand back from the cannon when lighting it.

Linstocks are not itemised in the *Mary Rose's* listings of equipment and so were likely to be the gunners' personal property. The elaborate carving suggests gunners spent time personalising their own linstock. Linstocks of this period are often carved with crocodiles or dragons like this one, where the animal grips the match between its jaws. ACS

PROV. The Mary Rose Trust

Length 685 mm (26.9 in), width 53 mm (2.1 in), diameter 43 mm (1.7 in)

{MR 81A1922}

{79}

VENT REAMER

Recovered from the wreck of the Mary Rose
English, mid 16th century

A vent reamer was a copper alloy wire used by gun crews to clean out the vent of the cannon of carbon debris between firings. It was important to do so as it might block the hole and prevent the cannon from being fired. They were made from square section copper alloy wire with one end twisted so it would collect any debris. The other end was looped to form a handle. Reamers recovered are about 12 in or 30.5 cm long.

Cartridges of paper or fabric containing gunpowder may have been used instead of loose powder in some cannons. The end of the reamer could then be used to pierce a hole in the powder cartridge to ensure ignition of the charge. ACS

PROV. The Mary Rose Trust

Length 305 mm (12 in)

{MR 79.1011}

Above: MR 81A1922
Below: MR 79.1011

{80}

GUNNER'S RULE

Recovered from the wreck of the Mary Rose
English, mid 16th century

The gunner's rule was found on the main deck and is made of brass. The gunner would need to know the weight of the shot appropriate to the bore of the gun in order to prepare the correct amount of gun powder required. The rule is designed to calculate the weight of a round shot from the direct measurement of its diameter. The scale of the rule was found to be is very accurate for iron shot up to 8 in (203.2 mm) and the assumption is the measurements on both sides are in English pounds.

Both sides of the rule are incised with lines and numbers. One side bears the letters 'ISERN' and the other 'BLI' which are likely to relate to gradations for iron (*isern*) and lead (*bleyern*) shot.

The numbers on both sides of the rule are two to five and then in tens up to 100. At the end closest to 100 the rule is bent backwards into a loop so it can be suspended. AS/JH/GR

PROV. The Mary Rose Trust

Length 290 mm (11.4 in), width 10 mm (0.4 in), thickness 5 mm (0.2 in)

PUB. Hildred 2009

{MR 81AO249}

ROUND SHOT

Recovered from wreck of the Mary Rose

English, mid 16th century

The shot on the left is made of cast iron. The cast line is still visible, and is indicative with casting by means of a two-part mould. A letter 'H' inside a circle, a pattern cut into the mould, is present at a point 90 degrees to the cast line. Metallurgical testing on a similar shot revealed evidence of a metal mould being used. The size of this shot fits it into the category of those that would have been fired from a culverin. One shot (81A1012) was found near a bronze culverin (81A1423) and has been linked to that gun by archaeologists.

The shot on the right is made from chiselled stone. It has been worked into a smooth spherical shape except for a flat bottom that may be due to wear over time rather than poor craftsmanship. Fine chisel marks are still visible on its surface. The stone is known as ragstone, a sandy limestone found in numerous quarries in Kent. It was used as building material as early as Roman times and was used extensively in the construction of the White Tower, William the Conqueror's Norman keep

The *Anthony Roll* listed 580 cast-iron shot and 390 stone shot aboard *Mary Rose*. However a total of 1,248 cast-iron shot

and 387 stone shot were recovered from the wreck. Most were found on the main deck, particularly in the two shot lockers. Shot could be made from iron, lead, composite iron and lead, or stone. All four types of were recovered from *Mary Rose*. Though iron shot cannot have been cast on board *Mary Rose*, there is evidence to suggest that lead casting and coating of iron shot with lead was being done. Stone shot is listed as being used solely for wrought iron guns. The presence of rough unfinished stone shot indicates that the final smoothing and finishing often took place on board rather than in a workshop ashore.

Mary Rose was armed with 96 guns of varying sizes; a sizeable amount of firepower for that period. Evidence from contemporary witnesses suggests that as early as the 1540s English ships were practicing an early form of broadside, in which all the guns from one side of the ship are fired at once for maximum effect. Despite this, guns were only the preliminary attack before the main aspect of naval combat: boarding the enemy ship for hand-to-hand fighting. JH

PROV. The Mary Rose Trust

81A1012: diameter 130 mm (5.1 in), weight 6.8 kg (14 lb 9 oz); E265: diameter 107 mm (4.2 in), weight 1.07 kg (2 lb 4 oz)

83A0023: weight 6.5 kg (14 lb 3 oz)

{MR 81A1012, 83A0023}

{82}

SHOT GAUGE

Recovered from the wreck of the Mary Rose
English, mid 16th century

Nine objects recovered from *Mary Rose* were identified as shot gauges. These gauges come in various forms such as rectangular or circular panels of wood and have a hole through which shot (i.e. cannon balls) were passed to ensure that they were of the appropriate size for specific guns. This one is made in the shape of a teardrop with a hole cut out of the widest part. It is made of oak and has a scored design from the hole along the edge up to the narrow end. There are six examples of this form, four made of oak and two of elm, with holes of varying sizes.

Different guns onboard ship used different diameters of shot.

Each gauge has a different diameter hole ranging from 100 mm to 184 mm, and this one appears to be for measuring 105 mm shot. The size of shot could be checked using this wooden measure. It was important to only use the right gauge of shot for the different guns; if the shot was too large it could get stuck in the barrel, if it was too small, although it could still be fired, it would not fire as effectively as shot close to the barrel diameter.

This gauge was found on the main deck towards the stern of the ship, but not near any artillery that would use the corresponding size of shot it measured. JH

PROV. The Mary Rose Trust

Length 287 mm (11.3 in), width 158 mm (6.2 in), thickness 10 mm (0.4 in), internal hole diameter 105 mm (4.1 in), weight 147.5 g (5 oz)

{MR 81A5662}

{83}

ARTILLERY POWDER CHARGE LADLE

Recovered from the wreck of the Mary Rose
English, mid 16th century

This object was used for decanting gunpowder into muzzle-loaded cannon and was part of the gun crew's equipment. It is made in four parts with a wooden handle and a copper alloy scoop attached to one end. It was found in the main deck in the centre of the ship.

The measure of powder required would depend on the gun barrel size and the weight and size of shot to be fired. Once determined, the powder would be poured into the ladle which was carefully inserted into the cannon muzzle and tipped out.

The powder would be pushed down into the breech of the cannon using a rammer; a simple, round wooden head on a long handle. The powder was held in place with wad before the shot was loaded.

Decanting powder this way would not be an easy task on a moving ship and powder cartridges would be preferable to using a ladle.

The ladle could also serve to clean out the barrel of the gun of any debris from previous firing. ACS

PROV. The Mary Rose Trust

Head length 135 mm (5.3 in), diameter 110 mm (4.3 in), ladle length 539 mm (21.2 in), handle-fragment length 210 mm (8.3 in)

{MR 80A0955}

{84}

INCENDIARY DART

Recovered from wreck of the Mary Rose
English, mid 16th century

The haft is of silver fir. The fletchings, made of a single thin sheet of oak, are slotted into the base of the haft. Traces of tar and nails survive to indicate how the fletching was fastened into place. It was found in two pieces and later reconstructed by conservators. Some fragments of pitch survive, underneath which are found traces of surviving fabric. Iron staining indicates the presence of the dart's original head. Around the collar are pairs of small holes that resemble staple marks. This dart was found in the carpenter's cabin next to a bronze demi-cannon.

Three incendiary darts were recovered from *Mary Rose*. They were initially labelled as paddles before being recognized for what they actually were. Wooden darts such as this would have been thrown by hand in the same manner as a normal military dart. Objects possibly comprising a toolkit for crafting incendiary darts were also found in the carpenter's cabin. Other incendiary devices found on board included 'lime pots' and 'mortar bombs' to be hurled at enemy ships to spread quantities of burning mixture over the decks.

Incendiary material, also known as 'wildfire', had been used in warfare for centuries. The 'Greek Fire' of the Byzantines was the most famous example of early incendiary technology. The sticky substance, once ignited, was difficult to remove and equally difficult to extinguish even in water. This being the case, its formidability in naval combat cannot be overstated. One method of constructing an incendiary dart comes from Vannoccio Biringuccio's *Pirotechnica* in 1540. The incendiary mixture was made from components such as ammonia, animal fat, arsenic, egg, juniper oil, linseed oil, mercury, naphtha, petroleum, pitch, quicklime, saltpetre, sulphuric acid, sulphur turpentine, un-distilled wine, vinegar, wax, and gunpowder. This mixture was placed in a linen bag and fixed to the end of the dart. Wooden fuse pegs were placed on the sides reaching into the mixture, and the whole area was covered with pitch. The pitch-coated section was lit and thrown, so that the mixture ignited and spread on impact. JH

PROV. The Mary Rose Trust

Length: 2000 mm (78.7 in), width: 200 mm (7.9 in), diameter 40 mm (1.6 in)

{MR 81A2866}

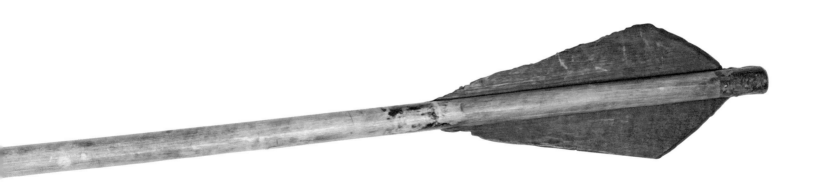

TO FEED THE KING'S MEN: CATERING FOR THE HENRICIAN ARMY AND NAVY

PETER BREARS

The provision of food and drink for the forces raised for Henry VIII's military expeditions presented enormous logistical problems. As this was neither a major standing army nor a permanent commissariat the required administration had to be set up at short notice as soon as the King had made a decision to go to war. Earlier in his reign Wolsey had headed the victualling organisation, but by the 1540s this enormous task was being undertaken by committees, of which Bishop Stephen Gardiner was a prominent member, earning him the nickname of 'Simon Stockfish'.[1] For practical advice they relied heavily on the experience of the royal household's officers, men who were experienced in the regular movement of the entire court from one palace to another. John Heath, Sergeant of the Royal Bakehouse, provided biscuit for the siege of Boulogne and served these as the army's standard-bearer, for example, while John Gwillim, Sergeant of the Woodyard, acted as a major contractor for the supplies of food required these.[2]

The size of the armies was vast in proportion to England's population and economy. Actions against France or Scotland frequently compromised 15,000 to 20,000 men, while the French campaign of 1544 more than doubled these numbers up to 43,000.[3] In theory every soldier was paid 6d. a day to feed himself, but the government had to provide the supplies for him to purchase. In practice the supplies were issued to each military company's victualler, who was supplied with the necessary credit. He was then paid by his captain, who deducted the required sums from the soldiers' wages.[4] In addition, the men might take the opportunity to live off the land, and thus save their money. In 1523, for example, a number who 'like fools' had been wandering about the country collecting sheep, pigs and cattle were captured by the French.[5]

In order to acquire all the necessary food and equipment in bulk, the government used the age-old practice of purveyance, essentially compulsory purchase at close to (but reputedly much lower than) market prices. Private victualling contractors were also employed.[6] Herds of oxen were driven to major ports such as King's Lynn and London, slaughtered, their heads, tails, feet and offal discarded and the remaining carcase split down the spine. Having been divided into 2 lb joints, they were then salted and packed into casks for transport. Most casks were 'pipes' of 105 gallons, each holding some 400 pieces. Here they tended to shrink as the salt extracted more of their juices, but when Lord Hertford complained of this in his 1544 campaign against

Scotland, he was firmly told that each joint still contained 'as much feeding, and more, than two pounds of fresh beef'.[7] 'Even so, quantities of salt beef were received in poor condition, much of that sent to France in 1547 being of 'corrupte lothesomeness, happening by myxture of the filthyness of a great numbre of coles ladend in the vesselles upon the same'.[8] However, after being washed, this was still sold to the troops. Salt pork, cured as bacon, was similarly processed and supplied, as was butter, salted down and packed into barrels.[9] Cheeses, both Essex and Suffolk, were made of skimmed milk, and hence so hard as to need no special packing.[10]

> Those that made me were uncivil;
> They made me harder than the devil,
> Knives won't cut me, fire won't sweat me
> Dogs bark at me, but can't eat me

For the fish days, the entire period of Lent and Wednesdays, Fridays and Saturdays, the staple was dried sides of cod, each around a yard long, called stockfish.[11] Much of this was supplied by John Gylmyn, Sergeant of the Woodyard, for Calais and Boulogne in 1545.[12] Other fish included ling, haberdine, greenfish (barrelled in salt when just caught off Iceland etc), white herring (gutted, salted and barrelled in the ports), and red herring, (salted and smoked to hardness).[13] A report received from France in July 1545, stated that the herrings had begun to go off, but even these were edible, 'if the time of the year might bear with men's stomachs to receive if for their ordinary victual...By persuasion and force, a great number of those herrings are spent amongst us since Lent'.[14]

Great quantities of cereals were required for the forces, the most important being wheat, harvested from the East Riding and the Great Ouse hinterland of East Anglia.[15] Much of this was baked into biscuit, 'such as was provided to serve at need, or in warres, that is twice baked, and without leaven or salt'.[16] John Payntell of Limehouse made large quantities for shipping across the channel, while Robert Donne appears to have baked almost 23 tons in Calais, ready to supply Boulogne. In order to keep them clean and dry, biscuits were carefully packed into either casks or canvas bags.[17] Vast quantities of wheat were also sent out in the form of bulk grain as bread-corn. For France in 1544, it was decided to introduce 100 mobile bakeries. Each had a mill mounted on a wagon, each with its own miller and carter and another wagon carrying a complete brick-built bread oven with its own baker and carter. Ten millwrights, ten cartwrights, six bricklayers, two mortar-makers and six pioneers provided the necessary support services. Even with their help, the project failed since *'the ovens being often heated, the mortar will fall from the brick, and small shaking will cause the bricks to fall under and break. I pray God send us no more lack of other things than of these ovens, for if they fail, others can be had…into this now not one loaf has been baked in the camp'*. The only alternative was to buy Flemish bread at inflated prices, as depicted in one of the Cowdray paintings (see cat. no. 76).[18]

Further supplies of wheat were required as 'head-corn' for brewing, along with malt, probably made from barley.[19] The large quantities of English beer sent across the channel were totally insufficient for the large number of troops, and so malt and hops were shipped out for brewing either in Calais, or in the field.[20] In contrast to the mobile bakeries the 50 mobile brewhouses appear to have worked relatively well, each being served by a brewer, an under brewer, two labourers and two carters.[21] Oatmeal, essential for thickening the liquid in which meat had been boiled, to make pottage, was shipped out in re-used barrels. 'Hambro' barrels presumably originating from Hamburg, were herring barrels from the fish trade, freed for use after their contents had been used up on fish-days and Lent.[22] In theory, these should have kept the meal in good condition, but much of that delivered to Boulogne was spoiled by bad packaging and taking in water en route, probably also absorbing a distinctly fishy flavour too.[23] Other essential dry foodstuffs required by the army included rye, most likely used as a bread-corn, and 'meat pease' and beans ready for soaking and boiling for pottages.[24] Finally, vast quantities of firewood had to be provided for fuelling the cooking fires, 250 loads of logs and 7,200 billets being consumed during just a single month's occupation of Boulogne.[25]

Controlling the distribution of such large quantities of food and materials presented an enormous challenge to the army's senior officers, who had to enforce strict rationing, prevent pilfering, and try to suppress gross profiteering by both its own staff and by its contractors. In 1544 they appointed a commissariat headed by two chief masters and two clerks, with six clerks for the sale of bread, ten for the sale of drinks, and twelve clerks and butchers for fish and meat. In addition there were twenty to supervise transport and security, 290 carters for 145 ton-and-a-half capacity wagons, and a support team of cartwrights, smiths and labourers carried in a further five wagons.[26] Even with a staff of 382 and 150 wagons, their task would have been enormous, especially when deciding how much of which food was to be sold each day, still observing all the fish-days, and making the best use of whatsoever was available.

The usual weekly diet for each man was generally accepted as comprising 7 lb biscuit, 4 lb beef, 2 lb pork, ¾ of a salt fish,

12 oz cheese, 2 pt peas, 6 oz butter, and 7 gallons of beer.[27] In May/June 1545 this was distributed as beef on three days, bacon on one day, and just butter or cheese or a piece of stockfish on each of the three fish-days, plus a daily allowance of bread or biscuit, and oatmeal, peas and beans for pottage, along with the usual ration of beer. Even though a plain diet, it must have been preferable to that provided at Lent. Then there was stockfish on two days in the week, with white salt herrings, red herrings, haberdines, sprats, and either ling or greenfish on the remaining five days.[28] As to the quantities, meat was served in 2 lb pieces at dinner and supper each day, which, when shared between four men, gave 8 oz of meat per meal, or one pound each per day.[29] The weight of cooked stockfish must have been similar, with two men consuming half-a-yard-long fish each day.[30]

Cooking the quantities of food required for an entire army could not be carried out in one central kitchen, the practical difficulties were just too great. In practice, the food for the senior officers and administrative staff appears to have been cooked in large mobile kitchens. The expedition to the Field of Cloth of Gold in 1520 took most of the royal household's culinary staff and its equipment with it. The painting of about 1545 of this great event shows its Lords' Side Kitchen, Boiling House and Pastry/Bakehouse in action with equipment identical to that used in the royal palaces.[31] The kitchens are housed in tents which have open panels in their roofs to let out the smoke and fumes of their fires. These were lent out as required for military use, the Earl of Warwick taking three to Scotland in 1547. They are described as being made up of breadths of canvas, the lighter variety being woven at Vitré in Brittany, and the coarse from nearby Le Vendelais. Assuming that they were woven around a yard or an ell in width, they measured up to some 80 x 35 ft, with an open-topped ridge terminating in semi-circular ends. This is close to the size of the Lords' Side and Hall Side kitchen of Hampton Court Palace, which regularly fed up to 1,200 a day in winter, but could never cope with a complete army.[32]

For each company in the army, the food issued each day would be set out by the staff of the commissariat and by its contractors. The latter were described in the 1540 *Ordinances and Instructions for Musters* as English victuallers called in Dutch *'Sutlers'*.[33] Both had to sell their wares at cost price, with the sutlers allowed a tuppence in the shilling (0.17%) mark-up on bread and beer to cover their expenses.[34] Even so, this still enabled corruption to flourish, as Pistol explained in Shakespeare's *Henry V*.[35]

'A noble thou shalt have, and present pay;
And liquor likewise will I give to thee,
And friendship shall combine with brotherhood:
I'll live by Nym, and Nym shall live by me
Is this not just? For I shall sutler be
Unto the camp, and profits will accrue'.

The food would then be carried back to the company for cooking around its individual fire. One of these is depicted on the Cowdray mural showing the army encampment at Portsmouth in July 1545 (see cat. no. 77). Here a Y-topped gallows-post has been driven into the ground at each side of the hearth to support a horizontal gallow-balk. From this a bow-handled open-topped kettle is suspended by a pot hook in order to simmer the joints of meat or pieces of fish to tenderness. The pre-soaked peas or beans might have been added at the same time as the beef, since they would also take about an hour and three quarters or two hours of slow cooking. Alternatively, oatmeal could be added some ten minutes before the meat was ready, then being stirred in to thicken the pottage and prevent it from burning onto the bottom of the kettle. No salt would be required, as this was more than adequately provided from the salt meat. In this way a good, hot and satisfying meal would be provided at dinner time, around 10 am, and supper time around 4 pm, unless other duties intervened.

In the navy, the diet was similar but the organisation of its preparation and service had to be carried out in a rather different manner.[36] The numbers were smaller, around 450 in a major warship, while the restricted space and circumstances made a single communal set of stores and a galley absolutely essential. Thanks to the enormous efforts of all involved in the excavation and raising of the *Mary Rose*, we now have an unrivalled body of physical evidence of how its catering was accomplished. Separate secure stores were established in various parts of the lower decks. Cereals, probably intended to include bread and biscuit, were housed in the bow and forward bays of the orlop deck, for example with most of the salt beef and fish casks further back, amidships, and beer and wine at the stern. Further beer casks lay in the stern half of the hold, the equivalent of a land-based cellar, with buttery above. Further casks of meat and fish, some probably for current use, lay in the fourth bay of the hold, at the foot of a companionway leading down from the deck.[37] This served as a scullery area, where joints could be taken from their casks, trimmed on an oak chopping block and carried on typical beech butchers' trays into the adjacent galley.[38] Here a brass furnace pan of 140 gallons capacity and a copper one of 80 gallons were mounted in brick furnaces, ready to simmer their meat or fish and integral pottages.[39] A copper skimmer was provided to remove the scum which rose to the surface, and a shallow-bowled paddle/ladle of beech to stir the contents and ladle them out.[40]

Although the serving dishes were apparently washed up and stored in the scullery after each meal, they could not have been filled and carried up the steep companionway without spillage, scalds and great confusion. The ship's inventory lists a 'carrying kettle' which served as a giant tureen to carry the combined 2 lb joints of meat, or the fish, in their respective pottages, up to the men waiting on the upper decks.[41] It was found in the excavation, a cylindrical copper vessel of 30 gallons, with loops for a bow handle.[42] Using this probably with a pair of small elm ladles, it would be easy to fill the food into the serving dishes previously carried up in wicker baskets.[43]

When dining in a house on land, the men would have used their own knives to cut pieces off the joints, transfer them to their personal trenchers, (five-inch squares of beech, pine or oak) and there divided them into mouthfuls, which they lifted to their mouths using their fingers.[44] This assumes the ready availability of a table, almost certainly lacking in sufficient numbers either at sea or in the field. Instead, the serving dishes appear to have acted as trenchers too. Each dish, probably filled with two 2 lb joints of meat and its bean, pea or oatmeal pottage, would be set down between four men on any flat surface. Taking out their knives, they would have cut off their share, then divided it into mouth-sized 'gobbets' and eaten it, leaving deep knife-scars across the base of the dish. The pottage could then be scooped up from the dish, either by using their personal spoons, or simply sipping it from the brim. These are not the polite etiquette of contemporary manners books, but would have been quite effective. As for the beer, this would have been served out of large coppered pitchers filled from the barrels in the hold, and poured into either coopered tankards or cups.[45] At this period cups usually took the age-old form of turned wooden bowls, rather than of a tall pottery vessels with a handle, a form then of relatively recent introduction.

The fact that an army marches on its stomach was just as true for the Henrician campaigns as it was in the Napoleonic or any other modern wars. However great the cause, and the effort and expense put into its planning and preparation, the outcome was always uncertain. On an international scale, Henry's wars were major undertakings involving vast expense, absorbing much of the fabulous wealth of the dissolved monasteries. An individual solider or sailor, however, might find it difficult to see where the money went. As reported from France in 1545 '*many people have dide amongst us in their sickness for lacke of succour of fresh meates, being driven to take unely of the provision of the store by the want of money to bye other victualles*'.[46] This was to be the experience of many English forces during the succeeding centuries.

Notes and references page 337.

{ 85 }

TIGG

Recovered from the wreck of the Mary Rose

England, mid 16th century

This wooden drinking vessel, known as a tigg, would have belonged to one of the ordinary sailors and contrasts with the valuable pewter flagons and tankards of the officers, which bear the initials or crests of their wealthy owners and the touch marks of their makers.

The vessel would have contained two pints and is made of pine staves which would have been bound together. The handle is made of poplar and it would originally have had a hinged wooden lid. It would have also been lined with pitch to seal it.

Vessel such as this were sometimes highly personalised so as not to be mistaken for someone else's. This one has an X incised on the base. Others have more intricate decoration and lettering, including one tigg inscribed with the Latin '*Sit deus cum quid contra nos*', which translates as; '*If God be with us, who can be against us*', from *Romans 8.31*. ACS

PROV. The Mary Rose Trust

Height 195 mm (7.7 in), base diameter 130 mm (5.1 in)

{MR 78AO270}

WOODEN DISH

Recovered from wreck of Mary Rose

English, mid 16th century

The *Mary Rose* has provided the largest assemblage of domestic wooden vessels yet recovered in the British Isles, amongst which are 184 bowls, dishes and platters. Wooden plates and containers were more practical on ship than breakable pottery, which was used mostly for storage and cooking. All the wooden vessels vary in size and are made of a variety of British woods including alder, beech, birch, oak and elm.

Of the wooden vessels found those vessels with a height less than one-third of, but greater than one-seventh of its diameter were classed as dishes. Of the dishes, 110 were made of beech, with five of alder and one of elm. Five dishes were branded with 'H' on the rim and 23 have incised lines on the base. All of the dishes have a distinctive internal rim which slopes down into the bowl that indicates they were likely to have been mass produced. ACS

PROV. The Mary Rose Trust

Height 50 mm (2 in), diameter 290 mm (11.4 in)

{ M R 8 I A 5 9 O 5 }

WOODEN COMB

Recovered from wreck of Mary Rose

English, mid 16th century

Combs are the most common personal possession recovered from the *Mary Rose* and 82 examples have been found. Eighty of these combs are double-sided and carved in one piece. All of the combs are made of boxwood except one of alder and one made of ivory, which was a highly prized material. Boxwood is a fine grained wood obtained from mixed deciduous woodland. This example shows the typical style of comb recovered, carved from a single piece of wood. The combs have one side with coarse teeth for detangling hair, and the other side has a row of finely spaced teeth. These teeth are useful for removing fleas and lice, which are likely to have been rife on board ship.

Eight of the combs were also found with a leather case. The majority of the combs and cases found do not have any decorative features. The combs are all fairly small and are quite utilitarian in appearance.

It is likely that most of the crew had their own comb and they were found distributed throughout the ship. Sixteen combs were found in chests and one in the barber surgeon's room, along with a number of razors. ACS

PROV. The Mary Rose Trust

Length 90 mm (3.5 in), width 70 mm (2.8 in)

{MR 81A4235}

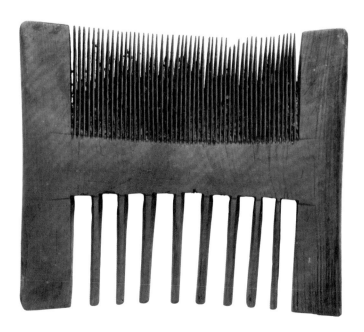

LEATHER COSTREL

Recovered from the wreck of the Mary Rose

English, mid 16th century

A range of vessels including flasks, bottles and costrels like this one would have been used to carry refreshment, such as wine or beer. These items could be carried about the person hung on cords or leather straps, or they could have been positioned at convenient places about the ship for communal use.

This particular example of a costrel was found inside a chest on the main deck, along with several personal items and wood-working tools. It is made from hardened leather and would have been double stitched with flax or hemp yarn, and has a wooden stopper to close it. The remains of a waterproof lining or coating were found on the inner surface and it has holes where it may originally have had a carrying thong.

These leather vessels were made by moulding wet leather into form and stitching the edges, most probably while damp, and then filling with sand to hold the shape until dry.

Eleven vessels like this one were found and all of them are decorated in a typical style of the late medieval period. They have three moulded raised ribs running from top to bottom, with decoration punched or incised in between these ribs. On this example both the front and back are decorated with five sets of double lines running top to bottom. These are framed by horizontal and diagonal sets at the neck. The base has two asterisks and two joining lines and there is also a saltire cross on each side. Some of these vessels may have originally been painted or dyed as well. ACS

PROV. The Mary Rose Trust

Height 135 mm (5.3 in), width 140 mm (5.5 in), width of base 40 mm (1.6 in)

PUB. Hildred 2009: 455

{MR 81A1214}

LEATHER SHOE

Recovered from the wreck of the Mary Rose

English, early 16th century

An estimated 425 examples of shoes and boots were found on the *Mary Rose*. They range from complete examples, like this one, to mere fragments. This particular shoe was found towards the front of the ship on the main deck. It is shaped like a slipper with a rounded front and is made from leather.

The shoes recovered from the *Mary Rose* fall into two main styles; high throated slip-on shoes and low-cut shoes, which often fasten over the instep with a buckled strap. The majority of the shoes like this example are high-cut slip-on shoes which are practical working footwear. This type is likely to have been worn by most of the crew. The low-cut shoes are generally considered to be dress shoes or for summer wear. Many of the high-cut shoes also have decorative slashing which was considered a fashionable feature of this period.

Within the shoes recovered there are also examples of ankle boots which either fasten at the front, or have a flap that wraps over the instep to fasten on the outside of the foot. In addition to these are nine pairs of thigh boots, found either amidships or towards the stern.

Variations between the shoes include the size, width of tread, and the degree of curve around the toes. As for the shoes' construction, most of them, including this example, were made using the welted method introduced at the start of the 16th century and still in use today. A small proportion of the shoes are turnshoes; a construction style where the shoe has a single sole and is made inside out. While the turnshoes from the *Mary Rose* tend to have rounded toes, the welted shoes can be divided into three main types; square, eared or round, like this example. ACS

PROV. The Mary Rose Trust

Length 275 mm (10.8 in)

{ MR 80A1312 }

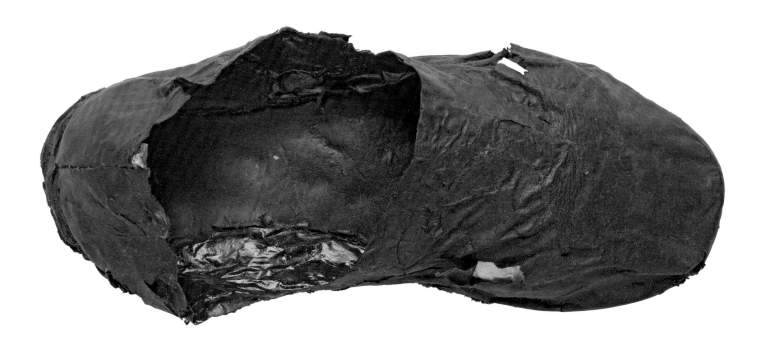

{ 5 }

HENRY'S
BODYGUARDS

THE GENTLEMEN PENSIONERS

GRAEME RIMER

In 1485, after the battle of Bosworth, the new King Henry VII raised a royal bodyguard of trusted soldiers; the Yeoman of the Guard. He may have been inspired to do so following a similar action by Louis XI of France, who in 1474 had raised a '*Compagnie de Cent Gentilshommes de la Maison du Roi*'.[1]

In the year of his accession Henry VIII sought to enhance further the protective ring of trusted men surrounding the monarch created by his father by raising a band of '*Spears of Honour*', a group of young men associated with noble families, each man with his own retinue, who would be retained at the King's expense to provide close protection for him. The Yeomen of the Guard were to be in an outer chamber to control access to the King, but members of his band of 'Spears' were to attend the King directly.

A copy of the '*Ordinances and Statutes of the Spears of Honour, 1509*', is preserved in the British Library,[2] which gives in detail the nature of the new guard and the requirements to be placed upon those chosen to form it:

'*...his highness hath ordeyned and appointed to haue a retynue daily of certaine Speres called men of Armes to be chosen of gentlemen that be commen and extracte of noble blod to thentent that they shall exercise the feate of Armes and be the more mete and able to serue theire prince aswell in tyme of werre as otherwise and to haue good wagis to leve upon accordingly...*'

This makes it clear that the term 'Spear' refers to the individual member of the guard and not to any weapon he might carry. The *Ordinances* then outline the expectation placed on anyone selected to become a Spear in the new guard:

'*ffurste euery of the said gentlemen shalhaue his harneys* [ie his armour] *complete and all other habiliments mete and necessary for him with twoo double horses at the leeste for himself and his page convenient and necessarye for a man of Armes. And also his Coustrell*[3] *with a Javelyn*[4] *or dymye launce well armed and horsed as it apperteyneth and they shall obeye in euery condicion the Captaine that shalbe ordeyned and deputed by the kinges highnes or his deputie lieutenaunte to haue the Rule conduite and governaunce of theim in all thinges that thei shalbe commaunded to doo on the kinges behalf.*'

In addition to providing a page and a Coustrell for himself each Spear was also required to provide two archers:

'*Item that euery of the aforesaid men of Armes shall furnyshe and make ready twoo good Archers well horsed and harnessed and to bring theim to muster before the kinges grace or suche persones as his grace shall appointe within a moneth at the*

furthest after the daye that they shalbe commaunded soo to doo by the kinges grace or theire Captaine or lientenaunte and not to faille soo to doo Vpon paine of losing theire Romes [ie the accommodation provided] *and theire bodies to be ponysshed atte the kinges pleasure.*'

The terms of the *Ordinances* make it clear that once in the King's service Spears and their retinue were to remain in accommodation provided for them and to be in a state of permanent readiness and to be available to the King at all times. Payment was to be made to each Spear, with which he was to maintain his retinue:

'*...euery Spere shalhaue and receive for himself his Coustrell his page and his twoo Archers three shillings & foure pens sterlinges by the daye...*'

This money was to be paid monthly, in arrears, by the Treasurer of the King's Chamber, which clearly indicates that the guard was to be a part of the royal household and not a military force like the Yeomen of the Guard. The original plan was to raise a body of one hundred Spears, but this was subsequently reduced to 50. Even so paying the wages of this new body meant an annual outlay by Henry of no less than £5,000.

It appears that, probably because of the enormous cost of keeping such an expensive elite guard, by 1515 it had ceased to exist. Henry's chronicler, Edward Hall, said that the Spears '*endured but a while, the apparel and charges were so great for there were none of them*'.[5] However, the improvements in Henry's financial situation following the dissolution of the monasteries may have been the spur to his inclination to revive the idea of a special personal guard at the time when he was anticipating marriage to Anne of Cleves.[6] As early as 1537 there had been ideas discussed about the forming of an elite guard of 50 '*speres*', and among the Henry VIII state papers of December 1538 thoughts were being given to raising a body of 100 'Gentillmen'.[7] For the first time the nature of their arms are suggested: '*And wheire the yomen* [ie the Yeomen of the Guard] *beire bylles or halbards the gentillmen might beire pollaxes...*' The pay for each member of this guard was to be paid £50 per annum, as in 1509, £30 of which was to pay for the maintenance of riding coats, horses and servants, £10 for livery gowns, for use in winter and summer, and £10 allowance for food and drink.

The order to raise this guard was carried out in 1539,[8] and it is clear that the new corps was to include trusted men formally in the employ of the Duke of Norfolk, the Duke of Suffolk and other distinguished members of Henry's court. In 1540 another list was drawn up of members of the guard, and for the first time the name of this unit as the '*gentilmen pencyoners*' appears.

It is clear that, given the cost of maintaining them and their high-profile presence in the court, the members of this band were very well-dressed and equipped, and must have made an imposing sight. A good contemporary example of their appearance is the portrait of a member of the Palmer family, possibly William Palmer (cat. no. 90). His rich velvet doublet is decorated with a heavy gold chain, and on his hat is a gold badge bearing an image of St George. He carries a basket-hilted sword of the type known to have become popular in England in the 1540s, and most notably carries a pollaxe, usually the mark of the Gentlemen Pensioners. These elements together give an air of strength and purpose to the image of this individual.

Despite their imposing demeanour there is little evidence that the Gentlemen Pensioners were tested militarily during Henry's reign. They are recorded as having been in attendance at Blackheath in 1540 during the events surrounding the marriage of Henry and Anne of Cleves, and that they accompanied the King to the siege of Boulogne in 1544, but there is no account of them engaging in combat. The Gentlemen Pensioners, however, continued in royal service after Henry's death. Indeed they existed as the Honourable Band of Gentlemen Pensioners until the 1830s, when the name was changed to the Honourable Corps of Gentlemen-at-Arms, a distinguished body which exists to this day and which can be seen in evidence at great state occasions still guarding the body of the sovereign.

Notes and references page 337.

Page 322: A watercolour by a Flemish artist working in England, possibly showing a 'Spere', second decade of the 16th century. The figure is of a man at arms wearing over his armour a gown decorated with the red cross of England in profusion, and he carries a pollaxe. The red cross was a distinguishing feature worn by the Band of Spears, while the Yeomen of the Guard wore the Tudor rose. The British Library, Cotton Augustus III f25.
© The British Library Board

(90)

PORTRAIT OF A MEMBER
OF THE PALMER FAMILY

Attributed to Gerlach Flicke

Oil on panel, English, about 1540

This panel portrait probably depicts William Palmer, Gentleman Pensioner, about 1539, with his pollaxe and basket-hilted sword, wearing a black gown and doublet, and a medallion of St George on the upturned brim of his hat. Henry VIII established a new body guard of fifty 'Spears' in 1509, a *'new and sumptuous Troop of Gentlemen composed of cadets of noble families and the highest order of gentry'.*[1] Under their captain Henry Earl of Essex they accompanied the King at the battle of the Spurs in 1513. Revived in 1539 as the Gentlemen Pensioners this body was renamed the Gentlemen at Arms in 1834, and today, numbering five officers and 27 gentlemen, the body survives as the second oldest guard in England, and the weapons are still in the custody of the Axe Keeper and Butler. Their characteristic weapon was the pollaxe with a spiked head, as they increasingly attended the King on foot. At the coronation of Edward VI they were *'apparelled all in red damask, with their pole-axes in their hands'*,[2] and versions of these are still carried by their successors, the Gentlemen at Arms, today. A pollaxe in the Royal Armouries, no. VII.2044, is the only known surviving example from the early period of the unit. The basket-hilted sword depicted in the portrait is close in form to an English sword of about 1540 in the Royal Armouries collection, no. IX.4427 (cat. no. 75), which in turn forms part of a small group of such early basket-hilted swords of the mid 16th century, mostly from English provenances or collections, including examples from the River Can, Chelmsford, Bolling Hall, Bradford, the Haarlemermeer in the Rijksmuseum, Amsterdam, and a hilt from Pembridge Castle in the Royal Armouries, no. IX.1404.[3]

William Palmer of Lemington, Gloucestershire, was recorded in the earliest list of Gentlemen Pensioners of 1539 and another of about 1540–5 transcribed by Pegge.[4] He was last recorded as a Gentleman Pensioner at the funeral of Edward VI in 1553, and died in 1573.[5] The arms of Palmer of Gloucestershire and Warwickshire, quarterly of four, 1, chequy or and azure a chief gules for Palmer, 2, argent three martlets sable for Godweston, 3, argent, on a chevron between three lions heads erased gules, a mullet for difference, for Rocliff, 4, quarterly argent and sable, 3 fleur-de-lys of the first for Garshall appear at the top right. The attribution to the German artist Gerlach Flicke was made by the Sabin Galleries in 1978. Born in Osnabrück he came to England and died there in 1558. He is best known for his Holbein-like portrait of Thomas Cranmer in the National Portrait Gallery, London.[6] TR

PROV. Purchased at Christie's, 24 November 1998, lot 3. From the Delbere collection at Southam House near Cheltenham, sold by Lord Ellenborough, Sotheby's 11 June 1947 lot 77, Captain E Spencer Churchill, sold Christie's, 25 June 1965 lot 10

996 x 704 mm (39.5 x 27.8 in)

REF. (1) Pegge 1791: 2–18; (2) Pegge 1791: 29; (3) Blair 1981: 207–15, Wilson 1986, Mazansky 2005: 4; (4) Pegge 1791: 27-8 (British Library Harleian MS 642), Blair 1981: note 70; (5) Blair 1981: note 71; (6) Hervey 1910

PUB. Bigland 1791: 377; Blair 1981: 173-5, fig. 77; Nevinson 1958: 4, 6, 12, pl. IIA; Starkey 1991: X.2; Chubb & Rowse 1983: 91, no. 90

{I.1548}

DECORATED POLLAXE

Probably English, early 16th century

The head consists of cast copper alloy (latten) apart from the axe blade, rear hammer of four points and top spike which are of steel, the whole originally gilded. The top spike, axe blade and hammer head sprout from the open mouths of three lions' heads which flank the hexagonal socket. Below these heads the socket is divided into two sections, firstly by a ridged band and lower down by a decorative band of pointed 'Gothic' arches. Beneath these are representations of flames or sun's rays bursting upwards from an engraved handguard in the form of a rose.

Weapons such as this were almost certainly for use in parades or the tournament, in foot combat at the barriers.

From at least the mid 19th century this pollaxe had been associated with Edward IV of England, Henry's grandfather, because of the rose within a sunburst decoration which was indeed one of his badges.[1] However, the sunburst was also used by other monarchs including Henry VIII and appears on the cuisses of Henry's 'silvered and engraved' armour (Royal Armouries II.5 cat. no. 21).

It has also been suggested[2] that it is this pollaxe that is mentioned in Henry VIII's Inventory of 1547[3] a possible identification also given to another example[4] from the University Museum of Archaeology and Anthropology, Cambridge (1948.1708) (AL.101.1: cat. no. 93). RCWS

PROV. In Paris since at least 1783; the Musée d' Artillerie, Paris, 1807

Overall length 1850 mm (72.8 in); weight 4 kg (8 lb 8 oz)

REF. (1) Les Collections 1845: 46, repeated in Penguilly l'Haridon 1862; (2) Laking 1900–22: Vol. III: 103–4; (3) Starkey 1998: 104, no. 3860; (4) Borg 1975: 297;

PUB. Anon 1845: 46 (cat. no. 467); Borg 1975: 297–298 (illus.); Carré 1783: pl. I.q (illus.); Dubois & Marchais 1807: pl VI.4; Laking 1900–22: Vol. III: 102–4; Penguilly l'Haridon 1862: 462; Reverseau 1982; Starkey 1998; Way 1847: 238

Musée de l'Armée, Paris

{K.84}

{92}

WREXHAM BUCKLER DECORATED
WITH THE ROYAL ARMS

Possibly originally belonging to or made for Henry VIII

English or Welsh, about 1510–30

The circular concave buckler is constructed of 24 closely set concentric iron rings, over some 184 iron laths, riveted together by 25 rows of numerous rivets, the prominent gilded heads of which create a decorative 'beading' effect. These rings and rows encircle the central conical iron boss which is prolonged into an onion-shaped knob from which projects a short, blunt and writhen spike. The boss is hollow on the inside to allow the hand to hold the transverse wooden grip, which is bound to the shield by thin iron strips and is reinforced by a strip of iron.

The boss is gilded and etched with the design of the sun in splendour around the base of the spike. On the main part of the boss is etched the Tudor royal arms (England and France quartered, with dragon and greyhound supporters). There are also three other separate devices, the portcullis, a crowned Tudor rose and the pomegranate badge of Katherine of Aragon.

This buckler is the finest surviving example known. Although early catalogues incorrectly stated that the buckler belonged to Henry VIII's father Henry VII it is clear that it was once the personal property of Henry VIII himself.[1] It therefore dates from sometime between his marriage to Katherine of Aragon (1509) and their separation (1531) and not earlier.

The buckler was in the Montmorency-Condé collection at Chantilly and is likely to have been a personal gift from Henry to a member of the French court. It has been suggested that it might have been given to Anne de Montmorency (1493–1567), *Grand Maître et Connétable de France*.[2] He visited the English court many times, was present at the Field of Cloth of Gold in 1520 and played a leading role in fostering an Anglo-French alliance.

Some Welsh buckler makers moved to London and in the 1520s one Geoffrey Bromefeld is known to have worked for Henry VIII.[3] In February 1530–31 he was made the King's '*boucler maker*' and it is possible that this buckler was made or more likely procured for Henry VIII by him.[4,5]

It is likely that bucklers, such as this example were not only made for Henry VIII and as gifts, but were also made for issuing to members of Henry's royal bodyguard. Very similar bucklers, also with gilded decoration, are depicted as being borne by various members of the King's retinue shown between the Archcliff and Black Bulwark forts at Dover in the painting of *The Embarkation at Dover*, of about 1545–50 (see page 8). RCWS

PROV. At Chantilly, France by 1783

Overall diameter 280 mm (11 in); weight: 2.3 kg (5 lb 7 oz)

REF. (1) Anon 1845: 33–4 (cat. no. 333); Penguilly l'Haridon 1862: 318; (2) Edwards & Blair 1982: 88–89; (3) Edwards & Blair 1982: 85; (4) Edwards & Blair 1982: 86; (5) Edwards & Blair 1982: 87–90;

PUB. Carré 1783 (pub. 1795): 392, 395. pl. XVI (illus.); Edwards & Blair 1982: 74–115; Laking 1900–22: 243 (illus. 614), 244–5; Penguilly l'Haridon 1862: 317–8 (cat. no. 1.5); Reverseau 1982

Musée de l'Armée, Paris

{I.6}

{93}

DECORATED POLLAXE HEAD

Possibly originally belonging to or made for Henry VIII
Probably English, early 16th century; end of top spike and most of the
shortened wooden haft modern restorations

The head consists of cast copper alloy (latten) apart from the upper halves of the rear fluke and top spike which were originally of iron, deeply sunk into the copper alloy core, the whole probably originally gilded. The extreme tip of the rear fluke is damaged. The latten base to the rear fluke bears an incised pomegranate. The hammer head consists of four rebated points, and downturned fluke sprouting from the open jaws of two lion's heads which flank the socket. Between these there is a winged cherub's face on either side. Below these the socket is divided into three sections by ridged bands. The upper section includes reliefs of the Tudor rose, surmounted by a crown and flanked by two supporting putti beneath which is a small fleur-de-lys. The middle section has a single larger fleur-de-lys, one on each side. The lowest section is pierced by a transverse bar, which secures the socket to the haft, the terminals of which consist of acorns (one now missing). Below the socket some 190 mm of the original wooden haft is preserved, with the remains of a silken tassel at the top. The sides of the haft are strengthened by four long langets of copper alloy, which are decorated in relief with applied fleurs-de-lys (some missing).

The crowned rose indicates English royal associations and has been compared to that which appears, with the HR monogram, on the harquebus (dated 1537) (Royal Armouries XII.1 cat. no. 46), and, also with putti supporters, on the three-barrelled cannon, (Royal Armouries XIX.17: cat. no. 52).[1]

It has been suggested that this existing pollaxe is the one described in the 1547 inventory:[2]

'*A polaxe the hedde party gilte the hammer hedde having iii pickes within the same a Rose gilte the staffe garnyshed with crymesyn velved and fringed with redde silke*'.[3] However this can only be so if one accepts a scribal error resulting in '*iii pickes*' rather than '*iiii pickes*'. (It should also be noted that at one time the similar pollaxe in the Musée de l'Armée, Paris (K.84: cat. no. 91), was also described as the pollaxe thus listed.[4] Although this identification is not at all certain the piece must be associated with Henry VIII as it bears the pomegranate decoration, the badge of Katherine of Aragon. It also points to a date between her marriage to Henry VIII in 1509 and their separation in 1531.

The pollaxe belongs to a small group of examples which similarly have heads partly of cast copper alloy.[5] They are probably of similar date (the first half of the 16th century) and possibly originate from England, though not necessarily from the same workshop. These include K.84 (cat. no. 91) which has an axe blade, the decoration of which includes a rose within a sunburst, a badge used by English monarchs including Henry VIII and which appears on the cuisses of Henry's 'silvered and engraved armour' (Royal Armouries II.5: cat. no. 21).

Weapons such as this were used for battle and tournament. This particular example was almost certainly for use in parade or in foot combat at the barriers. RCWS

PROV. Presented to the University Museum of Archaeology and Anthropology, Cambridge, by Lord Braybrooke in 1948.
Formerly the property of Sir Francis Vincent of Debden Hall, Essex, and purchased from his estate about 1847 by the
Hon. Richard Neville; it then became part of the Neville collection at Audley End, Essex

Overall length 1635 mm (64 in) (including restored haft); head length 375 mm (14.8 in) (including restored top spike
but excluding langets); weight: 4.2 kg (9 lb 4 oz)

REF. (1) Borg 1975: 296–7; (2) Borg 1975: 297; (3) Starkey 1998: 104, no. 3860; (4) Laking 1900–22: Vol. III 103–4;
(5) Borg 1975: 297–301; Marks & Williamson 2003: 198, no. 57 (illus.); Way 1847: 237 (illus.)

University Museum of Archaeology and Anthropology, Cambridge (1948.1708)

{AL.IOI.I}

NOTES AND REFERENCES

ESSAYS

{I} Henry VIII: Power and Personality –
   Cooper
1. Miller 1984: 101
2. Scarisbrick 1968: 417
3. Rebholz 1978:155
4. Elton 1972: 171, 207
5. Anglo 1992
6. CSP Venetian 1864–1947: vol 2, 918
7. Davies 1998: 237
8. Tudor-Craig 1989; Lloyd & Thurley
    1990: 29–32
9. Ullmann 1979
10. Hall 1550
11. Guy 1988:192
12. Davies 1977: 2, 7
13. Davies 1998: 248
14. Loades 2007: 75
15. Scarisbrick 1968: 128
16. Starkey 1991: 12
17. Loach 1994: 44
18. Starkey 1991: 48
19. Lloyd & Thurley 1990: 57
20. Thurley 1993: 39
21. Starkey 1991: 58–9
22. Lloyd & Thurley 1990: 44–51
23. Samman 1995
24. Starkey 1991: 118–25; MacCulloch
    1995:5
25. Bloch 1973: 104–5; 181; 185
26. Lloyd & Thurley 1990:32
27. State papers Henry VIII: vol 7, 283
28. Statutes of the Realm: vol 3, 427
29. Nicholson 1988: 21
30. British Library Cotton Tiberius E.VIII,
    fol. 89
31. Guy 1993: 38
32. Rex 1996: 863
33. Figgis 1914: 91–3
34. State Papers Henry VIII: vol 3, 233
35. State Papers Henry VIII: vol 3, 331
36. State Papers Henry VIII: vol 3, 340
37. Pollard 1902
38. Pollard 1902: 288, 296
39. Scarisbrick 1968: 506, 526
40. Pollard 1902: 289–90
41. Bernard 2002: 116
42. Marshall 1905: 292–3

{II} Faith and Politics – Wooding
1. Hall 1904: 64–5
2. Baldwin 1990: 41
3. Kingsford 1911
4. Leviticus ch.18, v.16; ch.20, v.21
5. Bernard 2005: 4–9
6. Erasmus 1978
7. Bernard 1999: 86
8. Thurley & Lloyd 1990: 29

{III} Warfare in Henry's Reign – Gunn
1. Tracy 1978
2. Knighton & Loades 2002: 24
3. Campbell 2007; 14–15, 27, 40, 100, 322,
    325, 327; Gunn 1987: 36–40
4. Gunn 1995: 22–53, 81–9
5. Miller 1986: 14–17, 133–61
6. Lander 1976: 228–30
7. Bowers 2002
8. Potter 2005
9. Hoyle 1995
10. Loades 1992: 55–65
11. Cruikshank 1969
12. Phillips 1999: 111–33
13. Loades 1992: 103–11; Gunn 1986
14. Phillips 1999: 138–45; Bernard 1985
15. Gunn 1991
16. Phillips 1999: 146–7
17. Ellis 1996
18. Hoyle 2001
19. Phillips 1999: 147–77
20. Hoyle 1995
21. Gunn, Grummitt & Cools 2007

{IV} Henry's Army and Navy – Loades
1. The militia, or levies, were intended
    mainly for defence against invasion.
    Cruickshank 1966: 12
2. A commission was an instrument
    delegating to named individuals certain
    aspects of the royal authority. It was
    extensively used in civilian government,
    particularly in the form of the
    Commission of the Peace. Chrimes 1972:
    68–96; Elton 1982
3. Loades & Knighton 2000: 119
4. Rose 1982
5. Oppenheim 1896: 143–54
6. Oppenheim 1896: 143–54
7. This is conjectural, because when the ship
    was rebuilt in 1536 a number of new gun
    ports were inserted. However,
    contemporary evidence suggests that
    originally there were two or three ports a
    side. Rule 1982: 120–22
8. Rodger 1997: 477; Loades & Knighton
    2000: 73
9. Bennell 2000: 34–8
10. Loades & Knighton 2000: 12–14
11. Schubert 1942: 131–40
12. Loades & Knighton 2008: 57–66
13. Corbett 1905: 20–24
14. Archivo General de Simancas E 165, f.29;
    Lloyd 1952: 1–84
15. Spont 1897: xxviii–xi
16. Fissell 2001: 5–6; Author 1862–1910
17. Phillips 1999: 109–32
18. Loades 1992: 68
19. Fissell 2001: 9; Hoyle 1993: ix–xv
20. Fissell 2001: 11; TNA E315/315, ff. 13–15
21. Gunn 1986: 596–634
22. Hoyle 2001: 306–38

23. Colvin 1982: 415–607
24. Bonner 1997: 36–53
25. Loades & Knighton 2008; Pollard 1903:
    37–52
26. The Scots refused to be intimidated, and
    called on the French for assistance. Mary
    was eventually betrothed to the Dauphin,
    Henry, in 1548.
27. Fissell 2001: 13–19
28. Fissell 2001: 14; Elton 1992: 15–16
29. Rodger 1997: 182
30. Loades 1996: 69–70
31. Loades & Knighton 2002: 116–20
32. In January 1557 the Lord Treasurer, the
    Marquis of Winchester, specified an
    'Ordinary', or standard budget of
    ££14,000 a year as a condition for
    assuming responsibility. Acts of the Privy
    Council, VI: 39
33. Individual letters of marquee had been
    granted before this, but this was the first
    application of privateering as a general
    policy. Hughes & Larkin 1964: 345

{V} The Treatment of Injury and Disease –
   Gruber von Arni
1. Cantlie 1974
2. Park 1997: 74–8; Garrison 1913: 80–3,
    97–103, 188–191, 210–11; Cantlie
    1974: 14
3. Gore 1879: 36–7
4. Parliamentary Act 32 of Henry VIII, 1541
5. Gale 1563
6. Gore 1879
7. Howell 1904; Brewer & Brodie 1965;
    Keevil 1974; Gore 1879
8. British Library Harleian Mss. 6844
9. Gardiner 2005
10. Cantlie 1974: 78–9
11. Marsden 2003
12. Gabriel & Metz 1992: 66
13. Howell 1904: 612
14. Grose 1786b: 273–4
15. Von Gersdorff 1517: 215–17
16. Von Gersdorff 1517
17. Copeman 1960
18. Lindeman 1999: 57
19. Elyot 1534
20. Boorde 1575
21. Gruber von Arni 2001

{VI} The Tower of London in the Reign of
   Henry VIII – Parnell
1. Holinshed 1588 Vol. I: 329
2. Haiward & Gascoyne survey, Royal
    Armouries I.573
3. Nichols 1850
4. Bayley 1825: appendix, ciii
5. Bayley 1825
6. TNA E101/474/13, f.11v
7. Merriman 1902 i: 351–2

8. Bodleian Library, rawl. Ms D775 f. 204r
9. Hamilton 1875–77 I: 37
10. BL, Add Charter 16334
11. BL, Add Charter16334
12. Dawson 1890–1907: 322–3
13. Starkey 1998
14. TNA E101/474/18
15. Parnell 1993: 59–60
16. Royal Armouries MS I.243

{VII} Food and Dining at Henry's Court –
Brears
1. Thurley 1993: 70
2. Society of Antiquaries 1790: 17
3. Society of Antiquaries 1790: 137–240
4. Society of Antiquaries 1790: 166
5. Society of Antiquaries 1790: 191–7
6. Society of Antiquaries 1790: 219
7. Thurley 1990: 1–28
8. Thurley 1993: 7, 8
9. Household Ordinances 1790: 153–4
10. Household Ordinances 1790: 162–70
11. Household Ordinances 1790: 191
12. Brears 1999: 102–5
13. Brears 2008: 147–71
14. Brears 2008: 423–8
15. Starkey 1998: 11624, 17615, 17624–5
16. Brears 1999: 174
17. Barclay 1518; Wright 1983
18. Household Ordinances 1790: 185–6
19. Brears 1999: 126–8
20. Household Ordinances 1790: 148
21. Household Ordinances 1790: 171
22. Household Ordinances 1790: 174–78
23. Nicolas 1827: 83
24. Thirsk 2007: 19–20
25. Thurley 1990: plans 7+8
26. Brewer 1861–3: 1540, 123b, 163b
27. Household Ordinances 1790: 154–8,
    152–3, 165
28. Household Ordinances 1790: 154, 156
29. Starkey 1998: 10407
30. Household Ordinances 1790: 215
31. Brears 2008: 474–82
32. Starkey 1998: 68
33. Starkey 1998: 1743–65
34. Starkey 1998: 112–55, 1202–48
35. Starkey 1998: 1685
36. Starkey 1998: 17220
37. Starkey 1998: 156
38. Household Ordinances 1790: 165
39. Starkey 1998: 1678–1742, 182
40. Household Ordinances 1790: 165;
    Starkey 1998: 11498–9, 11502–4
41. Brears 2008: 454–7
42. Starkey 1998: 1657–77, 1773, 1776, 1792
43. Starkey 1998: 427–43
44. Starkey 1998: 135; Byrne 1949: 77
45. Byrne 1949: 43, 590–96
46. Byrne 1949: 1923, 1927
47. Byrne 1949: 11471, 11481, 11482
48. Byrne 1949: 3438, 11155, 16022, 16863
49. Byrne 1949: 1096–1119
50. Byrne 1949: 1235, 1248, 1683–4
51. Cavendish 1962: 102–3
52. Cavendish 1962; 10953; Ashmole 1672:
    603

{VIII} Dress and Fashion at Henry's Court –
Hayward
1. Castiglione 1867
2. Sicca 2007
3. Norris 1938; Cunnington & Cunnington
   1954; Ashelford 1983: 14–15; Hayward
   2007a: 95–102
4. Hayward 2007a: 320
5. Hayward 2007a: 320–22
6. Hayward 2007a: 98
7. Castiglione 1967: 63
8. Plummer 1885: 125
9. Hayward 1996
10. Hall 1904b: 791
11. Hayward 2004: no.5
12. String 2009
13. Hayward 2002
14. Hayward 2007a: 89, 91–2; Carter 1984;
    Arnold 1988
15. Sutton 1991; Nicolas 1830
16. BL Harley MS 4217, ff. 1r–v
17. LP II: 1510
18. Hall 1809: 724
19. LP II: 1506–7
20. Hayward 2007a: 98
21. de Marly 1985: 33
22. Starkey 1998: 356–65
23. BL Harley MS 4217, f.25r
24. Hayward 2004: no.12
25. Castiglione 1967: 61
26. Blair 2005
27. Hall 1904b: 519
28. Starkey 1991: 63
29. Starkey 1998: no. 8384
30. Starkey 1998: nos 8602-17
31. Anglo 1968: 31
32. LP II: 1506
33. Hall 1904b: 722
34. Castiglione 1967: 135
35. Hayward 2009
36. Hayward 2007b
37. Blair 1965a
38. Hayward 2004: no.944
39. Starkey 1991: 64
40. LP IV. ii, 3746
41. Starkey 1998: no.2127
42. TNA E101/419/20, unfoliated

{IX} The Legacy of Henry VIII – Ives
1. Bain 1890–2: ii, 326; LP xix (I) 314
2. Bateson 1890
3. TNA, SP 10/8 no.4
4. Holinshed 1588: iii, 826
5. Ascham 1864–5
6. Daalder 1975: 185–6

CATALOGUE

Tournaments at the Court of King Henry VIII
– Watts

1. Anglo 1969
2. The manuscript is endorsed: 'Justes at
   Westminster the 12th of February by the
   King, my Lord Devon, sir Thomas
   Knyvet and Edward Nevill, A.1.H.VII.'

The format of this manuscript is
extremely unusual: it is a long continuous
roll, rather than a book. The roll shows
three separate scenes from the
tournament.

A. (membranes 2–23) the entry into the lists
   of a procession including the four Knight
   Challengers
B. (membranes 24–27) a view of the tilt
   itself, with the Challengers at one end the
   Answerers at the other, and the King
   tilting against an Answerer watched by
   the Queen, with ladies and gentlemen of
   the court in an ornate gallery.
C. (membranes 27–35) a procession returning
   from the lists after the day's tilting

A collotype reproduction of the manuscript,
*The Great Tournament Roll of
Westminster*, Oxford, 1968, with an
excellent historical introduction by
Sydney Anglo.

3. Hall 1904 Vol. I: 164–5
4. Hall 1904 Vol. I: 189–218; Groubaux &
   Lemoisure 1913
5. Blair 1959: 17–20
6. Hall 1904Vol. I: 215–16
7. Hall 1904 Vol. II: 83–88

Henry VIII's Hunting Interests – Rimer

1. Cayley 1808: 11–15; Wharton Vo.III:
   101; Strutt 1838: 8
2. Caxton 1926: 31
3. Giustiniani 1854: 312
4. For a more complete summary of King
   Henry's expenditure on hunting see
   Williams 2005: 49.

The Royal Armour Workshops at Greenwich
– Richardson

1. ffoulkes 1927; Richardson 2004
2. Brewer et al 1.2: 876, 1285
3. There is a large corpus of literature about
   the Greenwich armouries (the most
   important studies include Sharp 1929,
   Cripps-Day 1934–52; Mann 1951; Blair
   1963 (the present essay owes much to
   this account); Blair 1965; Blair 1985;
   Williams & de Reuck 1995 and
   Richardson 2006; for the pieces relating
   to Henry VIII see also Richardson 2002).
4. Blair 1965; Brewer et al 1.2: 1496; TNA
   E 36/1
5. Brewer et al 1.2: 1496
6. Brewer et al 1.2: 1497; Williams & de
   Reuck 1995: 46
7. Brewer et al 1.1: 330; 1.2: 1497; 2.1:
   875, 1479
8. Blair 1965
9. Blair 1965
10. Nickel et al 1982: 34–5, followed by
    Williams & de Reuck 1995: 28, 126–7;
    and with reservations by Blair 2002a:
    199–215; Terjanian 2006
11. Brewer et al 3.1: 408
12. Blair 1965; Brewer et al 2.1: 566; 2.2:
    1465

13. Brewer et al 2.1: 1548–50
14. Richardson 2000; Pyhrr 1984
15. Brewer et al 2.1: 1505; Blair 2002a: 199–200, who notes also that the eleven liveries were for the 'xi almayns late come owte of almayn'.
16. Brewer et al 2.1: 1583; Mann 1951: no. 97, appendix A
17. Brewer et al 2.1: 1533–4
18. Mann 1951: 57; La Rocca 1989: 8
19. TNA SP14/64; SP16/139; discussed at length in Cripps-Day 1944: 25–73
20. Brewer et al 3.1: 282–3
21. Blair 1995; Cat. no. 1
22. Boccia 1982: 283–90
23. Hall 1550: f. 155r
24. Blair pers. comm..
25. Watts 1992; Grancsay 1937
26. Blair 2002
27. Cripps-Day 1944: 24, 54–5
28. Cripps-Day 1944: 56–7
29. Hall 1550: f.241v
30. Starkey 1998: 161
31. Cat. no. 39
32. Williams & de Reuck 1995: 56–68
33. Blair 1963: 40; Williams & de Reuck 1995: 35; Nichols 1848: 298–312
34. Mann 1951: 57–8, appendix D dated to about 1553–4; Cripps-Day 1944: 25–6; changed by Blair 1963: 39; followed by Eaves 1999: note 63
35. Dillon 1905
36. Claude Blair's seminal study of the Jacob Album is yet to be published.
37. Blakeley 1997
38. Eaves 1999
39. Edge 1992
40. Mann 1951: 30–1, no. 23: 47 portrait no.79; Williams & de Reuck 1995: 109; Cripps-Day 1934: 105–7; Christie's 1981: 30–3, lot 132
41. Williams & de Reuck 1995: 38; Cripps-Day 1934 passim; Richardson 2004: 68
42. Williams & de Reuck 1995: 38–41
43. Cripps-day 1934: 114; 1944: 76
44. Williams & de Reuck 1995: 125; Richardson forthcoming; Richardson 1991
45. Williams & de Reuck 1995: 41; Richardson 2004: 24
46. Blackmore & Blair 1991
47. Borg 1976

The King and the Armourers of Flanders – Terjanian

1. In this essay the expression 'Low Countries' designates territories commonly referred to as 'Flanders' in 16th-century England, whereas 'Flanders' is reserved for the county of Flanders proper. In the absence of adequate nouns, however, people native of the Low Countries will be called 'Netherlanders' whereas the native of the 'Burgundian Low Countries', i.e. of the portion of the Low Countries that the Hapsburg inherited from the Valois dukes of Burgundy in 1477, will be described as 'Flemings'. The epithets 'Netherlandish' and 'Flemish' will be used to reflect the same distinction.
2. A historical account of the Greenwich workshops, including bibliographical references, is provided by Richardson's essay on the Greenwich armourers in this volume.
3. Blair 2002a: 199–200
4. Nickel & Phyrr & Tarassuk 1982: 34
5. Nickel & Phyrr & Tarassuk 1982: 34
6. Blair 1965b: 38
7. Nickel & Phyrr & Tarassuk 1982: 34
8. Terjanian 2005: 30, 31, notes 48–66
9. Blair 2002a: 199–202
10. Blair 1965b: 38
11. The accounts belong to the section of the chambre des comptes preserved in the Archives déepartmentales du Nord (henceforth abbreviated AD Nord), Lille. On this source and the armourers who worked for Philip the Handsome, see Terjanian 2006: 146–156.
12. Ffoulkes 1916, 1: 199–200; Dillon 1902: 85–88, plate IV; Laking 1920–22, 3: 190–194, fig. 1002; Blair 1965b: 37–38, plates XIII, d and XVI, a; Pyhrr 1989: 100–102; Gaier 1993: 17–18, fig. 14; Williams & de Reuck 1995: 127, ills; Richardson 2002: 11, ills; Williams 2003: 723, ills.
13. Ffoulkes 1916, 1: 95–99; Dillon 1902: 86–89; Laking 1920, 3: 193–194, fig. 1003; Blair 1965b: 16, 24–41, plates I; XIII, a–c; XV; XVI, d; XVIII, d; Eaves 1993: 12–16, figs 7, 9, and 12; Williams 2003: 724–725, ills; Richardson 2002: 12–15, ills.
14. Valencia de don Juan 1898: 3–4; Blair 1965b: 37, plate XVII, a–b; Godoy 1992: 132–133, ills; Terjanian 2006: 150. I am indebted to Alvaro Soler del Campo for the opportunity to study the pieces of these bards.
15. Boeheim 1889: 23, no. 60; Mann 1930: plate XXIX, fig. 2; Blair 1965b: 37–38, plate XIV, c; János 1971: 297–8, fig. 80; Temesváry 1982: 64: no. 15, fig. 15. I am indebted to Claude Blair for his comments on the composition and restoration of this armour, which he was able to superficially examine in its case, in June 1967. Personal communication from Claude Blair, 15 September 2006.
16. Kienbusch & Grancsay 1933: 129, no. 44, plate IV; Blair 1965b: 37, plate XIV a–b; Thomas 1984: 57–58; Gaier 1993: 18; Pyhrr 2000: 15, no. 18. I am indebted to Stuart W. Pyhrr for the opportunity to study this and the next three objects, as well as the corresponding files in the Department of Arms and Armor.
17. Chaffers 1875: 38, no. 1000; Laking 1920–2, 1: 261–2, fig. 307a and Laking 1920–2, 2: 114, 116, fig. 458; Cripps-Day 1925: 19, no. 430; Pyhrr 2000: 16, no. 19, ill; Blair 2002a: 210, note 2.

18. Kienbusch & Grancsay 1933: 130, no. 45, plate IV; Grancsay 1953, no. 22, ill.; Nickel & Pyhrr & Tarassuk 1982: 34–35, no. 8, ill.; Gaier 1993: 18, fig. 15; Pyhrr 2000: 15, no. 18, ill; Blair 2002a: 210, note 2.
19. Pyhrr 2000: 15, no. 18. The presence of the mark on this piece was first noted by Stuart W Pyhrr and recorded in August 1977 in the file for this object in the Department of Arms and Armor at the Metropolitan Museum of Art.
20. Blair 1965b: 37–38
21. Godoy 1992: 132–33; Terjanian 2006: 50
22. The armour bore the inventory number A. 77 while it was part of the collections of the Kunsthistorisches Museum. Thomas 1984: 57–58.
23. Personal communication from Dr Matthias Pfaffenbichler, 10 August 2006. I am grateful to Dr Pfaffenbichler for consulting for me the relevant files in the Hofjagd- und Rüüstkammer.
24. Laking 1920–2, 5: 250–1; Cripps-Day 1925: 19, no.430
25. Blair 1965b: 26–33, 37–8
26. Blair 1965b: 26–33
27. Blair 1965b: 37–8
28. Kretschmar 1909–11
29. On this helm, see ffoulkes 1916, 1: 170, no. 1; Dufty 1968, plate LXXXIII; Blair 1998: 292, note 12.
30. On this helm, see Blair 1998: 292–5, figs 5–6.
31. AD Nord, B 2191, fols 339v–340r and 357r.
32. AD Nord, B 2267, fol. 337v.
33. AD Nord, B 2294, fol. 337r. The detail of Margot's career and works will be the subject of a forthcoming publication.
34. On these armourers, see Blair 1965b: 34–35 and Thom Richardson's essay on the Greenwich armouries in this volume.
35. On Martin Rondelle and Lazare de St Augustin, see Blair 1998: 301–302, note 22.
36. Squilbeck 1953: 251–252, note 1. According to Squilbeck, the source of this information is in the papers of Alexandre Pinchart in the Bibliotheèque Royale de Belgique, Brussels. I consulted a large portion of these papers, which are presently uncatalogued, but was unable to locate Pinchart's notes on arms and armour.

Henry VIII's Gun Shields – Smithurst

1. The author wishes to acknowledge the assistance of Thom Richardson for providing the results of his current unpublished researches on the Tower Inventories

2. Dufty & Reid 1968: 8; Blair 1958: 182,183
3. Other examples may be found in Windsor Castle, Hampton Court Palace, the Victoria and Albert Museum, Edinburgh Castle, the Metropolitan Museum, New York, the Higgins Armory Museum, Worcester, Massachusetts, the Walters Art Gallery, Baltimore, the Art Institute of Chicago, the State Hermitage Museum, St Petersburg, and the Palace Armoury, Valetta, Malta.

Henry VIII's Firearms – Rimer
1. At this time the term *handgun* would have been used to describe any gun small enough to be picked up and fired from the shoulder, and did not mean the more recent interpretation of a pistol, or gun so small it could be fired from just one hand.
2. Blair 2002b: 22
3. Nicolas 1827: 104
4. Nicolas 1827: 159
5. Nicolas 1827: 127
6. Blair 2002b: 22
7. Blair 2002b
8. Starkey 1998
9. Wilson 1988
10. Morin and Held 1980: 27
11. Richardson 1998: 50–52
12. Monaghan and Bound 2001
13. This report examines finds from the wreck of a British military vessel of about 1590, so far unidentified, which demonstrate the marked changes in the types of ordnance and personal weapons which developed between the time of the loss of the *Mary Rose* and the late Elizabethan period.

Arming the Early Tudor Army – Richardson
1. Fissell 2001: 26 citing TNA E 351/212
2. Fissell 2001: 9–13
3. Stoate 1978
4. Brewer et al. 1.2: 1498, 1501, 2.1: 874
5. Brewer et al. 2.1: 1474, 1540
6. Brewer et al. 2.1: 1472
7. Brewer et al. 1.2: 892, 911 the last British Library MS Stowe 146: f69
8. Brewer et al. 1.2: 1514
9. Fissell 2001: 7
10. Brewer et al. 1.2: 1513
11. Starkey 1998: 103–4, 121, 113, 131–2, 129
12. Lumpkin 1960: pl XLVII
13. Lumpkin 1960: pl. XLVIII
14. Baynton-Williams 2007: 8–9
15. Lumpkin 1960: 163, Brewer et al. 14.1: 439
16. Lumpkin 1960: 152, citing Brewer et al 1.2: 1554
17. Fissell 2001: 26; Brewer et al. 1.2: 872–3, 876, 897, 1285; Starkey 1998: 111, 131, 133, 135, 141, 162, 163, 345

Artillery and Fortification – Hall
1. Bourne 1587
2. David Starkey, paper given at the Mary Rose Conference, 13 tbc October 2007. N A M Rodger observed that Henry VIII intended to revive the glory of Henry V's time (Rodger 2004: 164).
3. Rodger 2004
4. Rodger 2004: 168
5. Starkey 1998: 141
6. Blackmore 1976
7. Guicciardini 1966: 153
8. Starkey 1998: 104
9. Teesdale 1991
10. Rodger 2004: 207
11. Rodger 2004: 221–7
12. Lucar 1588
13. Lucar 1588
14. Blackmore 1976:ref
15. Smith 1993: 1
16. Hall 1998: 57-66; Hall 2001: 106-116
17. Eldred 1646: 88–9
18. Guicciardini 1966: 153
19. Shelby 1967: ref
20. Saunders 1989: 37–47
21. Saunders 1989: ref
22. Durer's work, *Etliche Underricht zu Befestigung der Stelt schloss unde Flecken* was published in Nuremberg in 1527. It was translated into Latin and published in England in 1535 as *De urbibus, arcibus castellisque cendendis*. Saunders discusses Durer and the design background to Henry's works of fortification.
23. Saunders 1989: 37
24. Millward 2007: 181
25. Biddle *et al* 2001: 347
26. Biddle *et al* 2001: 90
27. Rodger 2004: 168
28. Starkey 1998: 141
29. Bourne 1587
30. Machiavelli 1883: 293

To Feed the King's Men: Catering for the Henrician Army and Navy – Brears
1. Davies 1968: 240
2. Brears 1999:39, 45
3. Davies 1968: 234
4. Davies 1968: 238
5. Davies 1968: 236
6. L&P i.575; Gardiner & Allan 2005: 570
7. L&P XIX, i.275, 1023
8. Davies 1968: 242
9. Gardiner & Allan 2005: 574; L&P XXi. 8, 200
10. Wilson 1976: 145
11. Gardiner & Allan 2005: 578, 586
12. L&P XX, i, 612, 259
13. L&P XX, ii, 8, 200
14. L&P XX, ii, 1123
15. Davies 1968: 236
16. OED 1569
17. L&P XX, i, 1140; XX ii, 177, 430, 441
18. L&P XIX, i, 654, 738
19. L&P XX, i, 259

20. L&P XIX, i, 889; XXi, 259; XX ii, 200
21. L&P XIX, i, 272
22. L&P XX, ii, 200, 1123
23. Davies 1968: 242
24. L&P XX, i, 259; XX ii 200
25. L&P XX, ii, 262
26. L&P XXXIX i, 272/4
27. Davies 1968: 139; Gardiner & Allan 2005: 603
28. L&P XX, ii,8
29. Gardiner & Allan 2005: 604, 606; Brears 1999: 28
30. Gardiner & Allan 2005: 586; L&P XX ii,8
31. Royal Collection catalogue no. 23
32. Starkey 1998: nos 8798–9
33. OED
34. Davies 1968: 242
35. Act 2, Scene 1, lines 109–14
36. Gardiner & Allan 2005: 603
37. Gardiner & Allan 2005: 593, 569–70, 576–7, 417
38. Gardiner & Allan 2005: 379, 434–5
39. Gardiner & Allan 2005: 428–31
40. Gardiner & Allan 2005: 432, 349
41. Gardiner & Allan 2005: 490
42. Gardiner & Allan 2005: 431
43. Gardiner & Allan 2005: 440
44. Brears 2008: 435–37; Gardiner & Allan 2005: 443
45. Gardiner & Allan 2005: 457, 451, 480–84
46. Davies 1968: 242

The Gentlemen Pensioners – Rimer
1. Nevinson 1958
2. Glas Sandeman 1912a
3. Coustrell: an attendant to a man at arms (OED). Clearly in this context a coustrell was a fighting man in the service of a Spear. Note, however, that at least the end of the 16th century the word coustrell, (custrell, coistrel, coystrell, coystrill, &c), was a term of reproach, meaning a knave or base person. Perhaps from the French *coirstillier*.
4. Glas Sandeman 1912b: 3
5. Starkey 1991: 136
6. Glas Sandeman 1912b: 7
7. Glas Sandean 1912b: 10
8. For a 'javelin', or light spear, from the armoury of Henry VIII see cat. no.57

BIBLIOGRAPHY

Acts of the Privy Council VI

Archivo General de Simancas

British Library Cotton Augustus

British Library Cotton Tiberius

British Library Harleian

British Library MS Stowe

Calendar of State Papers (CSP) Venetian 1864–1947. London, HMSO

L & P Letters & Papers, foreign and domestic of the reign of King Henry VIII

Society of Antiquaries 1790

SP Dom Chas I

State papers Henry VIII 1830-52. London, John Murray

Statutes of the realm 1810-28. London, Record Commission

TNA

Anglo, S 1992 *Images of Tudor kingship*. London, Seaby

Anglo, S 1969 *Spectacle, pageantry and early Tudor policy*. Oxford, Clarendon Press

Anglo, S 1968 The Great Tournament Roll of Westminster. Oxford, Oxford University Press

Anon 1845 *Les Collections dont se compose le Musée de l'Artillerie*. Paris, Imprimiere de Bachelier

Arnold, J 1988 *Queen Elizabeth's wardrobe unlock'd*. Leeds, Maney

Ascham, R 1864-5 The whole works. J R Smith

Ashelford, J 1983 *A visual history of costume: The sixteenth century*. London, Batsford

Ashmole, E 1672 *Institution, laws & ceremonies of the most noble order of the garter*. London: Nathanael Brooke.

Ayloffe, J 1774 An account of some English historical paintings at Cowdry, in Sussex.

Bain, J (ed.) 1890-2 *The Hamilton Papers. Letters and papers illustrating the political relations of England and Scotland in the XVI century*. Edinburgh, H M General Register House

Baldwin, D 1990 *The Chapel Royal ancient and modern*. London, Duckworth

Barclay, A 1518 *The fyfte Eglog of Alexandre Barclay of the Cytezen and Uplondyshman*. London, Wynkyn de Worde

Bateson, M 1890 The Pilgrimage of Grace.*English Historical Review*

Bartsch, R A von 1803-21 *The Illustrated Bartsch*. New York, Abaris Press

Bayley, J 1825 *The history and antiquaries of the Tower of London*. 2 vols. London, printed for T Cadell

Baynton-Williams, A and M 2007 *Maps of war*. London, Quercus

Beard, C 1934 'An unrecorded Greenwich armour'. *Connoisseur* 93.389, January: 39–44

Beard, C 1931 An iconographic problem. *Connoisseur*, 87.365, June: 358–65.

Bennell, J 2000 *The oared vessels in the Anthony Roll*.

Bernard, G W 2005 *The king's reformation: Henry VIII and the remaking of the English church*. New Haven and London, Yale University Press

Bernard, G W 2002 'The tyranny of Henry VIII'. In Bernard & Gunn. Aldershot, Ashgate

Bernard, G W 1999 The piety of Henry VIII. In N Scott Amos, H van Nierop and A Pettegree (eds.) *The education of a Christian society*. Aldershot, Ashgate

Bernard, G W 1985 *War, taxation and rebellion in Tudor England: Henry VIII, Wolsey and the Amicable Grant of 1525*. Brighton, Harvester

Bernard, G W and S J Gunn, 2002 *Authority and consent in Tudor England: Essays presented to C S L Davies*. Aldershot, Ashgate

Biddle, M and J Hiller, I Scott, A Streeten 2001 *Henry VIII's coastal artillery fort at Camber Castle Oxford*. Oxford Archaeological Unit/English Heritage

Bigland, R 1791 *Historical, monumental and genealogical collections relative to the County of Gloucester, 1*. London, J Nichols

Blackmore, H L 1988 *Master Jacoco's culverin.Arms & Armour Society Journal* 12 [5]: 312-44

Blackmore, H L 1976 *The Armouries of the Tower of London: I Ordnance*. London, HMSO

Blackmore, H L 1965 *Guns and rifles of the World*. London, B T Batsford

Blackmore, H L and C Blair 1991 King James II's harquebus armours and Richard Holden of London. *Journal of the Arms and Armour Society* 13 September: 316–334

Blair, C 2005 A 16th-century reference to the making of a coat of mail. *Journal of the Arms and Armour Society*, **18.3**, 105-6

Blair, C 2002a The will of Martin van Royne and some lists of Almain armourers at Greenwich. *The Journal of the Arms and Armour Society* 17.4: 199-215

Blair, C 2002b *King Henry VIII's chamber-pieces*. Royal Armouries Yearbook 7. Royal Armouries, Leeds

Blair, C 1998 The Lullingstone helm. *The Antiquaries Journal* 78: 289-305

Blair, C 1995 King Henry VIII's tonlet armour. *Journal of the Arms and Armour Society* **15.2**: September: 85–108

Blair, C 1985 Greenwich armour. *Transactions of the Greenwich and Lewisham Antiquarian Society* 10: 6–11

Blair, C 1981 'The early basket hilt in Britain', in D Caldwell (ed.) *Scottish weapons and fortifications, 1100–1800*. Edinburgh, J Donald: 152–252

Blair, C 1974 'Comments on Dr Borg's 'Horned helmet'. *Journal of the Arms and Armour Society* 8.2: 138–85

Blair, C 1970, *A Royal swordsmith and damascener: Diego de Çaias. Metropolitan Museum Journal*, Vol.3: 149-198

Blair, C 1965a The Emperor Maximilian's gift of armour to King Henry VIII and the silver and engraved armour at the Tower of London. *Archaeologia*, 99, 1-52

Blair, C 1965b The silvered armour of Henry VIII in the Tower of London. London, Society of Antiquaries

Blair, C 1963 The Royal Armouries at Greenwich. *Third Congress of the International Association of Museums of Arms and Military History*. London

Blair, C 1962 *European and American Arms*. London, Batsford

Blair, C 1959 New light on four Almain armours. *Connoisseur*, August: 17-20

Blair, C 1958 *European armour*. London, Batsford

Blair, C and S W Pyhrr 2003 'The Wilton "Montmorency" armour: an Italian armour for Henry VIII'. *Metropolitan Museum Journal* 38: 95–144

Blakeley, E 1997 The tournament garniture of Robert Dudley, Earl of Leicester. *Royal Armouries Yearbook* 2: 55-63. Leeds, Royal Armouries

Bloch, M 1973 *The royal touch: sacred monarchy and scrofula in England and France*. London, Routledge & Kegan Paul

Boccia, L G 1982 *Le Armature di S. Maria delle Grazie di Curtatone di Mantova, e l'Armatura Lombarde del '400*. Busto Arsizio, Bramante Editrice

Boeheim, W 1889 *Kunsthistorische Sammlungen des allerhöchsten Kaiserhauses; Führer durch die Waffensammlung*. Vienna

Bonner, E 1997 The genesis of Henry VIII's 'Rough Wooing' of the Scots. *Northern History*, **33**: 36-53

Boorde, A 1575 *The breviary of health & Part II Extravagantes*. London,Thomas East

Borg, A 1976 Two studies in the history of the Tower Armouries. 1: Heads and horses from the Line of Kings. *Archaeologia* 105: 317–32

Borg, A 1975 'A royal axe?'. *Connoisseur*, April: 296-301

Borg, A 1974, 'The ram's horn helmet'. *Journal of the Arms and Armour Society* **VIII.2**, December: 127–37

Bourne, W 1587 *The arte of shooting in great ordnaunce: Contayning very necessary matters for all sorts of seruitoures eyther by sea or by lande.* London, Thomas Woodcocke.

Bowers, R 2002 The vernacular litany of 1544 during the reign of Henry VIII. In Bernard & Gunn 2002: 151-78.

Brears, P 2008 *Cooking & dining in medieval England.* Totnes, Prospect

Brears, P 1999 *All the King's cooks.* London, Souvenir Press

Brewer, J S (ed.) 1867 *Letters and papers foreign and domestic of the reign of Henry VIII,* Vol. III. London, Longman & Co.

Brewer, J S and Brodie R H (eds) 1965 *Letters and papers, foreign and domestic, of the reign of Henry VIII: preserved in the Public Record Office, the British Museum and elsewhere.* Vol. 1: 311-18. Vaduz, Kraus Reprint

Brewer, J S, J Gairdner and R H Brodie (eds) 1862–1910 *Letters and papers, foreign and domestic of Henry VIII, 1509–47.* 21 vols, London, HMSO

Brewer, J S 1861-3 (ed.) *Letters & papers: Foreign & domestic of the reign of King Henry VIII.* London, Longman

Byrne, M 1949 *The Elizabethan home.* London, Methuen

Campbell, T P 2007 *Henry VIII and the art of majesty: tapestries at the Tudor court.* Yale University Press

Cantlie, N 1974 *A history of the Army Medical Department.* Vol 1. London, Churchill Livingstone

Capucci, R 1990 *Roben wie Rüstungen.* Vienna.

Carré, J B L 1783 (published 1795) *Panoplie.* Paris & Chalons-sur-Marne, Chez Fuchs

Carter, A 1984 Mary Tudor's wardrobe. *Costume* **18**, (20), 9-28.

Castiglione, B 1967 *The book of the courtier.* Translated by G Bull. Harmondsworth, Penguin

Cavendish, G 1962 *The life of Cardinal Wolsey 1584.* CITY, PUBLISHER ONLY EDITION FROM 1962 IS:

Caxton, W 1926 *The Boke of the Ordre of Chivalry.* A T P Byles (ed.) London, EETS

Cayley, A Jr (ed.) 1808 M*emoirs of Sir Thomas More.* Vol I. 11-15. London, Cadell and Davis

Chaffers, W 1875 *Catalogue of the Londesborough Collection of arms and armour, with a descriptive account of the antiquities and works of art, the property of Lord Londesborough.* London

Charlton, J (ed.) 1977 *The Tower of London: its buildings and institutions.* London, HMSO

Chrimes, S B 1972 *Henry VII.* London, Eyre Methuen

Christie's 1981 *Important antique arms and armour.* London, 18 November

Chubb, R and A L Rowse 1983 *The Renaissance at Sutton Place: an exhibition to mark the 450th anniversary of the visit of King Henery viii to Sutton Place 18th May-15th September.* Guildford, Sutton Place Heritage Trust

Collins Baker, C H 1928 'Notes on pictures at Drayton House'. *The Burlington Magazine* **52.299**, February: 93-7

Colvin, H M 1982 *The history of the King's works,* Vol. IV. London, HMSO

Copeman, W S C 1960 *Doctors and disease in Tudor Times.* London, Dawsons

Corbett, J 1905 *Fighting instructions, 1530–1816.* London, Printed for the Navy Records Society

Crawford, A 1992 *The household books of John Howard Duke of Norfolk.* Alan Sutton, Stroud

Cripps-Day, F H 1934-52 *Fragmenta Armamentaria. An introduction to the study of Greenwich armour. 5 volumes.* London, Cripps-Day

Cripps-Day, F H 1925 *A record of armour sales 1881-1924.* London, G Bell and Sons

Cross, C, D Loades and J J Scarisbrick 1988 *Law and government under the Tudors.* Cambridge, Cambridge University Press

Cruickshank, C G 1969 *Army Royal: Henry VIII's invasion of France 1513.* Oxford, Oxford University Press

Cruickshank, C G 1966 *Elizabeth's army.* Oxford, Clarendon Press

Cunnington C W and P Cunnington 1954 *Handbook of English costume in the sixteenth century.* London, Faber and Faber

Daalder, J 1975 (ed.) *Collected poems of Sir Thomas Wyatt.* London, Oxford University press

Davies, C S L 1998 Henry VIII and Henry V: the wars in France. In John L Watts, *The end of the middle ages? England in the fifteenth and sixteenth centuries.* Stroud, Sutton

Davies, C S L 1977 The English people and war in the early sixteenth century. In A C Duke and C A Tamse, *Britain and the Netherlands,* vol. 6, *War and Society.* The Hague, Martinus Nijhoff

Davies, C S L 1968 Provisions for Armies, 1509-50; A study in the effectiveness of early Tudor government. *Economic History Review* XVII, 234-48: 240

Dawson, J R (ed.) 1890-1907 *Acts of the Privy Council of England.* 32 vols. London

De Marly, D 1985 *Fashion for men: an illustrated history.* London, Batsford

Dillon, H A 1910 *Illustrated guide to the Armouries, Tower of London.* London, HMSO

Dillon, H A 1905 *An Almain armourer's album: Selections from an original MS in Victoria and Albert Museum, South Kensington.* London

Dillon, H 1902 Horse armour. *Archaeological Journal* 59: 67-92

Dillon, H A 1888 Armour at the Tower, Westminster and Greenwich in 1547. *Archaeologia* LI: 219–80

Downman, J 1985 *A catalogue of portraits and other pictures at Butleigh Court.* Taunton. Taunton, F May

Dubois and Marchais 1807 *Dessins des Armures Complete, casques, Cuirasses, Bouciers...qui composent le Musée Impérial de l'Artillerie de France.* Paris, Chez les Auteurs

Dufty, A R 1974 *European swords and daggers in the Tower of London.* London, HMSO

Dufty, A R and W Reid 1968 *European armour in the Tower of London.* London, HMSO

Dunning, E G 1963 'Football in its early stages'. *History Today,* 13 (12): 838-847

Durer, A 1527 *Etliche Undderricht zu Befestigung der Steltschloss und Flecken .* Nuremberg

Eaves, I 1999 The Greenwich armour and locking-gauntlet of Sir Henry Lee in the collection of the Worshipful Company of Armourers and Brasiers. *Journal of the Arms and Armour Society,* 16 September: 133–64

Eaves, I 1993 'The tournament armours of King Henry VIII of England'. *Livrustkammaren*: 2–45

Eaves, I 1989, 'On the remains of a jack of plate excavated from Beeston Castle in Cheshire'. *The Journal of the Arms and Armour Society,* **XIII.2**, September: 81–154

Edge, D 1992 The Greenwich field armour of Thomas Sackville. *Park Lane Arms Fair* **9**, London: 5–11

Edwards I and C Blair 1982 Welsh Bucklers. *The Antiquaries Journal,* Vol. LXII, part 1.

Egan, G 1991 *Dress accessories: medieval finds from London excavations 3.* London. HMSO

Eldred, W 1646 *The gunners glasse.* London, Robert Boydel.

Ellis, H (ed.) 1809 *Hall's Chronicle.* London, J Johnson

Elton, G R 1992 War and the English in the reign of Henry VIII, in L Freedman et al., *War, strategy and international politics.* Oxford, Clarendon Press

Elton, G R 1982 *The Tudor constitution.* Cambridge, Cambridge University Press

Elton, G R 1972 *Policy and police: the enforcement of the reformation in the age of Thomas Cromwell.* Cambridge, Cambridge University Press

Elyot, T 1534 *The castel of health.* London, T Berchelet

Erasmus, D 1978 *Collected works of Erasmus.* Toronto, University of Toronto Press ffoulkes, C 1928 'Armour from the Rotunda, Woolwich, transferred to the Armouries of the Tower, 1927'. *Archaeologia*, 78: 61–72

ffoulkes, C 1927 *Some account of the Worshipful Company of Armourers and Brasiers together with a catalogue of the Arms and Armour in the possession of the company.* London: The Company, privately printed

ffoulkes, C 1916 *Inventory and survey of the Armouries of the Tower of London.* 2 vols. London, HMSO

ffoulkes C 1912 *Jousting cheques of the sixteenth century. Archeologia*, LXIII: 31-50

Figgis, J N 1914 *The divine right of kings.* Cambridge, Cambridge University Press

Fissell, M C 2001 *English warfare 1511–1642.* Routledge, London

Foister, S 2006 *Holbein in England.* London, Tate Gallery

Forster, H R 1848 *The Stowe catalogue priced and annotated.* London, David Bogue

Gabriel, R A and K S Metz 1992 *A history of military medicine.* Vol 2.

London, Greenwood Press

Gaier, C 1993 Une énigme: la production belge d'armures vers l'an 1500 et au-delà. *Le Musée d'Armes. Etudes et recherches sur les armes anciennes* 73-4: 2-48

Gale, T 1563 *An excellent treatment on wounds made with gunneshot.* London

Gale, T 1563 *Certaine Workes of Chirurgerie newly compiled and*

published by T.G. maister of Chirurgerie. London, R Hall

Gardiner J and M J Allan 2005 *Before the mast: Life and death aboard the Mary Rose.* Portsmouth, Mary Rose Trust

Garrison, F H 1913 *An introduction to the history of medicine.* London, W B

Saunders Company

Glas Sandeman, J 1912a Facsimiles *of the ordinances and statutes of the Spears of Honour 1509 and the oath and articles of the Gentlemen Pensioners, 1600.* Hayling Island

Glas Sandeman, J 1912b *The Spears of Honour and the Gentlemen Pensioners.* Hayling Island

Godoy, J-A 1992 La Real Armería. In J-A Godoy et al. *Tapices y armaduras del Renacimento. Joyas de las colecciones reales.* Exh. cat. Barcelona & Madrid: 99-193

Gore, A A 1879 *The story of our services under the crown.* London, Balliere, Tindall and Cox

Grancsay, S V 1937 *The armor of Galiot de Genouilhac,* New York, Metropolitan Museum of Art.

Grose, F 1786a *A Treatise on ancient armour and weapons,* London, S Hooper

Grose, F 1786b *Military antiquities.* Vol. 1 London, S Hooper

Gruber von Arni, E 2001 Justice to the maimed soldier: nursing, medical care, and welfare for sick and wounded soldiers and their families during the English Civil Wars and interregnum, 1642-1660. Aldershot: Ashgate

Guicciardini, F 1966 *History of Italy and history of Florence.* London, New English Library. First published 1561, Florence, Agnolo Guicciardini

Giustiniani, S 1854 *Four years at the court of Henry VIII: selection of despatches / written by the Venetian ambassador, Sebastian Giustiniani, and addressed to the Signory of Venice, January 12th 1515, to July 26th 1519 ; translated by Rawdon Brown.* London, Smith Elder

Gunn, S J, D Grummitt and H Cools 2007 *War, state and society in England and the Netherlands, 1477–1559.* Oxford, Oxford University Press

Gunn, S J 1995 *Early Tudor government 1485-1558.* Basingstoke, Macmillan

Gunn, S J 1991 Wolsey's Foreign Policy and the Domestic Crisis of 1527-8. In I D and P G Lindley, *Cardinal Wolsey: church, state and art.* Cambridge, Cambridge University Press: 163-77

Gunn, S J 1987 The French wars of Henry VIII. In J Black, *The origins of war in early modern Europe.* Edinburgh, Donald

Gunn, S J 1986 The Duke of Suffolk's march on Paris in 1523. *English Historical Review* CI: 596-634

Guy, J 1993 The Henrician age. In J G A Pocock, *The varieties of British political thought.* Cambridge, Cambridge University Press: 13-46

Guy, J 1988 *Tudor England.* Oxford, Oxford University Press

Hall, N 2001 Casting and firing a Mary Rose culverin. *Royal Armouries Yearbook* 6:106-116. Leeds, Royal Armouries

Hall, N 1998 Building and firing a replica Mary Rose port piece. *Royal Armouries Yearbook* 3: 57-66. Leeds, Royal Armouries

Hall, E 1904a *The triumphant reigne of King Henry the VIII.* 2 volumes, edited by C Whibley. London, J Johnson

Hall, E 1904b *The union of the two noble and illustre famelies of Lancastre and York.* 2 volumes, edited by C Whibley. London, J Johnson

Hall, E 1550 *The union of the two noble and illustrious families of Lancastre and York.* London

Hammond, P 1993 Royal Armouries Leeds [souvenir guide]. Leeds, Royal Armouries

Hammond, P 1986 Royal Armouries official guide. London, Royal Armouries

Hardy, R 1976 *Longbow, a social and military history.* Cambridge

Hayward, M A 2009 *Rich apparel: Clothing choices in Henry VIII's England.* Aldershot, Ashgate

Hayward, M A 2007a *Dress at the court of Henry VIII.* Leeds, Maney

Hayward, M A 2007b Unlocking one facet of Henry VIII's wardrobe: an investigation of the base. In M A Hayward and E Kramer (eds) *Textiles and text: Re-establishing the link between archival and object-based research.* London, Archetype, 45-51

Hayward, M A 2004 *The 1542 inventory of Whitehall: The palace and its keeper.* London, Illuminata

Hayward, M A 2002 Fashion, finance, foreign politics and the wardrobe of Henry VIII. In C Richardson (ed.) *Clothing culture, 1350–1650.* Aldershot, Ashgate

Hayward, M A 1996 Luxury or magnificence? Dress at the court of Henry VIII, *Costume*, 30, 37-46.

Hayward, J F 1962 *The art of the gunmaker.* London, Barrie and Rockliff

Hayward M A and E Kramer 2007 (eds) *Textiles and text: Re-establishing the link between archival and object-based research.* London, Archetype

Hervey, M S F 1910 'Notes on a Tudor painter: Gerlache Flicke II', *Burlington Magazine* XVII: 71–9

Hewitt, J 1864 'A tilting helm of the fifteenth century in the Royal Artillery Museum Woolwich', *Archaeological Journal* 21: 60–2

Hewitt, J 1862 'Contributions to the history of medieval weapons and military appliances: Unique example of a sabre with finger-guard, of the beginning of the sixteenth century. *The Archaeological Journal*, vol. XIX: 318-322

Hewitt, J 1859 *Official catalogue of the Tower Armouries, London.* London, HMSO

Hildred, A (ed.) 2009 *Weapons of Warre: the armaments of the Mary Rose.* Vol. 3 of The Archaeology of the Mary Rose: 455. Portsmouth, Mary Rose Trust

Holinshed 1588 *Chronicles.* VI vols. London (reprinted 1807)

Household Ordinances 1790 *Ordinances and regulations for the government of the royal household.* Society of Antiquaries

Howell, H A L 1904 *The army surgeon and the care of the sick and wounded in the British campaigns of the Tudor and early Stuart period. Journal of the RAMC* Vol. 2: 606-615

Hoyle, R W 2001 *The Pilgrimage of Grace and the politics of the 1530s.* Oxford, Oxford University Press

Hoyle, R W 1995 War and public finance. In D N J MacCulloch, *The reign of Henry VIII: politics, policy and piety.* Basingstoke, Macmillan: 75-99

Hoyle, R W 1993 *The military survey of Gloucstershire, 1522.* Gloucester, Bristol and Gloucestershire Archaeological Society

Hughes P L and J F Larkin 1964 *Tudor royal proclamations,* I. New Haven, Yale University Press

Impey, E and G Parnell 2000 *The Tower of London: The official illustrated history.* London, Merrell Publishers

Inglis, S 2005 A *load of old balls.* English Heritage

Innsbruck 1954 *Die Innsbrucker Plattnerkunst.* Tiroler Landesmuseum

János, K 1971 *Régi Magyar fegyverek.* Budapest

Keevil, J J 1974 *Medicine and the Navy 1200–1900.* Vol. 1. London, E & S Livingstone

Key, A 2001 *The Elizabethan Tower of London.* London, Topographical Society Publication No. 158

Kienbusch, C, O von Kretzschmar & S V Grancsay 1933 *The Bashford Dean Collection of arms and armor in the Metroplitan museum of Art.* Portland, Maine

Kingsford, C L 1911 *The first English life of King Henry the Fifth.* Oxford, Clarendon Press

Knighton, C S and Loades, D M 2002 *Letters from the Mary Rose.* Stroud, Sutton Publishing

Kretschmar, Colonel von 1909-11 Der Turnierteppich im Mueum zu Valenciennes. *Zeitschrift für historische Waffen- und Kostümkunde* 5.6: 166-171

Laking, G F 1900-22 *A record of European Armour and arms through seven centuries.* 5 vols. G Bell and Sons, London

Lander, J 1976 *Crown and nobility 1450-1509.* London, Edward Arnold

Lankester, P J 2000 Two maces from Henry VIII's arsenal?. *Royal Armouries Yearbook,* 5: 27-43. Leeds, Royal Armouries

Lindemann, M 1999 *Medicine and society in early modern Europe Cambridge,* Cambridge University Press

Loach, J 1994 The function of ceremonial in the reign of Henry VIII. In *Past and Present* CXLII: 43-68

Loades, David 2007 *Henry VIII: court, church and conflict.* Kew, The National Archives

Loades, D 1996 *John Dudley, Duke of Northumberland.* Oxford, Clarendon Press.

Loades, D M 1992 *The Tudor navy: an administrative, political and military history.* Aldershot, Scolar Press

Loades, D and C Knighton 2008 Lord Admiral Lisle and the invasion of Scotland, 1544. *Naval Miscellany,* VII: 57-66.

Loades, D and C Knighton 2002 *Letters from the Mary Rose.* Stroud, Sutton

Loades, D and C Knighton 2000 *The Anthony Roll of Henry VIII's navy.* Aldershot, Ashgate

London 1890 *Exhibition of the House of Tudor,* New Gallery, Regent Street, London

Lloyd, C and **Simon Thurley** 1990 *Henry VIII: images of a Tudor king.* Oxford, Phaidon

Lloyd, C 1952 (*ed.*) Spanish documents relating to the Armada. *Naval Miscellany,* IV: 1-84.

Lucar, C 1588 *Three bookes of colloqvies...* London, John Harrison

Lumpkin, H 1960 The pictures of Henry VIII's army in Cotton manuscript

Machiavelli, N 1883 Lettere familiare E Alvisi [*ed.*]. Florence

Mann, J G (ed) 1951 *Exhibition of armour made in the royal workshops at Greenwich,* London

Mann, J G 1932 'Two helmets at St Botolph's Church, Lullingstone', *The Antiquaries Journal* XII: 136–45.

Mann, J G 1930 The Sanctuary of the Madonna delle Grazie with notes on the evolution of Italian armour during the 15th century. *Archaeologia* 80: 117-142

Marks R and P Williamson (eds.) 2003 *Gothic. art for England 1400-1547.* (Exhib. cat.). London, V & A Publications

Marshall, H E 1905 *Our island story: a history of Britain for boys and girls.* Cranbrook, Galore Park

Marsden, P 2003 *Sealed by time, the loss & recovery of the Mary Rose.* Portsmouth, The Mary Rose Trust

Mazansky, C 2005 *British basket-hilted swords.* Woodbridge, Boydell

Melville, N 2001 'Towards the identification of a group of fifteenth century English two-handed swords'. *Eighteenth Park Lane Arms Fair* [guide]. London

Merriman, R B (*ed.*) 1902 *Life and letters of Thomas Cromwell.*

Miller, C H 1984 *The complete works of St Thomas More,* vol. 3, part 2, *Latin poems.* New Haven and London, Yale University Press

Miller, H 1986 *Henry VIII and the English nobility* Oxford, Blackwell

Millward, J 2007 The East Coast Martello Towers. *Fort the international journal of fortification and military architecture* 35: 173-184

Monaghan, J and M Bound 2001 *A ship cast away about Alderney.* Alderney Maritime Trust

Morin, M and R Held 1980 *Beretta; The world's oldest industrial dynasty.* Chiasso, Switzerland

Nevinson, J L 1958 'Portraits of Gentleman Pensioners before 1625'. *The Walpole Society, Vol. XXXIV, 1952–1954.* Glasgow, University Press

Nicholson, G 1988 The act of appeals and the English reformation. In Claire Cross, David Loades and J J Scarisbrick, *Law and government under the Tudors.* Cambridge, Cambridge University Press: 19-30

Nichols, J G (*ed.*) 1850 *Chronicle of Queen Jane, and two years of Queen Mary.* London, Camden Society

Nichols, J G (*ed.*) 1848 *The diary of Henry Machyn: citizen and merchant-taylor of London (1550–1563).* London. URL: http://www.britishhistory.ac.uk/report.aspx?compid=45531. Date accessed: 13 May 2008

Nicolas N H 1830 *Privy purse expenses of Elizabeth of York: Wardrobe accounts of Edward IV.* London

Nicolas, N H (*ed.*) 1827 *The privy purse expenses of King Henry the Eighth. November 1529-end of December 1532.*

Nickel, H and S W Pyhrr and L Tarassuk 1982 *The art of chivalry; European arms and armor from the Metropolitan Museum of Art.* Exhibition catalogue. New York

Norman, A V B and G M Wilson 1982 *Treasures from the Tower of London.* London, Lund Humphries

Norris, H 1938 *Costume and fashion: III.i The Tudors 1485–1547.* London, Dent

Oakeshott, E 1980 *European weapons and armour from the Renaissance to the Industrial Revolution.* Guildford & London, Lutterworth Press

Oppenheim, M 1896 *Naval accounts and inventories of the reign of Henry VII.* London, Navy Records Society

Ortiz, A D, C H Carretero and J A Godoy 1991 *Resplendence of the Spanish monarchy: renaissance tapestries and armor from the Patrimonio Nacional.* New York, NY, Metropolitan Museum of Art

Park, K 1997 Medicine and the Renaissance in I. Loudon (*ed.*) Western

medicine: An illustrated history. Oxford, Oxford University Press

Parnell, G 1993 *The Tower of London.* London, Batsford

Pegge, S 1791 *Curialia, or an historical account of some branches of the royal household part II.* London, B White

Penguilly l'Haridon, O 1862 *Catalogue des Collections composant le Musée de d'Artillerie.* Paris, Charles des Morgues Frères

Phillips, G 1999 *The Anglo-Scots Wars 1513-50.* Woodbridge, Boydell and Brewer

Plummer, C (*ed.*) 1885 *Sir John Fortescue on the governance of England.* Oxford

Pollard, A F 1903 *The late expedition into Scotland* (1544) in *Tudor Tracts.* Westminster, Archibald Constable

Pollard, A F 1902 *Henry VIII.* London, Goupil & Co

Potter, D 2005 Mid-Tudor foreign policy and diplomacy. In S. Doran and G. Richardson, *Tudor England and its neighbours.* Basingstoke, Palgrave: 106-38

Pyhrr, S W 2000 *European helmets, 1450-1650; treasures from the Reserve Collection.* Exh. cat. New York

Pyhrr, S W 1989 European armor from the imperial Ottoman arsenal. *Metropolitan Museum Journal* **24**: 85-116

Pyhrr, S W 1984 Some elements of armor attributed to Niccolò Silva. *Metropolitan Museum Journal* **18**: 111–121

Rangström, L (*ed.*) 1992 *Riddarlek Och Tornerspel [Tournament and the Dream of Chivalry].* Stockholm, Livrustkammaren

Rebholz, R A 1978 *Sir Thomas Wyatt: the complete poems.* London, Penguin

Reid, W 1976, *The lore of arms*, London, Mitchell Beazley

Reverseau, J-P 1982 *Musée de l'Armée Paris, les armes et la vie.* Paris, Musée de l'Armée

Rex, R 1996 The crisis of obedience: God's word and Henry's reformation. In *Historical Journal* **XXXIX**: 863-94

Richardson, T 2009 'An early Greenwich armet'. *Arms & Armour Journal of the Royal Armouries vol, 6, issue 1.* Leeds, Royal Armouries

Richardson, T 2006 The Greenwich Armouries. *The Court Historian* 11, December: 113–124.

Richardson, T 2004 *London Armourers in the 17th century.* Leeds

Richardson, T 2002 *The armour and arms of Henry VIII.* Leeds, Royal Armouries

Richardson, T 2000 Armour in the Church of St Lawrence, Hatfield, South Yorkshire. *Royal Armouries Yearbook 5:* 11–18

Richardson, T 1998 *Ballistic testing of historical weapons.* Royal Armouries Yearbook 3: 50-52

Richardson, T 1997 'The Bridport muster roll of 1457'. *Royal Armouries Yearbook* 2: 46–52

Richardson, T 1991 H R Robinson's 'Dutch armour of the 17th century'. *Journal of the Arms and Armour Society* 13, March: 256–78

Richardson T and Rimer G 1997 *Treasures from the Tower in the Kremlin.* Moscow

Rimer, G 2001, *Wheellock firearms of the Royal Armouries*, Leeds, Royal Armouries

Rimer, G and T Richardson 1997 *Treasures from the Tower in the Kremlin (Sokrovishcha Tauzra v Kremle)*, Royal Armouries, London and Moscow, State Museum of the Moscow Kremlin

Robert, L 1890 *Catalogue des collections composant le Musée de l'Artillerie en 1889,* Paris

Rodger, N A M 2004 *The safeguard of the sea.* London, Penguin/National Maritime Museum [First ed 1997 Harper Collins]

Rodger, N A M 1997 *The safeguard of the sea: a naval history of Britain.* London, Harper Collins, in association with the National Maritime Museum

Rose, S (*ed.*) 1982 *The navy of the Lancastrian Kings: accounts and inventories of William Soper, Keeper of the King's Ships.* London, Allen & Unwin

Royal Armouries 2000 Royal Armouries Tower of London [souvenir guide]. Leeds, Royal Armouries

Rule, M 1982 *The Mary Rose.* Portsmouth, The Mary Rose Trust

Samman, N 1995 The progresses of Henry VIII, 1509-29. In MacCulloch 1995: 59-73

Saunders, A 1989 *Fortress Britain.* Liphook, Beaufort

Scarisbrick, J J 1968 *Henry VIII.* London, Eyre & Spottiswoode

Schubert, H 1942 The first cast iron cannon made in England. *Journal of the Iron and Steel Institute,* 146: 131-40

Sharp, A D 1929 The story of the Greenwich armoury. *Transactions of the Greenwich and Lewisham Antiquarian Society* 3.4: 151–65

Shelby, L R 1967 *John Rogers, Tudor military engineer.* Oxford, Oxford University Press

Sicca, C M 2007 Fashioning the Tudor court. In M A Hayward and E Kramer (eds) *Textiles and text: Re-establishing the link between archival and object-based research.* London, Archetype

Smith, R 1993 Port pieces: the use of wrought-iron guns in the sixteenth century. *Journal of the Ordnance Society* 5: 1-10

Sotheby's 1961 *Catalogue of old master paintings and drawings,* 15 November

Sotheby's 1917, *Catalogue of superb prints, drawings, pictures and armour from the historical collections at Wilton House,* 5–10 July

Spont, A 1897 *Letters and papers relating to the war with France, 1512-13.* London, Navy Records Society

Squilbeck, J 1953 Le travail du métal à Bruxelles. In *Bruxelles au 15e siècle.* Exh. cat. Brussels: 245-271

Starkey, D 1998 *The inventory of King Henry VIII.* London, Harvey Miller/Society of Antiquaries of London

Starkey D R (*ed.*) 1991 *Henry VIII: A European court in England.* London, Collins and Brown

Strong, R 1967 *Holbein and Henry VIII.* (Trs. E W & C R Ives).

Strutt, J 1838 *The Sports and pastimes of the people of England.* London, Thomas Tegg

Stoate, T L 1978 *Dorset muster rolls 1539, 1542, 1569.* Bristol

String, T 2009 Projecting masculinity: Henry VIII's codpiece. In J N King, M Rankin and C Highley (eds) *Henry VIII in history.* Cambridge, Cambridge University Press

Sutton, A F 1991 Order and fashion in clothes: the king, his household and the City of London at the end of the fifteenth century. *Textile History,* 22.2: 253-76

Sylvester, R S and D P Harding 1962 (eds.) *The life and death of Cardinal Wolsey: two early Tudor lives by George Cavendish.* New Haven: Yale University Press

Tartaglia, N 1546 *Quesiti & inventioni diverse.* Venice, Venturino Russinelli/Niccolo Tartaglia

Teesdale 1991 *Gunfounding in the Weald in the sixteenth century.* Leeds, Royal Armouries

Terjanian, P 2006a 'The Master of the Roman M under a crescent and the horse armours of King Henry VIII in the Royal Armouries', lecture to the Arms and Armour Society, London, 6 July 2006

Terjanian, P 2006b La armería de Felipe el Hermoso. In Miguel Ángel Zalama *et al., Felipe I el Hermoso; la belleza y la locura.* Madrid: 141-162

Terjanian, P 2005 The armorers of Cologne: organization and exports markets of a foremost European armor-making center, 1391-1660. *Journal of the Armour Research Society* 1: 23-48

Temesváry, F 1982 *Waffenschätze und Prunkwaffen im Ungarischen nationalmuseum.* Translated by Valér Nagy. Budapest

Thirsk, J 2007 *Food in early modern England.* London, Hambledon Continuum

Thomas, B and O Gamber 1976 *Katalog der Liebrüstkammer I teil der Zeitraum von 500 bis 1530,* Vienna

Thomas, B 1984 Neues aus der Budapester Waffensammlung; eine Anküdigung. *Waffen- und Kostümkunde* **26.1**: 53-63

Thurley, S and C Lloyd 1990 *Henry VIII: Images of a Tudor king.* Oxford, Phaidon Press in association with the Historical Royal Palaces Agency

Thurley, S 1993 *The royal palaces of Tudor England.* New Haven and London, Yale University Press

Thurley, S 1990 Henry VIII's kitchens at Hampton Court. *Journal of the British Archaeological Association,* CXL 111: 1-28

Tracy, J D 1978 *The politics of Erasmus: a pacifist intellectual and his political milieu.* Toronto, University of Toronto Press

Tudor-Craig, P 1989 Henry VIII and King David. In Daniel Williams, *Early Tudor England.* Woodbridge, Boydell Press: 183-205

Ullmann, W 1979 This realm of England is an empire. *Journal of Ecclesiastical History* **XXX**: 175-203

Valencia de don Juan, Count of 1898 *Catálogo historico-descriptivo de la Real Armería de Madrid.* Madrid

van der Sloot, R B F 1985 'Het belang van de
    wapenfabricage in de Nederlanden
    gedurende de 16e en 17e eew, met
    bijzondere aandacht voor harnassen en
    helmen' *CL Themadag* 8: 5–17

Von Gersdorff, H 1517 *Feldbuch de
    Wundtartzney.* Strassburg, republished by
    Editions Medicina Rara Ltd

Watts, K 1992 Fit for a king. *Country Life* 20
    February: 66–7

Way, A 1847 'Illustrations of medieval manners
    and costume from original documents'.
    Archaeological Journal, Vol. IV: 237

Wharton ND *Wharton's History of English
    poetry.* Vol.III, 101

Williams, J 2005 Hunting and the Royal Image
    of Henry VIII. *Sport in History,* Vol.25,
    No.1, April 2005: 41-59

Williams, A 2003 *The knight and the blast
    furnace; a history of the metallurgy of
    armour in the Middle Ages & the Early
    Modern Period.* Leiden & Boston, Brill

Williams, A and A de Reuck 1995 The Royal
    Armoury at Greenwich, 1515–1649: a
    history of its technology. London

Wilson, C A 1976 *Food and Drink in Britain.*
    Harmondsworth, Penguin

Wilson, G M 1988 *Some important snap
    matchlock guns.* Arms Collecting Vol.26,
    No.1, February: 3-10

Wilson, G M 1986 'Notes on some early basket
    hilted swords', *Journal of the Arms and
    Armour Society* **XII.1**: 1–19

Wilson, G M 1985 A halberd head from the
    River Thames. *Park Lane Arms Fair* 2: 18.

Woolwich 1906 Official *Catalogue of the
    Museum of Artillery in the Rotunda,
    Woolwich.* London, HMSO

Woolwich 1889 Official *Catalogue of the
    Museum of Artillery in the Rotunda,
    Woolwich.* London, HMSO

Woolwich 1874 Official *Catalogue of the
    Museum of Artillery in the Rotunda,
    Woolwich.* London, HMSO

GLOSSARY

Compiled by Thom Richardson and Graeme Rimer

Accatery: An officer of the king's household, whose role was to act as a check between the clerks of the kitchen and the purveyors.

Almain rivet: A light half armour of plate for infantry, usually made in Germany, popular in the early–mid 16th century.

Anime: A form of cuirass, made of narrow horizontal plates or lames articulated together inside either with rivets or leathers or a combination of both to allow the wearer some movement, popular in the middle of the 16th century.

Armet: A form of helmet fully enclosing the head, with cheekpieces at either side which fasten together at the front and allow the helmet to be put on or taken off, and a visor, popular in the 15th–early 17th centuries.

Bacinet: A form of helmet protecting the skull of the head, worn with an aventail of mail protecting the throat and neck, and often with a plate visor, from the 13th–early 15th century, which evolved into the great bacinet.

Backplate: The rear plate of a cuirass, worn with a breastplate.

Ballock dagger: One whose hilt is in the form of male genitalia.

Bard: Defence of plate, mail or other forms of armour for a horse.

Base: A pleated skirt of rich fabric worn as part of male costume, often with armour, or of plate and part of an armour, fashionable in the early 16th century.

Basilisk: A large type of cannon, usually of bronze and of considerable length in proportion to the diameter of its bore.

Basket hilt: A sword hilt formed of a network of iron strips or bars forge welded together to form a guard enveloping the hand of the user.

Bellows visor: a form of visor embossed with horizontal ridges, hence resembling a bellows, popular in the early 16th century.

Bevor: A defence of plate for the throat and front of the face, worn in the 15th century with a sallet as a separate defence, in the 16th century as an integral part of a close helmet.

Bill: A staff weapon with a long hooked blade, sharpened on the inside and often with an additional spike on the back and at the top. Derived from the agricultural implement of the same name.

Breastplate: The front plate of a cuirass, worn with a backplate.

Brigandine: A defence of iron plates riveted inside a fabric doublet, popular in the 15th–early 16th centuries.

Brow plate: A reinforcing plate at the upper front of a helmet.

Buckler: A small, circular shield.

Buffe: A defence of plate for the throat and front of the face, used in the 16th century with a burgonet.

Burgonet: An open faced helmet with hinged cheekpieces, often worn with a buffe.

Burgonion Cross: The Burgundian Cross; a crest formed of two ragged, or rustic, wooden staves behind a fire-steel.

Cannon: In plate armour, one of the tubular defences in a Vambrace of plate, either for the upper arm (upper cannon) or forearm (lower cannon).

Cartridge: A tubular container holding a measured charge of gunpowder sufficient for one firing of a gun. It might or might not also contain a lead ball or other projectile.

Close helmet: A form of helmet fully enclosing the head, with a visor and bevor (or upper and lower bevors) pivoted at either side of the skull to allow the helmet to be put on or taken off, popular in the late 15th –16th centuries.

Codpiece: Groin defence for an armour, usually worn only when fighting on foot.

Combination weapon: One in which two or more types of weapon are combined in order to be used together.

Coronel: A lance head, usually of iron, formed with a point in the form of three or more short blunt spikes and used in the '*Gestech*' or joust of peace.

Corsèque: A staff weapon whose head is formed of one central symmetrical spear-like blade flanked by two others of almost similar size.

Couter: Elbow defence for a plate armour.

Crinet: Plate defence for a horse's neck.

Crupper: Plate defence for a horse's rump.

Cuirass: Defence for the thorax, part of a plate armour or worn separately, comprising a breastplate and backplate.

Cuisse: Defence for the thigh in a plate armour.

Culet: Defence for the rump in a plate armour.

Culverin: A type of cannon which, like the basilisk, was usually of cast bronze and long in proportion to its bore diameter.

Curette: Archaic term for a cuirass.

Damascening: A technique of decoration in which grooves forming a design are cut into the surface of a piece of metal, usually iron. Gold or silver wire is then hammered into these grooves and filed smooth, leaving the desired design inlaid into the surface.

Demi-cannon: The second largest, after the cannon, of the types of artillery piece commonly in use in the 16th and 17th centuries. Usually of cast bronze.

Enceinte: The continuous line of walls and bastions surrounding a fortification.

Estoc or Tuck: A type of sword with a long stiff blade of square or triangular section capable of being used only for thrusting.

False damascening: A decorative technique in which the surface of a piece of metal, usually iron, is very finely roughened by cross-hatching with a special tool. Carefully shaped pieces of gold or silver are then hammered onto this roughened surface and held there to form the required design.

Firesteel (or fusye): A piece of hardened steel against which a piece of natural flint may be struck to create sparks to ignite tinder. In heraldry firesteels are usually rendered as a rectangular bar with a ram's horn curl at each end.

Flanchard: Plate defence for a horse's flanks.

Fletchings: The flights of an arrow, made from three pinion feathers taken from the wing of a large bird, such as a goose or peacock.

Forte: The stiffest part of a sword blade closest to the hilt.

Fuller: A groove in a sword or dagger blade, made to lighten and stiffen it.

Galleasse: A heavily built military vessel larger than a galley and propelled both by oars and sails.

Garniture: Plate armour with interchangeable parts and extra pieces (or 'pieces of exchange') to enable it to be worn for different tournament events, such as the tilt, tourney or foot combat, or battlefield ('field') use, as heavy or light cavalry or as infantry.

Gorget (or collar): a plate defence for the neck, worn under the cuirass additionally helping to distribute the weight of the armour.

Grandguard: Plate reinforce for the left shoulder and left side of the face, worn with tilt armour.

Great bacinet: A form of helmet enveloping the head, neck and throat, with a plate visor, from the late 14–early 16th century, evolved from the bacinet.

Greave: Plate defence for the lower leg.

Guard: The part of a sword hilt designed to provide protection for the hand of the user (e.g. knuckle guard).

Halberd: A staff weapon whose head has an axe-like cutting blade, a shorter hooked blade, or fluke, at the rear, and a vertical spike for thrusting.

Harness: An alternative word for a plate armour.

Harquebus: A light form of infantry musket.

Helm: A cylindrical head defence, by the 14th century extending to the shoulders and frequently secured to the cuirass by straps, redundant on the battlefield by the late 14th century but still used in the tournament in the 16th century (see tilting helm).

'Holy water sprinkler': A type of long-hafted club whose head was fitted with short iron spikes. A term used popularly for a weapon thought to resemble the club-like *aspergillum* used by priests to sprinkle holy water.

Jack of plate: A textile doublet into which small square iron plates were sewn for additional protection, popular in Britain in the 16th century.

Lames: small plates of iron or steel used in a plate armour for protecting articulated joints or sections, joined by rivets or internal leathers either to larger plate components or to other lames (see anime for example).

Lantern shot: An anti-personnel artillery round. A tubular container made of slats of wood which was filled with sharp stones. It was designed to break up on firing causing the stones to spread out and cause the maximum damage to opposing troops.

Locking Gauntlet: A plate gauntlet used in the tourney in which the finger-plates were fastened to an extension of the inner cuff plate, locking a weapon in the hand.

Lower cannon: Plate defence for the forearm (see cannon).

Manifer: Plate reinforce for the left hand and forearm, worn with tilt armour.

Match cord: A twisted hemp cord impregnated with saltpetre (potassium nitrate), enabling it to smoulder evenly when lit to provide ignition for hand-held firearms or artillery pieces.

Match lock: A mechanical device fitted to the side of a firearm to hold a piece of match cord and, on pulling a trigger, to place the smouldering end of the cord into the pan to ignite the priming powder and fire the gun.

'Maximilian': A modern term applied to fluted armour of a style which became popular in German lands in the early 16th century, when Maximilian I was Holy Roman Emperor, inspired by the narrow pleating of civilian clothes fashionable at that time.

Nock: The horn tip found on either end of a longbow to protect the wood from the chafing of the bowstring, or; the notch in the rear end of an arrow to enable it to be fitted to a bowstring.

Partizan: A staff weapon with a long symmetrical two-edged thrusting blade, at the base of which are two short upward-curved wings or lugs.

Pasguard: Plate reinforce for the left elbow, worn with tilt armour.

Pauldron: Plate defence for the shoulder with wings extending over the cuirass at front and rear.

Peytral: Plate defence for a horse's front.

Pike: A long staff weapon, up to 18 feet (6m) long, with a small iron head and capable only of being used to thrust. Often used by closely ranked bodies of infantry.

Plackart: Reinforcing breastplate worn over the breastplate, often for the Tournament.

Pointillé: A technique, usually on metal, of using lines of finely punched dots to created decorative motifs.

Poleyn: Plate defence for the knee.

Pollaxe: A staff weapon with a striking part in the form of an axe blade or a rectangular or triangular group of three or four short spikes. The back of the head has a short spike or a serrated hammer face, while the top of the heads is fitted with a thrusting spike.

Port piece: A wrought iron breech-loading artillery piece.

Punchion spear: A type of spear with a head in the form of a spike, suitable only for thrusting.

Quillon: A guard projecting from the hilt of a sword or dagger usually at 90 degrees to the centre line of the blade at the point where the sword and hilt meet.

Raguly crosses: Raguly is the heraldic term for ragged, meaning rustic (see Burgonion Cross).

Ricasso: A blunted area of rectangular section formed in a sword or dagger blade adjacent to the hilt.

Rondel: A circular disk. in plate armour often attached to an armet to protect the strap of the wrapper, or to a manifer or shaffron.

Sabaton: Plate defence for the foot.

Sabre: A sword with a long, curved, single-edged blade.

Saddle steel: Plate covering for the tree of a saddle; the front section is called the bow, the central part of which is the pommel, the rear section the cantle or arson.

Saker: One of the lighter types of artillery barrel, usually of cast bronze. Named after the saker, a large species of falcon.

Sallet: A form of helmet covering the crown and sides of the head and flaring over the nape of the neck, often fitted with a visor and worn with a bevor, popular in the 15th–early 16th centuries.

Serpentine: One of the smaller natures of artillery piece, of bronze or iron, long in proportion to the diameter of the bore. Often but not invariably breech-loading. Also a late 15th-century term for a type of fine soft gunpowder.

Shaffron: Plate defence for a horse's head.

Shammer: A decorative cover made to simulate an article of household linen and used over or in place of it.

Sights: Slots pierced in the front of helmets or their visors (and sometimes bevors and buffes) which allowed the wearer to see out.

Sling: A relatively small nature of artillery, often of wrought iron, long in relation to its bore diameter. A term often applied to breech-loading swivel guns, i.e. those small enough to be mounted on a pivot or swivel placed into a socket in the gunwhale of a ship.

Spaudler: Plate defence for the shoulder in the form of a narrow series of plates and lames covering only the outside of the arm and cap of the shoulder.

Spear: A staff weapon with a symmetrical two-edged head primarily intended for thrusting. Used at times by both infantry and cavalry, either of whom might occasionally throw it at an enemy.

Splints: Simple plate arm defences or vambraces comprising spaudlers, upper and lower cannons and couters covering only the outside of the arm and articulated by internal leathers and rivets.

Stechzeug: The German term for an armour specially made for the Joust of Peace or *Gestech*.

Tang: The narrow tapered section of a sword or dagger blade onto which the hilt is fitted.

Tasset: Plate defence for the upper thigh, usually formed of articulated lames.

Tilting helm: A form of helm adapted with heavy plates for use in the tilt, popular in the 15th and early 16th centuries.

Toe cap: The plate defence for the toes, usually used with mail rather than plate sabatons.

Tonlet: A rare term popular in the early 16th century for the laminated base of an armour specially made of the foot combat.

Trephining (or trepanning): The process of cutting a hole in the skull to relieve pressure or to perform surgery upon the brain.

Trunnions: Pairs of cylindrical lugs formed one on each side near the point of balance of a cannon barrel to support it and to enable it to be elevated or depressed for firing at different ranges.

Upper cannon: Plate defence for the upper arm, see cannon.

Vambrace: Plate defence for the arm, see upper cannon, couter and lower cannon.

Vent: The touch-hole near the rear or breech of the barrel through which the powder charge of a cannon or other firearm was fired.

Ventral plate: A rare component of w plate armour worn inside the cuirass and designed to help distribute the weight of the harness.

Visor: Plate defence for the face, usually pierced with sights and usually pivoted at either side so it could be opened when not in action.

Wheellock: An ignition mechanism for firearms, using a spring-driven steel wheel to generate sparks from a piece of iron pyrites to ignite the priming powder.

Wrapper: Plate reinforce for the face of an armet, fastened with a leather strap round the back of the neck.

BIOGRAPHIES

Peter Brears
Peter Brears is a former director of museums in the cities of York and Leeds, and is a consultant food historian for organisations including the National Trust, English Heritage, Cadw and a number of private households. He is a Fellow of the Society of Antiquaries and of the Museums Association and his extensive list of publications includes *All the King's cooks* (1999), and *Cooking and dining in Medieval England* (2007).

Angela Clare Smith
Angela Clare Smith is as Researcher for the Royal Armouries, based in Leeds. She originally studied archaeology and later a Masters Degree by Research looking at women in military roles through history to today. Her research interests include women's history, historical portrayals and interpretation.

Bridget Clifford
Bridget Clifford is Head of Collections (south) at the Royal Armouries Museum based at the Tower of London.

J P D Cooper
J P D Cooper is Lecturer in History at the University of York. His first book, *Propaganda and the Tudor State* (2003), was published by Oxford University Press. He is historical consultant to the 'Henry VIII: Dressed to Kill' exhibition and co-editor of the catalogue. He is also an advisor to the *State Papers Online* project.

Dominic Fontana
Dr Dominic Fontana is a lecturer in GIS (Geographic Information Systems) in the Department of Geography at the University of Portsmouth. He has for many years been closely involved with the research into the loss of the Mary Rose and with the application of GIS-generated information into other coastal archaeological investigations.

Steven Gunn
Steven Gunn is Fellow and Tutor in History at Merton College, Oxford. He is author of *Charles Brandon, Duke of Suffolk, c1484-1545*, of *Early Tudor Government, 1485-1558* (1995) and, with David Grummitt and Hans Cools, of *War, State and Society in England and the Netherlands, 1477-1559* (2007)

Eric Gruber von Arni
Eric Gruber von Arn is an Independent Scholar and a Fellow of the Royal Historical Society who specialises in 16th and 17th-century military medical history. He has published widely on military hospital provision, including *Justice for the maimed soldier* (2001) and *Hospital care and the British standing army, 1660-1714* (2006).

Nicholas Hall
Nicholas Hall is Keeper of Artillery at the Royal Armouries, based at Fort Nelson, a 19th-century artillery fortification near Portsmouth. He is a Fellow of the Society of Antiquaries of London. He has worked closely with the Mary Rose Trust on research into Tudor gunnery.

Maria Hayward
Maria Hayward is Reader in History at the University of Southampton and a Fellow of the Society of Antiquaries. She has published on material culture at the Henrician court including *The 1542 Inventory of Whitehall: The Palace and its Keeper* (2004) and *Dress at the Court of Henry VIII* (2007)

James Hester
James Hester is a Researcher at the Royal Armouries Museum, based in Leeds. He has an MA in Medieval Studies from the University of York. His research interests include medieval and early modern weapons, armour and combat techniques. He also works with manuscripts and early printed books.

Eric Ives
Eric Ives is Professor of English History emeritus at the University of Birmingham, a Fellow of the Society of Antiquaries and a Fellow of the Royal Historical Society. He has published widely on the legal and political history of early-modern England, including *The life and death of Anne Boleyn* (2004) and *Henry VIII* (2007). In 2000 he was awarded the OBE for services to history and the University of Birmingham.

David Loades
David Loades is Emeritus Professor of the University of Wales and a Fellow of the Society of Antiquaries. He has written extensively on Tudor England including biographies of Mary I and Elizabeth I, the Tudor Navy and is currently writing a full-length work on Henry VIII.

Simon Metcalf
Simon Metcalf is Armourer and Senior Metalwork Conservator to the Royal Collection. He began his career working in various metal-working disciplines including jewellery and blacksmithing before training as a conservator while working in the Wallace Collection. He joined the conservation department at Royal Armouries then became senior metalwork conservator at the Victoria and Albert Museum. He is an accredited conservator-restorer with the UK Institute of Conservation.

Geoffrey Parnell
Dr Geoffrey Parnell is Keeper of Tower History at the Tower of London and a Fellow of the Society of Antiquaries of London. He has written widely on the archaeology of the Tower and the history of its buildings and institutions'.

Thom Richardson
Thom Richardson is Keeper of Armour and Oriental Collections at the Royal Armouries, where he has worked since 1984, and a Fellow of the Society of Antiquaries. He has published widely on historical armour, including *Arms and armour of Henry VIII* (2002) and *The London armourers in the 17th century* (2004).

Graeme Rimer
Graeme Rimer is Academic Director at the Royal Armouries, where he has been a member of the curatorial team since 1975. He is a Fellow of the Society of Antiquaries and in 2008 was appointed a visiting professor at the University of Huddersfield. He has lectured and published on a variety of arms and armour related subjects and his continuing research is focused on firearms of the 16th and 17th centuries.

Peter Smithurst
Peter Smithurst is a Senior Curator of Firearms at the Royal Armouries' National Firearms Centre, Leeds, and is also a Visiting Research Fellow at the University of Huddersfield. He is currently completing the making of a replica shield gun, which will be used to assess the ballistic capabilities of these weapons.

Pierre Terjanian
Pierre Terjanian is the J J Medveckis Associate Curator of Arms and Armor at the Philadelphia Museum of Art. His current research focuses on armour made for the courts of the Austrian and Spanish Hapsburgs, particularly in the Low Countries and the German lands.

Karen Watts
Karen Watts is Senior Curator of Armour and Art at the Royal Armouries. She is a Fellow of the Society of Antiquaries of London, Honorary Secretary of the Medieval Dress and Textile Society, Freeman of the City of London and Liveryman of the Worshipful Company of Gold and Silver Wyre Drawers. She teaches at the Louvre and at the University of Leeds.

Lucy Wooding
Lucy Wooding is Lecturer in Early Modern History at King's College London. She specialises in the history of the Reformation and her first book was *Rethinking Catholicism in Reformation England* (2000). She has recently published a biography of Henry VIII in Routledge Historical Biographies series.

Robert C Woosnam-Savage
Robert C Woosnam-Savage has been Curator of European Edged Weapons at the Royal Armouries, based at Leeds, since 2001. Previously he was Curator of European Arms and Armour at Glasgow Museums (1983-1997).

ACKNOWLEDGEMENTS

The Board of Trustees of the Royal Armouries express their gratitude to the following for their contribution to and support of this publication.

Editors: Graeme Rimer

       Thom Richardson

       J P D Cooper

Editorial Consultant: Adrian Budge

Production Editor: Debbie Wurr

Designer: Geraldine Mead

Photographers: Gary Ombler, Rod Joyce

Contributors & Supporters

Philip Abbott, Peter Armstrong, Brian Ball, Dave Beck, Peter Brears, Fiona Cahill, Angela Clare Smith, Bridget Clifford, J P D Cooper, Dominic Fontana, Ciara Gallagher, Michael Gilroy, Eric Gruber von Arni, Steven Gunn, Nicholas Hall, Maria Hayward, James Hester, Eric Ives, Stuart Ivinson, Suzanne Kitto, David Loades, Simon Metcalf, Graham Moores, Jonathan Morris, Geoffrey Parnell, Kathy Richmond, Thom Richardson, Graeme Rimer, Emma Schmuecker, Chris Smith, Peter Smithurst, Giles Storey, Pierre Terjanian, Karen Watts, Karen Whitting, Lucy Wooding, Robert Woosnam-Savage

Lenders & Supporters

Church of St Lawrence, Hatfield, South Yorkshire

College of Arms

Historic Royal Palaces

Hofjagd- und Rüstkammer, Kunsthistorisches Museum, Vienna

Metropolitan Museum of Art, New York

Musée de l'Armée, Paris

Museum of London

Society of Antiquaries of London

Stirling Castle

The Mary Rose Trust

The Royal Collection

The Wallace Collection

University of Huddersfield

Worshipful Company of Armourers and Brasiers